SAMS *Teach Yourself*

Microsoft® Office

Outlook® 2003

in 24 Hours

Diane Poremsky

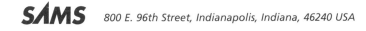

SAMS *800 E. 96th Street, Indianapolis, Indiana, 46240 USA*

Sams Teach Yourself Microsoft® Office Outlook® 2003 in 24 Hours

Copyright © 2004 by Sams Publishing

International Standard Book Number: 0-672-32554-3

Library of Congress Catalog Card Number: 2003108651

Printed in the United States of America

First Printing: August 2003

06   05   04   03   4   3   2   1

Sams Publishing offers excellent discounts on this book when ordered in quantity for bulk purchases or special sales. For more information, please contact

U.S. Corporate and Government Sales

1-800-382-3419

corpsales@pearsontechgroup.com

For sales outside of the United States, please contact

International Sales

1-317-581-3793

international@pearsontechgroup.com

Trademarks

Warning and Disclaimer

ASSOCIATE PUBLISHER
Greg Wiegand

ACQUISITIONS EDITOR
Stephanie J. McComb

DEVELOPMENT EDITOR
Todd Brakke

MANAGING EDITOR
Charlotte Clapp

PROJECT EDITOR
Dan Knott

COPY EDITOR
Mike Henry

INDEXER
Mandie Frank

TECHNICAL EDITOR
Vince Averello

TEAM COORDINATOR
Sharry Lee Gregory

INTERIOR DESIGNER
Gary Adair

COVER DESIGNER
Aren Howell

PAGE LAYOUT
Ron Wise

GRAPHICS
Tammy Graham
Tara Lipscomb

Contents at a Glance

Table of Contents

About the Author

Diane Poremsky is the owner and president of CDOLive, a messaging and collaboration consulting and solutions development firm. She is an associate editor and columnist for *OutlookPower*, an e-zine for Outlook and Exchange power users and reviews software for Fawcette Publications' *.NET* magazine.

Diane is a Microsoft MVP (Most Valuable Professional) in recognition for her support of Outlook in the Microsoft newsgroups and Internet community.

She spends her free time trying to keep up with the activities of daughters Jessie and Cecilia, and college students Rebecca and Liz. She often wonders what cute things grandson Joey is doing today.

Along with her husband, Phil, she enjoys the natural beauty in the mountains of upper east Tennessee. You can reach her at drcp@poremsky.com and visit her Web sites at www.poremsky.com and www.cdolive.com.

Dedication

This book is dedicated to my daughter Jessie, as her high school graduation gift. The future is an open book and you can write your own stories. And yes, Mom knows you can't drive a book, but you don't need a car either. Love, Mom

Acknowledgments

Yes, Mom, I'm finally done writing the book. Special thanks to Phil, Jessie, and Cece for their support during the time I was writing this book. It helped a lot when I didn't have to cook, even though I had to bribe Jessie and Cece to clean up in the kitchen.

To my fellow Outlook MVPs and friends in Outlook-Helpers and the BetaBros, thanks for humoring me and tolerating my whining. Outlook 2003 is the best version yet. Thanks Jensen, Ronna, Jeff, and all the Outlook developers.

We Want to Hear from You!

As the reader of this book, *you* are our most important critic and commentator. We value your opinion and want to know what we're doing right, what we could do better, what areas you'd like to see us publish in, and any other words of wisdom you're willing to pass our way.

As an associate publisher for Sams Publishing, I welcome your comments. You can email or write me directly to let me know what you did or didn't like about this book—as well as what we can do to make our books better.

Please note that I cannot help you with technical problems related to the *topic* of this book. We do have a User Services group, however, where I will forward specific technical questions related to the book.

When you write, please be sure to include this book's title and author as well as your name, email address, and phone number. I will carefully review your comments and share them with the author and editors who worked on the book.

Email: feedback@samspublishing.com

Mail: Greg Wiegand
         Sams Publishing
         800 East 96th Street
         Indianapolis, IN 46240 USA

For more information about this book or another Sams title, visit our Web site at www.samspublishing.com. Type the ISBN (excluding hyphens) or the title of a book in the Search field to find the page you're looking for.

Introduction

Outlook isn't the most intuitive program to use, even for people who've used it before. This book aims to change that or at least help you understand how Outlook works. It'll show you where to find things so that you don't feel lost and wish you had your old email client back.

If you're new to Outlook, you'll learn about all the features it offers, not only for email, but also for personal information management, which includes the Calendar, Contacts, and Tasks folders.

Outlook also has many hidden features that are hard to discover on your own. By the time you reach the end of the book, you'll be more organized then ever and be on the road to Outlook expert.

If you're upgrading from an older version of Outlook, you'll learn about the new features in Outlook 2003, as well as discover some new tricks.

There's so much to learn about Outlook that reading about using Outlook and trying it for yourself isn't enough to remember how to use all the features. After you've read through this book once, you'll want to keep it handy to use as a reference guide.

You'll quickly be well on your to way to power user status, learning many of the tricks discovered by other power users. By the time you're finished, you won't be asking whether you can do something in Outlook or how to use it—you'll be looking for more ways to put Outlook's power to use. You might even be showing friends and co-workers how to get the most out of Outlook. As fun as it is to be the resident guru, I'd like you to suggest they buy their own copy of this book.

Although this book is geared toward the new Outlook user, anyone upgrading to Outlook 2003 will learn many new things from reading this book. Filled with many tips and tricks familiar to Outlook power users, this book will put you well on the way to becoming a power user yourself.

What's in This Book

Beginning with an introduction to Outlook, you'll discover the features new to Outlook 2003, including the Navigation Pane, the Reading Pane, Search Folders, and Quick Flags. You'll learn the best way to set up your accounts and customize Outlook. Views comprise one of the best power user features in Outlook, I'll show you how to use the views that Outlook includes and help you create your own custom views. Managing your email is easier when you use Quick Flags, Search Folders, and rules.

Outlook is first and foremost an email client. It's very powerful when you know how to harness its power. Outlook is unlike any other email program. It supports a wide range of email protocols, from corporate email hosted on Exchange Server to free Hotmail accounts.

Although Outlook has its own email editor, you can work faster when you compose your messages in a familiar editor: Microsoft Word. You'll learn how to use stationery to send prettier messages and learn when it's better not to use formatted messages. You'll discover other features in Outlook that make it the most powerful messaging client available, including voting and delayed send.

Security is important in any email client—Microsoft made security its number one priority. Outlook protects you from snooping spammers who include Web beacons in HTML messages to track who reads the message. I'll show you how to make the most of Outlook's security, giving you the greatest level of protection with the fewest hassles.

Outlook automatically removes much of the spam you receive from your Inbox as it's downloaded, thanks to the new Junk E-mail filter. The accuracy rate is very high, eliminating much of the spam that fills your Inbox. The Junk E-mail filter even works on all accounts, including Hotmail.

Although Outlook is "just an email program" to many users, it's also a feature-filled personal information manager (PIM). You'll learn how to use these features to their fullest. Learn how to customize your contact forms, use categories to organize your contacts and calendar, and use your contacts in a mail merge.

No PIM is complete without a journal to record your activities. Use Outlook's journal to automatically record phone calls and email sent to your contacts and create journal entries for many activities.

After you get a handle on Outlook's basic features, you can move on to the advanced features, including designing custom forms, working with VBA, and creating custom toolbars. You'll learn what files Outlook uses and which ones to back up on a regular basis.

Integration with other Office programs and online services is important to many users. Use Outlook with MSN and SharePoint Services or use Outlook's contacts as a data source in Word. It's all covered in this book.

Conventions Used in This Book

This book uses several conventions to help you prioritize and reference the information it contains.

Tips highlight information that can make your Outlook use more effective.

Cautions focus your attention on problems or side effects that can occur in specific situations.

Notes provide useful sidebar information that you can read immediately or circle back to without losing the flow of the topic at hand.

In addition, this book uses various typefaces to help you distinguish code from regular English. Code is presented in a monospace font. Placeholders—words or characters used temporarily to represent the real words or characters you would type in code—are typeset in *italic monospace*.

Some code statements presented in this book are too long to appear on a single line. In these cases, a line-continuation character (➡) is used to indicate that the following line is a continuation of the current statement.

PART I

Introduction to Outlook

Hour

HOUR 1

Outlook Tour

Microsoft Office Outlook 2003 is nothing like you've seen before. It's eye-catching and for the most part, it's smartly designed. After using the new Outlook for just a short period of time, you'll fall in love with it. Outlook 2003 includes many customer requests, including a new preview pane on the right side of the screen, colored flags, and the ability to hide unused folder types.

You'll be able to manage your messaging, calendar, and contacts better. The Reading Pane presents more of your messages on the screen so that you can read many of your messages without scrolling. Using Quick Flags enables you to mark messages with different colored flags. Search Folders enable you to see all of your unread flagged messages or those with attachments. You can create your own Search Folders so that you can always find messages from your boss or co-workers, display multiple calendars side-by-side, and use smart grouping to group Outlook items by nearly any field.

This hour introduces you to Outlook's new interface and its many new features:

- The Reading Pane
- The Navigation Pane
- Using Outlook Today
- Getting Help using Outlook
- Using the Research pane

You'll learn how to use Reading and Navigation Panes, discover how get help with Outlook, and how to use the new Research pane to translate messages and look up words in an online dictionary or thesaurus.

Starting Outlook

When you open Outlook for the first time, your screen will look similar to the screenshot shown in Figure 1.1.

FIGURE 1.1

Outlook's new look uses three panes, one each for the Navigation Pane, list views, and Reading Pane.

Create shortcuts to Favorite Mail folders and Search folders

Outlook blocks possible Web beacons; click the InfoBar or right-click in the image place-holder to show blocked images

Select the folder type to view other Outlook folders

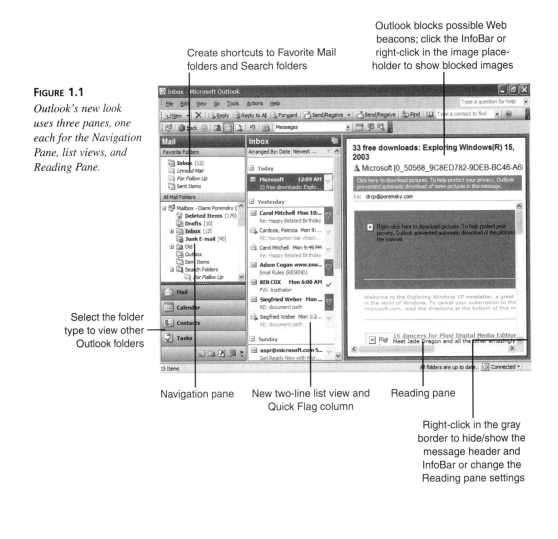

Navigation pane

New two-line list view and Quick Flag column

Reading pane

Right-click in the gray border to hide/show the message header and InfoBar or change the Reading pane settings

The list pane uses a two-line display so that you can see the sender, received date, and subject line in a narrow space, freeing more width for the Reading Pane. Slide the Navigation Pane's folder buttons down to one row to show more folders in the folder list.

The new look of Outlook includes the Navigation Pane on the left side with buttons to switch to display Outlook items by folder types.

When Mail folders are selected, the Navigation Pane includes the Favorite Folders section. Favorite Folders includes the Inbox and Sent folders by default, along with two predefined Search Folders: Unread Messages and For Follow Up. When you have HTTP or IMAP email accounts in your profile, those inboxes are listed on Favorite folders also. You can drag any mail folder, Search Folder, or public folder to Favorite Folders to create a shortcut.

> Don't worry if this hour overwhelms you with new and unfamiliar terms. Everything mentioned here, including using IMAP and HTTP email accounts, is discussed in greater detail in later hours.

The center section contains the message list, which displays the message information on two lines and uses smart grouping to group your items intelligently. Quick Flags enable you to flag important messages with different colors of flags. Search Folders make it possible for you to see all the flagged messages grouped together, even if they're in different folders.

The Reading Pane is on the right by default. As you can see in Figure 1.1, with the Reading Pane on the right, you can see more of a message before you need to scroll.

Outlook doesn't download images from the Internet unless you tell it to. This feature blocks *Web beacons*, which are images linked to your email address with codes that are transmitted to the sender when you view the message, as shown in Figure 1.1. Along with blocking Web beacons, all external content is blocked unless and until you allow it to be downloaded. You'll learn more about Web beacons in Hour 8, "Email Security ."

Using the Navigation Pane

The Navigation Pane combines the Outlook Bar and Folder view from previous versions of Outlook into one column. It provides the following layouts:

- A tree view of all mail folders with Favorite Folders shortcuts.

- Folder-only views for the Contacts, Notes, Tasks, and Journal folders. Folders are listed by name; subfolders are not indented or otherwise identified as subfolders.

- Folder view for Calendar folders only. Calendar thumbnails are included in the Navigation bar. Select check boxes to display multiple calendars side-by-side.

- Folder list view includes all folders. If you use Exchange Server, this is where you'll find your public folders.

- Shortcuts that provide the functionality of the Outlook Bar found in older versions of Outlook.

Buttons at the bottom of the Navigation Pane provide easy access to your Outlook folders. You'll probably want to slide the buttons down to provide more space for your folder lists. You can also select which buttons to show. Enabling the Current View selection list displays a list of the views available for your folder following the folder list in the Navigation Pane.

Customizing the Navigation Pane

By default, the Navigation Pane uses large buttons for Mail, Calendar, Contacts, and Tasks, with smaller icons along the bottom row for Notes, Folder List, and Shortcuts (see Figure 1.2).

FIGURE 1.2

Select buttons on the Navigation Pane to move between Outlook folder types.

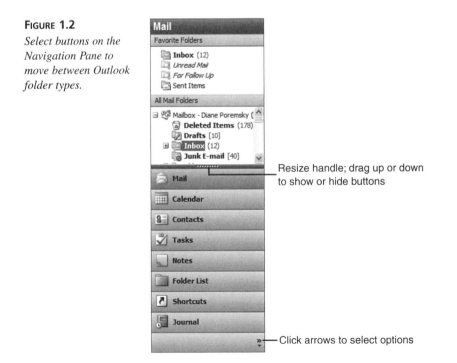

Resize handle; drag up or down to show or hide buttons

Click arrows to select options

When you use a high screen resolution, Outlook enables you to have larger buttons. You have fewer buttons when you use a low resolution, such as 800×600. Click the arrows at the bottom right to select which buttons are visible. By default, the Journal button is not shown; I added it for the screenshot.

You can also reduce the buttons to one row:

1. Hover the mouse cursor over the bar resizing handle at the top of the Mail button.
2. Click and drag down or up to show or hide the full-sized buttons.

You can also control which shortcuts Outlook shows on the buttons and the order in which they're listed:

1. Click on the arrow at the lower right of the Navigation Pane.
2. Choose Add or Remove Buttons and select the buttons you want to show and deselect the ones you don't want to see.
3. Choose Navigation Pane Options to rearrange the order of the buttons, as shown in Figure 1.3.

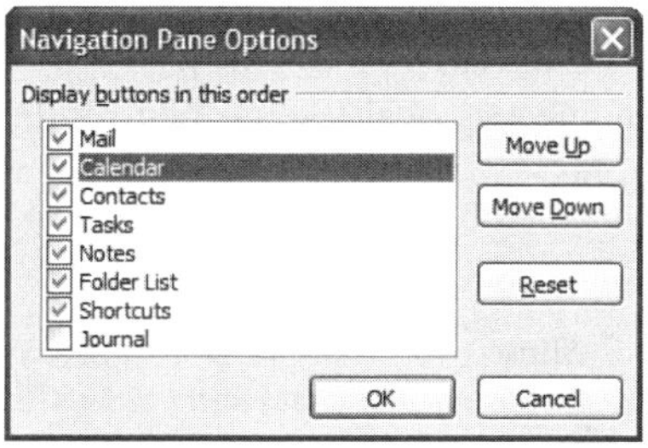

FIGURE 1.3

Select a button name and then use the Move Up and Move Down buttons to change the order in which the buttons appear. Uncheck any names for which you don't want to include buttons. You can use the Go menu instead of these buttons.

You're limited to using the buttons listed in Navigation Pane Options, so you can't add buttons of your own.

> The bottom button bar remains in the Navigation Pane, even if you remove all the buttons from it. If you do remove buttons, you can use the Go menu or keyboard shortcuts to move between folders.

Using All Mail Folders

Most people will spend the majority of their time in the All Mail folders view, or they will after they get used to it. This display works like the Folder list, except only mail folders are visible in this view.

You'll notice the Favorite Folders shortcut group at the top of the Navigation Pane. By default, it includes your Inbox, Sent folder, and two Search Folders. You can right-click on any mail folder to add it to the Favorite folders. Unfortunately, you can't add nonmail folders to it or remove it from the view.

The All Mail Folders section includes the Outlook Today folder and all mail folders in your profile. If you have HTTP (Hotmail) or IMAP accounts, those Inboxes are included in the Favorite Folders list.

Exchange Server Public Folders aren't included in this view, although you can add Public Folder Favorites to the Favorite Folders list.

Using the Navigation Bar with Outlook's Other Folders

The Navigation Pane looks much different when you're using Calendar, Contacts, Journal, Notes, and Tasks folders. Instead of a tree view of your folders, you'll see a list of the folders. When more than one message store is open, all the same type of folders are listed in the My (*folder*) group.

A message store is where your messages are stored. When you use an Internet email account, it's a Personal Folder store (PST). Exchange Server users have an Exchange mailbox or an Offline Store (OST) and can use a PST for archiving messages.

When you have shared folders opened, they'll be grouped below the ones in your message store in the Other (*folder*) group, as seen in Figure 1.4. This applies only to Exchange Server users and Contacts and Calendar folders for SharePoint Portal Server users.

Optionally, you can show the Current View selector at the bottom of the Navigation Pane. Turn it on or off using View, Arrange By, Show Views in Navigation Pane. The Navigation Pane scrolls when you have many folders or views, making it less useful to include views in the Navigation Pane. It's a per-folder group option, so you can turn it off for some folder types and turn it on for the folders on which you change views most often.

FIGURE 1.4

The Navigation Pane for all nonmail folders resembles this screenshot. This figure shows a Contacts folder from my public folder store as well as shared contacts from a SharePoint Portal Server.

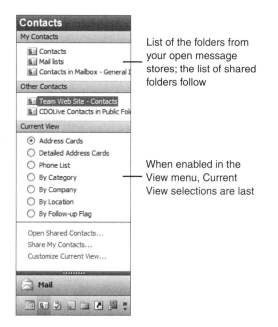

List of the folders from your open message stores; the list of shared folders follow

When enabled in the View menu, Current View selections are last

The final option found in the Navigation Pane is Customize Current View. You can't create new views using this link, but it brings up the Customize dialog, enabling you to modify or reset the current view.

Customizing views is covered in Hour 3, "Navigating the Outlook Interface."

The Open Shared (*folders*) link is present in all profiles, but only Exchange Server users can use it.

Outlook's Calendar

The Calendar's Navigation Pane has many changes from Outlook 2002 as well. As you can see in Figure 1.5, the most promising feature found in Outlook 2003 is the capability to select multiple calendars and view them side-by-side in one window.

The Navigation Pane displays a calendar thumbnail with two or more thumbnails shown on a high-resolution monitor. The width of the Navigation Pane is adjustable up to one-half of the screen width, which adds two or more thumbnails per row.

Add a check to the calendars you'd like to view
side by side; each calendar is color-coded.

Calendars from a mailbox

Figure 1.5

*Outlook's new multiple
calendar view displays
selected calendars on
your screen.*

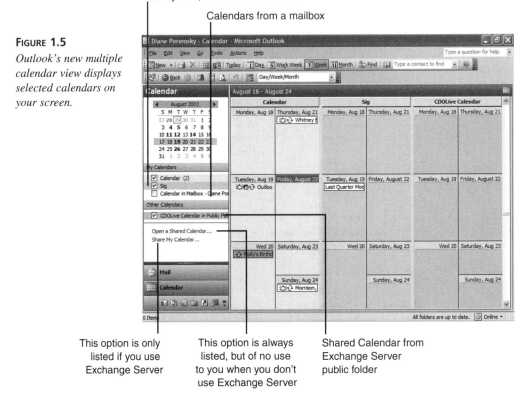

This option is only   This option is always   Shared Calendar from
listed if you use   listed, but of no use   Exchange Server
Exchange Server   to you when you don't   public folder
                             use Exchange Server

If you're familiar with the Calendar task pad and thumbnails on the right of the screen
from previous versions of Outlook and want to use it, you can restore that view by dragging the right edge inward the width of a calendar thumbnail. The task pad and thumbnails will appear on the right and the thumbnail in the Navigation Pane will disappear.

If you don't use Exchange Server, you won't be able to use Open a Shared
Calendar or Share My Calendar. If you're using a SharePoint server, you can
view a read-only copy of the SharePoint calendar in Outlook. The calendar
will update automatically, but it's just a one-way sync from SharePoint to
your computer.

If you need to share your calendar with other SharePoint users, you can
export your calendar from Outlook to CSV or Microsoft Excel format and
import it to the SharePoint calendar.

> More information on using the calendar is in Hour 11, "Using Your Calendar."

Using Shortcuts

The Shortcuts Navigation Pane replaces the Outlook Bar shortcuts used in older versions of Outlook (see Figure 1.6). Any type of shortcut, from Outlook folders to files and programs on your computer to Internet shortcuts works on the Shortcuts bar.

FIGURE 1.6

Place any type of shortcut in the Navigation Pane's Shortcuts group. Internet shortcuts open the Web page in Outlook's window; file system folders open in Windows Explorer. Other files open the appropriate program.

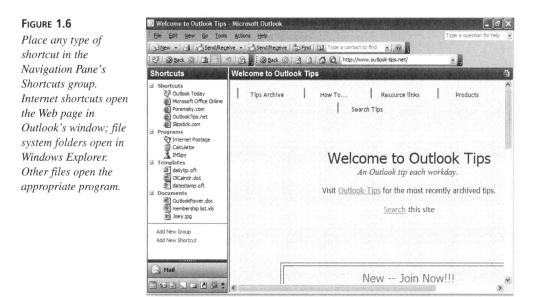

Select the Add New Group link to add a new group to the list. Groups are listed in the order you create them. To reorder the list, right-click on a group name and choose Move Up the List and Move Down the List.

Right-click on a group and choose Remove Group. When you remove a group, all the shortcuts in the group are also deleted.

Use Add a New Shortcut to add shortcuts to Outlook's folders. Create shortcuts to Windows files and folders by opening Windows Explorer and dragging files, folders, or existing shortcuts to the Shortcuts bar.

Using Smart Grouping

If you looked closely at the message list (middle section) in Figure 1.1, you noticed the date groups. Outlook uses a new view structure that groups messages by the sort field. You'll see natural language words describing the date groups: Today, Yesterday, Sunday, Saturday, Last Week, Two Weeks Ago, and so forth.

On occasion, you might even see messages grouped in Tomorrow. This happens when the sender's date is set ahead and you use IMAP or HTTP mailboxes and download only message headers. Outlook normally reads the received date, but when only headers are downloaded, it reads the sent field instead.

When a different field, such as the From field, is selected for sorting, the messages are grouped by the display name in the From field. Click on the Arranged By field at the top of the message list to select a different field to group by. Disable grouping by choosing Show in Groups on the menu; select the menu option again to re-enable it.

Select Custom to bring up the Customize View menu. The button at the very bottom, Reset Current View, resets all the current view settings to their defaults, except your group header shading.

Although the custom view settings are explained more completely in Hour 3, the Other Settings button contains the settings that control the look and feel of the list view and Reading Pane.

Use the options in the Other Settings dialog to change the look of the list view. You might want to select Shade Group Headings to add some color to the group headers so that you can see them more easily. Change the Reading Pane position and show or hide the headers in the Reading Pane using this dialog.

The Reading Pane

Microsoft replaced the Preview pane with what it calls the *Reading Pane*. By default, the Reading Pane is on the right side of the window, although you can move it to the bottom of the window or turn it off completely.

When the Reading Pane is on the right, more of the message is visible, which means less scrolling is required and your efficiency is improved when reading large volumes of email.

1

You can change the position of the Reading Pane using the Other Settings dialog, or by right-clicking in the gray border surrounding the Reading Pane.

Included on this menu is the Reading Pane Options dialog, as shown in Figure 1.7. It's used to toggle headers on and off, change the position of the Reading Pane or turn it off completely, and change the size of text used in HTML-formatted messages.

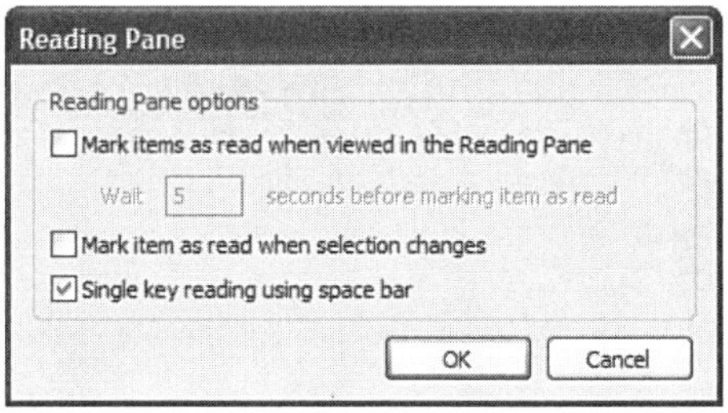

FIGURE 1.7

Open the Reading Pane Options dialog using Tools, Options, Other, Reading Pane or from Custom, Other Settings.

Reading Pane

Reading Pane options

☐ Mark items as read when viewed in the Reading Pane

    Wait 5 seconds before marking item as read

☐ Mark item as read when selection changes

☑ Single key reading using space bar

[OK] [Cancel]

This dialog controls whether messages are marked as read in the Reading Pane. Single spacebar reading eliminates the need to use the mouse. Choose this setting enables you to use the spacebar to scroll to the end of the message while in the Reading Pane. If the spacebar is pressed again at the end of the message, Outlook moves to the next message.

> Right-click on any edge of the gray border surrounding the Reading Pane to see the Reading Pane options.

> If you like reading your messages in the Reading Pane, but don't use it out of security concerns, stop worrying and utilize it.
>
> The Reading Pane is as secure as opening a message to read it and more convenient for most users. The Reading Pane is not active; that is, it doesn't display active content and scripts won't run. In fact, Outlook blocks all active content in messages, including form fields, in both the Reading Pane and in open messages.

Outlook Today

One of Outlook's popular features is Outlook Today. The Outlook Today page displays your upcoming events, tasks, and unread message counts in an HTML page. You can start Outlook directly in Outlook Today and return to it at anytime by choosing the top level of your default message store. If you have more than one message store, Outlook Today is in the top level of the message store that's identified by an icon containing a house and a clock.

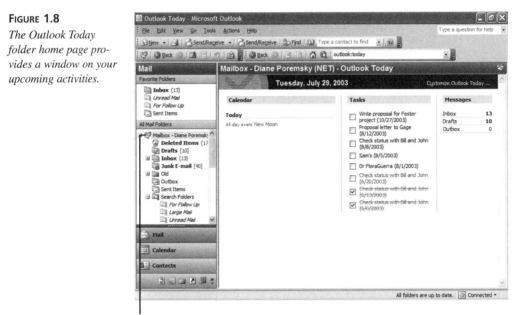

Icon identifies the Outlook Today message store

Outlook Today includes options for limited customizations, which are accessible from the Outlook Today page. Choose Customize Outlook Today at the top of the page to open the Customize Outlook Today dialog (see Figure 1.9).

You can choose to show all incomplete tasks or only those due today, and select from five basic styles or color schemes.

Although it's possible to edit the HTML page to further customize the included Outlook Today screens, it requires some HTML and programming knowledge because it uses a compiled HTML page. You can replace the Outlook Today home page with a home page you design. In most cases, a customized Outlook Today home page loads slower than the pages included with Outlook.

If you use the Winter style, the Save Changes button is at the bottom of the page. On all other pages, it's at the top of the page.

FIGURE **1.9**

Included in the settings you can configure for Outlook Today are whether Outlook starts in Outlook Today and how many days to show from your calendar.

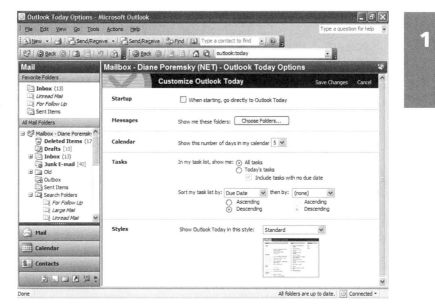

Using Folder Home Pages

You can use a home page on any folder, not just on the Outlook Today folder. To set a folder home page:

1. Right-click on the folder and choose Properties.

2. Select the Home Page tab and enter the file path or URL for your home page selection.

3. Check the box to Show Home Page by Default for This Folder.

4. Choose Offline Web Page Settings to make the folder home page available for offline use.

When the Show Home Page box is checked, the folder contents are hidden from view. You can use Search Folders, Advanced Find, or uncheck the box to view any items in the folder.

Use a local HTML page you create, possibly one using ActiveX controls that display your Inbox, weather, and stock market information for your folder home page. You aren't limited to using pages you create: You can use a Web page from your company's intranet or from any Web site you choose. Using Internet content requires an open Internet connection.

Hour 3 has more information about using and customizing Outlook Today
and folder home pages.

To remove the home page from the folder, open the Properties dialog and choose <u>R</u>estore
Defaults. Uncheck the Show Home Page Box if you want to temporarily disable the
home page.

Getting Help with Outlook

With the 2003 edition, the Microsoft Office family provides more online help files and
fewer offline, or local, help files. This enables you to receive the most up-to-date information, but requires an Internet connection to use. Although the default for searching
help is online, you can select offline from the search dialog or disable online help using
the Choose Online Content Setting link at the bottom of the Getting Started task pane.

Press F1 for Help or enter keywords in the Type a Question for Help dialog on the Menu
bar. Help loads into the task pane and returns the results in a new window, which docks
on the right side of your screen (see Figure 1.10).

Outlook's Help isn't always as helpful as it should be and you might need to look else-
where for advice and solutions. Choose from Slipstick (`www.slipstick.com`)—the pre-
mier site for anything related to Outlook—any Internet search engine, the Microsoft
Knowledge Base (`support.microsoft.com`), or Internet newsgroups.

The Microsoft Knowledge Base is full of information and might have exactly what you
are looking for, but locating the information you need is like finding a needle in a
haystack (and deciphering what it tells you is often not an easy task either). You'll generally get better results using an Internet search engine such as Google.

One of the best sources for assistance is the Microsoft newsgroup
`msnews.microsoft.com`. Quite often, someone already asked the same question that you
need an answer to. When you know where to look, it's faster to find the question and
replies than it is to post the question. Even when you post your own questions, the
replies to your question are often lost in the hundreds of posts made each day.

Drag the toolbar handle
to float the task pane   Type questions
or dock it on the left   in the help field

FIGURE 1.10

Help uses the task pane for the table of contents, search results, and Research windows. Selections load into a new window, which docks on the right edge of the screen. Choose the Tile/Untile button to float or dock the results window. Drag the task pane to float it or dock it on another edge.

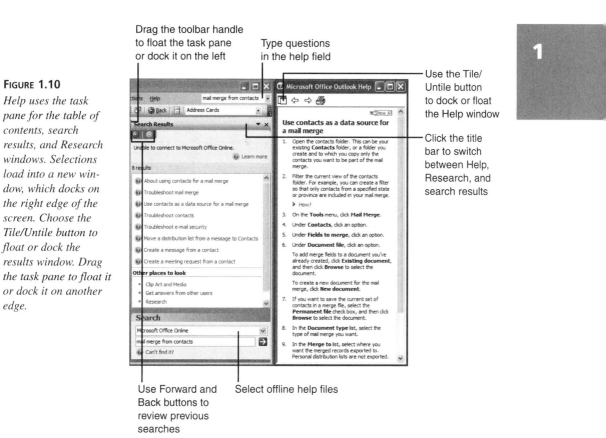

Use the Tile/
Untile button
to dock or float
the Help window

Click the title
bar to switch
between Help,
Research, and
search results

Use Forward and   Select offline help files
Back buttons to
review previous
searches

Task: Find Answers to Your Questions at Google

The answers to many questions can be found in the msnews.microsoft.com newsgroups, but finding the posts can be difficult using traditional newsreaders and impossible using the Communities interface. When you use Google to search newsgroups, you'll find the answer in seconds.

1. Go to http://groups.google.com.

▼ 2. Click the link for Advanced Groups Search.

▼   3. Enter your search terms in the Find Messages field. You want to be as specific as possible to narrow the results, but you must also ensure that you're using the same terminology others use. If you receive an error message, enter some of the words from the error message.

    4. Enter `Microsoft.public.outlook*` in the Return Only Messages from the Newsgroup field.

    5. Limit the search to dates within the past year or so to reduce the number of results returned.

    6. Select the number of posts to display. If you have broadband, you'll probably want to display more than 10 results at a time. Choose Sort by Date to see the most recent posts first.

▲   7. Click the Google Search button. In a few seconds, you'll have the results of your search.

There are a couple of things you need to keep in mind when you use Google. First, it takes about 12 hours for Google to archive the posts from the public newsgroups. If you use Google to look for answers to your questions, wait at least 12 hours before searching Google.

When you search for a problem and many of the results refer to older versions, don't discount the answers as not applicable because the versions are different. When the problem is the same as yours, the solution might work for you also.

When you can't find an answer to your problem, you can use Outlook Express or another newsreader to post questions to `msnews.microsoft.com`, a free service providing peer-to-peer assistance for users of Microsoft products. Occasionally someone from Microsoft will answer your questions, but most of the time the solutions come from people just like you.

If you've never used newsgroups before, you can use the Communities interface at `communities.microsoft.com` to read and ask questions on the Microsoft newsgroups using Internet Explorer. The Help task pane has a link to the Communities Web site.

The Communities interface has fewer features than a dedicated newsreader program and answers to your posts are often difficult to find. But when you use a public computer or your firewall blocks the NNTP port (the port which provides direct access to newsgroups), you can use the Communities interface to post to the Microsoft newsgroups. After posting a question, you can use Google to find replies.

Using the Research Pane

New to Office 2003, Research displays in the task pane and provides you with dictionary, thesaurus, encyclopedia, and translation services from the Outlook interface (see Figure 1.11).

FIGURE 1.11

The Translation Research pane is one of my favorites. Select the languages you need to translate in the To and From fields, and then select the text in a message. The translation window automatically updates with the translated text.

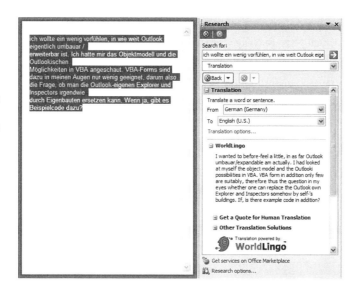

Select the Research options link at the bottom of the pane to change the sources used by Research (see Figure 1.12).

FIGURE 1.12

Use this dialog to add additional research services, update or remove existing services, and control the services children can use. A Research SDK (software development kit) is available for companies to create their own research services.

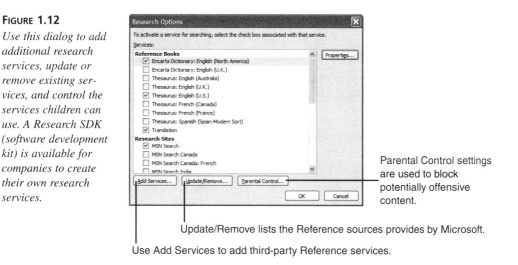

Parental Control settings are used to block potentially offensive content.

Update/Remove lists the Reference sources provides by Microsoft.

Use Add Services to add third-party Reference services.

Summary

In this hour, you discovered Outlook's new look, from the full-length Reading Pane on the right side of Outlook's window, to the ability to view multiple calendars side-by-side, to the uncluttered folder views showing you each Outlook item type in separate views.

You learned how to change the Reading Pane's orientation and configure the list views. Next, you were introduced to the Navigation Pane and learned about its features and how they work with the different Outlook item types.

You learned about Outlook's online help and where to find assistance when Outlook's help files don't have the information you need.

Q&A

Q Help! I messed up my rules and some messages were moved to Outlook Today before I realized my error. How can I get them back?

A If the messages are unread, look for them in the Unread Search Folder and drag them to a new folder. If you don't see them in the Unread Search Folder, you have two ways of recovering these messages. You can disable the Outlook Today folder home page and drag the messages out, or use Advanced Find and move the messages to another folder.

To disable the folder home page:

1. Right-click on Outlook Today at the top of your folder tree. Choose Properties for your message store from the bottom of the menu.

2. Select the Home Page tab on the Properties dialog.

3. Remove the check from the Show Home Page by Default for This Folder and choose OK to close the dialog.

With the home page disabled, the folder acts like any other folder and you can move the messages out. Repeat the steps to turn Outlook Today back on.

If you'd rather use Advanced Find, open it using Tools, Find, Advanced Find. Choose Browse and add a check beside Outlook Today at the top of the dialog. Remove any checks beside other folders and the one at the bottom beside Search Subfolders. Choose Find Now. Select all the found messages, right-click, and choose Move to Folder.

Q I did something and now my views aren't how I like them. I'd like to get the original views back. How do I do it?

A You just need to reset your views. You can reset each view independently or reset all views to their original settings, removing all custom views as well.

To reset individual views, open the Custom Views dialog. You can open it by clicking on the row of field names in the list view and choosing Custom. If you use a one-line list, the menu is called Customize Current View.

Choose Reset Current View from the Customize View dialog to restore the current view to its defaults.

Hour 3 has more information on resetting your views.

Q How do I remove folders from the Navigation Pane lists? I have some calendar folders I don't want on my list.

A Remove single calendars by right-clicking on the calendar name in the list and choose Remove <u>f</u>rom My Calendars. If you want to completely reset the Navigation Pane, you can start Outlook with the /resetnavpane switch.

In the Start menu, Run dialog, type **Outlook /resetnavpane**. This resets the Navigation Pane and removes all Favorite folders and other shortcuts you might have created.

Additional startup switches are listed in Appendix B, "Outlook's Command-Line Switches."

HOUR 2

Outlook Configuration Basics

Before you use Outlook, you must set up your email accounts. You might want to configure additional options and customize some of Outlook's features. This hour guides you though

- Setting up your profile
- Configuring your email accounts
- Using more than one Outlook profile
- Choosing the folder Outlook opens first

In many cases, following the wizards and using the default settings is suitable, although there will be times you'll want to tweak the settings, such as to leave your email on the server or control how often Outlook checks for new email.

Setting Up Profiles

The first time Outlook runs, you're presented with a setup wizard to guide you through setting up your first account and profile. The first screen asks whether you want to configure Outlook to connect to a mail server. Select Yes if you're going to use Outlook for email, or select No if you're using Outlook only for your calendar, tasks, and contacts.

This rest of this section assumes that you selected Yes and are setting up an email account. If you choose No, Outlook creates a no mail profile for you. To add email accounts later, follow the steps in the task "Add Additional Accounts to Your Profile," later in the hour.

The first thing you need to do is tell Outlook what kind of email account you're using (see Figure 2.1). If you use multiple mail servers or have more than one account, the wizard walks you through the setup of your default email account.

FIGURE 2.1

Choose your account type from the Server Type dialog and choose Next.

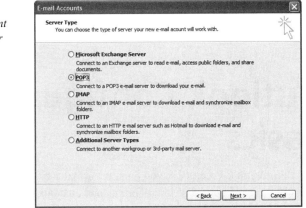

You have the following mail server choices:

- Microsoft Exchange Server—This option is normally used only in corporations. In most cases, the administrator preconfigures Exchange accounts for you.

- POP3—In a POP3 account, messages are typically downloaded from the server and stored locally. If you aren't sure what kind of email account you have, it's probably a POP3 account.

- IMAP—When you use IMAP, the messages are stored on the email server and Outlook downloads copies. IMAP accounts are common on college campuses.

- HTTP—HTTP is used to download Web-based email accounts to Outlook. Currently, only Hotmail and MSN addresses support HTTP accounts.

- Additional Server Types—Additional server types include Fax Services, Lotus Notes, Microsoft Mail (Workgroup Post Offices), and GroupWise. You won't have any services listed unless you've installed the appropriate software, such as the Windows Fax software or Notes connector. In most cases, you won't choose Additional Server types when setting up your default email account.

Select the appropriate account type for your main email account. If you're unsure what type of account you have, check with your ISP or email provider.

At this time, only Hotmail and MSN support HTTP access. Other Web-based accounts, such as Yahoo!, don't support the WebDAV protocol needed for HTTP access. If your Web-based mail service doesn't offer POP3 or IMAP service, you won't be able to use Outlook to check your email unless you use a third-party utility.

AOL uses proprietary email protocols, not POP3 or IMAP, so you must continue to use AOL's email client or use a third-party utility to pull the mail from AOL if you want to use Outlook.

Several enterprising developers have created utilities that enable you to use any popular email client with AOL or Yahoo! and other Web-based email servers. Search Google.com using the keywords `Yahoo AOL Outlook` for the latest offerings, including AOL2POP, Web2POP, and Izymail (POP3Hot).

MS Mail is not a supported server type in Outlook 2003. If you use an MSMail post office and are upgrading to Outlook 2003, see `http://www.outlook-tips.net/msmail.htm` for more information.

Task: Create Your First Outlook Profile

For this exercise, we're using a POP3 account because POP3 is the most popular account type. In most cases, the information required is the same for any account type: your display name, email address, server names. Outlook completes the setup based on the account type you select. If you have an IMAP or HTTP account, see "Add Additional Accounts to Your Profile," which follows this section.

1. Enter your name as you want it to appear on your outgoing mail in the Your Name field. In most cases, you'll want to use your full name, but some people use their email address or a nickname.

2. Press the Tab key to move to the next field: E-mail Address. Enter the email address you use for this account.

3. The next field is Incoming Mail Server (POP3). Enter the name of your POP3 server. If you're unsure what to use, check with your ISP or email service's online help. In many cases, the POP3 server name is `mail.domain-name.com`, where *domain-name* is the domain your provider uses (see Figure 2.2).

▼ FIGURE 2.2

Enter your basic account information on the Internet E-mail Settings dialog.

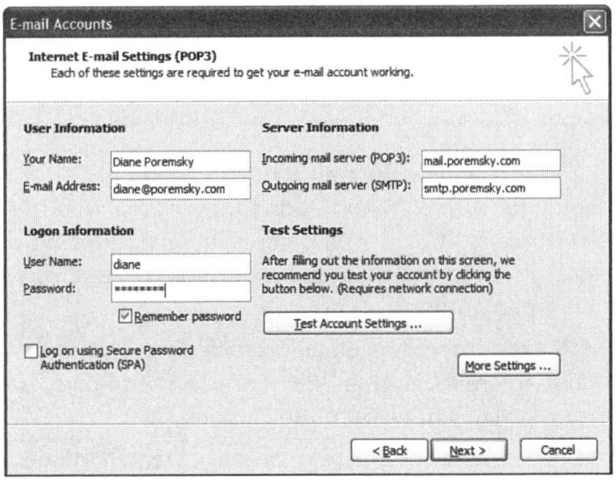

E-mail Accounts

Internet E-mail Settings (POP3)
Each of these settings are required to get your e-mail account working.

User Information

Your Name: Diane Poremsky
E-mail Address: diane@poremsky.com

Logon Information

User Name: diane
Password: ●●●●●●●●
                  ☑ Remember password
☐ Log on using Secure Password
   Authentication (SPA)

Server Information

Incoming mail server (POP3):   mail.poremsky.com
Outgoing mail server (SMTP):   smtp.poremsky.com

Test Settings

After filling out the information on this screen, we recommend you test your account by clicking the button below. (Requires network connection).

[Test Account Settings ...]

[More Settings ...]

[< Back] [Next >] [Cancel]

4. The Outgoing mail server (SMTP) is next. Again, if you're unsure of what to enter, check with your provider. In many cases, it's either `mail.domain-name.com` or `smtp.domain-name.com`.

5. Enter the User name and Password required to access your email account. Check the Remember Password box only if your computer is secure; otherwise, anyone can open Outlook and check your email.

6. If your email provider requires secure password authentication, add a check to the Log on Using Secure Password Authentication (SPA) box. If you aren't sure, leave it blank, you probably don't need it.

> Secure Password Authentication (SPA), also known as NTLM (NT LanMan), is a form of password authentication supported by Windows servers. Unless your email account is hosted on a Windows server and SPA is enabled, you won't use SPA. When SPA is required, your ISP or administrator will tell you.

7. Choose the Test Account Settings button to see whether your account information allows Outlook to connect to your mail server. When you click the button, a dialog appears like the one shown in Figure 2.3.

8. Choose the More Settings button. Although the account is usable after completing ▼ the E-mail Accounts screen, additional configuration options are available.

▼ FIGURE 2.3

Use Test Account Settings to verify that the information you entered is correct. If you entered an incorrect username, password, or server name, you'll receive an error indicating where the problem is.

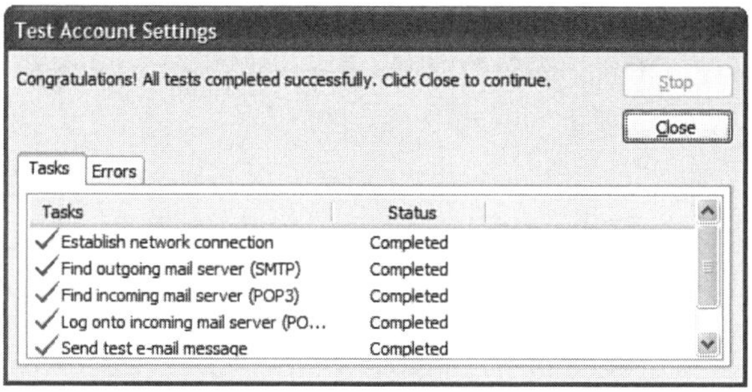

2

9. On the General tab, enter a friendly name for your account to replace the server name Outlook uses by default (see Figure 2.4). By default, Outlook uses your incoming mail server name for the account, adding a number to the name for additional accounts that use that server; for example, mail.server.com and mail.server.com (1). Suggestions include your email alias, name, or nickname.

FIGURE 2.4

If you use two or more email addresses and want all the replies to your messages to go to one address, enter the address in the Reply E-mail field.

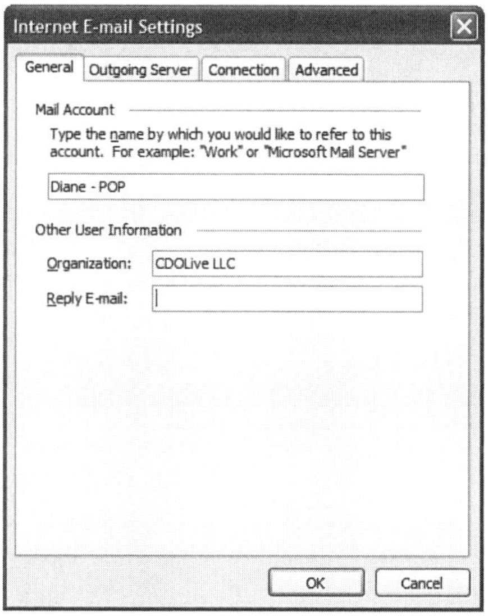

10. Complete the Organization and Reply E-mail fields. In most cases, the email address you entered on the E-mail Accounts screen is also your reply to address and you can leave this field blank. However, you can use this field to redirect replies to another email account. If you're using your account at work, you might want to include your company name in the Organization field; otherwise, most

▼ users leave it blank.

▼   11. Use the Outgoing Server tab if your SMTP server requires authentication or
        requires POP before SMTP, which means you must log on to the server to check
        mail before you send mail (see Figure 2.5).

In their fight against spam, many SMTP servers require authentication
before accepting outgoing email. Your ISP or email provider should tell you
if you need to enable outgoing authentication. If you can't send mail and
suspect authentication issues, try enabling POP before SMTP or outgoing
authentication.

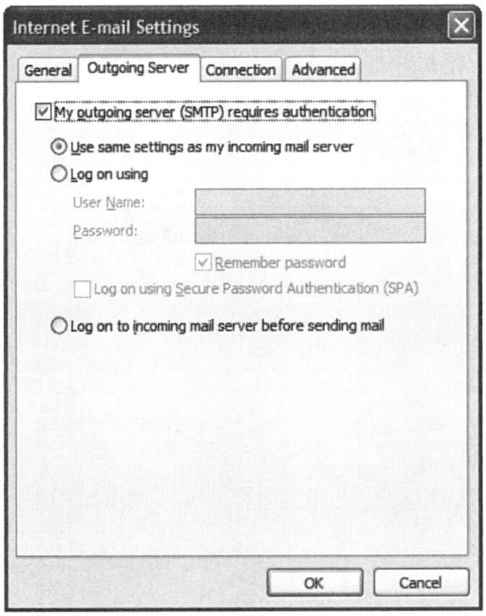

FIGURE 2.5

*Use the Outgoing
Server tab to configure
the settings needed to
connect to your outgo-
ing email server. If you
don't know if you need
to change these set-
tings, check your email
provider's help files
before making changes;
in many cases, the
default settings are
correct.*

Internet E-mail Settings

| General | Outgoing Server | Connection | Advanced |

☑ My outgoing server (SMTP) requires authentication

  ⊙ Use same settings as my incoming mail server
  ○ Log on using
     User Name:
     Password:
        ☑ Remember password
     ☐ Log on using Secure Password Authentication (SPA)

  ○ Log on to incoming mail server before sending mail

                          OK   Cancel

    12. The Connection tab controls how Outlook connects to the mail server (see Figure
        2.6). In most cases, you'll use the LAN option if you have cable or DSL service.
        Use Connect Using Internet Explorer or a 3rd Party Dialer if Outlook can connect
        using any active Internet connection. If you need to dial a specific account to check
        your mail, select Connect Using My Phone Line and select the Dial-Up networking
▼   connection from the Dial-Up Networking connection list.

FIGURE 2.6

Use the Connection tab to control how Outlook connects to your email server.

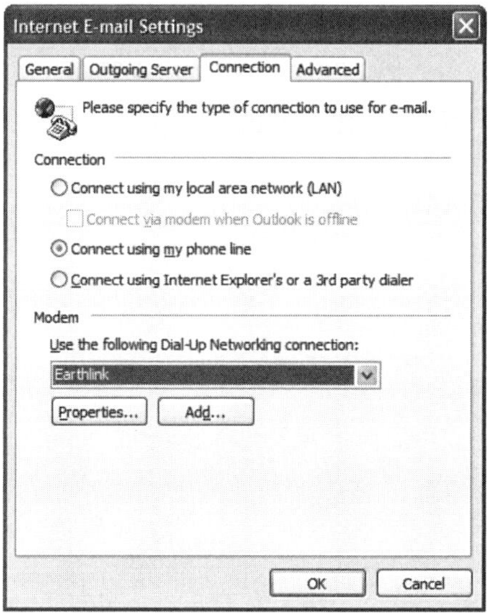

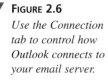

13. Use the Advanced tab to configure the ports Outlook uses to connect the email server (see Figure 2.7). In most cases, you'll use the defaults with ISP accounts. When alternative ports are required, your email provider will tell you. If you have a slow connection to your mail server, you might need to increase the Server Timeouts in intervals of 30–60 seconds. When you want to check your mail from more than one computer, you'll want to check the box to Leave a Copy of Messages on the Server. You can set Outlook to remove the messages after so many days or when you delete the messages from Outlook.

When you choose to delete messages from the server when they're deleted from Outlook, they're deleted from the server during the next send-and-receive cycle after emptying the Deleted Items folder or after using Shift+Delete to delete the items.

After you've selected the options you need, choose OK and then click Next, and you're finished setting up your account. A small dialog will display to tell you that it's setting up your message store. When it's completed that task, Outlook opens.

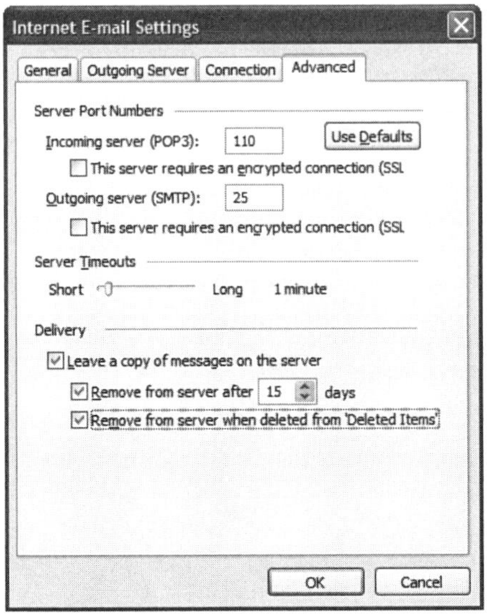

FIGURE 2.7

Use the Advanced tab to configure Outlook to leave copies of your mail on the server when you want to check your email for other computers. Unless you have an unlimited mailbox, you'll want to select one or both of the Remove from Server options.

Internet E-mail Settings

General | Outgoing Server | Connection | Advanced

Server Port Numbers

Incoming server (POP3): 110   [Use Defaults]

☐ This server requires an encrypted connection (SSL

Outgoing server (SMTP): 25

☐ This server requires an encrypted connection (SSL

Server Timeouts

Short ⊖———— Long   1 minute

Delivery

☑ Leave a copy of messages on the server

☑ Remove from server after 15 ⬍ days

☑ Remove from server when deleted from 'Deleted Items'

[OK] [Cancel]

If you have to set up additional accounts, open the E-mail Accounts dialog using Tools, E-mail Accounts and repeat the preceding steps for POP3 accounts or use the following steps for IMAP and HTTP accounts.

Task: Add Additional Accounts to Your Profile

Outlook doesn't limit you to one account per profile. Because many people have more than one email account, it's not unusual for people to have five or more accounts in a single profile.

For this exercise, we're going to add an IMAP account to an existing profile. If you use an IMAP account as your default account, select IMAP in the initial setup wizard and begin with step 3.

1. Choose Tools, E-mail Accounts to open the E-mail Accounts dialog.

2. Choose Add a New E-mail Account and then click Next.

3. Select IMAP from the Server type dialog, and then click Next.

4. The Account Settings dialog is almost identical to the one used for POP3 accounts, as shown in Figure 2.2. The exception is the lack of the Test Account Settings button. Enter your name, email address, and server names, as well as your username and password in the correct fields. Save your password if your computer is secure, and enable Secure Password Authentication if required.

▼   5. Click the More Settings buttons to access additional configuration settings for your account.

6. On the General tab, enter a friendly name for this account, an organization name, and a reply email address if needed. A friendly name is helpful when you use an IMAP or HTTP account because it's used to identify the message store in your folder list.

7. Select the Outgoing Server tab and configure your authentication settings. Many IMAP accounts require outgoing SMTP authentication, normally using the same settings as the incoming email account. If you use a different provider for your SMTP server, enter the username and password for that server here.

8. Use the Connections tab to configure your connection type. This is identical to the dialog used for POP3 accounts.

9. If your server uses nonstandard ports or you need to increase the server timeouts, make the appropriate change on the Advanced tab. This dialog differs only in that the delivery options shown in Figure 2.7 aren't here. In their place is a root folder path field. If your administrator gave you a root folder path, enter it on this tab;
▲   otherwise, leave this field blank.

Press OK and then click Next, then Finish and your IMAP account is ready to use. Outlook adds a new message store to your profile for each IMAP account. If you have only one account and it's an IMAP account, you'll have two message stores in your profile: the local store and the one that holds a local copy of your IMAP mailbox.

> When you need to edit your account settings, choose Tools, E-mail Accounts to open the E-mail Accounts dialog. Then choose View or Change Existing Accounts. Select the account in the E-mail Accounts dialog and choose Change or double-click on the account name. The Internet E-mail Settings dialog opens, as shown in Figures 2.2 and 2.5.

Configuring an HTTP Account

When you want to use Outlook to access your Hotmail or MSN account, choose the HTTP account option. Select Tools, E-mail Accounts to open the E-mail Accounts dialog, choose Add a New E-mail Account. Then click Next and choose HTTP as the account type.

1. Begin by entering your display name and email address in the name and email address fields. Outlook configures the server settings for you (see Figure 2.8). Although you can select an HTTP Mail Service Provider, you don't need to. Outlook chooses the correct provider based on the email domain.

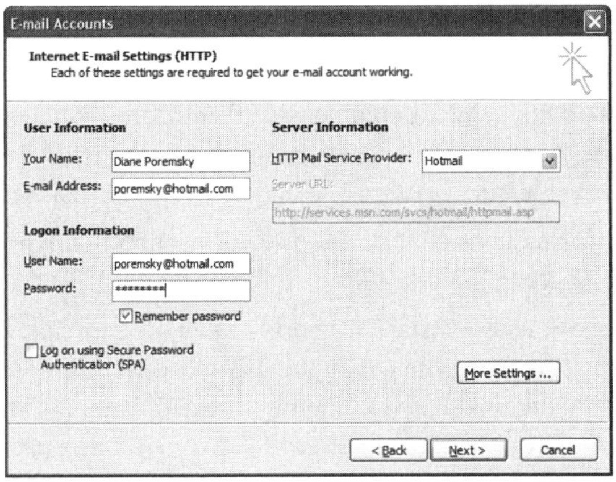

FIGURE 2.8

When you enter a Hotmail or MSN address, the server field uses the proper server URL.

2. If you choose More Settings, you'll discover that HTTP has just two settings tabs: General and Connection. These dialogs are identical to those used with IMAP and POP3. Enter a friendly name for your HTTP account, an organization name, and a reply to address on the General tab, and choose your connection settings on the Connection tab.

Choose OK and then click Next, and your HTTP account is complete. A new message store is created for each HTTP account in your profile.

As mentioned earlier, the only Web-based mail services that support HTTP access are Hotmail and MSN. However, if you use Exchange Server 2000 or Exchange 2003 and your administrator has OWA (Outlook Web Access) enabled, you can use Outlook to access your mail using the HTTP protocol.

After you enter your email address, the wizard detects that it's not a Hotmail/MSN address. The Server URL field is cleared, enabling you to enter an appropriate URL. When entering this URL, be sure to include your username at the end. For example, `http://ex2000.poremsky.com/exchange/diane/`.

Outlook's Calendar, Contacts, Tasks, and Journal folders are not supported by the HTTP protocol.

Configuring Exchange Server Accounts

The final account type included with Outlook 2003 is for Exchange Server. In most cases, your Exchange administrator will set up your profile for you, often by using configuration files to set up Outlook automatically. On the rare chance that you must set up Outlook yourself, access the server type dialog using Tools, E-mail Accounts to open the E-mail Accounts dialog. Choose Add a New E-mail Account, click Next, and select Microsoft Exchange Server from the list.

Enter your Exchange Server name and username, and then click Check Name. If Outlook asks for your username and password, you'll notice that there isn't a domain field in the dialog. You must enter your username in the format of *domain\username*. After Outlook connects to your server and resolves your name, your account is ready to use. Or you can click the More Settings button to configure additional options.

By default, Outlook creates Exchange accounts with Use Cached Exchange Mode enabled. This creates a local copy of your Exchange mailbox in an offline file (OST). You should leave this enabled unless your administrator disables it. When Outlook has problems connecting to the Exchange server, you'll still have access to the contents of your Exchange mailbox.

> You can add new accounts to a profile by selecting Tools, E-mail Accounts or Tools, Options, Mail Setup, E-mail Accounts.

Using Multiple Profiles

Using Outlook 2003, you can create as many profiles as you need. You'll most often create more profiles when more than one person shares a computer. Because Outlook 2003 supports multiple email accounts, you'll need more profiles only when you need to connect to more than one Exchange server or want to keep email from different accounts separated without using rules.

> Changing Windows logons just to check email can be annoying when you're using Windows 2000; it's easier to use one Windows logon and multiple Outlook profiles. Windows XP's Fast User Switching (FUS) allows other Windows users to log on without closing the first Windows session. They can switch to their Windows account and check their email.
>
> When using separate Windows user accounts, each user can have her own Outlook profile, including separate email signatures.

New profiles are also used for troubleshooting problems, such as when you have problems loading Outlook. One of the first things you should try when troubleshooting is a new profile (not a copy of your old one). Start with your default account and if Outlook loads properly, add any additional accounts to the profile, configure your signatures and other settings for the new profile, and then delete the old profile.

There are two ways to access the profile dialog:

- Use the Control Panel Mail applet by Choosing Start, Control Panel to open the Control Panel. If you use Windows XP and Control Panel categories, look in the User Accounts group for the Mail applet.

- Right-click on Windows XP Start Menu Outlook icon and choose Properties.

Choose Show Profiles to open the Profiles dialog as shown in Figure 2.9. Choose Add to create new profiles, or Properties to look at the settings of the selected profile. Either choice opens the dialogs shown.

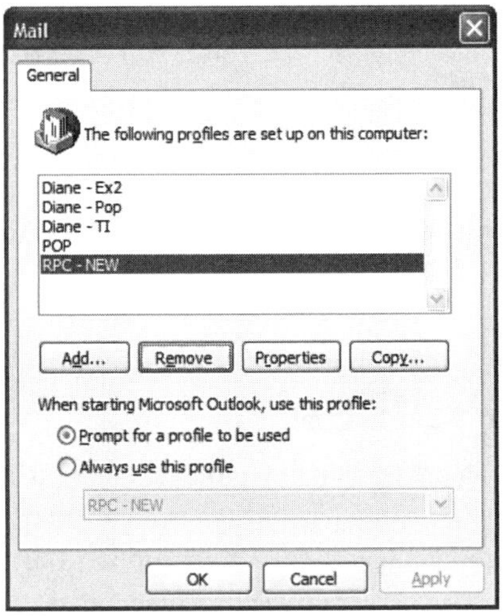

FIGURE 2.9

Use the Mail dialog to manage your Outlook profiles. Select a profile to use as your default profile, if desired.

If you have old profiles you no longer use, select the profile name and then click Delete to remove it. Use Copy to create a copy of an existing profile. However, it's often better to create a new profile instead of copying an existing one, especially if Outlook seems to hang or crash often.

Adding Address Books

If you're upgrading from a previous version of Outlook, you might have a Personal Address Book (PAB) to add to your profile. Although importing the contents of the PAB to your Outlook Contacts folder is highly recommended, you can add the PAB to your profile if you want to.

2

Now that Outlook supports distribution lists within the Contacts folder, there's little need for a Personal Address Book in Outlook. It just adds another file to keep track of and back up. If you're upgrading and previously used a PAB, you should import your PAB to the Contacts folder. If you never used a PAB before, don't start now. The PAB might not work with future versions of Outlook and won't work for mail merges or as an address book in other MAPI-aware programs, such as Internet postage programs.

Outlook supports the use of LDAP address lists. Although there are very few public LDAP servers, many universities have LDAP servers available for students and faculty to use and Windows 2000/2003 Active Directories are LDAP enabled.

Lightweight Directory Access Protocol (LDAP) is an Internet protocol that email programs use to look up contact information from a server. It's supported by most email clients and provides non–Exchange Server users with a shared address list.

- From the Tools, E-mail Accounts dialog, select Add a New Directory or Address Book.
- Choose Internet Directory Service (LDAP) if you use an LDAP server or Additional Address Books if you have a PAB to add to your profile.

If you chose LDAP, enter the server name and logon information for your LDAP server. Ask your administrator or look for online help files if you need the server name or search base information.

When you have an existing PAB to add to your profile, choose Personal Address Book from the next menu and then browse to select the PAB.

Using an Existing Personal Store

If you used Outlook previously, you might have an existing personal message store (PST) you'd like to use. But when you create a new profile in Outlook, it doesn't give you the opportunity to choose the message store to use—it creates a new one for you. You must go back into the menu and add your existing PST.

> Outlook 2003 uses a new message store format that provides Unicode support and can exceed the 2GB limitation found in Outlook 97–2002 format. As a result, you should consider moving or importing the contents of your existing PST into the new PST that Outlook creates for you.
>
> The exception is when you need to share the PST with older versions of Outlook. In that case, you'll want to keep using your existing PST.

If you want to use your existing PST, open the Tools, E-mail Accounts dialog and choose View or Change Existing Accounts. Click New Outlook Data File and browse for your existing message store (see Figure 2.10). Then select it from the Deliver New Mail to the Following Location list.

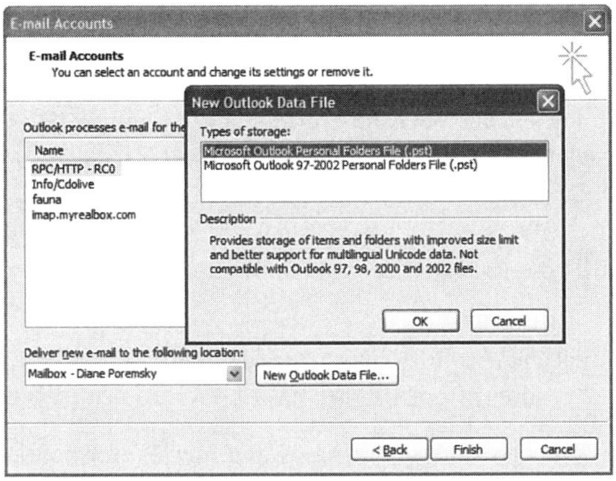

FIGURE 2.10

Click the New Outlook Data File button to create a new message store or use your existing message store. After adding a PST, select it from the Deliver New Mail to the Following Location List if you want to use it as the default delivery location.

> The New Outlook Data File button is confusing and misleading. You can use it to either create a new message store or use an existing store. If you select an existing PST, Outlook will use it. If you type in a name for a new PST, one will be created for you. The PST format selection applies only to new PSTs; your existing PST format does not change.

You can find and replace the PST Outlook creates with your old PST. If the PST names are the same, Outlook won't know the difference. You can find and rename the PST that Outlook created and reopen Outlook. When Outlook can't find the PST it was using, you'll be able to browse for the PST and point it to your old PST.

If you're using the new Unicode format PST, it's better to move the items to the new PST instead of using File, Import and Export. It takes a little bit more effort on your part, but links between contacts and other items are more likely to be preserved. If you use published custom forms, moving the folder also moves the forms. To move the items or folders yourself, open your existing PST using File, Open, Outlook Data File. Select the items or folders, right-click, and choose Move to Folder or Move "*foldername*".

Controlling Your Startup Folder

When you open Outlook, it normally opens to the Inbox folder. You can control which folder Outlook opens to by changing the Start Up In This Folder setting located in Tools, Options, Other, Advanced Options (see Figure 2.11).

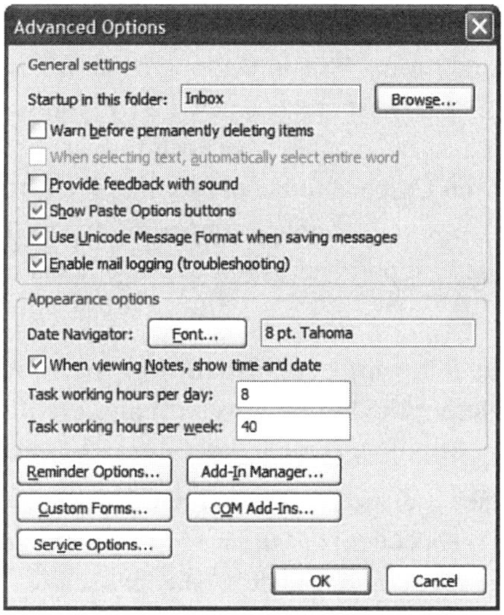

FIGURE **2.11**

New in Outlook 2003: You can select any folder in your profile to use as Outlook's default open folder, including Hotmail or IMAP inboxes. However, you can expect Outlook to open somewhat slower when a Hotmail or IMAP folder is set as the default folder.

You can also create shortcuts on your desktop to open Outlook in a different folder than the one set as the startup folder. Create a shortcut on your desktop with the full path to Outlook.exe and use the /select switch, followed by the folder name:

```
"C:\Program Files\Microsoft Office\OFFICE11\OUTLOOK.EXE "
/select outlook:Inbox\Mitchell
```

To make it easier to enter the correct folder name, especially for nested folders, show the Web toolbar (View, Toolbars), open the folder, and copy the folder name from the address bar.

 Look for the complete list of command-line switches in Appendix B, "Outlook's Command-Line Switches."

Summary

This hour showed you how to set up Outlook and create your profiles. You learned how to set up multiple accounts in one profile and how to set up multiple profiles. In many cases, this is all you need to do to begin using Outlook for the first time.

Q&A

Q Can I convert my PST between the new Unicode format and the old Outlook 97–2002?

A When you open an old format PST in Outlook 2003, it's not converted to a Unicode format PST. You must create a new PST if you want to use Unicode. There isn't a tool to convert your PST between formats because data loss can occur when you convert from Unicode to the old format. It's better to move, copy, or import and export. You won't be able to import or export from Unicode to the old format, but you can use import and export to move items from the old PSTs to the new PST format.

Q Outlook reports the following error when I try to connect to my hotmail account. I tried deleting the hotmail account and creating a new one but it didn't work.

The error says, `'Task Hotmail Folder:Inbox Synchronizing headers.' Reported error (0x800CCCF4): 'An unknown error has occurred. Please save any existing work and restart the program.'`

A This error is common when you're trying to connect to the Hotmail server from behind a proxy server that doesn't understand the WebDAV protocol. The result is that the responses from the Hotmail server are being stripped. The proxy server you connect through will need to be upgraded to one that supports the WebDAV protocol before you can use Outlook's HTTP protocol to access Hotmail or MSN email.

Q **I want to use the PST I used on my old computer in my new Outlook profile but when I try to open it I get this error:** `File access is denied. You do not have the permission required to access the file D:\Outlook.pst.` **What can I do?**

A It sounds like you burned the PST to a CD. When you copied the PST to your hard drive, you forgot to remove the Read Only flag from the file. Open Windows Explorer and browse to the location of the PST. Right-click on it and choose Properties and uncheck the <u>R</u>ead-only attribute at the bottom of the dialog. The file should now open correctly.

Hour **3**

Navigating the Outlook Interface

Finding your way around Outlook doesn't have to be difficult when you use views to show you the information you need. Views are fully customizable, with filters to control the information you display and formatting to control how it looks.

This hour shows you how to improve your experience with Outlook:

- Using views
- Customizing views
- Creating new views
- Using folder home pages

Views give you the chance to see some of the items in your Outlook folders while hiding the others. Outlook's print options use views to control what fields are printed. Or you can select all the items, copy the list, and paste it into Notepad, Word, or other programs.

Working with Views

Using Outlook views, you can control what fields and messages are visible, and highlight messages with different colors and fonts. You can use views for many more things, including displaying your Outlook items with specific fields showing, printing the items and fields shown in the format used in the view, filtering contacts you want to use in a mail merge, and copying the visible items and field to use in another program.

You can choose one of three ways to apply, customize, and define views. Choose the method that you're most comfortable using:

- Current View menu on the Advanced toolbar
- Selecting a view from the Navigation Pane Current View list
- Selecting a view using View, Arrange By, Current View menu

Each of these methods contains one or more customization options, including Customize Current View, for customizing the current view; Define Views, for creating new views; and Arrange By, for changing how your items group. For example, the view in Figure 3.1 is arranged by date.

FIGURE 3.1

When you enable View, Arrange By, Show Views In Navigation Pane, the views defined for the selected folder are listed at the bottom of the Navigation pane. You can also use the Current View toolbar button or the View menu to select a new view. Right-click on the Arranged By: field heading to change the grouping.

Custo<u>m</u> on the Arrange By menu opens the same Customize View dialog as Customize Current View on the Navigation Pane.

Arrange By is a smart grouping feature that's new to Outlook 2003. You can use it to quickly group by different fields. Arrange By isn't a new view; it's a different way of viewing the current view. When you expand or collapse groupings and then switch arrangements, the expanded or collapsed state of the Arrange By: groups isn't remembered. You must make a new view to save this and other settings.

Also new to Outlook 2003 is the two-line list view. When the list pane is fewer than 100 characters wide, the item's header information displays over two lines so that you can see more information about the message or item in a smaller space. When the list pane is greater than 100 characters wide, the list is on just one line, enabling you to see more items in the same amount of space.

Turn the Reading Pane off and on to switch between the one- and two-line lists.

Open View, Arrange By, Custom, Other Settings and change the character count to a lower number. Slide the Reading Pane to the right to switch to the one-line list and you can still use the Reading Pane. Use this dialog to disable or always force the two-line list.

The two-line list shows just the first six fields used in the view. By default, they are Importance, Icon, Attachment, From, Subject, Received Date, and Quick Flags. Changing the order of the fields changes the fields you'll see in the two-line list.

The Quick Flag column is always the rightmost column. You have to disable Quick Flags to move the flag column. Disable the Quick Flags column by right-clicking on the field names in the header row and choosing Custom. Select the Other Settings button, and then uncheck Show Quick Flags.

In most cases, changing the current view affects only the current folder's view. To change the view across all folders, you must modify the view, not customize it. Open the Custom View Organizer using View, Arrange By, Current View, Define Views and select the view by name (not <current view settings>), and then choose Modify. This opens the familiar Customize View dialog and applies the changes to all folders that use the same view (see Figure 3.2).

FIGURE 3.2

The Customize View dialog contains links to all the custom view options.

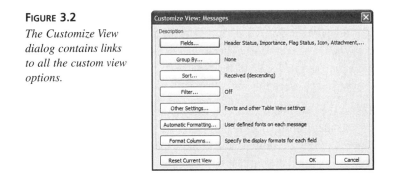

After changing the fields, arrangements, or other view options, restore the default view settings from the Customize View dialog or Reset Current View button, or reset the views from the Custom View Organizer.

> Outlook has a startup switch that you can use to reset all views to the default. Use this switch with care because all customized views are deleted.
>
> To reset all views, from the Start menu, select Run. In the Run dialog, type
> `"C:\Program Files\Microsoft Office\OFFICE11\OUTLOOK.EXE " /cleanviews`.

Message Views

Each Outlook item type includes several predefined views. For many users, those views are all they need. Using smart grouping, Message view may be the only view you'll ever need to use.

The default views for Mail and Post folders used for Exchange Server and POP3 mail accounts, as well as archives and personal folders, include Messages, Messages with AutoPreview, Last Seven Days, Unread Messages in This Folder, Sent To, and Message Timeline.

The local message store for IMAP accounts has additional default views, including IMAP messages, Hide Messages Marked for Deletion, Group Message Marked for Deletion, and Not Downloaded.

All new Mail and Post folders use the Message view, whereas IMAP folders use the IMAP Messages view by default.

Messages with AutoPreview and IMAP Message views display a three-line preview of the message body instead of using the Reading Pane. AutoPreview is 100% safe from viruses.

Calendar Views

Your Calendar folders offer the most view options. The Day/Week/Month and Day/Week/Month View with AutoPreview views are planner-style calendars, whereas the remaining views (Active Appointments, Events, Annual Events, Recurring Appointments, and By Category) use a table format. Use By Category to view all of your calendar items on one screen. You can drag items not assigned to categories to add them to a category.

The Day/Week/Month views use the Day Planner view by default, or you can choose Work Week, Week, or Month view within the view. Along with changing the day display, you can show or hide the TaskPad and move the calendar thumbnails from the left or right side of the screen.

Automatic formatting is available for calendar items, using labels on the Day/Week/Month view and font formatting in any Table view. You can use rules to set either type of automatic formatting and both are independent of each other. Labels can be applied using views or individually by selecting a label color on each calendar item.

In Figure 3.3, calendars in the mailbox and public folders are shown side-by-side using a Day Planner–style format.

The number of thumbnail calendars shown depends on your screen resolution. Making the Navigation Pane wider displays more calendars, as does removing the Current View list from the Navigation Pane and hiding the toolbars.

The Day/Week/Month views support multiple calendar viewing, provided you have more than one Calendar folder in your profile or use Exchange Server or SharePoint services and have permissions to view other calendars.

An Exchange public folder calendar is added to the Other Calendars list after you add it to Public Folder Favorites, right-click on it, and choose Add to Other Calendars. Remove a public folder calendar from Other Calendars by right-clicking on the calendar and choosing Remove from Other Calendars.

FIGURE 3.3

The Day/Week/Month calendar view provides many view customizations.

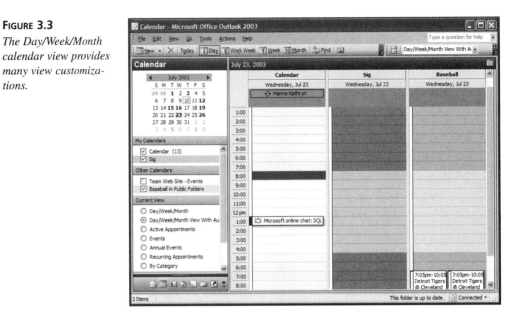

Drag the vertical bar on the right edge of the calendar inward to display the TaskPad and calendar navigators on the right side of the screen. When the TaskPad's calendars are visible, the calendar navigator on the left side is hidden. Adjust the bars separating the TaskPad and calendars to show more or fewer calendar navigators.

Even the view of the TaskPad can be changed to suit your needs. The TaskPad includes views for All Tasks, Today's Tasks, Active Tasks for Selected Days, Tasks for Next Seven Days, Overdue Tasks, Tasks Completed on Selected Days, and the option to Include Tasks with No Due Date. The TaskPad also supports Arrange By and custom views.

Right-click on the New Item row to select one of the predefined TaskPad views or right-click on a field name to use Arrange By or customize views.

Contacts Views

The default views for contacts are of two types: address card format and Table views. Table views enable you to view your contacts in groups, by category and by company, making it easier for you to locate the contact you need.

Address cards and detailed address cards are similar views, with more fields visible when using the detailed view. The remaining views are Table views, with Phone List the only view that does not use grouping. By Category, By Company, By Location, and By Follow-up Flag are the remaining default views and group your contacts by those fields.

Using views to filter contacts for mail merge enables you to begin the mail merge from Outlook and take advantage of Outlook's superior filtering capabilities.

Task Views

The default task views cover two areas: the Tasks folders and the TaskPad on the Calendar folder. The default views for Tasks folders include

- Simple List—Displays the subject and due date
- Detailed List—Includes Subject, Due Date, Status, % Complete, and Categories fields
- Active Tasks—Shows only the incomplete and not started tasks
- Next Seven Days—Displays the tasks due within the next seven days
- Overdue Tasks—Lists all tasks not yet completed and past due
- By Category—Groups tasks by category
- Assignment—Displays only tasks assigned to you
- By Person Responsible—Groups tasks by the task owner
- Completed Tasks—Shows only the completed tasks and the date they were marked complete
- Task Timeline—Displays the tasks in a timeline

The TaskPad displayed on the Day/Week/Month uses views that you can change and customize. Right-click on the Header row to access some customization options and on the New Task row to access view options.

Journal Views

The journal uses a timeline for most of its default views, grouping items by type, contact, or category. It also includes a Table view of all items in the journal, the last seven days, and journaled phone calls only.

In addition to viewing journal items in the Journal folder, many Outlook users use the Activities tab on contact forms to view journal entries for specific contacts. The Activities tab uses a view control and supports limited use of views.

Note Views

Not surprisingly, Notes has the fewest predefined views and the fewest available view options. Although the Reading Pane is not enabled for any of the default Notes views, it works well in the bottom position. AutoPreview is enabled only for Notes List view; however, it's nice to use with any Table view and permits you to read many notes without opening them.

The Icons view is similar to the Icons view you're familiar with in Windows Explorer and adds buttons to the toolbar to enable you to choose from large icons, small icons, or a list layout.

The remaining views (Last Seven Days, By Category, By Color) are variations of Table views. Enable AutoPreview on any of these views by choosing View, AutoPreview.

Automatic Formatting

Automatic formatting gives you the power to color-code Outlook items displayed in a Table view or Calendar items shown in the Day/Week/Month view.

You can create simple automatic formatting rules using the Organize pane or create more complex rules using Customize View.

Open the Organize pane using Tools, Organize and select Using Colors (see Figure 3.4).

FIGURE 3.4

Use the Organize pane to create simple color formatting rules. These are stored with the current view and can be customized or removed using Customize Current View.

Creating automatic formatting rules using Customize View enables you to use more conditions and create complex filters to apply formatting to the messages.

Calendar folders support two types of automatic formatting. The first is the same automatic formatting that you use in other folders. The second is labels that are used only in Day/Week/month view. You can choose labels for your calendar items from the calendar form or apply labels using rules. However, applying labels using views affects only items that don't have a label color selected on the appointment form (see Figure 3.5).

Choosing label colors on the appointment form creates persistent label colors that are not changed using views.

Figure 3.5

Use automatic formatting to set labels on existing calendar items.

Creating Custom Views

The power of views comes not from the predefined views, but from the ability to create your own custom views. You can customize the current view used on any folder, create new views, or customize any of the default views included with Outlook.

All custom view options are on the Custom View dialog. Open the dialog by right-clicking on the field names at the top of the list pane and selecting Custom.

The options you can choose from when customizing or creating views include

- Fields—Select the fields you want visible in your view, or remove fields you don't need, using the Show Fields dialog (see Figure 3.6). Use this dialog to control the number of lines used in the multiline layout. Not all of these options are available for all view types.

- Group By—Enables you to choose specific fields to group by or use the default of Automatically Group According to Arrangement (see Figure 3.7). Automatic grouping enables you to click on a field name and group by that field or select a grouping from the smart grouping menu. The Group By dialog also has the default Expand/Collapse setting for the view.

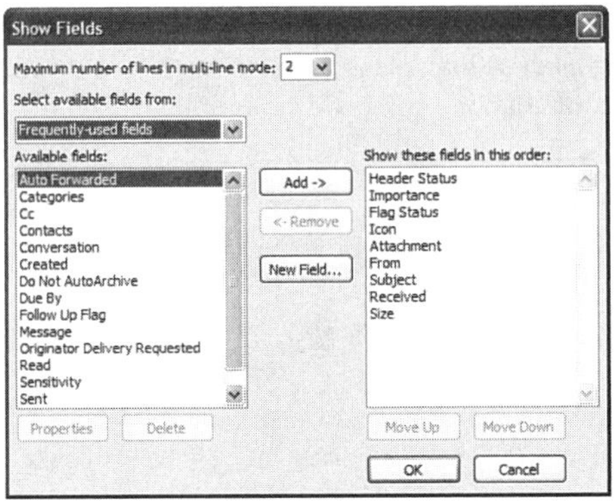

FIGURE 3.6

Use the Show Fields dialog to select and remove fields from your view. You can select any item type from the Select Available Fields From list for use on any other item type; how-ever, not all fields are available on all items.

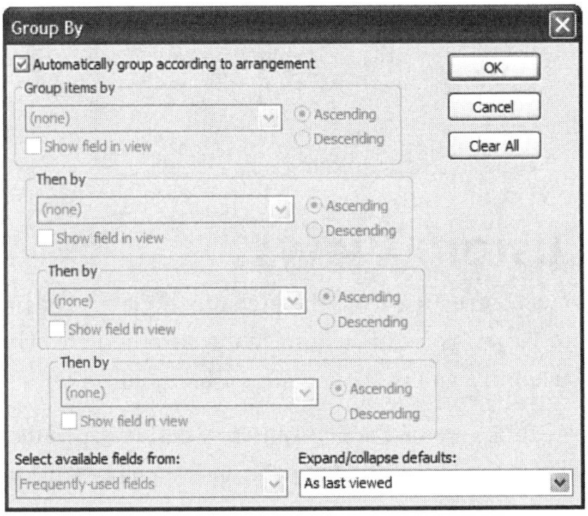

FIGURE 3.7

Use the Group By dialog to control how your view is displayed. Using automatic grouping enables you to change the grouping by right-clicking on the field names and choos-ing a new grouping.

Use grouping to group by fields that you need to change, and then drag the items between fields to change the groups. For example, group by the Private field, and then drag items between the Private: Yes and Private: No groups to change the Private setting on the items. You can also use grouping to change company names and add categories, but not remove categories.

- Sort—Enables you to choose up to four fields to sort by, in ascending or descend-ing order. Use this to create views that sort by sender, and then by received date, for example.

- Filter—Possibly the most powerful option available in views. It uses the same dialog, conditions, and actions that are used by Search Folders, automatic formatting, and Advanced Find.

- Other Settings—Provides you with many of the display options for the view, including the fonts used for the list items and field names, whether AutoPreview or the Reading Pane is enabled by default, and Quick Flag options (see Figure 3.8).

FIGURE 3.8

Use Other Settings to set column display and preview options for your view.

Other Settings

Column Headings and Rows

Column Font...	8 pt. Tahoma	☑ Automatic column sizing
		☐ Allow in-cell editing
Row Font...	8 pt. Tahoma	☐ Show "new item" row

Grid Lines and Group Headings

Grid line style: Solid   ☑ Show items in Groups
                            ☐ Shade group headings

AutoPreview

Font...   8 pt. Tahoma   ○ Preview all items
                          ○ Preview unread items
                          ⊙ No AutoPreview

Reading Pane

⊙ Right   ○ Bottom   ○ Off   ☐ Hide header information

Other Options

☑ Show Quick Flag column
☑ Use multi-line layout in widths smaller than [100] characters.
   ○ Always use single-line layout   ○ Always use multi-line layout
☑ Always show unread and flagged messages in Arrange by Conversation

OK   Cancel

> Enable Shade Group Headings to make your group headings smaller but easier to see.

- Automatic Formatting—Provides you with powerful options for displaying your Outlook items (see Figure 3.9).

   Automatic formatting uses the same filter dialog as filters and gives you the opportunity to display filtered items using different font formatting instead of simply showing or hiding the items. Using automatic formatting in conjunction with filters, you can create more granular filters by highlighting items that meet different conditions. For example, you could create a filter to show all email from your boss and use automatic formatting to colorize messages sent only to you in blue, messages cc'd to you in green, and messages sent to you and cc'd to others in red.

FIGURE 3.9

Choose Add and enter the condition and font formatting for your automatic formatting rule. Rules are applied in the order listed, and if two rules apply to one item, the item is formatted by the first rule.

Create simple automatic formatting rules by choosing Tools, Organize, and then Using Colors. Automatic formatting rules created this way are stored with the view you're using. If you change views, the messages lose the formatting.

- Format Columns—Use with the one-line view (Reading Pane off) to control how each field displays and change the name displayed for the fields shown in the view (see Figure 3.10).

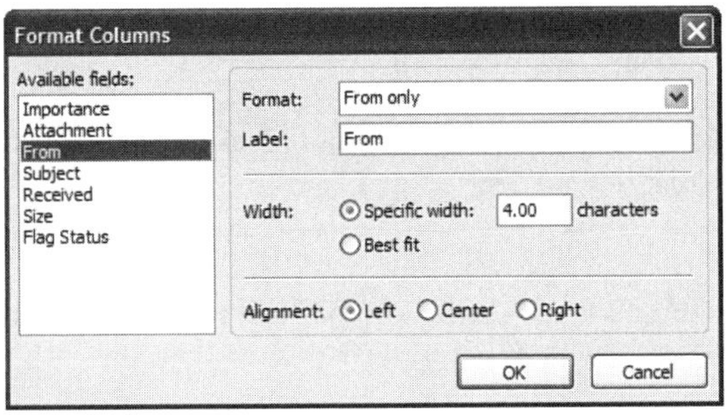

FIGURE 3.10

Change how the date and size fields display and whether to use icons or text for the Flag, Importance, and Attachment fields.

Use Format Columns to remove field names from group headings when using a one-line view.

- <u>R</u>eset Current View—Restore the default views to their original state. This button is disabled for custom views you create; you'll have to make a copy of your custom views before editing them if you want to restore the original view settings.

> Modifying the view by name won't apply to folders where the view is *one-offed*, which is when you customize the view on a folder and a copy of the view is stored in the folder. You'll have to reset the view on all folders that are one-offed and then customize the view again.
>
> To prevent one-offed views, use new views instead of changing the current view.

Task: Copy Data from a View

One advantage to using Table views is the capability to copy the information displayed and paste it into a document, which is often very useful for the calendar, contacts, and tasks.

1. Adjust the view on the folder to show all the fields you want to copy.
2. Select the first item and use Ctrl+A to Select All or hold Shift as you move down using the arrow keys.
3. Use Ctrl+C to copy the selected items, and then press Ctrl+V to paste them into a document for a nicely formatted table of Outlook data.

You can copy any list using this method, including contact's card format. By limiting the fields included in the view and using filters to control the records displayed, you can use this method to make a quick list of your Outlook items.

All fields included in the view are copied, not just the fields visible on screen, and all the items you select are copied.

Task: Create a New View

The steps for creating your own views are the same for any folder type. For this exercise, I'm creating a view that displays the last five days' email, color-coded by sender. You could use Search Folders and an automatic formatting rule to create a similar view, but I prefer using a view on the folder so that it can be applied to any folder at any time and display only items from the folder.

▼ 1. Open the Custom View Organizer using the Define Views menu located at the bottom of the Current View tool button list, located on the Advanced toolbar (see Figure 3.11). (Define Views is also on the View, Arrange By, Current View menu.)

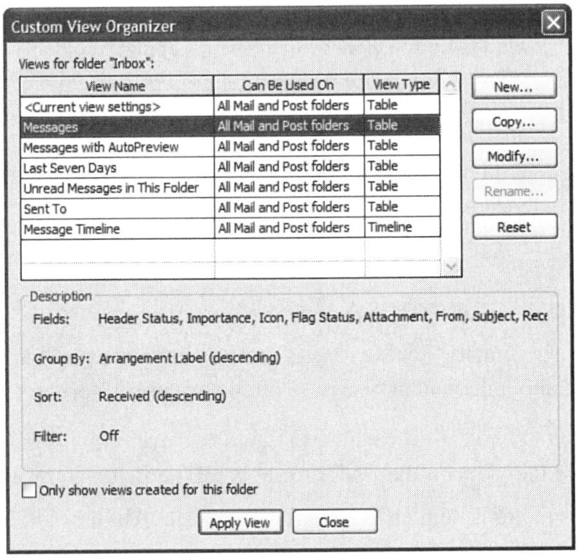

FIGURE **3.11**

Use the Custom View Organizer to create new views, and to copy, modify, delete, and reset existing views. When modifying views, select the view by name if you want the modifications to apply to all folders that use that view.

2. Select New to open the Create a New View dialog (see Figure 3.12). Enter a name for your view and choose the type of view you want to create. Finally, choose where the view will be used. I'm using a Table view to use on all mail and post folders.

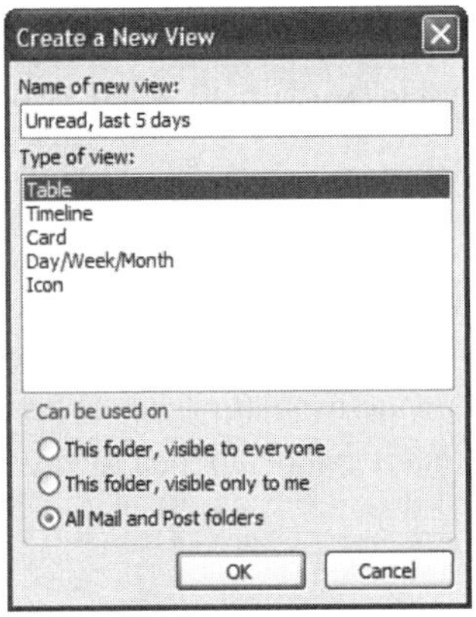

FIGURE **3.12**

Choose from all the available view types using the Create a New View dialog. You can use any type of view on any folder type, although some of the types offer limited functionality for most folder types. After you've selected a view type, you cannot change it—you'll have
▼ *to create a new view.*

▼

- Table views work well on all folder types for a variety of uses. This view provides the most configuration options, including automatic formatting, filtering, and sorting.

- Timeline is best suited for displaying journal items, with limited usefulness for email, calendar, and tasks. Automatic formatting and sorting are not supported in this view.

- Card view works best with Contacts folders and offers little functionality in other folders. It supports automatic formatting, but not grouping by fields.

- Day/Week/Month views are the default for calendar folders, but you can create Day/Week/Month views for any folder, including Tasks and Journal folders.

- Icon view is quite limited and most suitable for Notes folders because you cannot choose fields and are limited to sorting and filtering items.

> When creating new views, you can use any type of view for any folder type. Although some view types aren't the best choice for some folder types, such as an icon view for email, Outlook lets you create the view.

After choosing the view type, you need to select where you want to use the view: on the current folder or on all folders of same type as the current folder. You can make the view private so that only you can use it, or public, for anyone to use. In most cases, these options are best suited for Exchange Server users, for public folders, or for mailbox folders others have permissions to view.

3. After clicking OK, the Customize View dialog opens for you to configure the options you want to use in your view. For this example, I'm going to create filters and automatic formatting rules.

4. First, I need to create a filter that shows only the last 5 days' worth of messages. I could use the Time field, which is preconfigured for specific dates, but I'm going to use the Advanced tab and create my own time filter (see Figure 3.13).

5. Next, I'm creating the formatting rules to color messages from different senders. Choose the Automatic Formatting button from the Customize View dialog and click Add New Rules. Enter a name for the rule, and then choose Font to select the font effects for this rule. Select Condition and create a filter for the rule.

▲

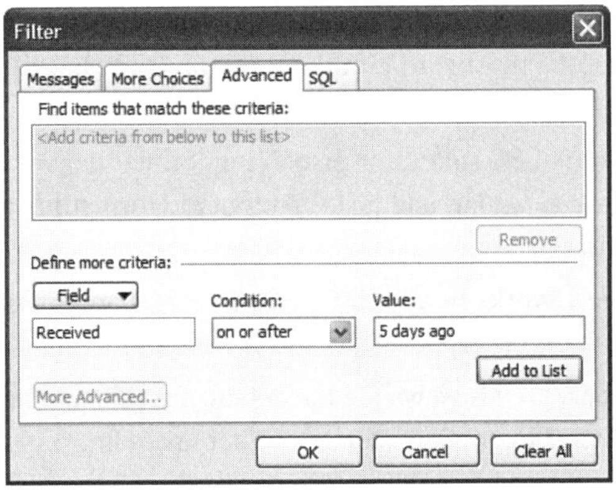

FIGURE **3.13**

Create the filter by selecting the Define More Criteria field, Date/Time fields, and then Received. In the Condition field, select On or After and enter 5 days ago *in the Value field. Choose Add to List and click OK.*

Filter [X]

Messages | More Choices | Advanced | SQL

Find items that match these criteria:

<Add criteria from below to this list>

[Remove]

Define more criteria:

[Field ▼]   Condition: Value:

[Received]   [on or after ▼]   [5 days ago]

[More Advanced...]   [Add to List]

[OK]   [Cancel]   [Clear All]

I'm making three formatting rules for my view. My first rule is for senders from certain domains. On the Messages tab, I create a rule using the From field and partial addresses in the field. I can use more than one domain or keyword in the field by separating the words with *or*; for example, `microsoft or quepub`.

> Not all fields by the same name are created equal. For example, the From field on the Messages tab looks at email addresses, whereas the From field on the Advanced tab looks at the display name.

My next rule is Family and uses display names as the criteria. On the Advanced tab, choose the From field. The condition is Contains and the value is the last names, separated by *or*: `worth or fisher`.

> Use the OR operator within conditions on the Advanced tab, and use AND to join conditions together.

My last rule is Has Attachments and uses the Only Items with One or More Attachments condition, found on the More Choices tab. Because unread mail not meeting these conditions is less important to me in the view, I uncheck the Unread rule.

The rules are applied to the items in the order they're listed, with messages meeting two or more of the rules using the formatting specified by the first rule. By adjusting the order of the rules, you can fine-tune the formatting. For example, because VIPs is the first rule, the message from Andrew Fisher is formatted by the VIP rule, even though his message also meets the conditions of the Family rule.

I switch to this view to catch up on my unread messages and switch back to Messages view when I want to see my complete Inbox (see Figure 3.14).

FIGURE 3.14

Use automatic formatting to highlight items in different colors.

Using Folder Home Pages

Use folder home pages to replace the view on a folder with a Web page, or use the Outlook View control to display different Outlook items in a folder.

You can choose any Web page for the folder home page, but using a locally stored home page is usually the best because it won't cause Outlook to hang if your Internet connection is slow.

Outlook Today is a folder home page, but the folder it's in has security restrictions on the type of controls that will display. Folders don't have the same restrictions and, as a result, they can display controls that Outlook Today cannot. For this reason, it's generally better to leave Outlook Today as is and create folder home pages when you want to use a custom Outlook Today page.

Open the Folder properties sheet by right-clicking on the folder and choosing Properties from the menu. Select the Home Page tab and enter the URL or browse for a local file. Display the home page by checking Show Home Page by Default for This Folder (see Figure 3.15).

FIGURE 3.15

Set a local file or page from the Internet as your folder home page. Although you can use any file type that displays in Internet Explorer, using HTML-formatted pages is more practical than using text or image files as your home page.

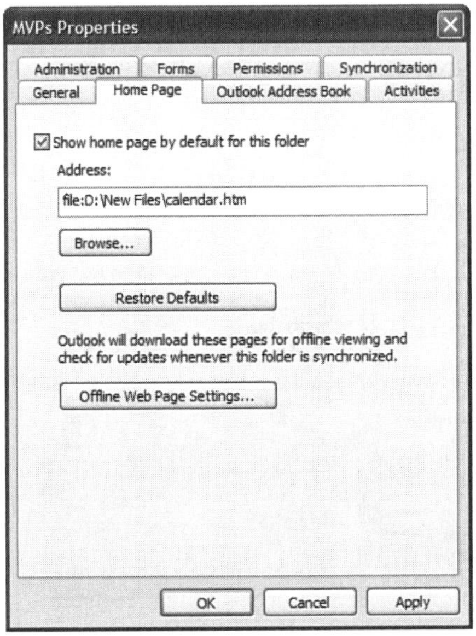

MVPs Properties

| Administration | Forms | Permissions | Synchronization |
| General | Home Page | Outlook Address Book | Activities |

☑ Show home page by default for this folder

Address:

file:D:\New Files\calendar.htm

Browse...

Restore Defaults

Outlook will download these pages for offline viewing and check for updates whenever this folder is synchronized.

Offline Web Page Settings...

OK   Cancel   Apply

When you set a local file as your folder home page, Outlook will complain about updating offline files. Choose OK to close the dialog and click OK again to close the property sheet, or click Cancel if Outlook continues to complain. The local file is set as your folder home page, even though you chose Cancel.

To view the contents of the folder, uncheck Show Home Page by Default for This Folder. To clear the filename, choose Restore Defaults.

 When you assign a folder home page to a Calendar folder, you need to use the folder list to view the folder home page. If you select the folder from Calendar's Navigation Pane, the folder contents display.

Although you can use any HTML page for the folder home page, you might like to use a page displaying other Outlook folders. Using the Outlook View control, you can display the contents of any folder in your profile in the folder home page.

Enter the following code into a new Notepad file. Adjust the height and width parameters to suit and replace Calendar with the folder you want to display. Save the text with an .HTML extension and use it for your folder home page (see Figure 3.16).

```
<HTML>
<HEAD>
<TITLE>My Folder Home Page</TITLE>
</HEAD>
<BODY BGCOLOR="#FFFFFF">
<OBJECT id=ViewCtlFolder height=225 width=500
classid=CLSID:0006F063-0000-0000-C000-000000000046>
<PARAM NAME="Folder" VALUE="Calendar">
<PARAM NAME="Namespace" VALUE="MAPI">
<PARAM NAME="Restriction" VALUE="">
<PARAM NAME="DeferUpdate" VALUE="0"></OBJECT>
</BODY>
</HTML>
```

If you show the Web toolbar, you can select a folder, and then copy the folder path from the Address field to use in the View control. Use the folder names following outlook:.

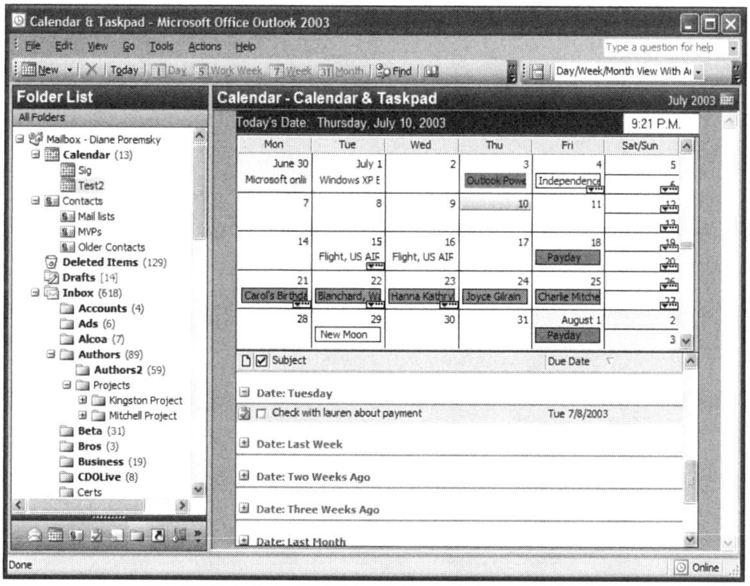

FIGURE 3.16

Two Outlook View controls embedded in an HTML page display a Calendar and Tasks folder as a folder home page.

For more information about using the Outlook View control to create folder home pages or desktop wallpaper, see http://www.poremsky.com/AD_DD.htm.

The toolbar for the first folder used in your home page is enabled, as shown in Figure 3.16. Changing the views for additional folders used in a View control is a bit more difficult; in many cases you can right-click on the field names in the View control and choose a new view. For a calendar, right-click anywhere on the calendar and choose Go to Date. Select a different view from the Go to Date menu.

Summary

This hour showed you how to use views to display your Outlook information in different ways. You learned how to customize your views, how to create a new custom view, and how to use automatic formatting to highlight items.

Views can help you become more efficient and make it easier to complete a mail merge with correct contacts. Views are used to control the information displayed on printouts, and make it easy for you to copy the just the information you need in reports and other documents.

In addition, you learned how to use folder home pages to display HTML pages in your folders.

Q&A

Q Can I back up my views or share them with other people?

A It's not easy, but it's possible to share views that were created for all folders. You can make a copy of your PST and delete all the Outlook items. This leaves only the views (and published forms) in the PST. Any views that are for this folder only or visible to you only must be copied as an All Folders, Visible to Everyone view.

To copy the views to another folder, select the folder where you want the view copied to. Select the view, and then choose Copy. Remove copy from the name (or rename the view) and then save the view. The copy is now stored in your folder.

Repeat for each view and folder type you want to copy.

Exchange Server users can also use Copy Folder Design, which is discussed in Hour 9, "Keeping Email Organized."

Q **How do I change the view used when I create new folders?**

A The default view used on new folders can't be changed, but you can customize the view. Open the Custom View Organizer and select the view by name, and then modify it.

Because a view can get messed up easily, always make a copy. You should also consider using a new custom view on a folder instead of customizing the default view. Views are easy to apply using the Custom Views toolbar button and there is less risk of resetting your customized view.

Q **I used Tools, Organize to color some messages and when I moved them to a new folder, the colors were gone. What happened?**

A The item properties aren't changed when you use Organize; a rule is created in the current view that displays the items using your selected colors. If you apply the view in the new folder, the items will be colored again.

3

PART II
Using Outlook for Email

Hour

Hour 4

Email Basics

This hour and the next hour show you how to use your email accounts effectively—from the basic configuration to choosing the best format for your messages.

- Working with email accounts
- Choosing message formats

If you're new to email, the different email account types, including Hotmail, POP3, and IMAP, might leave you confused. Although you'll need to check with your service provider to find out what type of account you have, this hour aims to help you understand the differences between the account types and how to use your accounts effectively.

Using Your Email Accounts

Outlook supports several common email protocols, including POP3, IMAP, HTTP, and Exchange Services. Many times you don't have a choice in the type of email account you'll use with your Internet access account, but you might have access to other account types through a Web hosting company or free email services.

The majority of Internet email accounts use *POP3*, which is short for *Post Office Protocol version 3*. POP3 is the Internet standard for email, and is supported by almost all mail server software. POP3 mail is typically downloaded from the email server and stored locally on your PC. *IMAP*, or

Internet Mail Access Protocol, is a server-based mailbox store that is growing in popularity and, like POP3, has support from many mail servers. Copies of the messages are downloaded to your email client and you can access your messages from anywhere. Although many mail servers support both POP3 and IMAP protocols, most Internet service providers configure only one, usually POP3, for subscribers to use.

Several years ago, Microsoft developed *HTTP*, a proprietary email protocol to use with Web-based email accounts. Like IMAP, messages are stored on the email server and a user downloads copies of her messages to her local machine. The difference is that HTTP uses port 80 to access the mailbox and IMAP uses port 143. Because port 80 is also used for Web browsing, only one port needs to be opened on the firewall, which increases network security. At this time, only Hotmail and MSN support HTTP access to email using an email program.

Exchange Services encompasses two types of access to your mailbox. Traditional MAPI access is typically used within LANs and supports special Outlook folders, such as Contacts and Calendars, which are not supported by IMAP and POP3. Security-conscious companies prevent access to mailboxes across the Internet, except when using a VPN (Virtual Private Network) connection. Outlook 2003 supports a new protocol: RPC over HTTP (Remote Procedure Call over Hypertext Transfer Protocol). RPC over HTTP provides MAPI (Messaging Application Programming Interface) access to your mailbox using port 80, the same port used by Web servers, thus providing the same email experience to remote users that is enjoyed by local users. Although RPC over HTTP sounds great, it has one major limitation. It's supported only in Exchange 2003 and Windows Server 2003 and requires Outlook 2003 to be installed on Windows XP SP2.

Simple Mail Transport Protocol, or SMTP, is the protocol that POP3 and IMAP accounts use to send email.

Set up the Send/Receive settings for your accounts using Tools, Options, Mail Setup, Send/Receive (see Figure 4.1). You can also access your Account Properties from the Send/Receive dialog.

If you don't know what type of email account you have, you'll need to ask your ISP or email administrator.

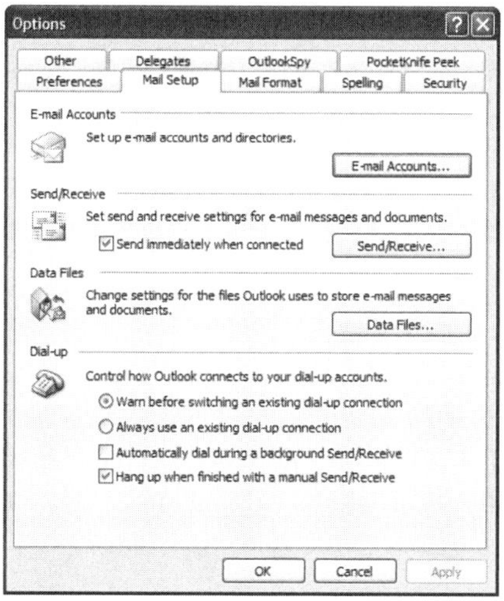

FIGURE **4.1**

*Use the Mail Setup tab
to configure Outlook to
send messages immedi-
ately when connected,
to control how Outlook
connects to dial-up
accounts, and to
access the Send/
Receive settings.*

All POP3 accounts share your default PST for message storage. IMAP and HTTP
accounts each use a local PST for local message storage because items stored locally are
synchronized with the IMAP or HTTP server—sharing one local folder would result in
messages from all accounts being stored on one or more servers. IMAP and HTTP
accounts require a second local PST to store calendar, contacts, and tasks because IMAP
and HTTP servers don't support the special folders.

Outlook uses a PST, or Personal Store, to store your messages, calendar, contacts, and
other Outlook items in one file on your hard drive. The PST file also contains forms,
views, and rules, which are stored as hidden messages in the PST. You can have any
number of PSTs in your Outlook profile. The default PST contains the special folders
used by the calendar, contacts, journal, tasks and notes and is where messages from
POP3 email accounts are delivered. Because a PST is a database, Outlook must have
read/write access to it. For this reason, you can't store a PST on a CD-R disc.

Using a POP3 Mail Account

If your Internet email account is POP3, select POP3 as the account type in the Tools,
Email Accounts Wizard. Enter your account information, including the display name you
use on outgoing email, your email address, your POP3 server name, and your outgoing
email server.

You might need to configure advanced options for your account, including outgoing
server authentication and the Leave Mail on Server setting. If so, choose the More
Settings button on the Internet E-mail Settings dialog.

You typically use POP3 to download messages to your local message store, and each time Outlook checks for new email, it deletes the messages from the server after it has finished downloading them. However, if you need to access your email on more than one computer, you can leave your messages on the server. Open the Internet E-mail Settings dialog using Tools, E-mail Accounts, View or Change Existing E-mail Accounts. Select the account by name and choose Change, and then choose More Settings.

Select the Advanced tab and add a check to Leave a Copy of Messages on the Server (see Figure 4.2). You should always add a check to Remove from Server When Deleted from "Deleted Items" to help keep the size of your mailbox under control. Unless you have a large mailbox and receive very little mail, you'll also want to check Remove from Server After *nn* Days. Without these settings, copies of your messages remain on the server and cause your mailbox to reach its maximum size, preventing the delivery of new messages.

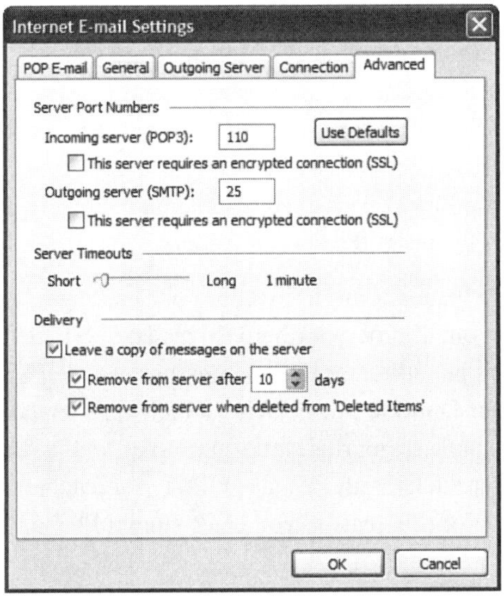

FIGURE 4.2

Configure Outlook to leave messages on the server after downloading so that you can access them from other computers.

If you're on a slow Internet connection, you might want to download only headers for your messages, shortening the time you need to remain connected. After the headers are downloaded, mark the messages for download or deletion and process the marked headers.

From Tools, Options, Mail Setup, click the Send/Receive button and then the Send/Receive group the account uses. Unless you created additional groups, your account is in the All Accounts group. Choose Edit and select your account in the Send/Receive settings dialog, shown in Figure 4.3.

FIGURE 4.3

Use the Send/Receive Settings dialog to choose headers only or complete items. You can choose Headers Only for large messages.

Finally, you should configure Outlook's send and receive settings. You can do this by account or by all accounts, if you have more than one account and want them to share the same settings. Open the Send/Receive Groups dialog using Tools, Options, Mail Setup, Send/Receive (see Figure 4.4).

4

FIGURE 4.4

Outlook can check for new messages on a regular basis, when you are online or offline. For best results, you should use check for new mail no more than every 8 to 10 minutes.

Choose Schedule an Automatic Send/Receive Every *nn* Minutes and Outlook will check for new mail when you open it and every *nn* minutes while it remains open.

After your account is configured, click Send/Receive to check for new email if you aren't using automatic send and receive.

Checking for mail too frequently causes excessive server load for your ISP. If you're downloading large messages, Outlook might stop collecting new mail if a send and receive is attempted before the current send and receive is finished.

If you're downloading only headers, right-click on the messages and choose Mark to Download or Delete to delete messages you want to remove from the server (see Figure 4.5). When you're ready to get the full message, choose Send/Receive.

The Junk E-mail filter removes spam from your inbox when you download the full message. See Hour 14, "Organizing Outlook," to learn more about junk email filtering.

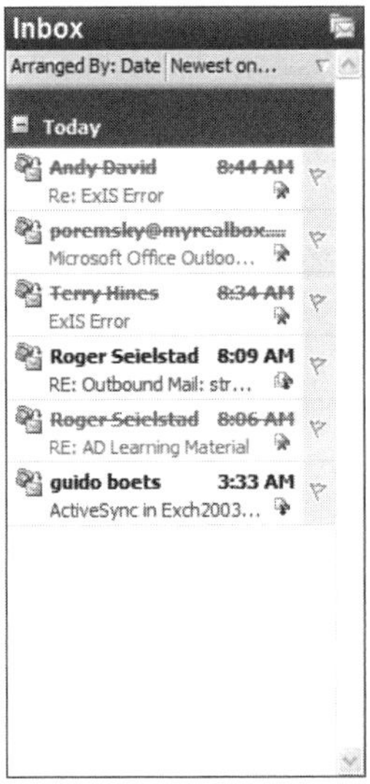

FIGURE 4.5

Using the Download Headers Only option, headers are marked to download later or marked for deletion. The next time you check for new mail, the messages are downloaded or deleted.

Inbox
Arranged By: Date Newest on...
Today
Andy David   8:44 AM
Re: ExIS Error
poremsley@myrealbox...
Microsoft Office Outloo...
Terry Hines   8:34 AM
ExIS Error
Roger Seielstad   8:09 AM
RE: Outbound Mail: str...
Roger Seielstad   8:06 AM
RE: AD Learning Material
guido boets   3:33 AM
ActiveSync in Exch2003...

You can access your account settings from the Tools, E-mail Accounts dialog. You can also access them by selecting Tools, Options, Mail Setup, Send/Receive button. Choose the Send/Receive group your account is in, choose Edit, select the account and then select Account Properties.

Using Your IMAP Account

When you use an IMAP account, select it as the account type in the E-mail Accounts Wizard. Enter your display name, email address, and server names in the appropriate fields.

If your Internet email account is IMAP, select IMAP as the account type in the Tools, Email Accounts Wizard. Enter your account information, including the display name you use on outgoing email, your email address, your IMAP server name, and your outgoing (SMTP) email server (see Figure 4.6).

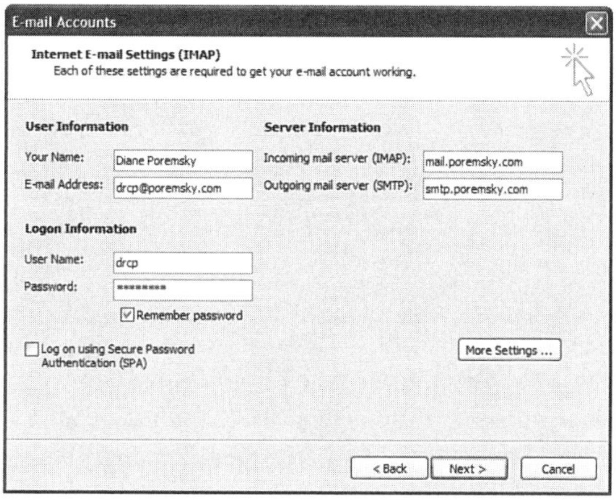

FIGURE 4.6

Configure the required fields for your IMAP account before you use it.

IMAP accounts generally don't require additional configuration, except for outgoing server authentication. If your email server requires authentication, enter the username and password information on the More Settings, Outgoing Server tab found in the Internet E-mail Settings dialog.

> Hour 2, "Outlook Configuration Basics," contains detailed instructions on setting up each type of email account.

Outlook downloads copies of IMAP messages to a local message store and the messages remain on the server until you delete and purge the folders.

When you're configuring a new IMAP account, you have to subscribe some folders for download before you can configure the send and receive settings for your IMAP folders.

If you previously used the IMAP account with another email program, the subscribed folders should display in Outlook after you add the account. You can change the list of subscribed folders by right-clicking on any IMAP folder and choosing I̲MAP Folders. Choose Query to show all available folders or enter a keyword to search for folders by name (see Figure 4.7).

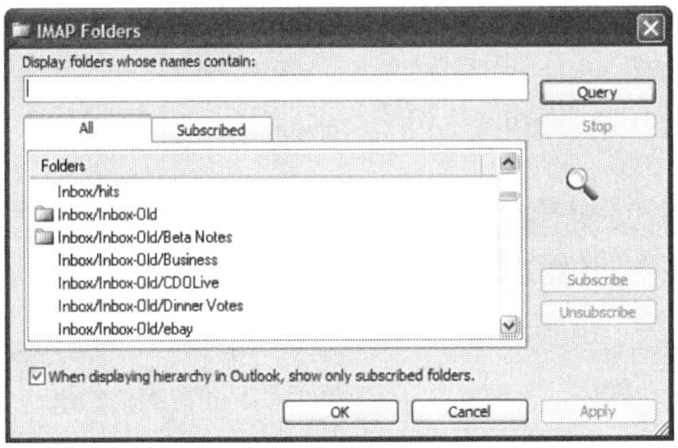

FIGURE 4.7

Use the IMAP Folders dialog to query the IMAP server for your email folders and sub-scribe or unsubscribe from them. The folder icon identifies sub-scribed folders. Select the option to show only subscribed folders in your folder list to restrict the size of your folder list.

If checked, remove the check from W̲hen Displaying Hierarchy in Outlook, Show Only Subscribed Folders to show all folders in the list in the Send/Receive Settings dialog. When you add a check to any folder in the Send/Receive Settings folder list, as shown in Figure 4.8, the folder is automatically subscribed and the contents are downloaded according to your send and receive settings.

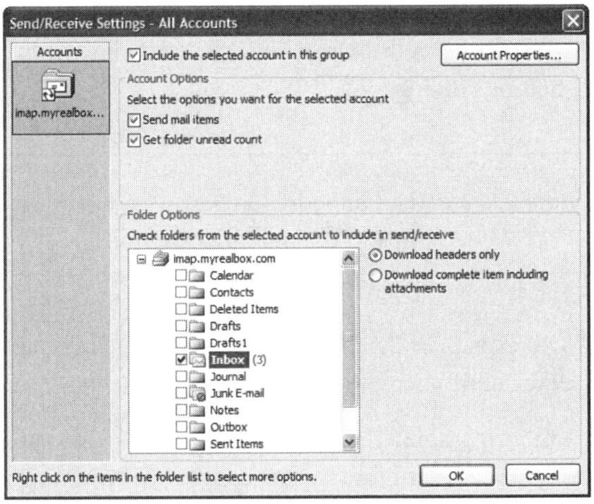

FIGURE 4.8

Send and receive settings control how Outlook handles auto-mated sends and receives for your IMAP accounts.

Each folder in your IMAP mailbox may have different send and receive settings, based on your needs. Regardless of the settings, selecting a folder while Outlook is online refreshes the folder contents and downloads the selected item.

> When you use IMAP to access an Exchange Server mailbox, you can view public folders if you subscribe to all folders in the path. For example, I need to subscribe to Public Folders, My Folder, and Old Email before I can access the folder located at \Public Folders\My Folder\Old Email\.

You can choose to download either headers only or full messages from any folder stored in an IMAP mailbox. However, Outlook's IMAP transport does not support downloading only the first *xx* KB of a message.

After subscribing to folders, choose Send/Receive to download your IMAP messages. If you're working online (File, Work Offline), selecting a downloaded message downloads the message body. When working offline, right-click and choose Mark to Download Message(s) and the message body will be downloaded the next time Outlook checks for new mail. Choose Delete to mark messages for deletion. However, messages aren't actually deleted from the IMAP server until you purge the messages using Edit, Purge Deleted Messages.

Outlook's rules, including the junk email rule, will process messages and delete junk email received in IMAP Inbox folders, after the message body is downloaded.

Outlook does not have an option to automatically purge deleted items from your folders, so you must remember to manually purge the folders occasionally.

> The default view for the IMAP folder uses AutoPreview. A recommended view is Group by Deleted Group Messages marked for Deletion. This puts the deleted items out of sight, but not completely hidden from view, lessening the chances that you'll forget to purge deleted items.

IMAP doesn't support Outlook's special folders, including Calendar, Contacts, Tasks, Notes, and Journal. Exchange Server users can view the folders, but editing the contents converts the items to mail items and results in data loss.

A third-party application, InsightConnector, is available from Bynari (http://www.bynari.net/) and works with any IMAP server. InsightConnector stores Outlook's special folders on the IMAP server, enabling you to synchronize the special folders with the IMAP server.

4

Using HTTP Accounts

An HTTP account uses HTTP port 80 to connect to a mailbox that you normally access using a Web browser. Not all Web-based email accounts support the HTTP protocol by using WebDAV, which is required for HTTP support. At this time, only Hotmail and MSN are accessible using HTTP.

Using the HTTP protocol is a convenient way to access Hotmail and MSN accounts because it removes the need to log on to a Web page to read your mail. Copies of the messages are stored locally, so you can read them offline at any time after downloading the full message.

Set up your HTTP account using Tools, E-mail Accounts and selecting HTTP. Enter your display name and email address. When Outlook detects a Hotmail or MSN address, it completes the server URL automatically (see Figure 4.9).

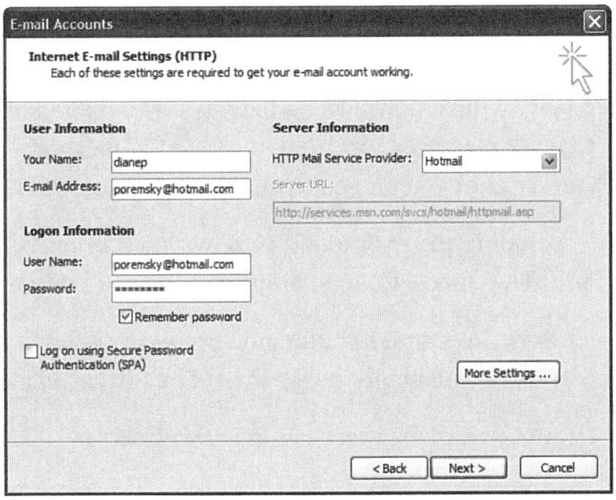

FIGURE 4.9

When you choose HTTP and enter a Hotmail or MSN address, Outlook selects the correct server URL for you.

Configure send and receive options for the HTTP account using Tools, Options, Mail Setup, Send/Receive. Outlook's default configuration is to check for new mail on the accounts every few minutes and download the headers to a local message store. The messages remain on the server, accessible from any computer, until you delete the message from the local store.

Junk mail filters remove junk mail from your mailbox after you download the message body. Junk filters are unable to filter messages using headers only.

The Rules Wizard is not supported using the HTTP protocol. Some third-party rules add-ins might move your email to local folders, provided that you download the message bodies before running the rules. My personal favorite is ExLife (www.ornic.com). A complete set of current applications is at http://www.slipstick.com/addins/housekeeping.htm.

> Although Exchange 2000 and Exchange 2003 do not officially support the HTTP protocol, you can use the Outlook Web Access (OWA) URL to access your email using Outlook. Enter your OWA URL in the Server field, including your mailbox username in the URL, as shown in this example: http://mail.poremsky.com/exchange/sallyl/.

Working with Exchange Server

Outlook was designed to work with Exchange Server accounts. In fact, many of Outlook's features work best with Exchange Server.

Set up your account using the instructions you received from your administrator. In many cases, your profiles are created for you when you log on to your computer. If not, select Exchange Server as the email account type in the E-mail Account Wizard. In most cases, the default account settings are suitable. However, if you need to open additional mailboxes, you have to select More Settings, Advanced tab and add the mailboxes to your profile.

Under most circumstances, you don't need to configure send and receive settings for your Exchange account. However, if you're using Offline mode, you'll need to select the folders you want available offline and set up filters and a synchronization schedule.

Cached Exchange mode doesn't require send and receive configuration. However, you could create filters for folders, just as you do for Offline mode (see Figure 4.10). I don't recommend filters unless you routinely use two different profiles or computers and use filters only with the second profile; otherwise, you might forget the filters are on.

Using Exchange Server's RPC over HTTP

Outlook 2003 supports a new feature called RPC over HTTP, which allows Outlook to connect to Exchange mailboxes over the Internet, using HTTP port 80. By using port 80, administrators can leave the ports closed that are normally needed by Outlook for a normal MAPI connection to Exchange Server.

You need to speak with your administrator to find out whether RPC over HTTP is supported. You might be able to use RPC over HTTP if you connect to Exchange 2003, which is installed in a Windows Server 2003 network.

4

FIGURE 4.10

Use the Synchronization settings to set up filters for Offline mode.

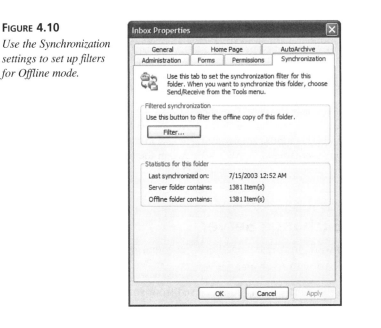

In most cases, your administrator configures your Exchange accounts for you. Always speak to your administrator before changing your account information.

Unfortunately, just because your company has migrated to Exchange 2003 doesn't mean that you can use RPC over HTTP. A number of other conditions must be met; for example, all the servers Outlook needs to communicate with must run on Windows Server 2003.

If your network supports RPC over HTTP, the next requirement is Outlook 2003 must be installed on Windows XP SP2. You cannot use RPC over HTTP with Outlook 2003 installed on Windows 2000. See http://support.microsoft.com/?kbid=331320 for more information.

If your network supports RPC over HTTP and your computer has Windows XP SP2, you need to enable RPC support in your Exchange Server profile.

Check for your version of Windows by typing **winver** in the Start menu, Run dialog. You can get more detailed information about your computer by selecting System Information in the Help, About menu choice of any Office application.

Open your account settings using <u>T</u>ools, E-mail <u>A</u>ccounts, <u>V</u>iew or Change Existing
Email Accounts. Select the Exchange account and choose Change, <u>M</u>ore Settings to
open the Microsoft Exchange Server dialog.

On the Connection tab, add a check to Connect to My Exchange Mailbox Using H<u>T</u>TP.
Then choose <u>E</u>xchange Proxy Settings to set up your server information (see Figure 4.11).

FIGURE 4.11

*Ask your administrator
for the correct settings
to enable on the
Exchange Proxy
Settings dialog, includ-
ing the URL to your
Exchange server.*

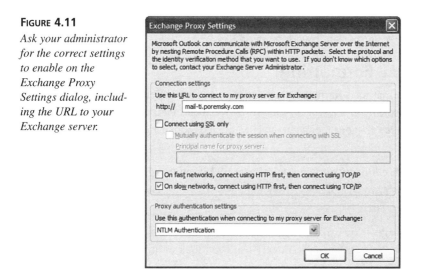

Rules, junk rules, and all other features that work with Exchange Server accounts work
with RPC over HTTP.

Choosing Your Message Format

By default, Outlook is configured to use Word as the email editor and to use HTML
stationery.

Outlook has three message formats you can choose from:

- Plain text
- HTML
- Rich text format (RTF)

Each format has advantages and disadvantages. Plain text is, well, plain. It results in the
smallest message size, which is important for people still using dial-up accounts or who
have size limits on their mailboxes.

Using HTML format enables you to format fonts and embed graphics so that they display inline. As a result, messages tend to be quite a bit larger than plain text messages—as much as four times larger. When you're emphasizing a point, you can use bold or italic fonts to draw attention to it, just as you can on printed letters.

The final format Outlook offers is rich text format. It's a format that only Outlook can use; therefore, RTF-formatted messages should be avoided for all but other Outlook users. You need to use RTF format when you send meeting requests, task requests, and voting forms or the forms won't work properly.

Using HTML Formatting

Using HTML format for your messages enables you to use different fonts and control the layout of your text in your message. Nearly every popular email client can render HTML-formatted messages, so your recipients will see the message using the formats you selected.

Outlook's HTML editor supports only the basic HTML editing functions, and many users find it's easier to design newsletters in an HTML editor and insert it into Outlook to send.

For prettier messages, you can use HTML stationery. Outlook includes several ready-to-use stationeries or you can create stationery using Outlook or any HTML editor.

Choose stationery for your message using Actions, New Mail Using menu. If you've never used stationery, choose More Stationery; otherwise, choose one of the recently used stationeries (see Figure 4.12).

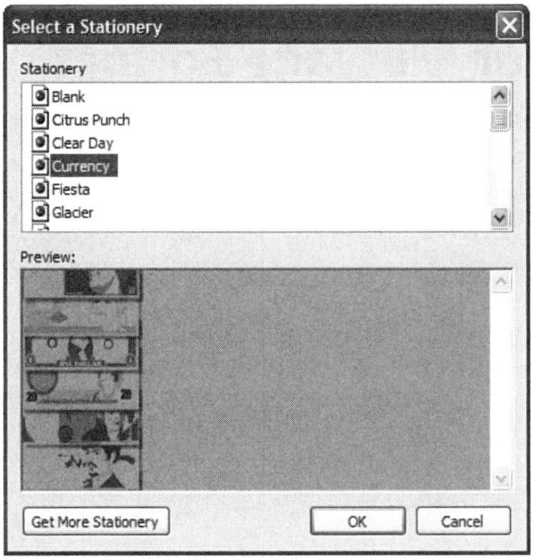

FIGURE 4.12

Preview the stationery or Get More Stationery using the Select a Stationery dialog. Get More Stationery opens a search page at http://office. microsoft.com/ downloads/.

You can also find stationery at many Web sites, including `http://thundercloud.net/`. Any stationery designed for Outlook Express will work with Outlook.

Save your stationery to `C:\Documents and Settings\username\Application Data\Microsoft\Stationery` to display it in the Select a Stationery dialog. For messages created with HTML or stationery saved to other locations, open a new message form, choose File, Insert, and then choose Insert As Text from the file browser dialog (see Figure 4.13).

Figure 4.13

Use any HTML file as stationery when you select Insert As Text.

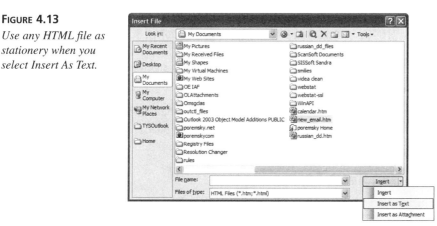

Insert As Text is not the only way to add HTML to Outlook's messages. You can copy rendered HTML (as displayed in a Web browser, not the raw HTML code) and paste it into a message.

When to Use RTF Formatting

RTF wraps the message in a Transport Neutral Encapsulation Format (TNEF) wrapper, which only Outlook can decode. For this reason, you should avoid using it for email messages. Specific message types, including meeting requests and voting ballots, require RTF to work correctly.

TNEF is a proprietary format that Outlook uses when sending messages formatted as rich text format. Outlook extracts all the formatting information and encodes it in a special TNEF block. On the receiving side, Outlook processes the TNEF block and reformats the message.

Unfortunately, other clients, including Outlook Express, cannot decipher TNEF blocks. Consequently, when someone receives a TNEF-encoded message with any other email client, the TNEF part appears as a long sequence of hexadecimal digits, either in the message itself or as an attached file (usually named `WINMAIL.DAT`). Recipients using Outlook Express might notice the message size is large but usually don't know why because OE is programmed to hide the `WINMAIL.DAT` file. These `WINMAIL.DAT` files serve no useful purpose and can be deleted unless there was an attachment included on the message. In that case, the attachment is wrapped in the TNEF file. The message either must be re-sent as plain text or the recipient has to get a program that can decode the `WINMAIL.DAT`. To avoid this problem, never send RTF.

Outlook 2003 is smart enough to know that many Internet users can't use RTF-formatted messages; by default, Outlook doesn't allow RTF message to Internet addresses, it converts them to HTML instead. You can change this behavior In Tools, Options, E-mail format, Internet Options or on individual contacts that you know can accept RTF. You can change the Internet format before sending a message by clicking on the addresses and choosing Rich Text Format in the Internet Format field.

There are times you'll need to use RTF on messages to the Internet. Voting forms and meeting or task requests won't update the forms and calendar as designed unless you use RTF. Read receipts also won't automatically process unless you use RTF.

When Plain Text Format Is Best

All the netiquette experts say you should always use plain–text-formatted messages, but plain text is boring. Because plain text doesn't support text formatting as HTML and RTF do, you can't use formatting to make a point or highlight message text.

Because HTML is set as the default message format in Outlook and Outlook Express, we tend to use it instead of changing to a new default message format.

Plain text should always be used for messages sent to mailing lists unless you know for certain that the list supports HTML and the list members are not opposed to HTML-formatted messages. HTML messages are included in digests as plain text, with all the HTML code visible.

Some older email clients, especially the clients used on Unix and Linux systems, can't render HTML. The messages are displayed as plain text, with all the HTML tags visible, which makes the message difficult to read. Always use plain text if you believe the recipient is using a Unix email client such as Pine.

An HTML-formatted message is at least 25% larger than a plain-text message. In some cases, an HTML message is as much as four times the size of the same message sent as plain text. For people on slow dial-up accounts or in areas where Internet access is still charged by the minute, every byte counts. If your recipient is using dial-up account, be kind and use plain text.

Outlook helps us in our quest to be kind to our correspondents by providing an option on the contact form to always use plain–text-formatted messages. Open the contact form, double-click on the person's email address, and choose Send Plain Text Only in the Internet Format drop-down list.

Outlook always replies in the format that the original message used. It's a safe bet that if a person is sending HTML-formatted messages, she can also receive them, so you don't have to worry about the format used for replies.

Summary

In this hour, you learned about the different types of email accounts and how to use them. You learned about the different types of email formats and why plain–text-formatted messages are the best, whereas rich text formatting should be used only when sending messages to other Outlook users.

This hour introduced you to stationery, and you learned how to use stationery with Outlook even if it's not stored in your stationery folder.

Q&A

Q I sent a message with attachments and the recipients didn't receive them. The attachments are on the sent message in my Sent Items folders. What happened to them?

A Sounds like you're using the RTF message format and your recipients aren't using Outlook. Resend using plain-text formatting and verify that the contacts' email addresses are set to the Internet Format: Send Plain Text Only or let Outlook decide the best format for sending.

If you're using plain-text format and the recipients still get `winmail.dat` attachments, find and rename the NK2 file for your profile, located at `C:\Documents and Settings\`*username*`\Application Data\Microsoft\Outlook`.

Q **When I use the voting option in Outlook, the recipients don't have voting buttons on their messages. What's going wrong?**

A This is one area where you need to use RTF for the message format for the feature to work. If you aren't sending the message to very many people, double-click each address and choose Send Using Outlook Rich Text Format.

If a recipient uses the voting buttons but you receive her vote as a normal message, it's an RTF problem. Unfortunately, there isn't too much you can do about it except count the votes yourself.

HOUR 5

Working with Email

This hour teaches you how to use email, from choosing your email editor to addressing email and creating signatures and just about everything in between.

- Choosing your email editor
- Creating and editing email
- Using stationery and HTML formatting
- Using Outlook's address books
- Creating signatures

From choosing which email editor to use, to the message format, signatures, and other features found in Outlook, you'll learn about many of the things Outlook can do.

Choosing an Email Editor

Outlook has two email editors to choose from, with Word set as the default email editor. The Outlook editor, which is included with Outlook, offers basic editing and word processing capabilities. The Word Editor, which has all the editing features of Word, including grammar and spell check as you type, and signatures that automatically change with the account type.

To select an email editor, choose Tools, Options, Mail Format (see Figure 5.1). To make Outlook your email editor, clear the check box labeled Use Microsoft Office Word 2003 to Edit Email Messages.

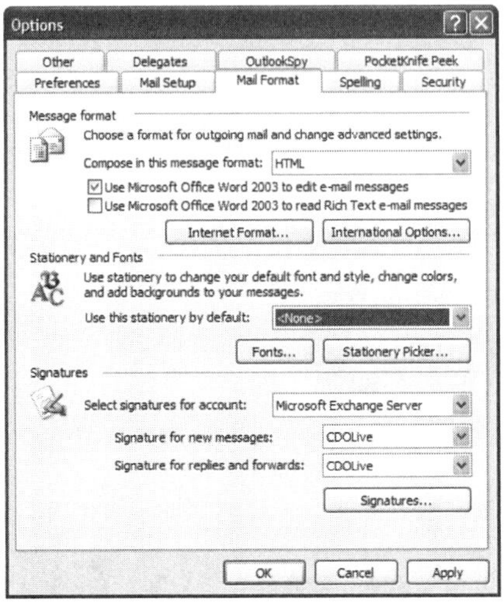

FIGURE 5.1

Choose your email editor and message format using the Tools, Options, Mail Format dialog.

With the exception of features found only in Word, such as spell checking as you type, the Outlook Editor and Word have the same basic features, although they're often found on different menus.

One example is Options. In Word, the Option button includes options for E-mail Signature, Stationery, and Show/Hide the From and BCC headers. Using the Outlook editor, these options are on the View menu (headers) and the Insert menu (signatures). A second example is message format. Using Word, you can choose between HTML, RTF, and plain text from a toolbar button and can quickly change formats on the fly (see Figure 5.2). With the Outlook editor, you have to use the Format menu and switch to Plain Text when switching between HTML and Rich Text options.

Using Outlook's Email Editor

Outlook's editor is generally believed to be faster and to use fewer resources, although most people won't notice any difference in speed. This editor has limited spelling and AutoCorrect capabilities. You have to check your spelling using F7 or configure Outlook to spell check before sending; it doesn't spell check as you type. AutoCorrect works only with plain text and RTF, not HTML-formatted messages.

The Outlook editor provides basic email signatures, including the ability to assign different signatures to different email accounts, but it doesn't automatically change the signature when you select a new sending account.

You have to use the Outlook editor when designing custom forms.

FIGURE 5.2

Although there are many minor differences between Outlook's editor and Word's interfaces and the location of menus and options, there are many similarities as well.

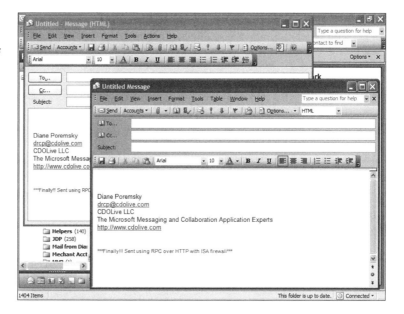

Using Word As the Email Editor

The Word editor provides you with a full-featured word processor for composing your email. Although it might be overkill, many people spend a large part of their workday sending email and the features they've come to rely on in Word can be used in Outlook, too.

Outlook has supported the Word editor since Office 97, but it was buggy, crashed often, and was the cause of many resource leaks. In short, using Word was not a pleasant experience for many Office users. As a result, Word as an email editor has a bad reputation. Fortunately, it has improved a lot since then. If you tried the Word editor with a previous version and were disappointed, give it a second chance—you'll be pleasantly surprised.

Word offers several advantages, beginning with spelling and grammar checking as you type. AutoCorrect works on all message formats, including HTML.

You can assign signatures by account, and choosing to send the message using a different account automatically changes the signature. You can select new signatures using a right-click in the signature block.

Create a blank signature to use when you don't want to use a signature, and then right-click on the signature block to change signatures instead of deleting the signature.

Open a new message form and choose <u>T</u>ools, <u>O</u>ptions, General and select E-m<u>a</u>il Options to access Signature, Stationery, and HTML options (see Figure 5.3).

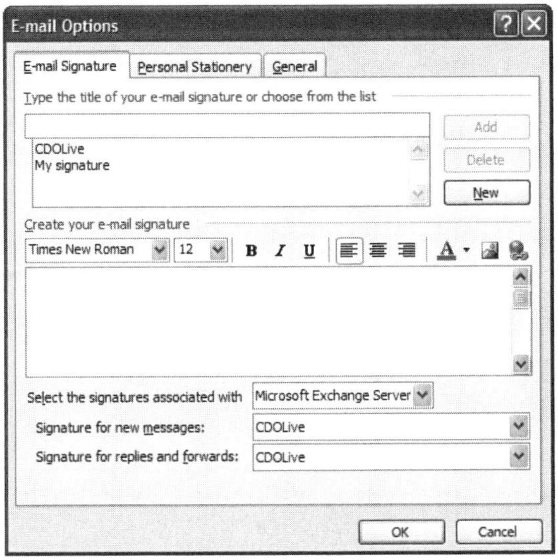

FIGURE 5.3

Use E-mail Signature to view and change your signature settings.

Use Personal Stationery settings to select a theme for your HTML email and to choose fonts and colors for new mail and replies (see Figure 5.4). When Word is your editor, you can let Word choose a new color for each reply, making it easier to read a long thread.

Font Settings and Mark My Comments are available for both Word and Outlook editors, and are also in Outlook's Tools, Options dialog. Look for Font Settings on the Mail Format tab and Mark My Comments on the Preferences tab of the Email Options dialog.

When you use Word as your editor and use HTML formatting, the messages are often much larger than they should be. Select HTML Filtering Options on the General tab. In most cases, you'll want to use Medium or High filtering to reduce the message size.

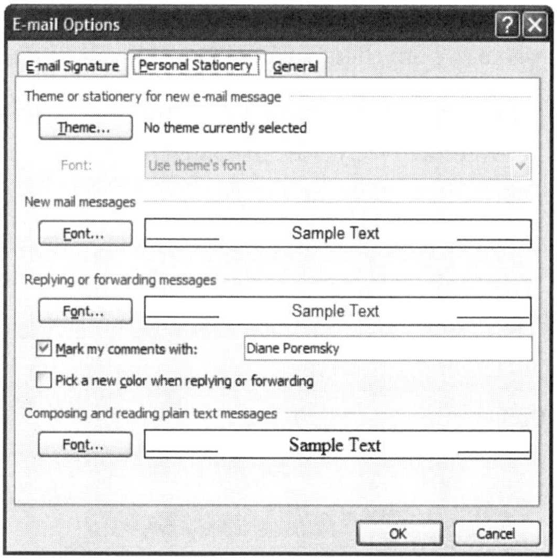

FIGURE 5.4

Choose Personal Stationery settings, including fonts and colors.

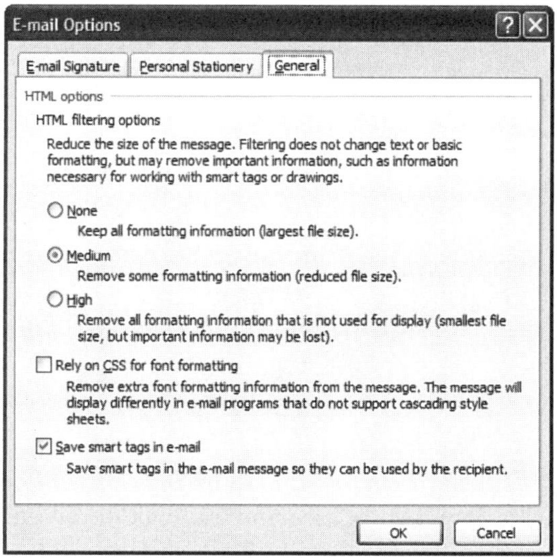

FIGURE 5.5

The HTML filtering options associated with the Word email editor can help you control the size of HTML email messages.

Creating and Editing Email

Creating and editing messages is a fairly simple task with either Word or Outlook as your email editor.

1. Open a new message form by selecting File, New Message or select a received message and choose Reply

2. Begin typing in the message body. The Outlook editor has simple word processing features, whereas Word editor enables you to use all of Word's features.

3. When you're finished, click the Send button or use the keyboard shortcut, Ctrl+S.

That was easy, but you'll probably want to configure spell checking, fonts, and other options.

Spelling has its own tab on the Tools, Options dialog (see Figure 5.6). Things to consider when enabling the spelling options include

- Always Check Before Sending is not necessary if you use the Word editor and enable Spell Check As You Type.

- Ignore Original Message Text in Reply or Forward fails if you reply to a plain text message and use the option to prefix the original message.

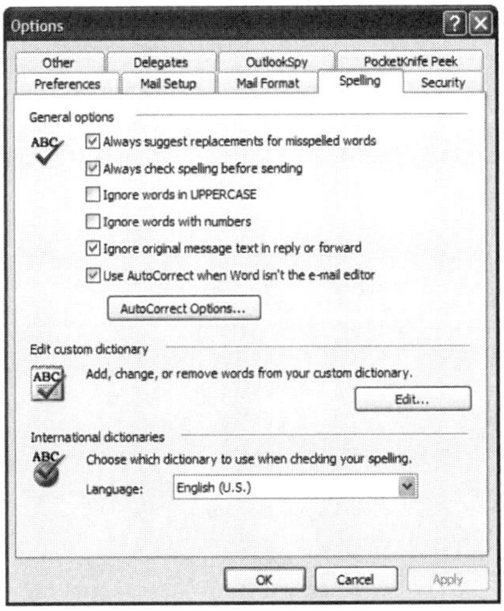

FIGURE 5.6

Configure your spelling and AutoCorrect options using the Tools, Options, Spell Check dialog.

Outlook's editor supports some AutoCorrect features, but they only work for plain text and RTF messages, not HTML. Changes to the AutoCorrect settings in Outlook do not affect the AutoCorrect settings in Word, enabling you to use different configurations in each program.

Use Ctrl+Z to undo AutoCorrect's changes.

Configure the fonts used on new messages, replies, and plain text messages in Tools, Options, Mail Format, Fonts (see Figure 5.7). You can configure these settings from a new message form when using Word as your editor by choosing Tools, Options, General, E-mail Options.

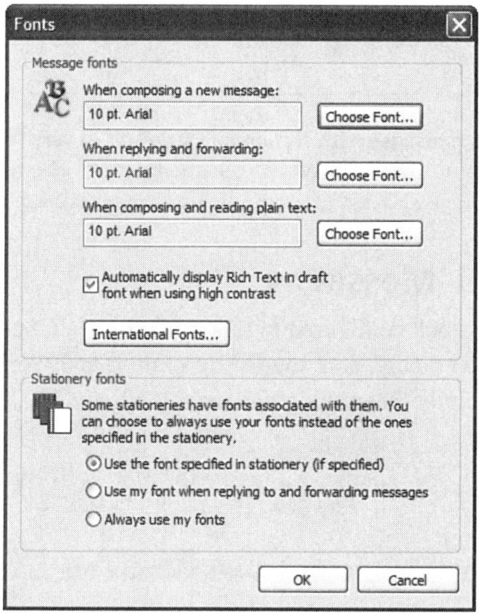

FIGURE 5.7

Choose the fonts and colors used when composing and replying to messages. The plain text font also affects the font used in the Reading Pane.

Using Stationery

If you'd like to send a graduation or birthday wish on pretty stationery instead of a drab white note, choose Actions, New Mail Using, More Stationery and select from the list of installed HTML stationeries. Choosing Get More Stationery opens your Internet browser to the Office downloads site at Microsoft.com with the currently available stationery listed.

You aren't limited to using Microsoft stationery; in fact, many other Web sites have prettier stationery available. You can use your favorite search engine and the keywords `outlook stationery` to find these sites, including `thundercloud.net`.

Any stationery created for Outlook Express also works with Outlook.

You can save your downloaded stationery to the stationery folder, located at `C:\Documents and Settings\username\Application Data\Microsoft\Stationery` or save it to any folder you prefer. When it's saved to the Stationery folder, it's listed in the stationery picker. Or you can use Insert, File to browse for the stationery and use Insert as Text.

You can create your own stationery using any HTML editor or save existing messages as stationery using File, Save As and choosing HTML.

> Sending messages with stationery can result in very large email messages. Avoid using stationery when you email people who have a dial-up account.

Creating HTML Messages

Many people leave Outlook configured to send HTML email, but rarely use any special HTML formatting, even though both the Outlook editor and Word offer basic HTML editing functionality via the Formatting toolbar (see Figure 5.8).

FIGURE 5.8
Use the tools on the Formatting toolbar to create simple HTML messages.

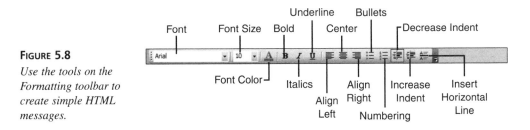

If you want to create complicated HTML messages or stationery, you'll probably want to use an HTML editor.

Using RTF Formatting

Rich text formatting should only be used in-house, where everyone uses Exchange Server and Outlook because other email clients do not support it and Outlook converts RTF to HTML when sending a message to an Internet address.

> Using Outlook's editor and HTML as your default format, you first need to switch to Format, Plain Text, and then select Rich Text, which is also on the Format menu. The Outlook editor can't switch between HTML and rich text.

RTF is required to use voting buttons, meeting or task requests, and to send hyperlinks to files using the Insert command.

As with HTML, RTF supports font formatting such as different size fonts, multiple colors of text, and background colors.

Adding Signatures to Your Email

Outlook can be configured to automatically add a block of text to your outgoing messages. Each email account in your profile can have a different block of text, or signature, and you can create one signature for new messages and a different one for replies and forwards.

Task: Create a Signature

Before Outlook can add a signature to your messages, you need to create one or more signatures and tell Outlook which signature to use and when to use it.

1. Choose Tools, Options, Mail Format tab, and then click Signatures at the bottom of the dialog to open the Create Signature dialog, as seen in Figure 5.9.

FIGURE 5.9
Use the Create Signature dialog to create new signatures or edit existing signatures.

Create Signature

Signature:

CDOLive

Edit...
Remove
New...

Preview:

Diane Poremsky
drcp@cdolive.com
CDOLive LLC
The Microsoft Messaging and Collaboration Application Experts
http://www.cdolive.com

Finally!! Sent using RPC over HTTP with ISA firewall

OK   Cancel

5

2. Choose New and enter a name for your signature. For this task, use Start with a Blank Signature and choose Next (see Figure 5.10).

▼ FIGURE 5.10

Create your signature
using a blank signature,
an existing signature
as a template, or an
existing file as a
template.

Create New Signature

1. Enter a name for your new signature:

My signature

2. Choose how to create your signature:
   ⦿ Start with a blank signature
   ○ Use this existing signature as a template:

   CDOLive

   ○ Use this file as a template:

   [   ]

   Browse...

   [Next >]   [Cancel]

3. Enter the text you want to use as a signature in the Edit Signature dialog (see Figure 5.11).

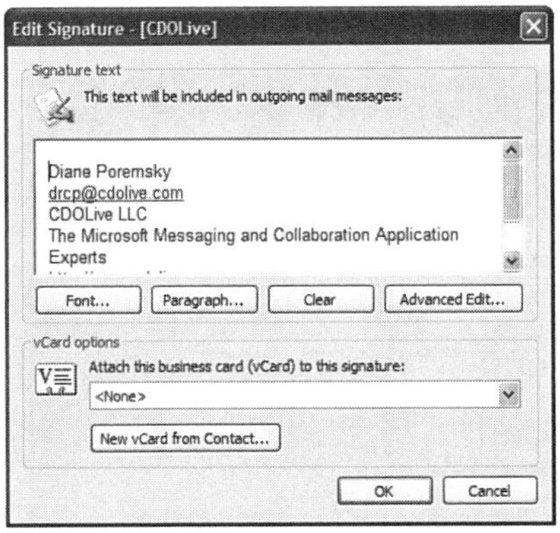

FIGURE 5.11

Use formatting to cus-
tomize your signatures
with different fonts and
colors or set your
paragraph alignment
to left, center, or right.
Advanced Edit opens
your HTML editor,
which is usually
FrontPage.

Edit Signature - [CDOLive]

Signature text

This text will be included in outgoing mail messages:

Diane Poremsky
drcp@cdolive.com
CDOLive LLC
The Microsoft Messaging and Collaboration Application
Experts

[Font...]   [Paragraph...]   [Clear]   [Advanced Edit...]

vCard options

Attach this business card (vCard) to this signature:

<None>

[New vCard from Contact...]

[OK]   [Cancel]

You should limit your signature to three to five lines, with each line no longer than 75 characters long. Don't use a vCard with signatures you use all the time—use it on a signature you use the first time you correspond with someone.

4. When your signature is satisfactory, choose OK and you're returned to the Create Signature dialog, where you can preview it. If you need to edit the signature, choose Edit.

5. After you finish creating your signatures, choose OK to return to the Mail Format dialog.

Adding Signatures to Email Messages

After you've created email signatures, it's time to assign your new signatures to your email accounts by selecting the same or different signatures for new messages and replies.

Assign signatures to your email accounts using the Mail Format dialog, shown earlier in Figure 5.1. If you closed the dialogs after creating your signatures, reopen the Options dialog using Tools, Options and selecting the Mail Format tab.

For each account listed in the Select Signatures for Account drop-down list, choose a signature for new messages and a signature for replies and forwards.

> Assign a signature to each account and to new mail and replies, even if it's only a blank signature and you'll be able to take full advantage of Outlook's signature handling features.

When you create a new message, the signature is added to the message body. When you reply, the correct signature for the account is added to the message body.

When you use Word as your editor and have more than one email account configured, you can use different signatures for your accounts and the correct signature is used when you choose a secondary account from the Accounts button. Using Outlook's editor with multiple email accounts, the correct signature is added only on replies.

Outlook stores three copies of each signature at `C:\Documents and Settings\username\Application Data\Microsoft\Signatures`; one each in HTML, plain text, and RTF format.

> When you use Outlook's editor, create a blank signature to use on all replies and forwards, and then use Insert, Signature to select the signature you want to use.

Using Word as your editor, you can right-click on a signature and select a different signature. Create a blank signature and use it when you don't want to include a signature, instead of deleting the signature.

Addressing Email

After you create a message, you need to send it. Although it's easy to commit some email addresses to memory, you'll need an address book to store less frequently used addresses.

After creating contacts that contain the addresses, the Contacts folder must be enabled as an address book. Even though it's enabled by default when you create a new profile and a new PST, you might need to configure it when you use an existing PST. If you use more than one Contacts folder, you can enable those as address books, too.

Right-click on the Contacts folder in your message store and choose Properties, select the Outlook Address Book tab, and add a check to the box to Show This Folder As an E-mail Address Book. You can enter a friendly name for this folder when it's displayed as an address book—the name of the folder in the message store won't change.

After sending a message to an address, the address is added to the resolver cache. The next time you send a message to the person, you can type just a few letters of the address and select it from the AutoComplete list. When you have many addresses to remove or just want to reset the list, delete the `*.NK2` file for your profile, located at `C:\Documents and Settings\username\Application Data\Microsoft\Outlook`.

Remove addresses that you no longer need or contain errors by using the arrow keys to move down the list, select the bad address, and then press Delete.

Configure the AutoComplete settings using Tools, Options, Preferences, E-mail Options, Advanced E-mail Options. In the Advanced E-mail Options dialog, enable the Suggest names While Completing To, Cc, Bcc Fields check box (see Figure 5.12).

Using the Outlook Address Book

The concept of the Outlook Address Book confuses many people. It's not a real address book, but rather a container for your Contacts folders, much like you would use a shoebox to store all of your address books together. Along with the Outlook Address Book, you can add other address lists to your profile, such as LDAP providers or corporate directories.

FIGURE 5.12

Configure addressing options using the Advanced Options dialog, including using a comma to separate names in the address fields and automatically resolving names typed into the address fields.

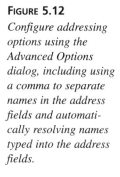

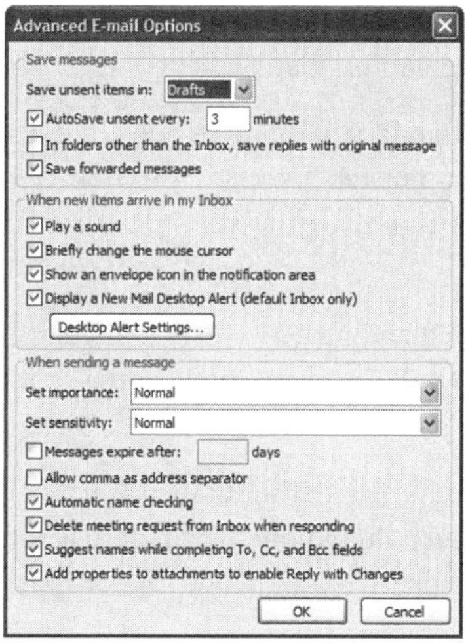

When you set up your profile, the Outlook Address Book is automatically added to your profile. You can add other address book providers, including LDAP services, by choosing Tools, E-mail Accounts and selecting Add a New Directory or Address Book or View or Change Existing Directories or Address Books.

Open the address book using Tools, Address Book. Then select Tools, Options to open the Addressing dialog, shown in Figure 5.13.

FIGURE 5.13

Use the Addressing dialog to select the folder that Outlook uses first and the folder Outlook stores your personal addresses in, and to set the order in which your address lists are searched.

Unless you enter email addresses or select names from your address book, Outlook must resolve the names you type in the address fields with contacts before it sends messages.

Outlook checks the first address list in your address book, and if no match is found, it searches the next address list. If no match is found, it moves to the next list. When Outlook finds a match, it doesn't stop searching until it reaches the last record in that address list.

So, if you type **John** in the To field and have two Johns in your Contacts folder and three in a second address list, Outlook will find both Johns in the first list but none of the Johns in the second list.

After the names are resolved, Outlook underlines them. It uses a solid underline when there is only one match, and a green dotted line when there is more than one potential match. A red wavy line indicates that Outlook found one or more matches and you have choose which contact is correct.

Using a Personal Address Book

One word about using a personal address book: Don't. If you have a personal address book (PAB), you should import it to a Contacts folder and learn to use the Contacts folder as your address book. Microsoft will discontinue support for the PAB in future versions of Outlook.

When to Use To, CC, and BCC

Outlook, like all email editors, enables you to send messages directly to a recipient by entering the address in the To field, or as a carbon copy by using the CC field. You can also hide the identity of a recipient by sending a blind carbon copy of a message if you put the address in the BCC field.

Most of the time, you'll use the To field. Use the CC and BCC fields just as you would for printed letters; that is, when you need to copy someone on the message. There is one time that you should always use the BCC field: when you send a message to a group of people, especially people who might not know each other. The purpose of this is twofold. First, it hides everyone's email addresses from the others. Second, it prevents the recipients from using Reply to All.

 When you use the BCC field, add your own address to the To field. Many anti-spam filters treat email with no address in the To field as spam.

For example, if you want to send a birth announcement to a group of your friends, put their addresses in the BCC field.

> Don't send things you think are cute or funny to your friends. Many of them have already seen the jokes and graphics. If you feel you must forward something to a group of your friends, use the BCC field, so that someone doesn't Reply to All to complain about your messages.
>
> When you're on the receiving end of messages from friends and family members who don't use the BCC field, use Reply—not Reply to All—and ask them to use the BCC field.

Sending, Checking for, and Receiving Email

Outlook uses Send/Receive groups to control which accounts to check and when to check them. In addition to using a Send/Receive group to check for new mail automatically, you can use the Send/Receive toolbar button to check one account or all of your accounts between automatic polling times.

> Hour 4, "Email Basics" explains how to configure send and receive settings in more detail.

The Send/Receive menu includes choices for

- Send/Receive All—Checks all accounts for new messages and sends all outgoing messages.
- This Folder—Used with IMAP, HTTP, or offline Exchange accounts, this option checks for new mail in the currently selected folder.
- Send All—Sends all messages waiting in the Outbox, without checking any accounts for new messages.

The next group of menu options is for your Send/Receive groups. The All Accounts group is listed first and any other groups you create are listed after it (see Figure 5.14).

Following the Send/Receive groups are your individual email accounts. Each item includes a fly-out menu listing Inbox, Download Inbox Headers, and Process Marked Headers.

The next section contains menus specific to the selected account type. Exchange Server includes Free/Busy Information and Download Address Book, whereas IMAP lists only Free/Busy Information.

Next on the list are the selections you'll use when working with headers, including Download Headers in This Folder, Mark to Download Messages, Unmark Selected Headers, and Unmark All Headers. The last header menu is Process Marked Headers in This Folder.

The final items on the menu are the Send/Receive configuration menus.

Responding to and Forwarding Email

After receiving your email, you might need to reply to it or forward it others.

As you probably already know, you choose Reply, Reply to All, or Forward and a message form opens for you to add your thoughts to the message before Sending the message.

In most cases, the original message is included in the message body, often with greater than carets (>) preceding each line. This is called *quoting* and you can control how Outlook quotes.

You should always include some of the original message when replying so that the recipient knows what the conversation is about. It's often a good idea to trim the message, leaving off signatures and other information not pertinent to the conversation.

Choosing Your Quoting Format

Open Tools, Options, E-mail Options and choose your quoting options at the bottom of the dialog.

The choices for replies and forwards are

- Do Not Include Original Message—Used on replies only, not forwards. Does not include the original message in the message body.

  Do Not Include Original Message is not recommended in most situations. It's almost always better to include the original message and you can always Select All (Ctrl+A) and begin typing to remove the original message.

- Attach Original Message—Attaches the original message to the message as a message (*.msg).

  Including the original as an attachment is better, but the recipient has to open the message to read it and it's not convenient when replies include the original message as an attachment. This option works well when you're forwarding messages. Recipients can open the message and reply to the original sender, mimicking a redirect, or they can drag attached messages into an Outlook folder.

- Mark My Comments With—The text in the field is inserted in HTML- and RTF-formatted messages when you add comments inline with the reply.

  If you changed the default message format to plain text (Tools, Options, Mail Format tab), this setting is disabled. You'll have to change your default message format to HTML to change the text.

- Include Original Message Text—Includes the original message text in the message body.

- Include and Indent Original Message Text—includes the original message text and indents it.

- Prefix Each Line of the Original Message—Prefixes the original message with a character, usually >. The character is user configurable. This is considered the Internet standard for replies.

The last three choices are all good because the original message is included in the message body, where it's easy to read it if necessary. Of the three options, include and indent is the least desirable because it's difficult to read after a couple of replies back and forth, with each reply indenting the quoted message more.

The options to include message text and prefix message text are both good choices, so select the method you prefer. If you choose to use a prefix, you can change it, but using the > is an Internet standard and is preferred by many users.

To see how the Mark My Comments With option works, enable it and reply to any HTML message. Begin typing anywhere in the original message body and the text is inserted before your comments.

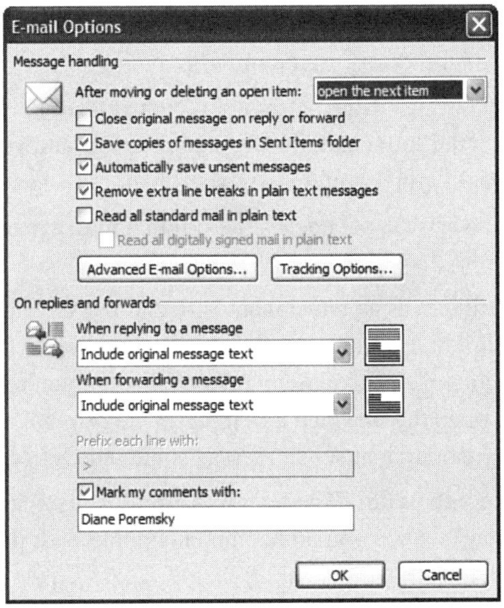

FIGURE 5.15

Use the E-mail Options dialog to configure how your reply to or forward messages.

Some recipients might not be able to read messages that include attachments because not all email clients can handle a `.msg` attachment.

You can forward messages as attachments at any time by selecting more than one message, right-clicking, and choosing Forward. If you need to forward only one message as an attachment, select two and delete the second message from the new message form or use Insert, Item to insert the message in your reply.

Choosing Reply or Reply to All

Knowing when to use Reply (to reply only to the sender) and when to use Reply to All (to send replies to all the recipients) is sometimes difficult to determine. When only the sender needs to receive your reply, use Reply. When you're discussing something with others, use Reply to All so that everyone has the complete discussion.

For example, if someone likes to send jokes and other things he finds cute to a group of people, but you think the material is annoying, use Reply to reply directly to the sender asking him to stop—don't use Reply to All.

> Reply to All can create a mail storm when the recipient list is large and everyone uses Reply to All.

Delayed Send

Outlook enables you to prepare messages now and send them later.

To send a message at a later time and date, open the Options dialog using the Options button on the toolbar or View, Options when using Outlook's editor, shown in Figure 5.16. Select the time and date you want the message delivered, click OK, and Send. If your server supports delayed send, the message will be sent at the time and date specified, when Send Immediately is enabled, or at the next Send/Receive operation.

> You can use shortcuts to enter the time and date in the fields. For example, to send the message tomorrow, enter **1d**. Enter the time as **315** or **10.15a**.

When the message sends, it uses the time you sent it to the Outbox as the sent time, not the time Outlook actually sends it.

> When you configure Outlook to send the message at a later time, you must have Outlook open at the designated time for the message to be sent. When you close Outlook while a message is waiting to be sent, Outlook will ask whether you want to close Outlook with messages in the Outbox.

FIGURE 5.16
Choose Options and add a check to Do Not Deliver Before, and then select a date and time. The message should remain in your Outbox until the time and date selected.

Recall Sent Messages

The ability to recall messages after they are sent is limited to Exchange Server users. In fact, it's limited to Exchange Server users who are sending a message to other users on their Exchange Server. For it to work correctly, the recipient can't read her mail as soon as new mail arrives because it only works on unread messages. In short, recalling sent messages doesn't work reliably for anyone.

To use Recall, go to your Sent Items folder and open the message you'd like to recall, and then choose Actions, Recall This Message. The Recall This Message dialog opens, as shown in Figure 5.17.

FIGURE 5.17
When you use Recall, you can delete unread copies or replace unread copies with a new message.

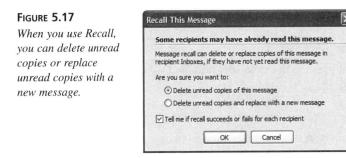

The recipient receives a message with Recall: in the subject line and `[sender] would like to recall the message, "[subject]"`. Human nature being what it is, most people will see this and read the original message to find out why you wanted to recall it. For this reason, don't rely on Recall; it's better to wait to send messages in the first place.

When the recall succeeds, the recipient will see a message that states `[sender]` `has` `recalled` `the` `message,` `"[subject]"` when he opens the recall message in his Inbox and you'll receive a message indicating that the recall succeeded.

Summary

This hour taught you many of the ways you can use Outlook for email. After deciding which email client you want to use and selecting your preferred mail format, you learned to create HTML messages and signatures. You now know Recall doesn't work, but you know how to create a message and let Outlook send it for you tomorrow.

Q&A

Q I changed the email address of some of my contacts but when I send them messages, Outlook tries to use the old address. What's wrong?

A It's the resolver cache remembering the older email address. Find and delete the `*.NK2` for your profile and your messages will go to the right address. The file should be at `C:\Documents` `and` `Settings\username\Application` `Data\` `Microsoft\Outlook`.

HOUR 6

Working with Email Attachments

We all get email attachments, even if we don't want some of the attachments friends like to send us. Most people prefer to send files through email because it's a convenient way to share documents and digital pictures with anyone. For most people, the only concern is a full mailbox.

In this hour, you learn how to manage the attachments you receive, including

- Where Outlook stores attachments
- Why the way you open attachments matters
- How to find and remove large attachments without deleting the message
- How to retrieve blocked attachments
- How to control where Outlook creates temporary attachment files

Using Email Attachments

As more and more people get broadband connections to the Internet and mailbox size limits increase, including attachments, especially large ones, on email messages is something few of us think twice about these days. It's easier for the sender to attach the file to the email than it is to provide a link to a download on a public server. And it's often easier for the recipient to download the file with his email than to download it from a server.

Many corporations delete all attachments from incoming email in an effort to prevent the spread of viruses.

After you've downloaded the message and attachment, Outlook stores the attachment in your mailbox or message store. Attachments you send are kept in your Sent Items folder. If mailbox size is a problem, you can delete the attachments and save the message. See "Removing Attachments" later in this hour to learn how to delete attachments.

An attachment isn't included on a reply; you must use Insert, File if you need to send the attachment back. The reasoning behind this is that the sender already has the file and she doesn't want a copy of it back. Forwarding a message with an attachment keeps the attachment on the message, unless it's a blocked attachment. In that case, you must forward the message as an attachment. There are two ways to forward messages: inline, in which the forwarded message body is seen in the message body, and as an attachment, in which the forwarded message is included as an attachment. When messages are forwarded as attachments, the recipient needs to open the message to read it, but can easily reply to the original sender.

To forward a message as an attachment when inline forwarding is your default:

- Select two messages: the one you want to forward and another.
- Choose Forward.
- After the new message form opens, delete the extra attachment.

You can also open a new message form, and then use Insert, Item if you're using the Outlook editor, or the Insert button (which has a paperclip icon), Insert Item when Word is your editor to insert one or more Outlook items to forward.

When the Insert Item browser dialog opens, select the Outlook folder from the Look In: folder list and the item you want to insert in the Items: list. Use Shift+Click or Ctrl+Click to select and insert multiple items.

The Insert As format choices offered are affected by the message format used. The message format in Figure 6.1 is HTML, so Insert As Attachment is the only option available.

Use the Insert, File menu selection to send files from your hard drive. Select the file from the Insert File explorer and choose Insert to add the attachment to your message or use Shift+Click or Ctrl+Click to select multiple files.

FIGURE 6.1

*Use the Insert Item dia-
log to attach Outlook
items to your email.*

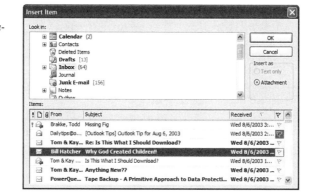

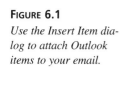

When the file is a plain text format, including HTML, you can use Insert As
Text, which sends the file as text in the message body.

After you add an attachment to a message, the Attachment Options task pane opens. If
you're using SharePoint services, you can add the files to your document workspace;
otherwise, ignore it. When your message includes images, select a picture size from
Picture Options.

You can disable the task pane by unchecking Show When Attaching Files at the bottom
of the pane. You can show it again at any time using Ctrl+F1.

Editing Attachments Opened from Outlook

The easiest way to open an attachment is with a double-click from the email message.
From the standpoint of viruses and security, it's just as safe to open it this way as it is to
save it to your hard drive first. But when you're editing an attachment, it's generally better to save the attachment to your drive first and then edit the copy saved on your hard
drive. If you don't, you risk losing your edited file when you close it. If you don't need
to save the edits back to the copy on the message, you don't gain much by opening the
attachment from Outlook.

If you regularly receive attachments by email for your work and are worried
that opening attachments from an email message leaves you at greater risk
for virus infections, stop worrying. How you open attachments is less important than keeping your antivirus scanner running in autoprotect mode with
the latest virus definitions and using common sense when you decide which

attachments to open. This is because Outlook saves attachments to the hard drive when you view the message and your antivirus scanner will scan it. You don't gain additional antivirus benefits if you save the attachment to your drive first because Outlook beat you to it. So, go ahead: Open the attachment from the Reading Pane or from an open message—your antivirus scanner has already scanned it.

Keep in mind, however, that this doesn't mean you should open every attachment you receive. You need to be cautious with attachments you aren't expecting or didn't request. Bypass Outlook's attachment blocking feature only for file extensions you must use for work and keep the remaining extensions blocked. If the message is suspicious, don't open the attachment before asking the sender for more information.

Right-clicking a message in the list pane and choosing View Attachments opens the attachment in read-only format. If you edit the attachment and try to save it, you'll be asked to use a different filename.

Saving Changes to Attachments

When you open an attachment in Outlook, if you do it right, you can edit the attachment and your changes will be saved back to the attachment.

The right way: Open the message, and then open the attachment, and close the attachment before closing the message. The message must remain active, either opened or in the Reading Pane, until you've finished editing the document. When you open the message, you don't have to remember not to read more email until you're finished editing the document.

The wrong way: Open the attachment from the Reading Pane and later go back to Outlook to read more email or check your calendar. As soon as the message is no longer in the Reading Pane, the temporary file is deleted and Outlook forgets which message the document belongs to.

Because you're (hopefully) already in the habit of saving early and often, saving and closing the attachment before closing the message will be easy to remember. When you close the message, a dialog will ask whether you want save changes. Choose Yes. If you choose No, the document won't be updated.

Outlook can update attachments in your message store because it saves the attachments to a temporary folder and remembers which attachment belongs with which message. As long as you don't do something to confuse Outlook, such as close the message or switch to another message in the Reading Pane, Outlook remembers where the attachments belong.

You aren't limited to just one open attachment at a time, either. As long as you remember not to close the messages, you can edit several attachments at once and the attachments on the messages are updated with your edits.

Saving Attachments Before Opening

If you don't need to save changes back to the attachment on the message, it's better to save the attachment to your hard drive before opening it. This ensures that you know where the saved file is. When you open an attachment from Outlook, the attachment is saved to a temporary directory that is well hidden in a subfolder under the Temporary Internet Files folder.

When you edit and save the document, the file is saved in the temporary directory unless you use Save As. There's a chance it might be deleted when the message is closed, or it could be overwritten if you open the message a second time. If you leave the message open, changes will be saved back to the document unless you choose No when asked to save changes.

How many times have you edited an attachment, saved it, and then wished you could revert to the original? When you save attachments to the drive and edit that copy, you're assured that you'll always have the original in your message store.

Selecting a Default Attachment Folder

When you save email attachments using the File, Save Attachments menu selection, Outlook always defaults to your My Documents folder. Your ability to change this location is limited to moving My Documents to another location (which affects all programs) or adding folder shortcuts to the places bar. To add a place to your places bar:

1. Open any Outlook item and choose File, Save As to open the Save As file explorer dialog box.

2. Browse to the folder you want to put on the places bar. You can use local or network folders.

3. Select the folder, but don't open it.

4. Choose the Tools menu, and then select Add to "My Places" from the drop-down menu.

Use Shift+Click or Ctrl+Click to select several folders, and then choose Tools, Add to "My Places" to add all the folders to the places bar at once.

The customization options for the places bar are on the right-click menu. You can change between large and small icons, rename your icons, and move the icons up and down.

6

The default places can't be removed, but the Office Explorer dialog is resizable and the places bar scrolls up and down so that you can find all the places you add (see Figure 6.2). The places on Outlook's places bar are the same across all office applications; any places you add using Outlook are usable in Word and Excel, for example.

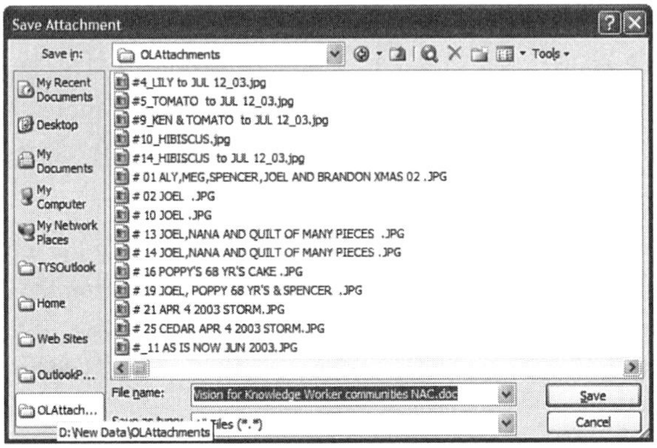

FIGURE 6.2

When you use the Open or Save As file explorers, choose your Outlook attachment folder from the places bar and save your attachment.

You can add at least 155 additional places to the places bar, using both local and network addresses. I ran out of folders before I ran into a limit imposed by the software. My personal limit is about 10 top-level folder places for maximum usability because it's faster to browse subfolders than to scroll the places bar.

> If you'd like to back up your places list, you can export the following Registry key:
>
> HKEY_CURRENT_USER\Software\Microsoft\Office\11.0\Common\Open Find\ Places\UserDefinedPlaces

If you want to remove a place, right-click on the icon and choose Remove from the context menu. To delete all the places, you can delete the UserDefinedPlaces key in the Registry. The key is re-created when you add new places to your places bar.

Understanding the SecureTemp Folder

As I mentioned earlier, Outlook saves attachments to a temporary folder when you open or preview a message. That temporary folder is called the *SecureTemp folder*. Attachments remain in this folder as long as the message or the attachment is open. This happens whether or not you open the attachment.

The reason Outlook uses the SecureTemp folder instead of the Windows temp folder is that SecureTemp provides a level of security to these attachments because no one, not even you, can see the folder the attachments are saved in.

Outlook creates the SecureTemp folder in the Temporary Internet Files folder—a hidden system folder with special attributes that uses a `desktop.ini` file to hide all subfolders. If you delete the folder used for SecureTemp, Outlook creates a new one the next time it runs. If you have to reinstall Outlook or have more than one user logging on to the computer, you might have multiple SecureTemp folders in the Temporary Internet Files folder.

Pitfalls of the SecureTemp Folder

When you're looking at an attachment and close it before changing messages within Outlook, the temporary file is usually deleted when you view another message. If you leave the attachment open and open more email, the temporary file will not always be deleted when you close the file. After awhile, you'll have quite a few documents stored there. You can delete the files one of two ways: by determining the path to the folder and typing it in Windows Explorer's address bar or by using Command Prompt and DOS commands.

To use Windows Explorer:

1. Open an attachment from Outlook. Most document types will work for this purpose, except images.

2. Use the File, Save As menu selection to see the full pathname. Write it down. It should be in this path: `C:\Documents and Settings\`*username*`\Local Settings\ Temporary Internet Files\` and the last folder in the path begins with OLK. Remember to replace *username* with your Windows logon.

3. Open Windows Explorer and type the full pathname to the SecureTemp folder. Select and delete the files. You won't be able to browse for other folders using this method.

Windows Explorer hides all the folders under Temporary Internet Files, so if you want to check for other folders, you must use the Command Prompt window:

1. At Start, Run, Open, type **cmd** and click OK.

2. The prompt should show C:\Documents and Settings\username>.

3. After the >, type **cd "C:\Documents and Settings***username***\Local Settings\ Temporary Internet Files\"** and press Enter. Don't forget to use your Windows logon username in place of *username*.

6

4. Type **dir** after the next prompt and you'll see a list of files and folders, as shown in Figure 6.3. The Outlook SecureTemp folder begins with OLK. If you have more than one OLK folder, you can use the del command on all the folders.

5. At the command prompt, type **del** followed by the OLK folder name and press the Enter key to delete all files in the folder. You'll be prompted to enter Y or N. Enter Y to delete the files. Repeat this step for each OLK folder. This deletes only the contents of the folder, not the folder itself.

FIGURE **6.3**

Use the command prompt to delete Outlook's hidden temp files.

Moving Your SecureTemp Folder

As you've learned, Outlook stores temporary files in a hidden folder beginning with OLK under C:\Documents and Settings\username\Local Settings\Temporary Internet Files\. If you reinstall Office, a new temporary attachment folder is created and the old one is left on your drive. Cleaning up the Temporary Internet Files folder or using the Windows Disk Cleanup utility won't delete the folder or its contents. For this reason, if you plan to open attachments from Outlook, you'll probably want to move the folder to a better location. You can do this by editing a Registry key.

1. Create your new attachment folder. If the folder doesn't already exist, Outlook reverts to the default SecureTemp folder.

2. From Start, Run, type **regedit** in the Open: field to open the Registry Editor.

3. Navigate to the HKEY_CURRENT_USER\Software\Microsoft\Office\11.0\Outlook\ Security key. Do this by clicking on the plus (+) sign beside HKEY_CURRENT_USER to expand it, then expanding Software, Microsoft, Office, 11.0, Outlook, and finally, Security.

4. Look for the value Name OutlookSecureTempFolder in the right pane.

5. If the key doesn't exist, right-click and choose New, String Value and then name it OutlookSecureTempFolder.

6 Change the value Data to the folder you want to use. If the folder doesn't exist, create it before you change the `OutlookSecureTempFolder` key (see Figure 6.4).

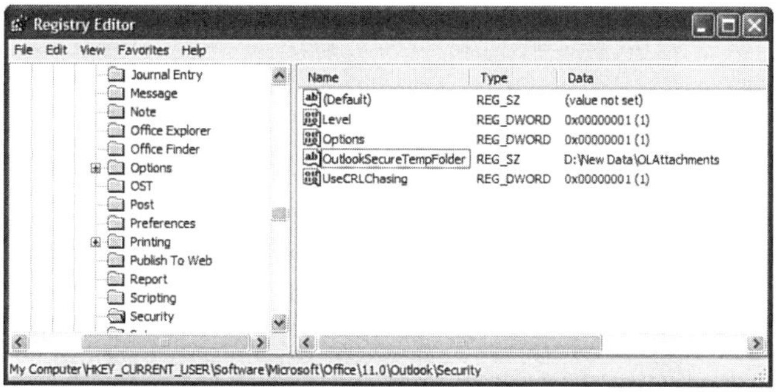

FIGURE 6.4

*Use a custom
SecureTemp folder
for your attachments.*

If the value exists and it contains a valid path, Outlook 2003 uses that location for its temporary files. Make sure that you create the folder before you change the Registry key or Outlook will revert to using the default folder under Temporary Internet Files.

Moving the SecureTemp folder enables you to use a folder that you can access and clean up regularly. If you forget to save a file, you might get lucky and find it in the temporary folder, which is easier when you use a custom folder location.

I don't recommend using your My Documents folder directly because the temporary files aren't always cleaned up correctly. But a subfolder under My Documents works great, as does your Windows temp file, usually found at `C:\Documents and Settings\username\ Local Settings\Temp`.

Removing Attachments

Attachments sent by email are stored in your mailbox or personal message store along with the message. When someone sends you a large file attachment and you want to keep the message but not the attachment, you can delete the attachment from the message:

1. Open the message that has the attachment.

2. Select the attachment in the Attachments field of the header.

3. If you need to save a copy of the attachment, right-click and choose Save As.

4. Right-click and choose Remove.

5. When the dialog asks whether you want to save changes, choose Yes to save the message without the attachment.

6

When you use the Large Messages Search Folder, all messages with attachments are grouped together by size and you can begin by deleting the
largest attachments first.

Deleting attachments one at a time is monotonous and time-consuming when you have
many attachments to remove. Several third-party utilities are available, or you can write a
VBA procedure to delete the attachments. Some of the utilities save the attachment to
your hard drive and include the filename in the message body. For the most complete and
current list of utilities, see `http://www.slipstick.com/addins/housekeeping.htm`.

If you'd like to see how big your mail folders really are, right-click on the
top level of your mailbox, choose Properties of Outlook Today, and then
click the Folder Size button.

When the attachment is a blocked file type, you must edit the Registry first to unblock
the file type and then delete the attachment. Afterward, you should delete the Registry
key for maximum security. See "Accessing Blocked Attachments" in the following section for more information about editing the Registry.

Outlook and Attachment Security

Some of most common attachments you receive, such as JPG and GIF images, are
entirely safe. Others, such as Word or Excel documents, are usually safe but could carry
macro viruses. Other attachments, including those with `.exe`, `.js`, and `.pif` extensions,
might be safe, but they're just as often viruses. Because it's impossible to know for sure,
it's important that you not only install a virus scanner, but also use its autoprotect feature
and keep the virus signatures current. You should never open files you aren't expecting,
even if your antivirus scanner gives them a clean bill of health—the virus might be too
new to be in your virus definitions.

Just in case you're lax when it comes to keeping your antivirus scanner up-to-date,
Outlook offers some built-in protection against email viruses, including blocking all file
types that have the potential to carry viruses and are executable. Although you can
unblock any or all the file types, you should unblock only the file types that you really
do need or use other methods to retrieve the attachments.

Many corporate firewalls block the same extensions that Outlook blocks, and you might have to change the extension or zip the file before sending attachments to some contacts. If you'd like all of your attachments zipped before sending, look for ZipOut, the WinZip Outlook add-in or other utilities at http://www.slipstick.com.

When you send blocked file types as attachments, you should get in the habit of changing file extensions to a safe, nonexecutable type or zipping the file. Outlook 2003 won't warn you when you attach a blocked file type, but it will warn you before you send it, as shown in Figure 6.5. Choose <u>N</u>o, zip or add an underscore to the filename, and then reattach. This ensures that the person you send it to can access it also.

FIGURE 6.5

When you send attachments that could carry viruses, Outlook alerts you before sending. If you edited your Registry to allow some file types, you won't see the warning when you send these file types.

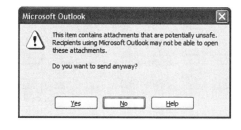

Blocked Attachment File Types

When you receive a file with any of the extensions listed in Table 6.1, Outlook hides the attachment from you to prevent you from opening it and infecting your computer system. In reality, you can still retrieve the attachment in several ways, including editing the Registry to allow access to a specific file type, accessing your mailbox using a different mail program, or asking the person to zip the file and resend it.

6

TABLE 6.1 File Attachment Types Blocked by Outlook 2003

Attachment Extension	Program Associated with the Extension
.app	Visual FoxPro Application
.ade	Microsoft Access project
.adp	Microsoft Access project
.bas	Microsoft VB/VBA code module
.bat	Batch file

TABLE 6.1 continued

Attachment Extension	Program Associated with the Extension
.chm	Compiled HTML help file
.cmd	Microsoft Windows NT command script
.com	Microsoft MS-DOS program
.cpl	Control Panel extension
.crt	Security certificate
.csh	C Shell program
.exe	Executable program
.fxp	Visual FoxPro compiled program
.hlp	Help file
.hta	HTML program
.inf	Setup information
.ins	Internet naming service
.isp	Internet communication settings
.js	JScript file
.jse	JScript-encoded script file
.ksh	Korn Shell program
.lnk	Shortcut
.mda	Microsoft Access add-in program
.mdb	Microsoft Access program
.mde	Microsoft Access MDE database
.mdz	Microsoft Access wizard program
.msc	Microsoft Common Console document
.msi	Windows Installer package
.msp	Windows Installer patch
.mst	Visual Test source files
.pcd	Photo CD image or Visual Test compiled script
.pif	Program information file
.prf	Microsoft Outlook Profile Settings
.prg	Visual FoxPro Program
.pst	Outlook Personal Folders file
.reg	Windows Registry entries
.scf	Windows Explorer command

TABLE 6.1   continued

Attachment Extension	Program Associated with the Extension
.scr	Screen saver
.sct	Windows script component
.shb	Shortcut into a document
.shs	Shell scrap object
.url	Internet shortcut
.vb	VBScript file
.vbe	VBScript-encoded script file
.vbs	VBScript file
.wsc	Windows script component
.wsf	Windows script file
.wsh	Windows script host settings file
.xsl	XML file that can contain script

When you receive a message that contains a blocked attachment, Outlook places the text shown in Figure 6.6 in the message header. The attachment icon is visible and all messages with blocked attachments are included in the Large Messages Search Folder.

FIGURE 6.6

Outlook's InfoBar alerts you to the fact that a blocked attachment is in the message and includes the filename.

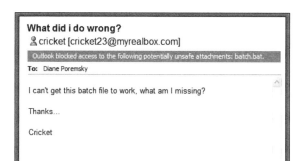

Accessing Blocked Attachments

Many people find it easiest to edit the Registry and always allow some file types, especially when they use the Attachment Options add-in from `http://www.slovaktech.com`.

6

Editing the Registry to allow all files isn't the brightest idea in the world and could result in a virus infection. For this reason, unblock only the extensions for the attachment types you need to access regularly, not all the file types. If you don't normally get any blocked attachment types, remove or rename the `level1remove` key when you save the attachment you need.

Outlook is programmed to block certain file types that Microsoft calls *Level1 attachments*. These attachment types are considered dangerous. Less dangerous attachments are Level2 attachments and have to be saved to the hard drive before opening. You can move Level1 attachments to Level2 by editing the Registry. You cannot remove attachment types from Level2.

If you'd like to edit the Registry to add the `Level1Remove` key yourself:

1. Open the Registry Editor and navigate to `HKEY_CURRENT_USER\Software\Microsoft\Office\11.0\Outlook\Security`.

2. Right-click on the right pane and choose <u>N</u>ew, <u>S</u>tring Value.

3. Enter **Level1Remove** for the name of the new value.

4. Double-click on `Level1Remove` value name and enter the extension of the file types that you don't want blocked, in `.mdb` format. If you're unblocking multiple file types, separate the extensions with semicolons and don't use spaces, as in `.pst;.prf`.

Exit the Registry Editor and restart Outlook. You can now save the files you unblocked to your hard drive and open them (see Figure 6.7).

FIGURE 6.7

Add the `Level1Remove` *key so that you can access blocked attachments.*

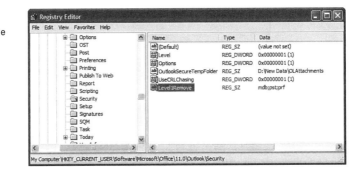

 If you want to force yourself always to save certain file types to the hard drive before opening, add their extensions to the `Level1Remove` value and force them to be considered Level2 attachments.

You should encourage people to zip files before sending them. Not only does this enable you to leave the extensions blocked, but it also reduces the size of the message.

Viruses and Email Attachments

Some people like to send out joke programs to their friends and opening these is risky. You have no way of knowing whether the file is safe. Opening every file Aunt Carol sends often results in your computer being infected with a virus, trojan horse application, or spyware.

Many times your friends are not aware they're infected until you alert them. The newest viruses get email address from any source—they listen to data that your modem sends and receives to get email addresses from your incoming and outgoing email, Web pages, and files in your Internet cache folder.

Many viruses also include their own outgoing mail server so that you won't notice Outlook sending messages.

Overall, Outlook 2003 is much more secure than previous versions of Outlook. The Outlook Object Model (OOM) puts up a warning when a program attempts to read email addresses or message bodies. When you try to mail merge to email, you might have to approve every message. The Preview pane is inactive and scripts won't run in email. There's no way Outlook will cause your system to become infected without a lot of help from you. But that doesn't mean you're home free. You still need to be careful, especially with email attachments.

You know what viruses are, but what are trojan horses and spyware?

Trojan horses are small programs that permit hackers to take control of your computer. At the very least, hackers can use your computer to attack other computers. At the other end of the scale, they might have full access to all the files on your drive, including any personal financial data you might have.

Spyware is also known as adware, and although it usually isn't destructive, it downloads files to your drive and is often responsible for crashes.

6

The first and possibly most important thing you can do is not open every attachment you receive, even if it's from your beloved Aunt Carol. Remember, cleaning up after a virus won't be nearly as funny as the joke she sent you. If the attachment isn't necessary for your work or personal business, don't open it. When you stop opening every attachment that friends send you, you reduce your chances of infection to almost nothing.

> Remember to check for security updates regularly at Windows Update and Office Update (office.microsoft.com).

Summary

This hour taught you all there is to know about editing and saving an attachment you receive in your email, including how to open and edit the attachment and save changes back to the message stored in your PST or mailbox. You should now understand why your attachments default to the Temporary Internet files folder when you choose File, Save As. More importantly, you now know how to use the places bar to easily save the files where you want them saved.

You also learned how Outlook's attachment security protects you from viruses and how to disable it when you need attachments that Outlook blocks.

Q&A

Q I'd rather not edit the Registry to access attachments that Outlook blocks. What other ways can I use to get blocked attachments?

A Other than telling the sender to resend the attachments, either in a zipped file or with a changed extension, hacking the Registry is one of the easiest ways to access blocked attachments. If you don't want to edit the Registry yourself, use Attachment Options (http://www.slovaktech.com/attachmentoptions.htm).

Another easy way is to import the message to Outlook Express (OE) after moving the message to a new folder. Use the import option in OE to import just that one folder. If you use OE 6, you must disable its attachment block in Tools, Security or choose Forward and save the attachment.

If you use Exchange Server, speak with your administrator. She can configure Exchange to enable you access to the attachments.

For a complete list of the methods available to access blocked attachments, check out http://www.slipstick.com/outlook/esecup/getexe.htm.

Q I'd like to edit a Word document and have the attachment updated, but it doesn't seem to work for me all the time.

A When you want to update an attachment, make sure that you open the message—don't open the attachment from the Reading Pane. Don't close the message until the document is saved and closed, and then save and close the message. Don't right-click on the message and choose View Attachments; doing so opens files with the Read Only flag set. If the document is zipped, you should leave the zip archive opened as well.

Hour 7

Outlook's Advanced Email Features

Outlook offers you more messaging options than just plain old email. Outlook offers basic Windows Messaging integration, enabling you to see whether the sender of a message is logged in to Windows Messenger.

You can send faxes to numbers stored in Outlook contacts or send faxes by email. You can vote on silly or serious issues and tally the ballots automatically, getting the correct results even if the voters try to cheat by voting often.

The personal address book is a holdover from early Exchange Server days and should not be used. It's better to import the contacts to your Contacts folder.

Send/receive groups give you complete control over when and how often you check for new mail on each of your email accounts.

This hour covers the following features:

- Using Messenger
- Email voting
- Sending faxes
- Using the personal address book
- Using send/receive groups

Using Windows Messenger Integration

Because many Outlook users also use Windows Messenger, Outlook contacts provide integration between Windows Messenger contacts and email.

You can enable Windows Messenger integration from the Tools, Options, Other tab. The Person Name smart tag, as shown in Figure 7.1, is enabled by default when you install Outlook. Check Display Messenger Status in the From Field to include the Messenger status icon with the smart tag.

FIGURE 7.1

The sender's Messenger status displays in the message header when the Person Name smart tag and Display Messenger Status are enabled.

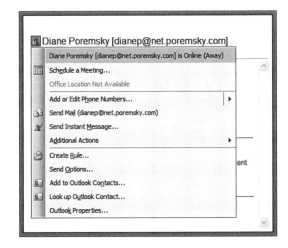

When the sender is in your contact list, the Messenger icon displays her status. The icon is gray when the sender is not in your Messenger contact list, when Display Messenger Status is disabled, or when you are not signed into Windows Messenger.

> Disabling the Person smart tag removes many of the options available when you click on names or addresses in the message header. However, you can still right-click on the names and choose Add to Contacts and Look Up Contacts.
>
> When Messenger integration is disabled, the smart tag includes many of the same menu options, except for the ones requiring Messenger.

When the sender is on your Messenger contact list, you'll see the menu shown in Figure 7.1. This menu shows the person's online status and includes options to send them an email message, send an instant message, create a new contact, or open the person's contact.

Additional Actions lists actions for other smart tags you've installed that work with contacts. A sample smart tag, Find People, searches all of your Contacts folders for matching names. It's available at `http://www.cdolive.com/samples/`.

The smart tag works automatically when the sender's email address is his Messenger address and is on your Messenger contact list. However, many Messenger users use Hotmail or another email address as their Messenger address; in that case, you have to add that user's Messenger addresses to the IM field on his contact form. After you do this, the Person Name smart tag shows his Messenger status and you can send him an instant message by selecting Send Instant Message from the Person Name smart tag menu.

Smart tags are functions that detect keywords in a document and provide options based on the type of keyword. For example, a Stock smart tag detects all potential stock symbols. Smart tags remain hidden until you hover your mouse over the text; at that point, a small button becomes visible. When you click on the button, several options are available on a menu. Office comes with several preinstalled smart tags; look for the list at Tools, AutoCorrect Options, Smart Tags. When Word is used as the email editor, smart tags are available in your messages.

Paste Options and AutoCorrect Options look like smart tags, but are technically just options buttons because they can't be enhanced.

The Messenger icon is red and the Send Instant Message item is dimmed on the Person Names menu when the sender is offline.

If the sender isn't on your Messenger contact list, the Person Names menu contains the Add to Messenger Contacts option and the Messenger icon is gray. Choosing Add to Messenger Contacts initiates a connection to the Passport server to confirm that the address has a Passport account. If a Passport account exists for the address, Outlook adds the address to your Messenger contact list. When the address is not associated with a Passport, a dialog informs that you the address does not exist in the Passport database. Only valid Passport addresses can be added to the Messenger contact list.

The Person Name smart tag also works in Word. However, the Messenger contact's display name must match the name entered into Word and contain the first and last names for the tag to be enabled. For example, DianeP as a display name in Messenger doesn't enable the Person Name smart tag, but the tag does work with Diane P.

Voting by Email

Outlook 2003 enables you to do more with email than just send and reply to messages. Along with meeting and task requests, you can use Outlook to send and compile votes. The requirements for voting include

- Recipients must use Outlook.

- Messages must be sent using RTF (rich text format).

When these conditions are met, your message will be sent with voting buttons. When the recipients vote, their votes are sent back to you and Outlook tallies the votes.

Open the Options dialog and add a check to Use Voting Buttons (see Figure 7.2). This automatically creates voting buttons using the text in the field. By default, Outlook includes selections for `Approve;Reject`, `Yes;No`, and `Yes;No;Maybe`. You aren't limited to using these choices: You can type any text you want to use to label your voting buttons in the field as long as you remember to use a semicolon as the delimiter between button names.

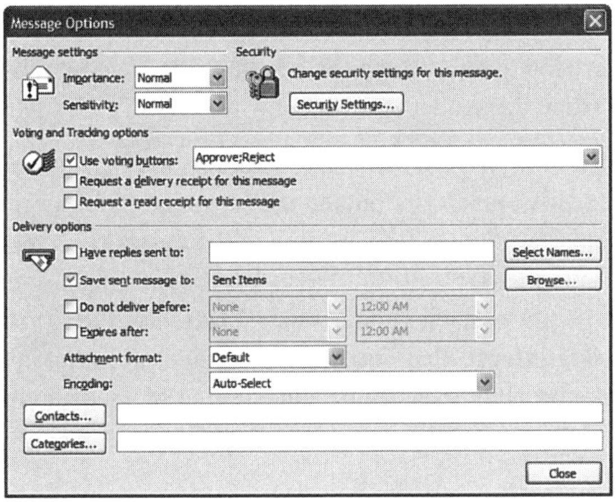

FIGURE 7.2

When enabling voting buttons, select a predefined set of voting button text or enter your own text, separating the button text with semicolons.

When the recipient opens the message, she'll see buttons at the top of the form (see Figure 7.3). Outlook 2003 users can also vote from the Reading Pane by clicking in the InfoBar and choosing one of the voting selections from the menu.

FIGURE 7.3

Recipients click on the button to vote and Outlook sends their responses to you. A recipient can change his mind and cast a new vote as often as he wants; however, only the last vote is included in the tally.

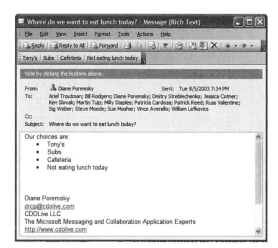

Choosing <u>E</u>dit the Response Before Sending opens a reply so that the recipient can reply as if it were a normal message (see Figure 7.4). This doesn't affect the vote results and gives the recipient the chance to explain her choice, ask questions, and make a comment.

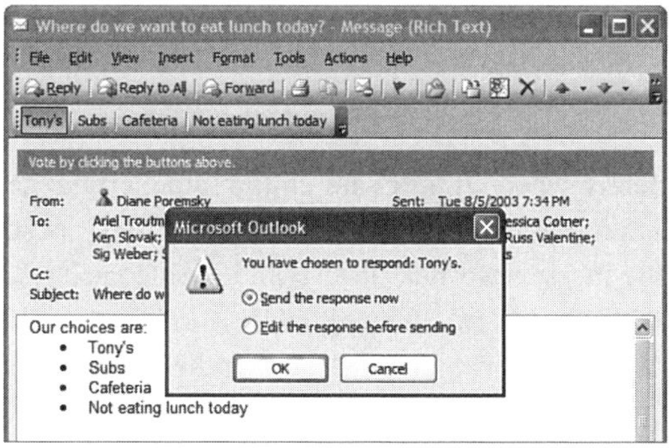

FIGURE 7.4

After choosing the vote selection, Outlook offers the choice of immediately returning the ballot or opening a message form to include a reply with the vote.

When votes come back to you, Outlook keeps a tally on the original message in the Sent Items folder (see Figure 7.5).

FIGURE 7.5

After the first vote is returned to you, the original message in the Sent Items folder displays a Tracking tab. The message must remain in the Sent Items folder for tracking to work with new voting responses. When it's time to end voting, move the item out of the Sent Items folder.

Recipient	Response
Ariel Troutman	
Bill Rodgers	
Diane Poremsky	Tony's: 8/7/2003 1:30 AM
Dmitry Streblechenko	
Jessica Cotner	
Ken Slovak	
Martin Tuip	
Milly Staples	
Patricia Cardoza	
Patrick Reed	
Russ Valentine	
Sig Weber	
Steve Moede	
Sue Mosher	
Vince Averello	
William Lefkovics	

This message was sent on 8/6/2003 9:23 PM.
Reply Totals: Tony's 1; Subs 0; Cafeteria 0; Not eating lunch today 0

The tracking list prints when you print the message, although the tally in the InfoBar is not included in the printout. You can also copy and paste the list into a file. Select the first item in the list, hold the Shift key, and select the last item using the Down Arrow key, the Page Down key, or your mouse. After selecting the list, use Ctrl+C to copy and paste it into another program file, such as Excel or Notepad, or even a message or post form.

Occasionally, votes are not returned in RTF format and Outlook cannot tally them. Unfortunately, Outlook doesn't enable you to edit the voting responses on the original message, and you'll have to count the votes yourself.

Voting works perfectly when all users are on the same Exchange Server, but when done properly, it works equally well for POP3, IMAP, and HTTP accounts. You just have to remember to set the message format to RTF and enable each recipient for RTF. To accomplish that, double-click on an email address to bring up the E-mail Properties dialog. If this opens a contact form, double-click on the contact's email address to open the Properties dialog. Choose Send using Outlook Rich Text Format from the Internet Format field and close the dialog. Repeat this for each address to which you're sending the message. Coupled with choosing Rich Text format for the message, this enables your voting buttons to work when sent to other Outlook users.

If you need to send a voting form to many Internet addresses, open Tools, Options, Mail Format, Internet Format and change the Internet Format to Send using Rich Text

Formatting. Make this change before creating the message and change it back to plain text or HTML format after voting ends to prevent problems if you accidentally compose an RTF message to send to non-Outlook users.

Using Windows Fax Service

Faxing from Outlook is as easy as sending email, but instead uses the Windows Fax service. In fact, that's why the Fax field in a contact displays as an email address in the Outlook Address Book.

Before you can send a fax, you must set up the Windows Fax service and add the fax service to your Outlook profile. The Windows Fax service must be installed and configured before you can add it as a service in Outlook.

> If Fax is not listed in Printers and Faxes, open the Printers and Faxes folder and choose Set Up Faxing from the Windows Explorer task pane. You might need your Windows CD to complete the installation.

If this is your first time using Windows Fax, double-click on the Fax icon and follow the wizard to set up Windows Fax for sending and receiving.

When you're finished installing and configuring the fax service, you need to add it to your Outlook profile. The fax service is added to Outlook using the same method that you use to add new accounts.

1. Choose Tools, E-mail Accounts, and then choose Add a New E-mail Account. Select Next, Additional Server Types.

2. From the Additional Server Types dialog, choose Fax Mail Transport and complete the wizard.

3. Select Fax Mail Transport in the E-mail Account list and select Change.

4. The Fax Mail Transport options include cover page selection, delivery receipt settings, and the default message font (see Figure 7.6).

When you're finished selecting the options, close the dialog and restart Outlook to enable the service in your profile.

FIGURE 7.6

Select a cover page style for your faxes using the Fax Mail Transport dialog.

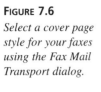

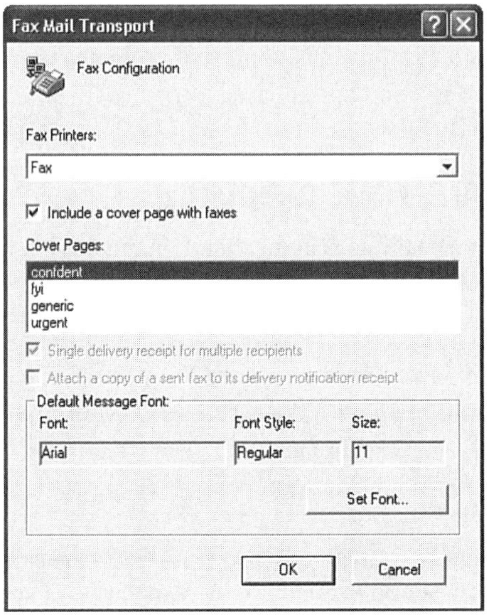

You're now ready to send faxes from Outlook. Open a new message, attach the files you want to fax, choose the fax numbers from the Outlook Address book, and choose Send. The attachments are rendered by the fax printer driver in TIFF format and placed in the fax console's Outbox and sent using your modem.

> You can mix fax numbers and email addresses on messages. The message is sent by email to the recipients with email addresses, and then faxed to the fax recipients.

When the fax numbers you want to send to aren't in your Contacts folder, you can enter them in the To: field in what is commonly known as *one-off format;* for example, `[fax:14235551212]`. Outlook understands this is a fax number and resolves it to 14235551212, and then sends it to the fax transport to dial.

> To fax a file from Outlook without including a cover sheet, leave the subject and message body blank.

Task: Send Faxes from Outlook

When you use the Windows Fax service, you can send documents from Outlook and the text in the message form is included as the cover letter. If you'd like a more professional looking cover letter, you can use a Word template and send it using the Office envelope, even if Word isn't your default email editor.

1. Open Word and select the fax cover sheet template of your choice using File, New. Then select Templates on My Computer in the New Document task pane.

2. Select the fax template of your choice from the Letters and Faxes tab.

3. Complete the fields on the cover sheet with your information.

4. Choose the email button on the Standard toolbar or File, Send To, Mail Recipient to display the email fields to open the Office envelope as shown in Figure 7.7.

FIGURE 7.7

Use Word to create a fax cover sheet and send using the Office Envelope.

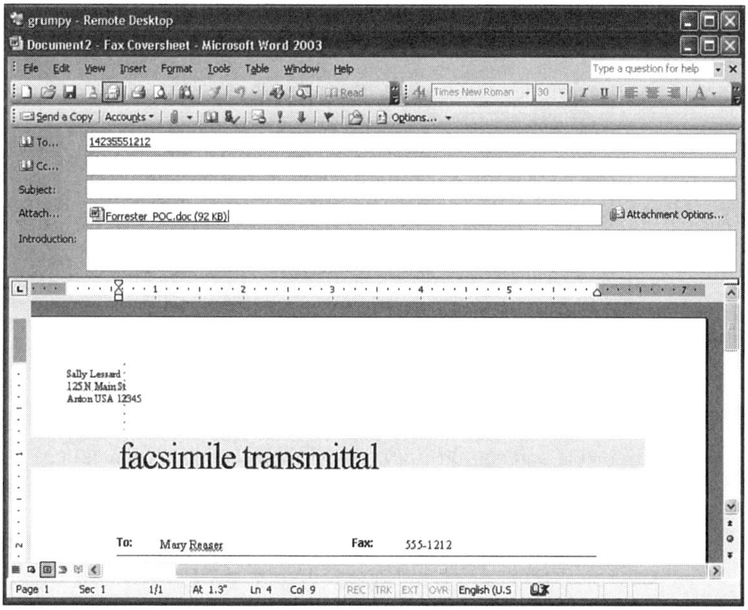

5. Select fax numbers from the Outlook Address Book or enter them in one-off format.

6. Leave the subject line blank in the email message so that the fax transport doesn't add a cover page.

7. Attach the files you want to include with the Fax and click Send a Copy.

7

The message goes to the Outbox. The attachments are rendered and printed using the fax printer driver, and then put into the fax console outbox and sent. Two copies of the fax are saved by default: one as the email message in Outlook's Sent Items folder and the fax image in the fax console Sent Items folder.

Using Other Fax Systems with Outlook

When you computer doesn't have a fax modem or you are unable to use it for faxing, you can send faxes by email, for a fee. Two popular Internet fax services that offer Office integration are Venali and eFax. When these services are installed, you can use the File, Send To, Recipient Using Internet Fax Service menu to send your faxes from many Office programs. Internet faxes are sent as attachments to email using Outlook, provided that you properly format the fax number as an email address. Check the documentation provided by the Internet fax service for the correct format, which will probably be in `fax_number@fax_domain.com` format; for example, `14135551212@venali.net`. You must send the message from the email account you've associated with the service.

The first time you select File, Send To, Recipient Using Internet Fax Service, you'll be redirected to the Office Web site where you can select the Internet fax provider of your choice.

Check out the Office Marketplace (`www.microsoft.com/office`) for a complete list of Office-integrated Internet fax services.

Using the Personal Address Book

Outlook 2003 supports the Contacts folder as an address book service as well as the personal address book (PAB). Although Outlook supports the use of a PAB, it's a depreciated service and should not be used under most circumstances. If you don't have a PAB now, don't create one. You should use only the Contacts folder for your address book.

If you upgraded to Outlook 2003 from a previous version of Outlook and are using a PAB, you should allow Outlook to import the PAB into its Contacts folder. If Outlook doesn't offer to import it, use the File, Import and Export menu to import the records and convert them to contacts.

1. Select Import from another program or file, and then click Next.

2. Choose Personal Address Book as the file type to import and then click Next.

3. Browse to locate your `*pab` file.

4. Select a destination folder and finish the import.

The contents of your personal address book are imported into the selected folder.

See Hour 19, "Managing Your Data," for complete instructions on using Import and Export.

In past versions, the PAB was the only way you could have distribution lists in Outlook, but because Outlook 2003 supports distribution lists in the Contacts folder, there's little need for the PAB now.

To connect an old PAB to your Outlook profile, choose the Tools, E-mail Accounts menu and select Add a New Directory or Address Book. Select Additional Address Book, and then select Personal Address Book from the next dialog. Browse to locate your PAB and connect it to your profile. The PAB is now ready to use and the addresses will be available for addressing messages.

After adding the PAB to your profile, you might need to adjust the order in which Outlook searches the PAB and Contacts folders and which address book is listed first. Open the address book using Tools, Address Book, and then choose the Tools, Options menu to display the Addressing dialog (see Figure 7.8). From this dialog, you can choose the address list that's displayed first and the address list where your personal addresses will be stored.

FIGURE 7.8

Use the Addressing dialog to select the address list that displays in the Address Book window when the address book is opened, to set the Contacts folder where global address list addresses are saved locally when you choose Add to Contacts, and to set the order in which address lists are searched when Outlook resolves addresses.

Addressing

Addressing

Show this address list first:

Contacts

Keep personal addresses in:

Contacts

When sending mail, check names using these address lists in the following order:

Contacts
Global Address List
MVPs
Diane's Address Book

Add...   Remove   Properties

OK   Cancel   Apply

7

The final field in this dialog controls the order in which Outlook searches the address books when resolving addresses. The address list search order is important because Outlook stops looking for addresses when it reaches the end of the address book where at least one possible match has been located. When address resolution doesn't seem to work as you expect, try changing the search order of the address lists.

If some of your address lists are missing from the fields on the Addressing dialog, choose the Add button to add the missing folders to the Outlook Address Book. Use the Remove button to remove address lists from the address book.

Working with Send/Receive Groups

Use send/receive groups to control when and how often your email accounts are polled and whether the full messages are downloaded or just headers. Although many people are satisfied with the default send/receive settings and have just one send/receive group, you can have as many groups as you need to control your email accounts. Send/receive groups are especially useful for travelers because they enable you to create different groups based on where you are.

When you choose to download full messages, you get just that: the full messages, including attachments. You can read, delete, and reply to messages as soon as Outlook has finished downloading your messages.

When you download headers only, you have to download the message body before you can read the message. In most cases, you can delete the message header and the message will be deleted from the server the next time Outlook checks for new mail.

To set up your send/receive groups, you must first access the Outlook Options dialog. Select Tools, Options and then select the Mail Setup tab (see Figure 7.9).

First, configure your dial-up settings on the Mail Setup tab to control how Outlook connects to your mail server using dial-up accounts. If you use more than one dial-up connection, select Warn before switching an existing dial-up connection to prevent Outlook from disconnecting you.

To work with send/receive groups, click the Send/Receive button (see Figure 7.10). Configure your send/receive group settings to control when and how often Outlook checks for new mail .

Figure 7.9

Use the Mail Setup tab to reach the configuration dialogs for your email accounts and send/receive settings, to set the location of your data files, and to control how Outlook handles dial-up accounts. Check Send Immediately when Connected and messages are transferred by SMTP as soon as you press the Send button.

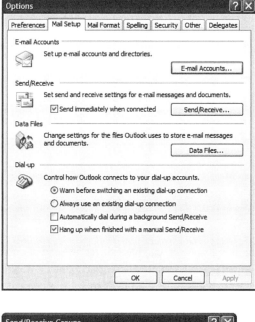

Figure 7.10

When automatic send/receive is enabled, Outlook checks for mail as soon as it is loaded and every nn *minutes. To reduce the load on your email server, you shouldn't check mail more frequently than every 8 to 10 minutes.*

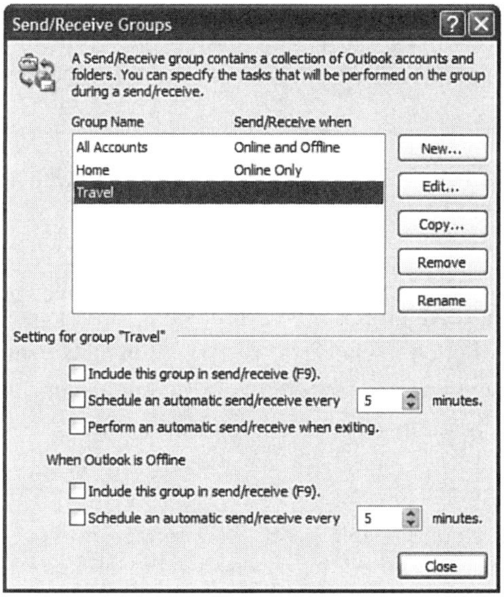

Outlook includes a default group that contains all of your email accounts. All accounts in your profile are enabled for send and receive using the default settings for the account type. Select the group and choose Edit to change the settings or select New to create another send/receive group (see Figure 7.11) .

FIGURE 7.11

Use the Send/Receive Settings dialog to configure your send/receive groups. Create as many groups as you need to control how Outlook checks for new mail on each account.

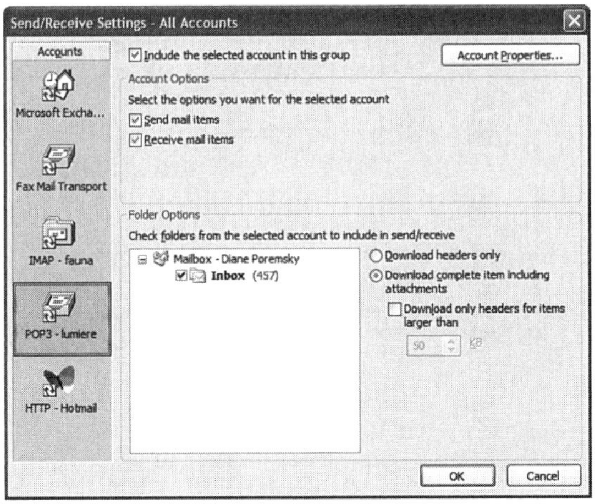

Each mail account in your profile can have different send and receive settings. Configure IMAP, HTTP (Hotmail), and Exchange Server accounts to download specific folders with full messages or headers only, with the capability to download full messages up to a certain size on POP3 and Exchange Server accounts.

When a send/receive group isn't enabled for online or offline mail checks, you can still use the group by choosing Tools, Send/Receive and selecting the group by name.

The send and receive options available for use with an account are different for each account type.

After your send and receive groups are set up, you can press the F9 key or click the Send/Receive toolbar button to check for new email in all accounts included in a send/receive. When you want to check for new mail in a single account, use the Tools, Send/Receive menu choice to select the account or folder .

IMAP accounts enable you to check for new mail per folder or per account. Use Shift+F9 to check for new mail in the selected IMAP folder, or use F9 to check for new mail in all the folders in the current account.

Summary

In this hour, you learned about the services available in Outlook that aren't used as often as Outlook's other features. Some of these features are needed by only a small subset of Outlook users; other features are new to Outlook and many users aren't aware of the features or don't understand how they work. This hour showed you how to use these services.

You might not use Windows Messenger service to send instant messages to friends or need the fax services to send documents now, but if you ever have the need to use either feature, you now know how to use it.

Other less-used features found in Outlook include voting and the personal address book. Voting is fun and usable by everyone, for serious or silly votes. By contrast, the personal address book shouldn't be used by most users.

The final feature covered in this hour was send/receive groups. Although this feature is very important because it controls your connections to your mailbox server, it's often forgotten and many users continue to use the default settings.

Q&A

Q I don't have the Person Name smart tag working in the Office applications. What am I doing wrong?

A First, ensure that the Person Name smart tag is enabled in Tools, AutoCorrect Options, Smart Tags.

Next, the Person Name smart tag works only with two-word names, which means that your Messenger contacts can use only two-word display names. If your messenger contacts use a longer display name, the smart tag won't work.

Finally, the Person Name smart tag works only in Word and Outlook. It's not supported in Excel or PowerPoint.

Q I'm having a problem sending faxes. They just sit in the fax console outbox.

A Do you have fax enabled for sending? Open the Configuration Wizard from the fax console's Tools, Configure Fax dialog. Enable Send must be enabled on the second screen of the wizard.

If sending is enabled, verify that the phone line is plugged in to the modem and that the modem is properly installed by choosing Control Panel, System, Device Manager.

Q Why don't my voting ballots always include the voting buttons?

A Voting buttons require rich text format. When you're sending RTF messages to the Internet, Outlook converts the messages to HTML format by default. For this reason, you must set the properties for each address to use Outlook rich text format.

Hour **8**

Email Security

As email grew in popularity over the years, many people wanted to send pretty messages using fonts and colored text. When more email programs supported using HTML-formatted messages, HTML eventually became the quasi-standard format for email. Unfortunately, the ability to embed sounds and images in HTML-formatted messages also makes it an easy way to deliver viruses. Some people took the opportunity to see how much damage they could do to the computers of unsuspecting users by creating viruses that took advantage of Outlook's power and programmability.

Unfortunately, after virus creators took advantage of Outlook's programmability, Microsoft tightened the security of Outlook to the point it annoyed many users. Many of the most popular features, including mail merge, some VBA code, and COM add-ins, triggered a dialog every time an address was accessed. Sending and receiving attachments became more difficult because Outlook blocked many attachment types. The security features in Outlook 2003 are somewhat relaxed compared to earlier versions—trusted code runs without annoying dialogs while still providing the highest level of protection to users.

Viruses are not the only worry. Mass mailers discovered they could track how many people read their messages by including Web beacons in the HTML and identifying the addresses that read the message.

Security goes beyond protecting your computer from viruses and Web beacons. It also includes ensuring important messages aren't tampered with and controlling what happens to messages after you send them.

This hour features all aspects of Outlook's security, including

- A secure object model
- Safety in the Reading Pane
- Using digital signatures
- Understanding Information Rights Management

By the time you're done with this hour, you'll know how to use Outlook securely without risking a virus infection on your computer. You'll know how to use a digital signature and you'll understand rights managements.

Understanding Outlook's Security

One of Outlook's strengths is its programmability. Outlook supports VBA, enabling you to use procedures to automate many mundane tasks. When you need more than VBA provides, you can install COM add-ins to provide features that Microsoft didn't build into Outlook.

A Component Object Model (COM) add-in is an application that uses the host program's object model to access the host program's interface. COM add-ins add features missing from the program or improve on existing features.

Extended Reminders (www.slovaktech.com) is an example of a COM add-in that adds a feature that Outlook is missing—the ability to use reminders in any folder.

After a COM add-in is installed, it's listed in Tools, Options, Other, Advanced Options, COM Add-ins.

This programmability comes with a high price tag: Anything you can do, virus writers can do too, and they usually have destruction on their minds, not helping Outlook users work smarter.

Outlook 2003 provides a good mix of security and usability. Microsoft assumes that you know not to install add-ins or use VBA code that comes from questionable sources, so it allowed Outlook to trust COM add-ins and project code. That means code now runs without triggering annoying dialogs, such as the one shown in Figure 8.1.

FIGURE 8.1

*The object model secu-
rity dialog warns you
when a program is
trying to send mail
on your behalf.*

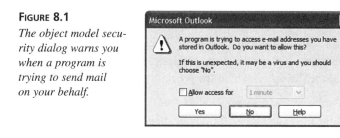

8

The responsibility to ensure that unsafe add-ins aren't installed now falls on your shoulders, not Microsoft's. Plenty of safeguards are still built in, but in the end, keeping your system secure and free from viruses, trojan horses, and worms is your responsibility, and that's how it should be.

Even though Outlook is very secure, don't use it as an excuse to stop using common sense when you receive questionable messages. Don't open attachments you don't need. Always use an antivirus program and keep the virus definitions current. Auto-protect settings will protect you if a virus tries to run.

Outlook's first line of defense is Outlook Object Model (OOM) security. If you're using a COM add-in that's not updated for Outlook 2003, you'll notice the most visible effect of the OOM security: A warning dialog alerts you that something is trying to access email addresses or send mail on your behalf (see Figure 8.2).

FIGURE 8.2

*A second warning dia-
log displays as new
messages are created.
After the green bar
completes, you need to
choose Yes or No to
send the message.*

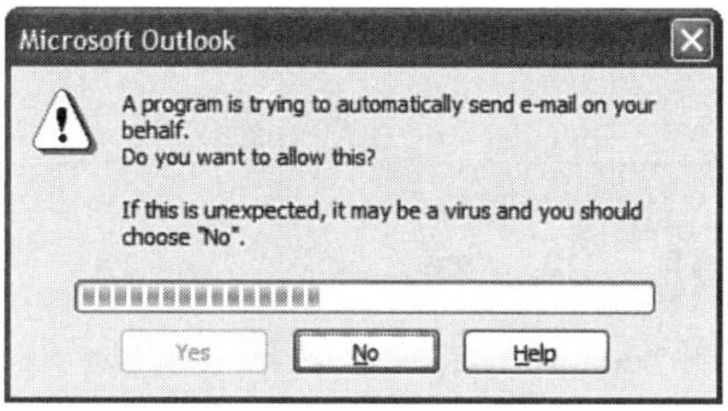

As you can see from this figure, the dialog asks whether you want to allow it to send email. In most cases, you'll want to choose Yes and allow it access for 1 to 10 minutes. However, if you're not sure what's causing the warning dialog to appear, play it safe and choose No.

Outlook Object Model Security

Outlook's object model security protects you by preventing untrusted code from accessing your messages and address lists. When a program attempts to access your Outlook data, you'll see one or both of the dialogs shown in the previous section in Figures 8.1 and 8.2.

However, published Outlook forms, Visual Basic for Applications code, and properly written Outlook COM add-ins won't trigger the security prompts for standalone users. Exchange administrators will still be able to manage Outlook security through the Outlook Security Settings folder and form.

The Office Resource Kit (available online at Microsoft) includes the security form for Exchange Server and instructions on using it. Exchange administrators install and administer the form, giving permission to selected domain users and groups to avoid the security prompt.

If you use Exchange Server and want to avoid the security prompts, you'll need to speak with your administrator.

Any attachment type that's executable is blocked by default. That means any attachment that the computer can run directly, and shortcuts to programs are blocked. This includes attachments with exe, scr, and pif extensions. Files such as text files (txt) and images (jpg, gif) open, but can't be run directly. You can edit Windows Registry to unblock the extensions you need to access. Refer to Hour 6, "Working with Email Attachments," to learn more.

Security in the Reading Pane

The Reading Pane is secure because it doesn't support active content. All potentially dangerous attachments are blocked (including scripts) and Outlook no longer allows iframes to display in email.

Open messages offer the same level of protection that you have with the Reading Pane, so if you like using the Reading Pane, go ahead and use it.

Many HTML elements are disabled in email, including forms, submissions, and other active content. Open the message and choose <u>V</u>iew, View in Internet <u>Z</u>one if you need to make the content. The message is displayed using the Internet Zone settings normally used for browsing the Internet.

Never lower the security settings using the <u>T</u>ools, <u>O</u>ptions, Security tab—it's not safe to do so. If the source is trustworthy, use the <u>V</u>iew, View in Internet <u>Z</u>one menu selection when you need to reduce the security level on your email. Don't view messages from unknown sources in the Internet zone.

Understanding Web Beacons

Also known as *Web bugs*, Web beacons are images with a URL that includes a code to identify the email address it was sent to. Every time the image loads, the sender is informed of the email address that viewed the message. This lets the sender know that the email address is active and ripe for future mailings.

Although Web beacons are often used by spammers to verify valid email addresses, they're also used by legitimate mailers, including many newsletters and advertisers, to learn who reads the messages and which layouts or ad campaigns result in the highest levels of readership.

> Although Web beacons are a popular method for spammers to track who reads their messages, they aren't the only ones who use them. Many legitimate companies who send HTML-formatted email use them to track their readers. Twice I've received messages from companies asking why I don't read their email or stating that since it appears I don't read their email, I'll be dropped from their mailing list. They didn't know I was reading the mailings; I just wasn't letting the Web beacon report back.

You can selectively show the images that are blocked by Outlook or disable Web beacon blocking for all messages from specific domains or disable it for all email you receive. Click on the InfoBar or right-click on any image placeholder in the message and select Download Pictures to display the images in an individual message (see Figure 8.3). Choose <u>C</u>hange Automatic Download Settings to change the global options.

FIGURE 8.3

*Messages containing
external images show
only the picture place-
holders and text
informing you why the
images are missing.*

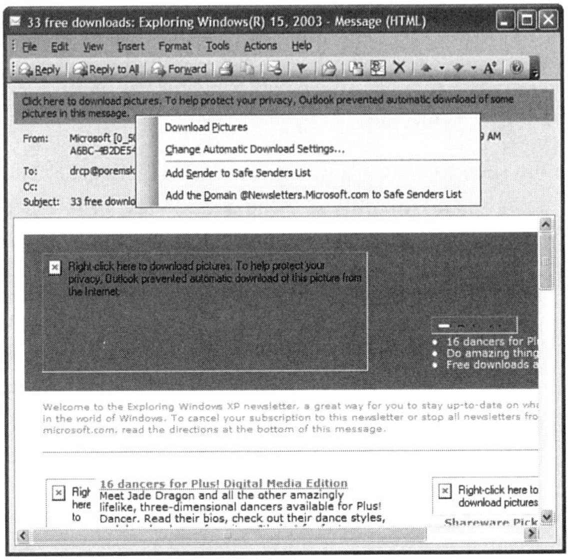

Click here to download pictures. To help protect your privacy, Outlook prevented automatic download of some pictures in this message.

Download Pictures

Change Automatic Download Settings...

Add Sender to Safe Senders List

Add the Domain @Newsletters.Microsoft.com to Safe Senders List

You have four methods you can use to change how Outlook uses external content:

- Enable External Content Per Message—Click on the InfoBar or right-click in the picture placeholder and choose Download Pictures.

- Enable External Content by Domain—Allow external content from domains on the Safe Senders list or in the Internet Zone's Trusted list.

- Permit External Content for Trusted Senders—Allow content from addresses on the Safe Senders list and in your Contacts folder to download automatically.

- Disable External Content Blocking—Download all external content automatically. Not recommended.

Although I recommend against disabling the feature completely, trusting senders or domains is an acceptable option.

Both the Junk E-mail filter and the Web beacon feature use the Safe Senders, Safe Recipients, and Blocked Senders lists are.

In most cases, using the Safe Senders and Safe Recipients lists is preferable to changing your Internet Zone settings. Doing so gives you better security when browsing the sender's Internet site, while allowing their images and external content to display in your email.

8

One of the Safe Sender options is Also Trust E-mail from My Contacts. I recommend against choosing this option for several reasons:

- Most Outlook users include a contact for themselves in the Contacts folder. Spammers are beginning to send messages to your address and using your address in the From field. This allows the external content to download because Outlook thinks it's from you, as well as prevents it from being treated as junk mail.

- Messages containing viruses that are sent from people in your Contacts folder would be trusted—a bad move because many viruses fake their From address with addresses found on the infected computer. Although there is no known exploit that could take advantage of this feature, we don't know what the future might bring and the risk isn't worth it.

- I don't need it—no one in my address book sends me messages containing external content and I don't add newsletter and advertisers addresses to my address book.

Clicking once per message takes a second or I can add individuals or their domains to the Safe Senders list as needed.

Recently, a spammer tried to trick me into adding his address to my address book. The message was sent from Chris and the subject mentioned he had a new email address. The only visible text in the message asked me to update his address. I was suspicious and checked the message source by right-clicking on the message body and choosing View Source. I discovered a disclaimer in the HTML, formatted as white text so that no one would see it, and a Web beacon so that the spammer could see whether I read his message.

It's a good thing I didn't fall for his trick. Adding the address to my address book would allow his messages to remain in my Inbox and the external content to display.

I immediately added his domain to the Blocked Senders list.

Outlook, Outlook Express, and Internet Explorer share the security zone settings. That means when you add a domain to the trusted zone, browsing the domain's Internet site is also in the trusted zone. Use this option only when you already trust the Internet site because adding the domain to the Safe Senders list provides more protection with the least amount of hassle.

Finally, if you really don't like Outlook blocking your external content on any of your messages, you can disable the feature completely. This is not recommended; it's safer to trust senders.

After you enable external content on a message using the InfoBar, it remains enabled on that message and will download each time you view the message because external content isn't cached locally.

> When you use a dial-up Internet connection and work offline, blocking external content prevents your modem from trying to dial every time you select a message.

Change Automatic Download Settings

There are two areas where you can change the settings that control the download of external content: Automatic Picture Download settings and the Safe Senders list. Unless you completely block all downloaded content, which I do, you'll need to configure options in both areas.

You can open the Automatic Picture Download Settings dialog when you click to download images on any message or from the Tools, Options, Security dialog. Choose Change Automatic Download Settings to open the dialog as shown in Figure 8.4.

FIGURE 8.4

Configure the options to allow some images to be downloaded automatically.

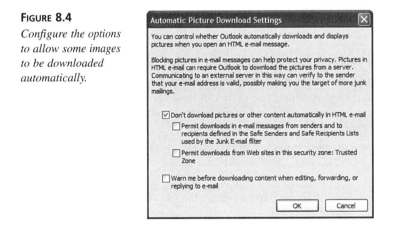

It's highly recommended that you leave the setting enabled for Don't Download Pictures or Content Automatically in HTML E-mail. However, you might want to permit pictures and content for addresses or domains included in the Safe Senders list, which is also used by the Junk E-mail filter.

You can permit pictures and content for sites listed in your Trusted security zone. Choose this option to use with Internet domains you already trust; don't add domains to the Trusted zone for email only. Use the Safe Senders list instead.

When you edit, reply, or forward messages containing external content, the content is downloaded. You can disable the warning notification from this dialog.

Configuring Your Safe Senders List

The Safe Senders list is part of the Junk E-mail filters. If you choose to allow external content from addresses listed in your Safe Senders list, you need to check the configuration of the list.

You can add addresses and domains to the Safe Senders list directly from an email message. Click on the InfoBar or right-click in any image placeholder, and select Add Sender to Safe Senders List or Add the Domain @[*domain-name*] to Safe Senders List. The sender's fully qualified domain name is listed in the menu selection, as shown previously in Figure 8.3.

Open your Safe Senders list using Tools, Options, Preferences, Junk E-mail and select the Safe Senders tab (see Figure 8.5). Near the bottom of the dialog is an option to Also Trust E-mail from My Contacts. You should leave this disabled and add senders from whom you receive messages with blocked content to the Safe Senders List.

FIGURE 8.5

You can allow content in messages from addresses and domains listed in the Safe Senders list to automatically download.

Using the right-click menu is the easiest way to add new addresses to the list. However, you'll need to use this dialog to remove or edit addresses from the list. The list doesn't support wildcards, so you can't enter addresses in the format of @*.microsoft.com. You have to enter the entire text following the @ when you add addresses to the list.

After you've created a Safe Senders list, you can export it for use on other computers where Outlook 2003 is installed or use it as a backup copy if you need to reinstall Outlook or Windows.

Using Digital Signatures

When email is signed with a digital signature, it provides a level of proof that the person using the email address sent the message. More importantly, it also ensures that no one tampered with the message.

A digital *signature* is a digital code that can be attached to an email message to uniquely identify the sender. Like a written signature, the purpose of a digital signature is to guarantee that the individual sending the message really is who he claims to be. To be effective, we need to be assured that a digital signature is not forged, and there are a number of different encryption techniques that guarantee this level of security.

Encryption is a more secure form of a digital signature, and encodes the message so that only someone with the sender's secret key or password can read the message. Encrypted data is also referred to as cipher text.

Every digital signature has two levels of signing: a simple digital signature that identifies messages that have been tampered with, and an encrypted signature that encodes the message and attachments so that only the person the message is sent to can read it.

Before you can digitally sign your email, you must obtain a digital certificate. Although many corporations provide digital certificates to their employees, anyone can get one free or at a low cost from several Internet sites. Most certificates are issued for one year and must be renewed or reissued when they expire.

If you use Outlook at work, your employer might issue a digital certificate for you to use. The certificate is valid only when you send email using the address that's included in the certificate. If you use several email addresses, you'll need a certificate for each address you want to use to send digitally signed messages.

Don't routinely sign all of your messages, especially on personal messages or those sent to mailing lists. Not all email clients can read signed messages. Reserve the use of digital signatures for important messages.

Task: Set Up a Digital Signature

Before you can use a digital signature, it must be installed and set up in Outlook.

1. Open the Tools, Options, Security dialog.

2. If you already have a current digital certificate, use Import/Export to install your digital ID.

3. If you need a digital signature, choose Get a Digital ID. This opens your Internet browser to a list of digital ID providers who partner with Microsoft. The steps necessary to get your digital ID vary with each service, but most will install the certificate for you at the end of the process.

4. Once your digital ID is installed, select the Settings button in the Encryption section of the Security tab.

5. Type a name for your security settings in the Security Setting Name field (see Figure 8.6). Select the Choose button to select the certificate to use. You should leave the other settings at their default. Click OK when you're done.

▲

FIGURE 8.6

Configure the setting for your digital signature on the Change Security Settings dialog.

Change Security Settings	
Security Setting Preferences	
Security Settings Name:	
Diane Poremsky	
Cryptographic message	S/MIME
☑ Default Security Setting for this cryptographic message format	
☑ Default Security Setting for all cryptographic messages	
Security Labels...	New	Delete	Password...
Certificates and Algorithms	
Signing Certificate:	Diane Poremsky	Choose...
Hash Algorithm:	SHA1
Encryption Certificate:	Diane Poremsky	Choose...
Encryption Algorithm:	3DES
☑ Send these certificates with signed messages	
OK	Cancel

Don't change the default security settings when you install certificates. Using the wrong setting prevents others from reading your messages.

If you have more than one certificate or need to configure alternative security settings, choose the New button and type a new name in the name field.

Your digital signature is ready to use.

Task: Send Signed and Encrypted Messages

After you've obtained a digital certificate, signing a message is as easy as pressing a toolbar button to enable signing and or encryption.

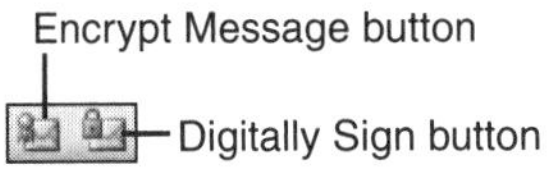

Encrypt Message button

—Digitally Sign button

FIGURE 8.7
The Digitally Sign and Encrypt Message buttons are automatically added to the toolbar when you install a digital certificate.

Before you can send encrypted messages, you must have the recipient's digital certificate associated with his contact record. If the person hasn't sent you signed email yet, ask her to send you a digitally signed message. Right-click on the sender's display name and choose Add to Outlook Contacts to add the digital certificate to her contact record. Confirm that the digital signature was added to the contact by looking on the contact's Certificates tab (see Figure 8.8).

When the recipient's certificate isn't associated with her contact record, Outlook won't allow you to send encrypted messages. Instead, you'll receive a message like the one shown in Figure 8.9. You can still send a digitally signed message.

When someone sends you a signed message, you'll see a red ribbon on the envelope icon and a larger red ribbon icon on the right side of the header area on a message form, as shown in Figure 8.10. Select a button to display information about the certificate used to sign or encrypt the message. A signed and encrypted message won't display in the Reading Pane; you have to open the message to read it.

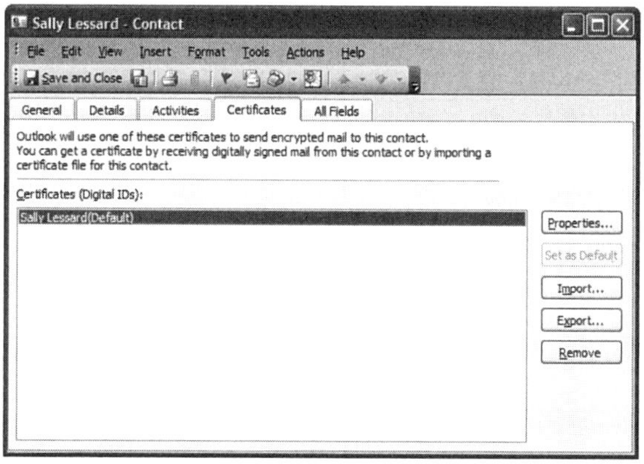

FIGURE 8.8

Your contact's digital IDs are listed on the Certificates tab of her contact record.

FIGURE 8.9

You need to have the recipient's digital ID associated with her contact before you can send her encrypted messages.

FIGURE 8.10

Signed messages have a red ribbon button and encrypted messages include a blue padlock button.

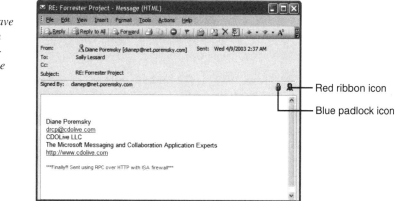

When there's a problem with the digital ID, the message header includes a warning message that the signature has a problem, as shown in Figure 8.11. Many times the problem is caused by an expired digital ID, or the company issuing the certificate is not in your trusted Certificate Authority (CA) list. This often happens when the sender's employer issues its own certificates. In almost all cases, it's safe to trust the certificate if you know and trust the sender.

FIGURE 8.11

Outlook warns you when there's a problem with the digital certificate. Most of the time, it's either expired or the issuing authority isn't on your trusted list. You'll also see this warning if the message contents were changed after the message was sent.

| From: | Sally Lessard [sallyl@digidashlive.com] | Sent: | Sat 8/2/2003 1:01 AM |
| Signed By: | There are problems with the signature. Click the signature button for details. | | |

Click on the signature button to the right of the warning message and a dialog opens that contains information explaining why Outlook is unable to trust the certificate.

Choose the Details button to view more information about the sender's certificate or choose the Trust button to immediately trust the certificate.

From the Message Security Properties dialog, view additional information about the certificate and click the Edit Trust button to change how Outlook trusts the certificate. This opens the View Certificate dialog shown in Figure 8.12. You can choose from three options:

- Inherit Trust from Issuer—This is the default setting and trusts certificates installed on your computer. You can open the Certificates dialog and view trusted Certificate Authorities (CAs) by choosing Internet Explorer's Tools, Internet Options, Content, Certificates menu option.

- Explicitly Trust This Certificate—Choose this option to trust certificates used by people you trust when their certificates aren't initially trusted by Outlook.

- Explicitly Don't Trust This Certificate—Use this option when you don't want to trust the sender.

After you trust the certificate, the message header looks like a normal signed message. Selecting the Digital Signature or Encrypted Message button on the message opens a dialog like the one shown in Figure 8.13.

A digital signature isn't absolute proof that the person is who he says he is. Anyone can make up a name and get a digital signature. However, if it's someone you know and trust, a digitally signed email is proof enough that the person you know really did send the message and whether it was tampered with.

FIGURE 8.12

Use the View Certificate dialog to learn more about the certificate. Only when you trust the sender should you select Explicitly Trust This Certificate.

8

> **View Certificate** [?][X]
>
> General | Details | Certification Path | Trust
>
> Trust Status indicates whether you trust the individual, group or corporation to whom this certificate is issued. The certificate can then be used for the specified purposes such as sending/receiving e-mail, trusting a web site having the certificate, etc.
>
> ┌─ Certificate trusted for ──────────────────────┐
> │ E-Mail Encryption and Authentication   │
> │   │
> │   │
> └──┘
>
> ┌─ Edit Trust ───────────────────────────────────┐
> │ ⦿ Inherit Trust from Issuer   │
> │ ○ Explicitly Trust this Certificate   │
> │ ○ Explicitly Don't Trust this Certificate   │
> └──┘
>
> [OK]

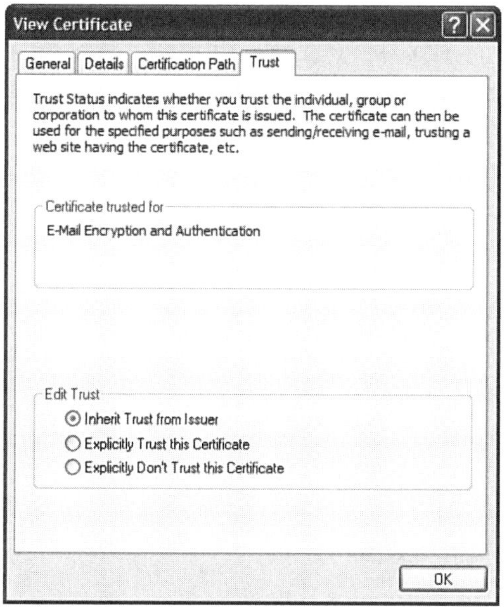

FIGURE 8.13

The Digital Signature: Valid dialog. Click the Details button to learn more about the certificate.

> **Digital Signature: Valid** [X]
>
> Subject:
> From: Sally Lessard
>
> Ⓠ The digital signature on this message is Valid and Trusted.
>
> For more information about the certificate used to digitally sign the message, click Details.
>
> [Details...]
>
> ☐ Warn me about errors in digitally signed e-mail before message opens.
>
> [Close]

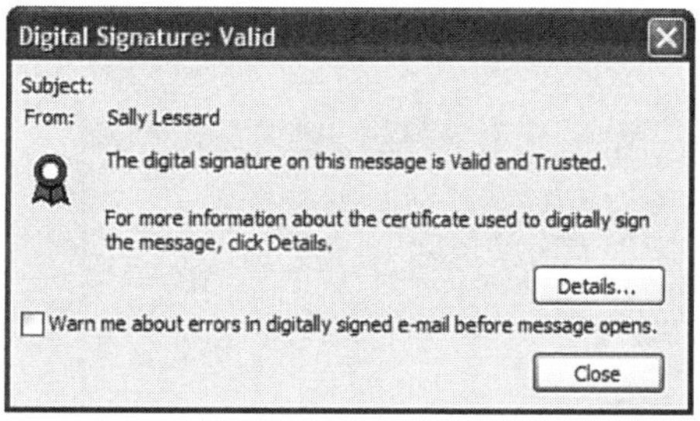

You should use a clear text signature for most signed messages you send, especially if you aren't sure what email client the recipient uses or when you know she uses an older client that doesn't support S/MIME messages.

> S/MIME, short for Secure/MIME, is a version of the MIME protocol that supports encryption of messages. It works with many newer email programs and is used for digitally signing messages. Fortunately, you don't have to understand it to use it; you only need to know that it's the type of digital signature Outlook uses.

To enable clear text for all signed messages, choose Tools, Options, Security and add a check to the box to Send Clear Text Signed Message When Sending Signed Messages. This allows recipients whose email clients don't support S/MIME signatures to read the message without verifying the digital signature.

You can change the settings on a per-message basis from the Options dialog when you compose a message. Open the Options dialog using the Options button on the toolbar and then click the Security Settings button.

The Security Properties dialog, shown in Figure 8.14, includes options to

- Encrypt Message Contents and Attachments—This is checked when you select the Encrypt Message toolbar button.
- Add Digital Signature to This Message—This is checked when you select the Digitally Sign toolbar button.
- Send This Message as Clear Text Signed—Selecting this ensures that the message can be read using any email client.
- Request S/MIME Receipt for This Message—This is a digitally signed read receipt. After the recipient who has a digital ID opens the message, you'll get back a receipt that is signed with the recipient's digital ID .

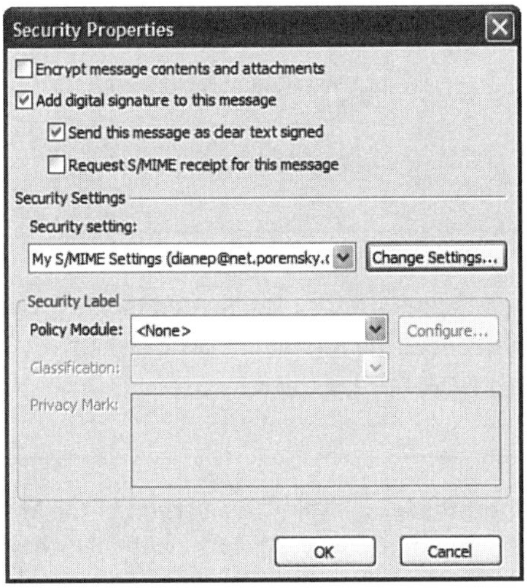

FIGURE 8.14

Use the Security Properties dialog to enable or disable clear text signed messages, request signed read receipts, and to select a different security setting.

The Security Setting selection contains the digital signature configurations you created, as shown earlier in Figure 8.6. By default, it contains Automatic, Default, along with the security settings you created and named.

8

The Security Label section is for corporate users only. When your administrator has policy modules set up, you can select them from the list and add a sensitivity label, such as Internal Use Only, to the message header.

Understanding Information Rights Management

New to Outlook 2003, Information Rights Management (IRM) enables you to secure a message, including any attachments, to prevent the recipient from printing, forwarding, or copying the message or attachment. The recipient can open the message only after she confirms her identity by logging on to her Passport account.

Although there are similarities between digital signatures and IRM, they're two distinct methods you can use to secure your messages. You can digitally sign and encrypt IRM-protected messages.

A digital signature is used to prove you are the person sending the message; encryption prevents someone who doesn't have your private key from opening the message.

IRM ensures the confidentiality of the message and attached documents by preventing the recipient from printing, forwarding, or copying a message that's sent with IRM enabled.

Office 2003 applications that support IRM are Word, PowerPoint, and Excel. Microsoft will release a server add-on for corporations that want to deploy IRM internally. Anyone with a .NET Passport account can control permissions for their messages and read restricted messages or documents. Other documents are partially restricted in that they're restricted when attached to a message that's protected by IRM. The File and Save dialogs are disabled, along with Print and Forward. However, you can save the attachments to your drive and use them as you normally would. When you send a message or document using restricted permissions to someone who doesn't have Office 2003, he'll have to install an Internet Explorer add-in to read the message or view the attachment.

Don't confuse using document protection with IRM. Both can prevent others from using the document, but each method has advantages and disadvantages.

- Document protection uses a password to protect the document from prying eyes. Anyone who knows the password can open the document and you can't control what happens to it.

- IRM protects the document using a digital certificate and only those people you give permission to can open the document. You retain complete control over the document, including whether someone can edit, copy, or print it. In the case of email, you can prevent others from forwarding the message.

> A popular trick to reduce mailbox size is to remove large attachments from messages and then save the message. However, when a message has restricted permissions assigned, you're unable to remove the attachments and save the message. If you need to keep the message, you'll also have to keep the attachment with it.

Using Information Rights Management

To protect your message with IRM, choose the Permission button sometime before sending it. The Permission button is the envelope icon with the red circle on it, as shown in Figure 8.15.

Permission button

FIGURE 8.15

Select the Permission button to enable IRM. The InfoBar message reminds you that the message has restricted permissions.

The first time you use IRM, either to send a restricted message or to read one, the IRM software is downloaded from the Microsoft Office Web site and installed. It's about 340KB in size and shouldn't take more than a few minutes to download, even on a dial-up connection.

After the client software is installed, a .NET passport is required to send or read messages with restricted permissions. If you don't have a passport for your email address, you must get one to use IRM. The first time you use IRM, the Passport Wizard opens and you can get a passport for your email address or associate your existing passport with the service and receive a rights management (RM) certificate.

If you don't have a passport account for your email address, the wizard leads you through signing up for a passport and associating it with the rights management service.

If you use several different email addresses, you'll need a .NET Passport and certificate for each address with which you send or receive protected messages.

After the RM certificate is installed and you open the message, you'll receive a warning that the Office program needs to connect to the RM servers to verify your identity (see Figure 8.16). If you aren't signed in to the Passport service, the passport logon dialog displays.

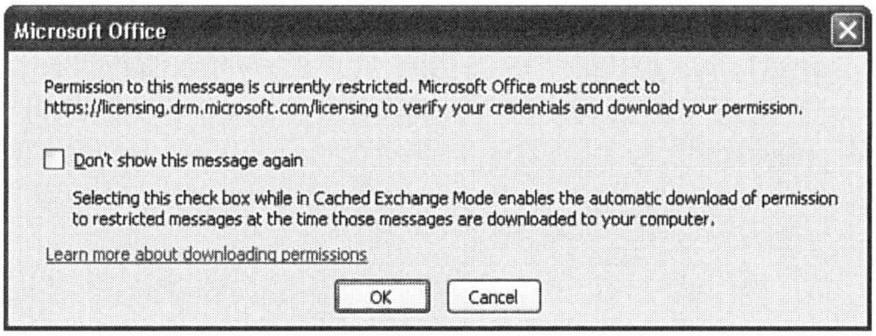

FIGURE 8.16

Before opening an RM-protected message, your credentials must be verified.

Microsoft Office

Permission to this message is currently restricted. Microsoft Office must connect to https://licensing.drm.microsoft.com/licensing to verify your credentials and download your permission.

☐ Don't show this message again

Selecting this check box while in Cached Exchange Mode enables the automatic download of permission to restricted messages at the time those messages are downloaded to your computer.

Learn more about downloading permissions

[OK] [Cancel]

> If the address doesn't match the address used on the message, Outlook will display a message asking whether you want to open it using a different set of credentials. Answering Yes opens the Select User dialog for you to choose a different passport. When you need to associate a new address with an RM certificate, you can get a new passport using the Add button. Choosing No closes the dialog and the RM-protected message is not opened.

You need to sign in to the licensing service using a .NET Passport associated with the same email address used on the message. After you get the RM certificate, you must open the message to read it because the Reading Pane is disabled along with the Copy, Forward, and Print commands.

> Corporations might have a rights management server available. Instead of using a passport, you'll follow the instructions to log on to your corporate server. As always, speak with your administrator if you have any questions.

If you use Outlook to add restricted permissions to an attachment, the attachment can be read but not edited. When attachments are assigned restricted permissions in Word, Excel, or PowerPoint, you'll have more control over the permissions that readers have. The File, Save menu option is disabled, but you can right-click on the attachment in the opened message and choose Save As.

You can enable permissions on a message at any time before sending the message. The message is signed using the passport with which you're currently signed in. If it doesn't have an RM certificate, Outlook guides you through the required steps. If you have an RM certificate associated with a different passport account, select the passport using File, Permission, Restrict Permission As. The Select User dialog opens for you to select the passport account to use.

If you have a Word, Excel, or PowerPoint document attached to the message, you'll receive a warning that the attachment will also have restricted permissions. If you don't want permissions assigned to the attachment, choose Cancel and the send operation will be canceled. You must disable permissions or remove the attachment if you don't want it to be protected.

> Don't use IRM as a matter of routine and enable it on every message you send. It's annoying when it's used on unimportant messages because the recipient can't read the message without first connecting to the certificate server.

Summary

This hour covered many of the security features Outlook offers you to protect your computer from viruses, including external content blocking, which prevents images and other content from downloading as soon as you select a message. You also learned about other security features in Outlook, including the security features built into Outlook's object model, which prevent viruses from accessing your mailbox.

Also included in this hour's coverage were using digital signatures to sign and encrypt the messages you send, and using Information Rights Management to prevent the recipient from printing, forwarding, or copying the message or attachments.

Q&A

Q I have an add-in that worked perfectly in older versions of Outlook. Now it triggers the dialog seen in Figure 8.1 when I use it.

A Check the add-in's Web site for a newer version. There were some minor updates to the object model security and the developer must update his program to avoid the security prompts.

Q Can I send email with restricted permissions to someone who doesn't use Outlook 2003?

A Yes, you can restrict permissions to anyone. She'll need to install the Internet Explorer Rights Management client add-in to read the protected content if she doesn't use Outlook 2003. The Internet Explorer add-in is available at Windows Update.

8

HOUR 9

Keeping Email Organized

Like many users, you probably get a lot of email. Maybe not enough to say you have email overload, but you get enough that you need to organize it. Too much of your mail is spam or ads and you delete those as they arrive. Other messages are important and you might add flags to them or move them to other folders. Then you can't find them without using Advanced Find or custom views. To make organizing and locating your messages easier, Outlook 2003 has three new features: Quick Flags, Search Folders, and Favorite Folders.

This hour introduces you to these new features in Outlook 2003 as well as helps you make better use of all the folder management features, including

- Using Quick Flags
- Making the most of Search Folders
- Using Favorite Folders
- Creating and deleting folders

Using Quick Flags

Because flagging every message that needed action with an identical red flag meant every message was flagged, many users adopted the unread method of mail management. All unread messages needed action and Outlook's feature of automatically marking mail viewed in the preview pane as read is disabled. Flags and reminders were reserved for only the most important messages.

Quick Flags will change message management for many users. Flagging your messages with different-colored flags means that every message no longer has an identical flag. You can customize the mail list view and remove the flag field from your normal view, and use Search Folders to view only the flagged messages. Using customized Search Folders, you can see filtered views of all the messages in your mailbox.

Quick Flags are cool. Click on the flag block in the message list and a flag is added to the message, using the default flag color (see Figure 9.1). If you want to use a different color flag, that's easy enough: just right-click the block and choose a new flag color. Click once again to mark the flag as complete.

FIGURE 9.1

Use Outlook's Quick Flags to mark messages for follow up.

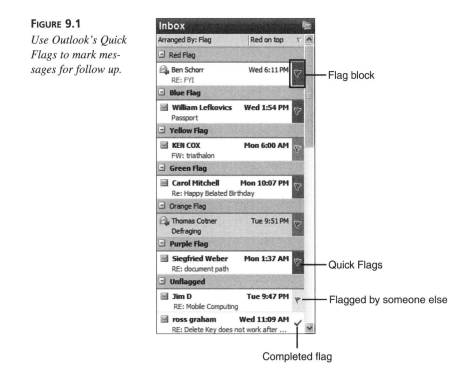

Flag block

Quick Flags

Flagged by someone else

Completed flag

Quick Flags come in six colors: red (default color), blue, green, orange, yellow, and purple. You can change the default color from red, but the colors and labels aren't customizable. If you want to see the red flag labeled Important, you must create a custom toolbar. See "Create a Quick Flag Toolbar" later in this hour to learn how .

The Quick Flag block works only on messages. You can flag other Outlook items, including notes, using the colored flags displayed in the Flag Status column.

Outlook's Original Flag

Outlook's original red flag is still alive and well in Outlook 2003, and is used on items flagged using older versions of Outlook or when flagged messages are sent to you. Nonmessage items support the new flag colors but not the Quick Flag box.

9

 Customize the view on any folder to include the Flag Status field. In the Show Fields dialog, select All Mail Fields in the Select Available Fields From: list and add the Flag Status field to the view. Don't let the fact that it's in All Mail Fields keep you from using it—it works on all folder types.

Messages flagged with red flags aren't listed in the By Follow Up Search Folder. You must create a custom Search Folder, using the Only Items Which: Have Been Flagged by Someone Else selection on the More Choices tab as the Criteria. See "Create a Custom Search Folder" later in this hour for help in creating a custom Search Folder.

Existing flags can be converted to Quick Flags by using rules to flag messages and then choosing the Run Rules Now option in Tools, Rules and Alerts.

The flags can be changed for several messages at once by selecting a group of messages and clicking in the Quick Flag box to apply a flag to all the selected messages.

Flags, Rules, and Reminder Spamming

Quick Flags can be set using rules and alerts. By doing this, important messages are flagged for you as they arrive in your inbox.

If you upgraded from a previous version of Outlook and are using rules to flag messages, you must update the rules to use Quick Flags because old rules use the old flags.

1. Open Tools, Rules and Alerts.

2. Choose Start Creating a Rule from a Template, select the Flag Messages from Someone with a Colored Flag template, and then choose Next.

3. Remove the check from People or Distribution List and add one to Flagged for Action. If you want the rule to apply the same color flag to all flagged messages you receive, click on Action and choose Any. Otherwise, choose an action to use.

4 On the next screen, select the action. For this rule, we want to flag messages with colored flags. Click on a color flag in the rule description field and choose a flag color (see Figure 9.2).

FIGURE 9.2

Use the Rules Wizard to change the flags on incoming messages to colored flags.

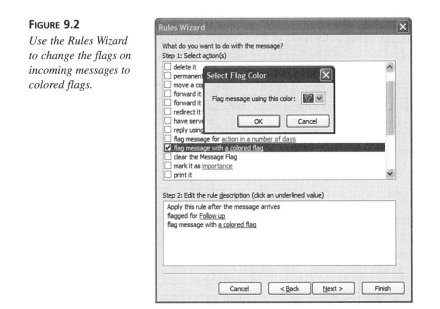

5. Add exceptions to the rule, if needed. Choose <u>N</u>ext if you want to run the rule on messages already in your mailbox, or click Finish to save the rule and exit the wizard.

In the Rules Wizard example shown in Figure 9.2, I'm changing the flag on all incoming messages that are flagged for Follow Up by the sender to the purple flag.

In addition, you can use rules to add flags to any messages based on the conditions you specify. For example, you might want to flag all messages from some people with purple flags and messages with certain words in the subject with a blue flag.

Flags and Views

Quick Flags are always displayed on the right side of the list view, as shown previously in Figure 9.1. The Quick Flag column is always docked on the right and can't be moved to the more familiar left side unless you uncheck Show Qui<u>c</u>k Flags Column in <u>V</u>iew, <u>A</u>rrange By, Cust<u>o</u>m, <u>O</u>ther Settings (see Figure 9.3).

FIGURE 9.3

Enable or disable the Quick Flag field from the Other Settings dialog.

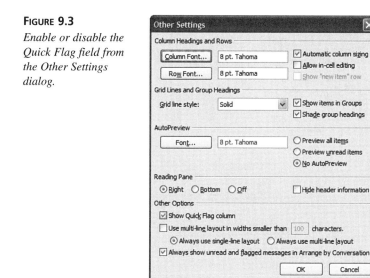

When the Quick Flag column isn't used, you can move the Flag Status column to another position. The flags display in this column as colored flags on a white background, whereas the Quick Flag column uses a background color that matches the flag color.

When you disable Show Quick Flags, you can still set Quick Flags and use Search Folders or other views to display the flags by color.

Quick Flags are supported on POP3, IMAP, and Exchange Server accounts, as well in all personal folder stores (PSTs), but not on HTTP accounts (Hotmail and MSN). You'll have to move these messages to your Personal Folders if you want to use flags.

When the Quick Flag column isn't shown in your folder view, you can flag messages with any color flag by right-clicking the message, choosing Follow Up, and then selecting a flag color or Add Reminder to set a reminder and choose the flag color. If you added the Flag Status field to your view and enable in-cell editing, you can select flag colors by clicking in the Flag Status cell and selecting a flag from the drop-down list.

When you're working in an opened message, choose the Flag icon on the toolbar to bring up the Flag for Follow Up dialog (see Figure 9.4).

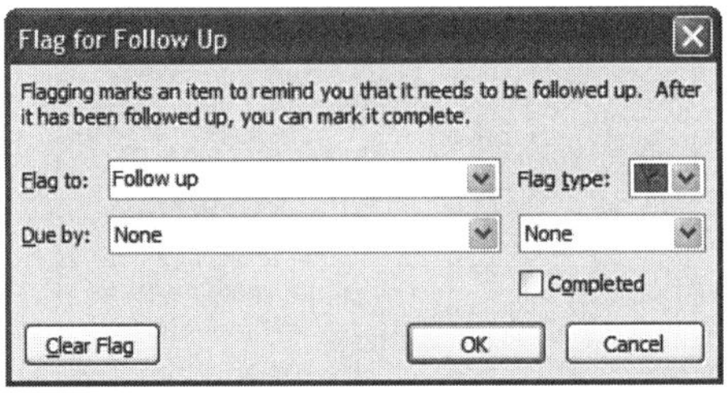

FIGURE 9.4

Set reminders and choose flag actions and colors using the Flag for Follow Up dialog. If you need a different flag action, type it in the Flag To field. The field accepts up to 256 characters and displays it in the InfoBar.

 The date and time fields in the Flag for Follow Up dialog accept natural language and shortcuts. You can enter holiday names or shortcuts such as *2 weeks* or even *2w* and Outlook will convert them to the correct date format for you. Enter a time as *115p* or *1.15p* and Outlook will convert it to the correct time format.

Task: Create a Quick Flag Toolbar

▼ TASK

Adding Quick Flags to messages is easy when you're using the default flag color: just click on the flag field in the mail list. When you want to use one of the other flag colors, you must right-click the item, select Follow Up, and then the flag color. It's enough extra steps for most people to use the default flag for everything.

By taking the time to choose flag colors for your messages, you can use colored flags to categorize your messages. Red flags might be used for urgent messages, whereas yellow flags are used for messages you need information from later. The next problem is how to remember what each color means.

Sue Mosher, from slipstick.com, had a wonderful idea that makes using different color Quick Flags easier: create a custom Quick Flag toolbar. The flags are in full view at all times and you can name each flag for its purpose. Remembering that blue flags are used for personal messages and purple marks messages from clients is much easier when the flag is labeled Personal or Clients.

1. Open the Customize Toolbar dialog using <u>T</u>ools, <u>C</u>ustomize.

2. Select the Tool<u>b</u>ars tab, click the <u>N</u>ew button, and name your toolbar.

3. Select the <u>C</u>ommands tab (see Figure 9.5), choose Actions from the Categories list, and then scroll the Comman<u>d</u>s list to find the flags.

▼ FIGURE 9.5

Add the Flag com-
mands to a new tool-
bar so that you can
easily select new flag
colors.

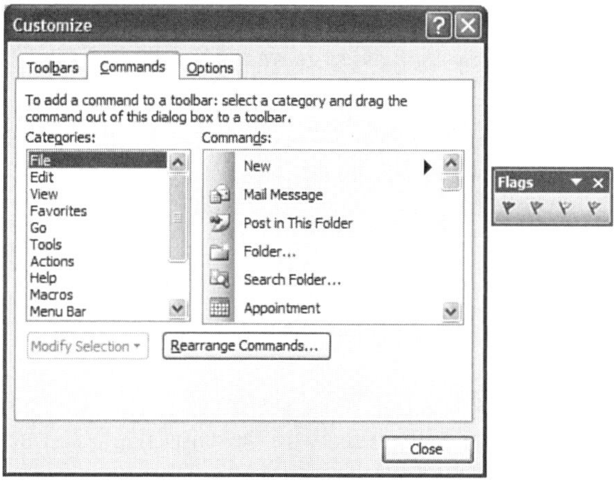

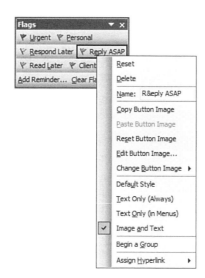

9

4. Drag each flag color and the Clear Flag and Add Reminder commands to the new toolbar. You don't need to add Flag Complete because one click on the flag sets the flag as completed.

5. Right-click on the command button and choose Image and Text to display the flag icon and name on the button.

6. Right-click each flag again and change the name to something meaningful, such as Urgent, ASAP, Personal, Read Later, and so forth. If you want to use a keyboard shortcut to add the flags, insert an ampersand (&) before the letter you want to use as an Alt+ keyboard shortcut (see Figure 9.6).

FIGURE 9.6

Customize the flag
commands by using
names that help you
remember the types of
messages indicated by
the flags.

▼   7. Close the Customize dialog when you're finished and drag your new toolbar to
          dock with the other toolbars or leave it floating (see Figure 9.7).

FIGURE 9.7

*A Quick Flags toolbar
makes it easier to
apply different flag
colors to your items
and reminds you what
the colors represent.*

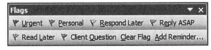

When you're ready to quick flag a message, select it and choose one of the flag buttons.
If you need to flag several messages with the same flag color, hold Ctrl or Shift as you

▲   make your selections.

Using Search Folders

Another new and cool feature in Outlook 2003 is Search Folders. These are virtual views
of your message store, using the same filtering capabilities as Advanced Find and Views.
Because these are virtual folders, the messages you see in Search Folders are not duplicates of the originals; they're pointers to the original. If you mark a message in a search
folder as read, flag the message, or delete it, the message in your Inbox will reflect what
you did in the search folder.

Outlook creates three Search Folders for you:

*   For Follow Up—Searches all folders for flagged messages; the default folder view
    groups the messages by flag color.
*   Large Mail—Groups all messages in your mailbox by size. Use this Search Folder
    to help you find messages with attachments.
*   Unread Mail—Shows all unread messages in your mailbox. Use rules to file mes-
    sages in folders as they arrive and read them from this folder

The criteria used for the default For Follow Up and Unread Mail folders cannot be
changed, but you can change the folders that are searched. The criteria for the Large
Mail folder, Show Mail Greater Than:, defaults to 100KB and is configurable. Right-
click on the Search Folder and choose Customize This Search Folder.

Use the By Follow Up Search Folder to show all of your flagged mail items at a glance,
with the messages grouped by flag color. Collapsed groups include a message count so
that you know how many messages are in each group. You can create custom Search
Folders or custom views to restrict the flag colors shown.

Use the Large Mail Search Folder to help you keep your mailbox size under control. Because it groups messages by size, Huge (1–5MB); Very Large (500KB–1MB), and Large (100–500KB), you can easily find messages with large attachments and remove the attachment.

The final Search Folder, Unread Mail, was often requested. As new mail arrives, you only need to check the Unread folder to read the messages, not all the folders that rules move messages to. As you mark messages read and refresh the view, the pointers to the messages marked as read are removed from the Unread view. You can use F5 to refresh it while reading messages.

9

Task: Create a Custom Search Folder

One of the reasons search folders are so great is because you can create your own search folders by using the same criteria you use in custom views or with Advanced Find. You won't need to use Advanced Find to find messages in other folders and the search results are always available and current.

1. Right-click on the Search Folders header in the Navigation Pane and choose <u>N</u>ew Search Folder. The New Search Folder dialog opens, as shown in Figure 9.8.

FIGURE 9.8

Although the New Search Folder dialog contains some simple predefined searches, you can also create powerful custom searches.

New Search Folder

<u>S</u>elect a Search Folder:

Reading Mail
Unread mail
Mail flagged for follow up
Mail either unread or flagged for follow up
Important mail
Mail from People and Lists
Mail from and to specific people
Mail from specific people
Mail sent directly to me
Mail sent to distribution lists
Organizing Mail

<u>C</u>ustomize Search Folder:

S<u>e</u>arch mail in: Mailbox - Diane Poremsky

OK   Cancel

2. Because a Search Folder is limited to searching one mailbox or personal store, you'll need to select the message store to search in if you have more than one message store in your profile.

▼   3. Select one of the predefined searches or scroll to the bottom of the list to Create a custom Search Folder. For this task, we're going to choose Create a Custom Search Folder.

4. Select Choose to open the Custom Search Folder dialog (see Figure 9.9).

5. Type a Name for your folder; let's use *Last 3 days* as the name of our Search Folder.

FIGURE 9.9

Use the Custom Search Folder dialog to create your filters and select the folder to search.

6. To limit the search to specific folders in your message store, click Browse and select the folders you want searched. Skip this step to search all the mail folders.

7. Select Criteria and the Search Folder Criteria dialog opens. The dialog and options are identical to the filter used for views and Advanced Find.

8. Enter the criteria for the search. We're going to use the Advanced tab for this search. Choose Field and select Date/Time fields, Received. As the Condition, choose On or After, and type **3 days ago** in the Value field. Then choose Add to List (see Figure 9.10).

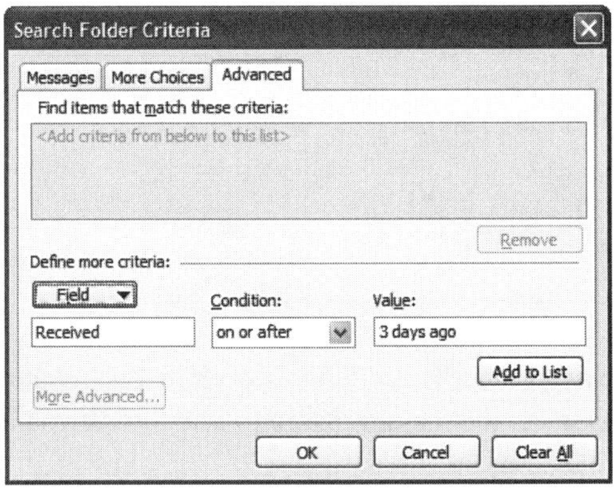

FIGURE 9.10

The Search Folder Criteria dialog includes commonly used criteria on the Messages and More Choices tab. Using the Advanced tab to create your own searches enables you to create more powerful searches.

9. Click OK on all open dialogs and then select your new Search Folder in the Navigation Pane. If your message store is large, it might take a few minutes for the search to complete. However, once it does finish, all messages that meet your criteria will be listed in the folder.

▲

If you need to make changes to your search, right-click the Search Folder and choose Customize This Search Folder. This opens the Customize dialog you read about in step 6.

That's all there is to it; your Search Folder is ready to use. If you use saved Advanced Find in older versions of Outlook, you'll probably want to convert your advanced searches to Search Folders.

9

You can add your Search Folder to your Favorite Folders list so that you don't have to look for it when you want to use it.

Using Favorite Folders

Favorite Folders are new to Outlook 2003, replacing the folder shortcuts found on the Outlook bar in older versions. When you view your mail folders using the Mail button at the bottom of the Navigation bar, you'll notice the Favorite Folders group at the top of the screen.

By default, there are four folders already in your Favorite Folders:

- Inbox
- Unread Mail Search Folder
- For Follow Up Search Folder
- Sent Items Search Folder

Each IMAP or HTTP (Hotmail) Inbox in your profile is added to your Favorite Folders by default. Inboxes for your POP3 accounts aren't listed because they share the Personal Folders Inbox folder.

These default folders can be deleted from the Favorites list and you can add your other favorite folders to it (see Figure 9.11). For practical reasons, you don't want to put too many folders on the Favorite Folders list; doing so makes it harder to find the folders you're looking for. Any folder that is visible in the All Mail Folders list, including Search Folders, can be added to the Favorite Folders list, the other Outlook folder types are not supported.

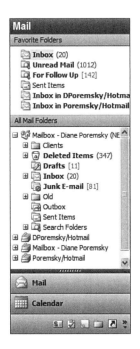

FIGURE **9.11**

Hotmail and IMAP inboxes are included in the Favorite Folders list by default. As you add your own favorites, the Favorite Folders list expands.

The number of favorites in the Favorite Folder group determines the height of the Favorite Folders and All E-mail Folders groups. Once Favorite Folders expands to about two-thirds of the height of the Navigation bar, it begins to scroll. Your monitor resolution and the number of toolbars you display in Outlook control how many Favorite Folders you can see on screen before it begins scrolling.

If you need more space for folder shortcuts, try Shortcuts on the Navigation Pane. You can mix types of folders and shortcuts and use the entire height of your Navigation Pane for shortcuts, reducing the need to scroll.

Managing Favorite Folders

Outlook creates some Favorite Folders for you, but you might have additional folders that you want to use as favorites and you'll need to add those to Favorite Folders yourself.

Select the folder you want added as a favorite from the All Mail Folders portion of the Navigation Pane, left-click, and then drag it to Favorite Folders. Drop it when the cursor includes a plus (+) sign.

You can also select a folder, right-click, and choose Add to Favorite Folders from the context menu that appears.

You can also remove the default folders that Outlook created in the Favorite Folders list: select the folder, right-click, and then choose Remove from Favorite Folders. Don't choose Delete unless you want to delete the folder from your message store.

9

The list of Favorite Folders is stored in an XML file located at C:\Documents and Settings\username\Application Data\Microsoft\Outlook. Each profile has its own XML, which is named for the profile. You can delete the file to reset the Favorite Folders and the Shortcuts lists to their defaults; Outlook creates a new one the next time it runs. Interestingly enough, Outlook creates the XML file when it closes, not when it opens or as you add folders to the list, as it does for many other files it uses.

Outlook also uses the command-line switch /resetnavpane to reset the Navigation Pane. This switch has the same effect as deleting the XML file, and resets the buttons to their default positions. It removes any Shortcuts you added.

To start Outlook using the command line, from the Start Menu, Run dialog, enter OUTLOOK.EXE /resetnavpane or "C:\Program Files\Microsoft Office\OFFICE11\OUTLOOK.EXE " /resetnavpane and click OK.

More information about starting Outlook using the command line is in Appendix B, "Outlook's Command-Line Switches."

You can remove all the items from the Favorite Folders group, but you cannot remove the Favorite Folders group from the interface.

Although Favorite Folders are for Mail folders only, Exchange Server users can put Public Folders in the Favorite Folders, provided they're already in the Public Folder Favorites and are Mail and Post folders. You can also add secondary Exchange Server mailboxes to Favorite Folders if they're included in your profile. Secondary mailboxes aren't added to Favorite Folders automatically, as Hotmail or IMAP Inboxes are—you must create the shortcut yourself.

Organizing Favorite Folders

When you drag a folder to Favorite Folders, you can drop it in any position on the folder list. As you drag it over the favorites already in the list, you'll see a dark blue line that indicates the position of the folder at that time. When you select a folder, right-click, and then choose Add to Favorite Folders, the folder shortcut is always added at the bottom of the list.

Existing folders can be rearranged by selecting them and either dragging to a new position or using the right-click menu and choosing Move Up in List or Move Down in List.

> Included in the menu options when you right-click on a favorite are Rename and Delete. These actions apply to the folder the favorite points to, not just to the shortcut in the Favorite Folders list. If you rename the folder in Favorite Folders, the folder in your message store is also renamed. Likewise, if you choose Delete, the source folder and all of its contents are deleted. Use Remove from Favorite Folders when you want to remove the folder from the Favorites list, not Delete.

Managing Folders

Even with the message management benefits offered by Quick Flags and Search Folders, you'll still use folders to organize your messages.

You might end up using more folders because it's so easy to find your messages with Search Folders. The Unread mail folder is especially handy—you can create rules to file your messages as they arrive and use a Search Folder to view them in one folder. The end result is your messages are neatly filed away and you don't have to browse your folders looking for new mail.

Adding a New Folder

Outlook includes just one folder for each item type when it creates a message store for a profile, along with Outbox, Sent Items, Deleted Items, and Drafts folders.

Although there's nothing wrong with keeping all your mail in your Inbox folder, most people create some folders for filing messages as they're finished reading them. A good filing system makes it easier to find the messages you need when you need them. Even with a bad filing system, Outlook 2003 helps you find your messages.

Don't use the Deleted Items folder as a filing folder. You don't file papers you need in a trashcan, so why would you store email you want to keep in the Deleted Items folder? Outlook 2003 supports more than 65,000 folders with 65,000 messages per folder—why not use a few?

Before adding new folders, plan your filing system. After you have a system in mind, it's time to create some folders.

1. Select any folder in your message store.

2. Right-click and choose New Folder.

3. Type a name for the folder.

4. Select the type of Outlook item you're going to store in the folder from the Folder Contains drop-down list.

5. Select where to place the folder. You can place any folder type in any folder (see Figure 9.12). Select Mailbox or Personal Folders to add a new folder at the same level as the default Outlook folders.

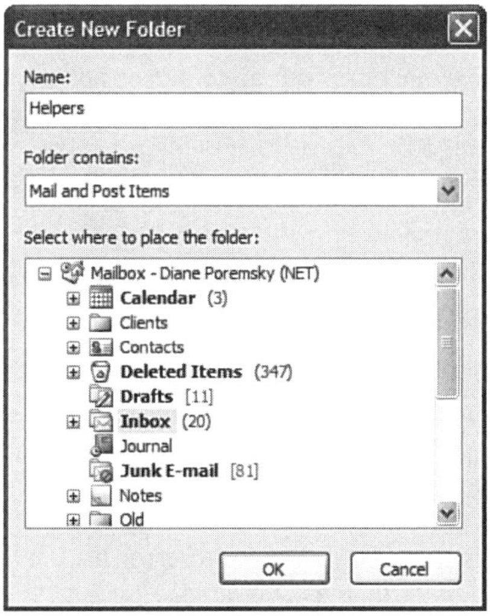

FIGURE 9.12

Use the Create New Folder dialog to add more folders to Outlook. You can create new folders in any folder. For example, you can create a Calendar folder in your Inbox folder.

Deleting Folders

The default folders that are in your mailbox when you first use Outlook cannot be deleted. However, you can delete any folder you create. Right-click on the folder and choose Delete "*[folder]*", where *[folder]* is the name of your folder. You'll have to respond to a dialog asking whether you really want to delete the folder and all of its contents. If you say <u>Y</u>es and then change your mind, you can still recover the folder provided that you haven't emptied the Deleted Items folder. Just select the deleted folder from within the Deleted Items folder and drag it back to its original location. But after you empty the Deleted Items folder, you cannot recover deleted items (except Exchange Server users under limited circumstances).

In addition to using the right-click menu, there are additional ways to delete folders:

- Select and drag the folder to the Deleted Items folder. You won't get the warning dialog reminding you that all the folder contents will be deleted.

- Select the folder and press the Delete key or Ctrl+D. You'll get the warning dialog when you use the keyboard.

To delete the folder and bypass the deleted folder, hold the Shift key when you delete. When a folder or item is deleted this way, it's gone for good. Fortunately, Outlook warns you before it deletes the folder and you can change your mind.

When the Deleted Items folder is emptied or if you hold the Shift key when deleting, the deleted items can't be recovered. If you don't have a backup, you're out of luck and the items can't be recovered.

Exchange Server mailboxes can be configured to use Deleted Items Recovery, in which case deleted items can be restored. If you connect to Exchange Server, look for <u>T</u>ools, Recover Dele<u>t</u>ed Items. If you don't see it or it doesn't contain any items, speak to your Exchange administrator.

Moving Your Folders

After adding a folder, you might decide that you'd rather have it somewhere else in the folder tree. When you're moving a folder around your message store and have only a few folders, the easiest way to move it is to select and drag and drop, especially if you're using the Folder list in the Navigation bar.

When you're moving folders between message stores or have a lot of folders, right-click on the folder and choose Mo<u>v</u>e Folder. The Move Folder selection dialog opens, enabling you pick the folder or message store you want to move the folder to (see Figure 9.13).

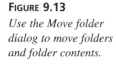

FIGURE 9.13

Use the Move folder dialog to move folders and folder contents.

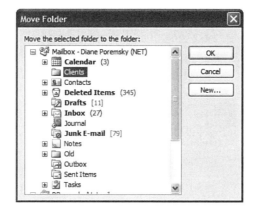

It usually takes only a few seconds to move a folder. However, if there are a lot of items in the folder, it could take several minutes, especially on a slow machine.

Copy Folder, also found on the right-click menu, works like Move Folder but creates a copy of the folder and folder contents, instead of moving it.

Copy Folder Design

A common complaint by many Outlook users is the inability to share custom views. Although this is true for Internet mail users, Exchange users can copy their views to a PST and share it with other Exchange users.

1. Select the folder that you want to copy another folder's designs to.

2. Choose File, Folder, Copy Folder Design to open the Copy Design From dialog (see Figure 9.14).

3. Select the folder to copy the design from and select the elements you want to copy, choosing from Permissions, Rules, Description, and Forms & Views.

Not all elements will be available for copying. Forms & Views is the important selection because it enables you to move custom views and forms published to specific folders between folders and message stores.

FIGURE 9.14

Use Copy Folder Design to copy views and forms to new folders after using Import and Export.

Summary

This hour introduced you to the new email management features in Outlook: Favorite Folders, Search Folders, and Quick Flags. Included were some ideas on how to make the most of these features, such as creating a Quick Flag toolbar to make it easier to apply flags. Custom Search Folders can filter on any field available in Outlook, giving you the opportunity to create Search Folders using complicated conditions for the search.

Q&A

Q I have three POP3 email accounts and I'd like to have Favorite Folders for the email from those accounts.

A There are several different ways you could solve your problem. Because Search Folders can be added to the Favorite Folders list, I recommend setting up a Search Folder for each account.

Follow the steps used in "Create a Custom Search Folder," earlier in this hour, using the custom search option. On the Advanced tab, choose All Mail fields, Email Account from the Field drop-down list, use contains for the Condition, and enter all or part of your account name in the Value field. Your email account name is the name of the account in Tools, Email Accounts, View or Change existing email accounts and click Next. The account names are listed on the Email Accounts dialog.

Add the Search Folders to your Favorite Folders list and you can view the messages by account.

Q **I set up a rule to flag messages and did something wrong and a lot of messages I didn't want flagged are flagged. Because there are so many of these messages, changing each flag individually will take days. Is there a way to remove the flags quickly?**

A Create a Search Folder that contains only the flag color you want to remove from messages. If you can fine-tune the Advanced Filter tab to show only the messages that were flagged incorrectly, you can select all the messages in the Search Folder, right-click, and choose Follow Up, Clear Flag. If you can't create a filter to show only the messages that were flagged incorrectly, hold the Shift or Ctrl key as you select the messages that need the flag cleared. Right-click and choose Follow Up, Clear Flag periodically—don't wait until you have all the messages selected to clear the flags.

9

PART III

Using Outlook As a PIM

Hour

HOUR 10

Outlook As a Contact Manager

Contact management is the number two reason people choose to use Outlook. Not only do you use contacts to store email addresses, you can also store phone numbers and mailing addresses in contacts, along with personal information including birthdays, anniversaries, and spouse's or children's names.

In addition to using your contacts as an email address book, you can also use them for mail merges to address letters and envelopes. Many third-party programs access addresses in the Contacts folder.

This hour introduces you to many of the features that make Outlook an excellent contact manager tool. The topics include

- Understanding contact forms and fields
- Using categories and views to manage your contacts
- Creating distribution lists
- Using mail merge

By the time you reach the end of this hour, you'll be managing your contacts like a pro.

Overview of Contact Features

Using contacts, you can store names, postal and email addresses, phone numbers, personal information including spouse and children names, and assistant and department information. You can use this data to address email, make phone calls, and address letters and envelopes.

The contact form has five tabs:

- General—Contains name, postal, email, IM addresses, and phone fields.
- Details—Contains office information, personal information, and NetMeeting and Internet Free-Busy server settings.
- Activities—Lists other Outlook items that are linked to the contact.
- Certificates—Lists all digital certificates associated with the contact.
- All Fields—A List view of all Contact fields. Fields are editable.

Many people only use the first tab, General, for contact data (see Figure 10.1). The contact form used by Outlook 2003 now also includes an image control so that you can add photos to each contact. The Activity tab is not user-editable and lists the items linked to the contact using the Contact field found on all Outlook forms.

You can customize the view used on the Activity tab using the same options you would use to customize any folder view. To access the Customize View dialog, right-click on the row of field names and choose Customize Current View, or select one of the other options from the context menu.

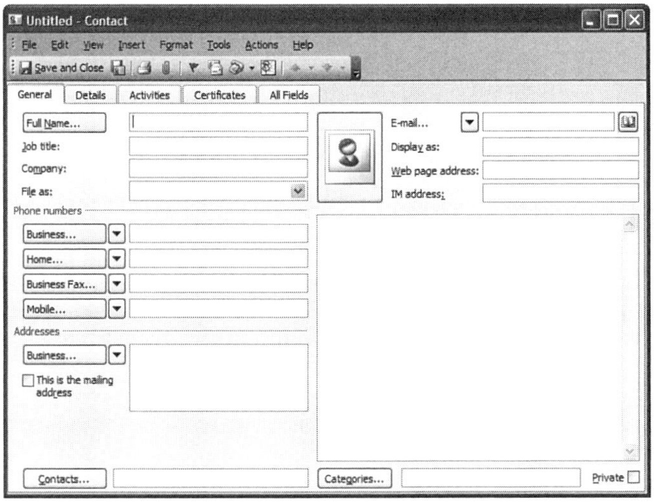

FIGURE 10.1

The General tab of the contact form includes fields for your contact's name, three physical addresses, nineteen phone numbers, and three email addresses as well as Web site and instant messenger addresses.

The Details tab contains fields for personal information, including the contact's birth date and spouse's name. Recurring events are added to your calendar automatically when you enter the birth date and anniversary to a contact.

Making the Most of the Contact Form

After you create a contact form and save it, use the Actions menu to make use of contact information. You don't even have to open the contact to use the data: Select the contact and then choose an action from the Actions menu. Some of the menu items are enabled only when one contact is selected; other menu items, including New Message to Contact, work equally well when you select several contacts.

The Actions menu on an opened contact contains four additional actions not available on the Actions menu in Outlook: New Instant Message, Display Map of Address, Explore Web Page, and Add Picture. If you have MapPoint installed, Outlook displays the contact's address in MapPoint. If you don't have MapPoint installed, Outlook will connect to `mappoint.msn.com`.

Using the Actions menu, you can automatically use the contact data for the following actions:

- Address a letter using Microsoft Word's letter wizard.

- Send an email message to the contact.

- Create meeting requests, appointments, tasks, or journal entries with the contact entered in the item's Contact field.

- Link the contact to any Outlook item or file. When you link to a file, a journal entry is created that contains your contact information. When any other Outlook item is linked, the contact is added to the item's Contact field. When you want to see a history of your interaction with the contact, open the contact record and look on the Activities tab.

- Call contact using a phone number entered on the contact form.

- Map the contact's address. When MapPoint is installed, it's used for address mapping; otherwise, MSN.com maps are used, which requires an open connection to the Internet.

- Open contact's Web page (when there is a URL on the General tab).

- Create a new contact using the company information from the selected contact.

One item on the Actions menu is New Distribution List. Although you would expect this to create a new distribution list containing the selected contact as the first entry, this isn't how it really works. It only opens a new, empty distribution list form. You must add contacts to create the list.

Task: Add a Photo to Your Contacts

Outlook 2003 includes an image control on the General tab of the contract form, enabling you to include a photo of the contact or the logo of the contact's company. If you don't like the icon used as the image placeholder but don't have photos for your contacts, you could use one image for personal contacts and a different one for business.

When contacts are printed, the photo is not included on the printout.

1. Locate the photo or image you want to use on the contact. You'll get best results with a vertical image with an aspect ratio of about 75%, but you can use any size image.

For best results, don't choose group pictures. If you do, you should crop the image to remove most of the background.

2. Open the contact form and click on the image control. You can also open the Add Contact Picture dialog using the Actions, Add Picture menu selection.

3. Select the photo and choose OK. The image control reduces the photo to fit (see Figure 10.2).

FIGURE 10.2

Adding an image to your contact helps you to remember the faces of clients and adds just a couple of kilobytes to the file size of each contact.

▼   4. Save and close the contact.

      If you need to change the image, double-click on the image or use the Actions, Change
▲   Picture menu selection. Remove the picture using Actions, Remove Picture.

> The image control is sized 70 pixels wide by 95 high; however, you aren't
> limited to using an image this size. The image control will maintain the
> aspect ratio while shrinking a photo to fit, as shown in Figure 10.2. The orig-
> inal size of the photo was about 780×625.

Managing Contacts

When you have a large number of contacts, it's sometimes difficult to find the contact
you need just by browsing. Occasionally the contact you need is filed using a different
format than the rest of your contacts or you forget part of the contact's name. Outlook
offers several ways to quickly find any contact.

- From any folder, type part of the contact's name in the Type a Contact to Find field
  of the Find a Contact button and press Enter. The field is located on the Standard
  toolbar. This brings up the Choose a Contact dialog, which contains a list of all
  matching contacts, as shown in Figure 10.3.

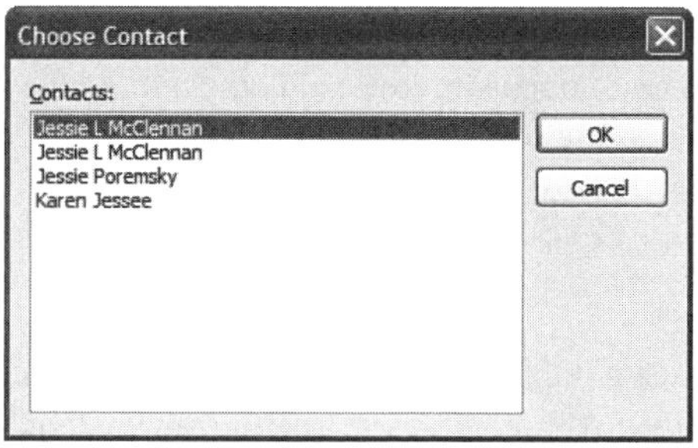

FIGURE 10.3

*Use the Find a Contact
dialog on the Standard
toolbar to bring up
contacts with matching
first, middle, or last
names.*

In the example shown here, I entered **jes** and all contacts with a first, middle, or last
name beginning with *jes* were displayed. You should enter at least three letters, especially if you have a large number of contacts.

When you know part of the contact's name but aren't sure of the spelling, use initials or letters contained in their name. For example, in my Contacts list, entering **j p** or **j por** will return the contacts for Jessie Poremsky, Jim Porter, and Reja Aportee.

Note that when you use a space in the search, Outlook searches differently, depending on where the first letter is found. Outlook uses pattern matching and if the first letter at the beginning of the word, it looks for the second letter at the beginning of the next word.

If the first letter is found in the middle, Outlook looks in the middle of the second word. Because j is in the middle of Reja, Outlook looks in the middle of Aportee for a match with por. Mark J LaPorte won't be found searching for **j por**, but AJ LaPorte and Jim Porter will be found.

- Use custom views and filters to limit the contacts that are visible in the folder.
- Use Find or Advanced Find.

Views and Advanced Find use the same filter dialog and the same criteria. Use views when you're working in the Contacts folder and need to see items from only one folder; use Advanced Find when you use multiple contacts folders and need to search in them all.

Open the Advanced Find dialog from anywhere in Outlook using Tools, Advanced Find. Choose the Contacts folder and contact items, enter your criteria, and find the items.

You can flag contacts with colored flags and set follow-ups, which will fire if the contact is stored in the default Contacts folder.

Quick Flags are not supported on contact forms.

The Find dialog might seem redundant with the Find a Contact command, both of which are on the Standard toolbar. Although this is true to some extent, Find is still useful for finding contacts. Like the Find a Contact command, you can use Find from any folder and search for contacts. By selecting which folders to search in, you can find all messages, calendar items, and contacts meeting the criteria entered in the Look For: field. The Find a Contact command finds only contacts.

For more information about using Find, see Hour 15, "Searching Outlook."

Using Categories

Categories might be one of the most underused features found in Outlook. Many people choose to use multiple folders to categorize their contacts, with one for personal contacts and another for business contacts. Other people go so far as to create one contact folder per company or organization.

When you learn how to use categories effectively, you'll discover using multiple folders is often the worst way to manage your contacts. One of the biggest problems you encounter when you use multiple folders is maintaining multiple copies of contacts who are filed in more than one folder, such as someone who is both a personal and business contact.

Another problem concerns how the automatic resolution feature of the address book works. When Outlook is trying to resolve a name, it searches all the address books in order and stops at the end of the first address list in which it finds a match. For example, if you have Wayne Johnson in your business contacts folder and John Archer in personal contacts and type **John** in the To field, Outlook stops searching for matches to John after finding Wayne Johnson in the business contacts folder. When both men are in one contacts folder, Outlook finds both and enables you to choose the correct person to whom you want to send the message.

Figure 10.4 shows a contact list grouped by category. Although it might seem that there are duplicates of the contact, it's really just one contact. If you need to remove it from one category, open the contact and delete the category from the Category field. Don't delete the contact from the category in the List view.

Pocket PC users should use categories instead of multiple folders to limit which contacts are synchronized with the Pocket PC device. Open ActiveSync's options, select Contacts and then Settings to choose the categories to synchronize.

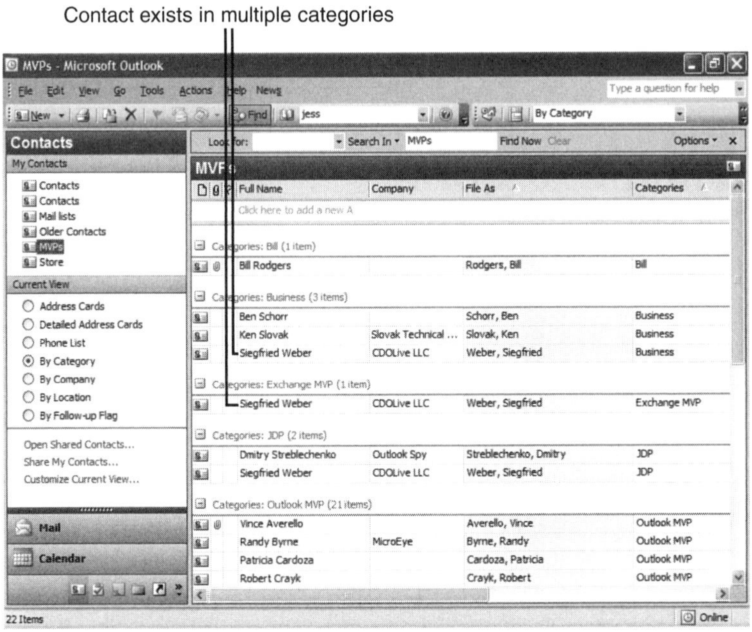

Contact exists in multiple categories

FIGURE 10.4

When you use categories, you can add multiple categories to a contact. When you use the Group By Category view, the contact is shown in all categories it belongs to.

Outlook includes a predefined list of categories, but you can also enter your own categories (see Figure 10.5).

FIGURE 10.5

Select categories for your Outlook items using the Categories dialog.

Open the Categories dialog by choosing the Categories button on any Outlook form. Add a check beside the category you want to use or enter a new one in the Item(s) Belong to This Category field. Choose Add to List to add the category to the master category list.

Categories not included in the master list are identified by (not in Master Category list) when you open the Categories dialog.

Choose the Master Category List button to add or remove categories from the master list stored in the Registry (see Figure 10.6). Although you can add categories to the master categories list while using the Categories dialog, you need to open the Master Categories dialog to remove categories from the master list.

FIGURE 10.6

Use the Master Categories List to manage your categories.

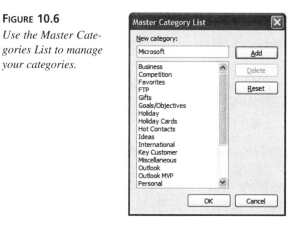

You can add categories to your contacts using the category picker or by typing categories in the Category field. These categories are not included in the master list and cannot be selected for use with other contacts or Outlook forms. Until the category is on the master list, you must continue to type it into the Category field. You'll also see this designation often when you move Outlook items between computers.

When you use a lot of custom categories, you'll want to export the Registry key. When you get a new computer or need to reinstall Windows, you can restore your custom categories.

Using Views

When you have a large number of contacts, using views to limit the contacts that are visible is often necessary to find and manage your contacts. The things you can use views for include

- Selecting contacts for mail merge
- Changing some contact fields

- Limiting the display to contacts that meet specific conditions
- Controlling the layout for printed lists

The default views include

- Address Card—A card layout that displays basic contact data, including all address and phone numbers.
- Detailed Address Card—A card layout that displays all fields.
- Phone List—A table layout that includes phone numbers.
- By Company—Groups contacts by company.
- By Category—Groups contacts by category.
- By Location—Groups contacts by country as selected in the Address field. Click on the Business, Home, or Other button to see the Country/Region selector.
- By Follow-Up Flag—Groups contacts by Flagged, Completed, and (none).

All these views have in-cell editing enabled, allowing you to make changes to visible fields without opening the contact for editing. In most cases, when you group contacts by a field, you can drag contacts to other groups to change that field for the contact. This is helpful when you need to change a field used by many contacts, such as for company name changes or when you're categorizing contacts.

 Create a view that has all the fields you want included in a printed list, select File, Print, and choose a table style printout. The printout will include the fields shown on the screen.

The default views are customizable or you create custom views. To change the current view, right-click on the row containing the field names. Depending on your view, choose Customize Current View or Custom to open the Customize View dialog.

 See "Creating Custom Views" in Hour 3 for more information about creating custom views.

Task: Change Contact Data Using Views

Making changes to multiple records can seem like a daunting task, but depending on the field that must be changed, Outlook might be able to make the changes for you.

▼ For example, one of your major customers recently merged with another company and you need to change the company name in many records. Changing each record individually could take hours or it can take just minutes.

1. Apply the Group By Company view to your Contacts folder, selecting it from the Current View command on the Advanced toolbar. Collapse the groups using the Views, Expand/Collapse Groups, Collapse All Groups menu selection to make it easier to see all the company names (see Figure 10.7).

Not all fields support grouping or can be updated by dragging to a new group. Outlook will return an error if the field doesn't support grouping.

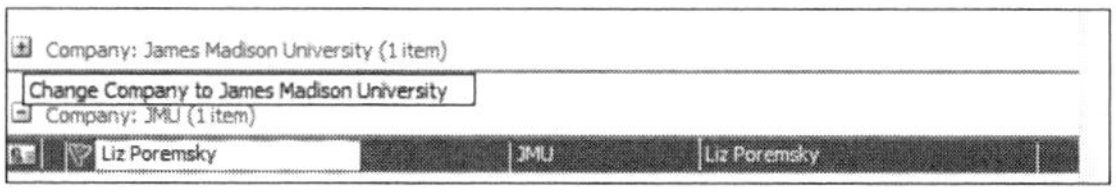

FIGURE 10.7

Use Group By views to change fields without typing. Although Outlook includes some Group By views, you can drag most fields to the Group By box to group by most fields.

| Company: James Madison University (1 item) |
| Change Company to James Madison University |
| Company: JMU (1 item) |
| Liz Poremsky | JMU | Liz Poremsky |

2. Change the company name on one contact if a contact does not exist for the new company.

3. Select all the records for the old company and drag the records to the new company's group.

▲ 4. Drop the contacts on the new company's group when you see a ScreenTip display Change Company to [*new name*].

You can use this method to change many fields, including Category, Job Title, and Private fields, not only on contacts, but also Tasks, Journal, and Calendar. It won't work with all fields, such as phone number fields.

To use grouping to change fields that don't have a Group By view, create a new view and group by the field you want to change. You can change any view to a Group By view by right-clicking on the row of field names and choosing Show Group By Box. Drag the field you want to group by the Group By box.

10

Task: Import and Export Contacts

One of the easiest ways to move contacts between users is using the Import and Export menu.

1. Use File, Import and Export to open the Import and Export Wizard.
2. Choose Import from Another Program or File.
3. Select Personal Folder File (.pst).
4. Browse to find the personal folder you want to import. When you import records, you have the option to replace duplicates, allow duplicates to be created, or don't import items that are duplicates (see Figure 10.8). Outlook's capability to determine what is a duplicate often leaves much to be desired, so I usually allow duplicates and delete them later.

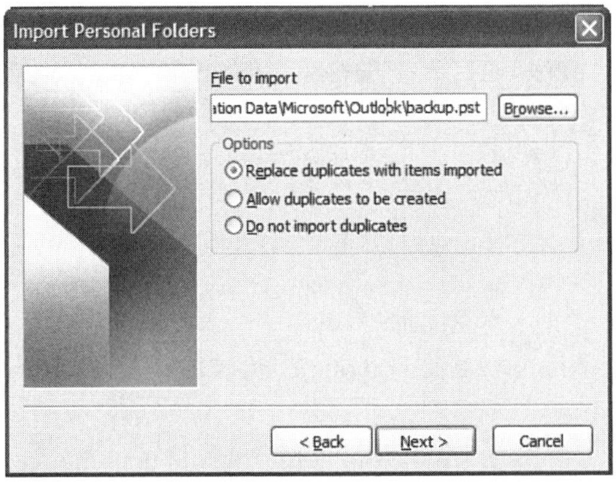

FIGURE 10.8

Use the Import/Export Wizard to import contacts to your current message store.

5. Select the folder from which you want to import (see Figure 10.9). Add a check to the Include Subfolders box if you also want to import subfolders.
6. Set up a filter if you want to limit the items that are imported. The Filter dialog uses the same criteria used with views, Advanced Find, and Search Folders.

Click Finish when you're ready to import the items. Exporting items from Outlook to a PST file works in much the same manner, except it exports the items rather than importing them.

Import and Export supports a variety of file formats, including CSV, tab-delimited text, and Excel format. Exporting to Excel is useful when you need to edit a large number of records.

FIGURE 10.9

Choose between importing items into the current folder or into the same folder in a message store. When you choose to use the same folder, Outlook will create a new folder if one doesn't already exist.

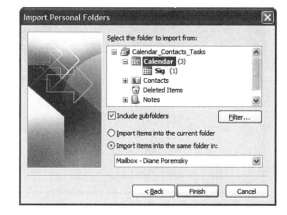

When you use File, Import and Export to copy items into your mailbox, the links between contacts and associated items are broken. This prevents associated items from showing on the Activities tab. Although you can restore the associations, it requires less effort to move items between message stores than it does to import and export and then repair the associations.

Move items or folders by opening the PST using File, Open, Outlook Data File. Select a folder, right-click, and choose Move Folder. To move items in the default folders, select the items to move, right-click and Move to Folder, selecting the new folder from the folder picker.

Task: Create a Distribution List

When you send a message to a group of users, you can create a distribution list (DL) and enter the name of the DL in the address field instead of selecting each contact individually.

1. Use the New, Distribution List menu selection to open a new distribution list form (see Figure 10.10). You can also use Ctrl+Shift+L to open a new form.

2. Enter a name for your distribution list. Although it's helpful to have a long, descriptive name, a shorter name is easier to type when you're addressing messages.

3. Choose the Select Members button to open the Select Members address picker dialog. You must use this dialog to address members; you can't drag contacts to the DL form.

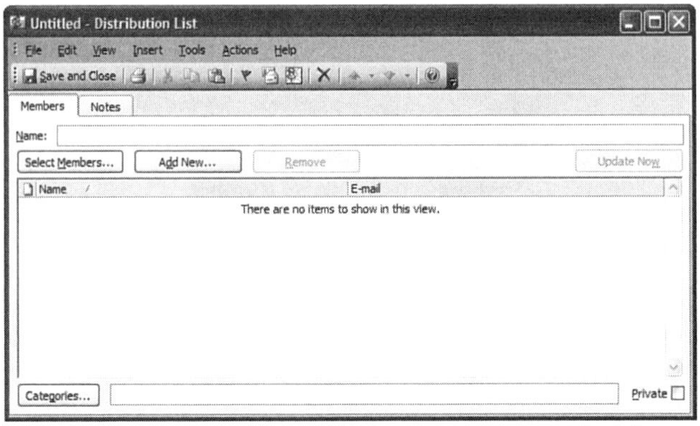

▼ FIGURE **10.10**

The distribution list form includes few fields. Choose Select Members to add existing contacts to the DL, or click the Add button to add members who aren't already in your Contacts folder.

4. Select the contacts you want added to the DL. A contact is listed for each valid electronic address listed. Click the Members button to add the names to the DL list (see Figure 10.11). When you're finished selecting members, click OK.

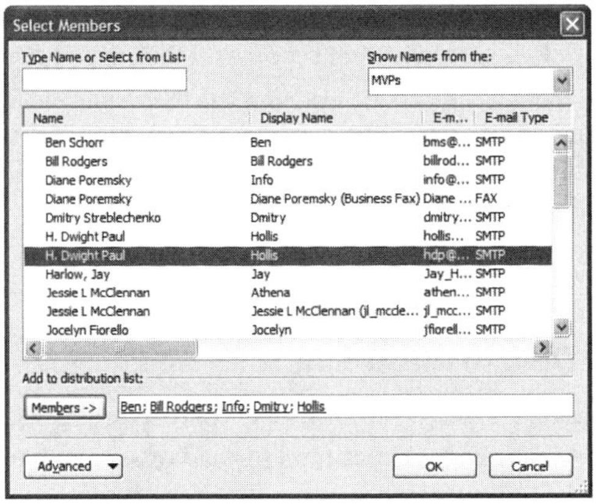

FIGURE **10.11**

Select more than one name at a time by holding down the Shift or Ctrl key as you select names or by double-clicking on a name to add it to the Members field.

5. If you want to add an email address to the DL without first creating a contact record, choose the Add New button. Add a check to Add to Contacts Dialog to create a contact record.

Save the distribution list when you're finished adding addresses to it. To use it, type the DL name or part of the name in the To, CC, or BCC field of a message. If you'd like to see all the individual names, click on the plus sign beside the DL name (see Figure 10.12).

FIGURE 10.12

Expand the distribution list when you want to remove someone from the mailing temporarily, such as if you're planning a surprise party for them.

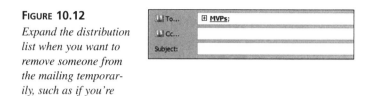

When a contact changes her email address, the DL isn't automatically updated with the new address. You must open the distribution list form and choose the Update Now button. When you choose the Update No<u>w</u> button, any changed addresses are updated. When a contact is missing, you can choose to remove, ignore, or repair the missing member's record by trying to match to an existing contact (see Figure 10.13).

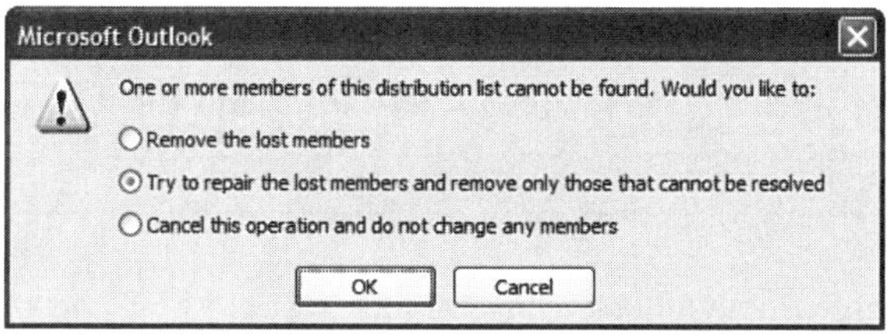

FIGURE 10.13

Choose the Update Now button to update the distribution list with your contacts.

> **Microsoft Outlook**
>
> ⚠ One or more members of this distribution list cannot be found. Would you like to:
>
> ○ Remove the lost members
> ● Try to repair the lost members and remove only those that cannot be resolved
> ○ Cancel this operation and do not change any members
>
> [OK]   [Cancel]

Many times it's better to send group mail by assigning categories to your contacts than by using the Group By Category view. Select the category's group header and then use the <u>A</u>ctions, New Message to Contact menu selection. The benefits of using this method are that the list is dynamic, the addresses are always current, and deleting a member is as easy as removing it from the category. This method works well for mailing lists where the distribution list membership is always changing.

Using this method, it's more difficult to add members to any message and to add them to the CC or BCC fields. You can choose Select All and cut the addresses from the To field and paste them in another field.

The benefits of using a real distribution list are that it's easier to put the DL in the CC or BCC field, and you can begin the message from any folder or add them to a reply. When the list membership is stable, it works very well.

Using Contacts for Mail Merge

One of the advantages to using Outlook for contacts is the ability to use your contacts for a mail merge. The benefits of mail merge include customizing and personalizing a form letter for each recipient. It's also used for sending a group of people the same email message, enabling you to put the individuals address in the To field without exposing all the email addresses to the other recipients.

How Mail Merges Work

Outlook and Word work together when you're doing a mail merge, and you can start the merge from either Outlook or Word. Where you begin the merge is important because it determines the fields you'll be able to use in the mail merge.

Along with the additional fields you'll have available to use, you'll have better filtering from Outlook and will be able to select exactly the contacts you want to use in the mail merge.

Regardless of the method you use to begin the merge, the steps used to complete the merge are the same.

Start the merge from Outlook using Outlook's Tools, Mail Merge menu selection. When you begin the merge from Outlook, you can filter the contacts using views and select the contacts you want to use for the merge. Although all contact form fields can be used in a mail merge when you start the merge from Outlook, only a limited set of fields are used when you start the merge using Word's Tools, Letters and Mailings, Mail merge menu selection.

If you're more comfortable using the Mail Merge Wizard, show the mail merge task pane after the contacts are processed and Word opens. Select Word's Tools, Letters and Mailing, Mail Merge menu to show the Mail Merge Wizard.

Starting the merge using Word's mail merge menu has two limitations:

- You lose the ability to use filters or categories to restrict records included in the merge.
- The number of Outlook fields available is limited to name and address fields.

Word has specific options that enable you to choose document types, including templates. Although Outlook's mail merge options are limited, after the contacts are processed and Word opens, you can show the Mail Merge task pane and change the template or document type.

> Choose View, Toolbars and show Word's Mail Merge toolbar. It has several commands that you might need.

1. Open the Mail Merge dialog using Tools, Mail Merge. If you select contacts before opening the dialog, you can use just the selected contacts in your merge (see Figure 10.14).

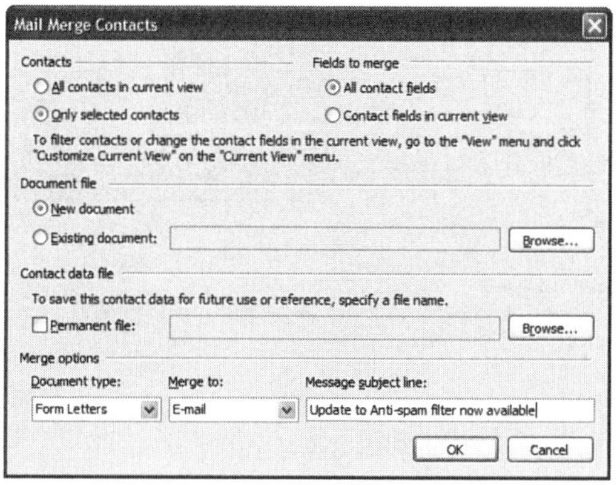

10

FIGURE 10.14

When you mail merge from Outlook, select the contacts you want to use in the merge. When you use a Group By view, you'll have to select the contacts in the group, not just the group header.

Mail Merge Contacts dialog box screenshot

2. Choose a document type and merge to type. Choose from Form Letters, Mailing Labels, Envelopes, and Catalogs. You can merge to a New Document, Printer, or E-mail. If you decide on a different document type, you can change the document type or merge to type from Word's Mail Merge task pane.

   After you make your selections, Outlook needs a few minutes to convert the contacts to a document, OMM0.doc, which it uses for the mail merge data source. When the conversion is completed, Word opens. If you show the Mail Merge task pane, you'll see you're at step 3 in the Mail Merge Wizard. Move back to step 2 if you need to change the document type.

3. If you need to filter your list, open the Mail Merge Recipients dialog. You can the drop-downs lists at the top of each column to set the criteria or remove the checkmarks from rows that you don't want included. However, it's usually faster and easier to filter in Outlook and then select the filtered records before beginning the merge.

4. Compose your mail merge document. Use the Mail Merge toolbar to insert fields or show the Mail Merge task pane and choose predefined merge fields, including an address block or greeting line, or insert the fields you need using the More Items selection (see Figure 10.15).

FIGURE 10.15

Use the Mail Merge Wizard to guide you through a mail merge, or enter the fields you need and complete the merge using the Mail Merge toolbar.

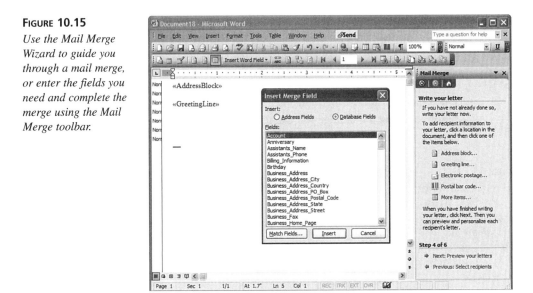

5. When you're finished composing the message, choose Preview Your Letters from the task pane wizard or the Mail Merge toolbar.

6. When you're satisfied with the document, complete the merge. The toolbar has options to merge to new documents, merge to printer, or merge to email.

Mail merge to email is often better than sending BCC messages. Many anti-spam filters are configured to treat messages in which the user is blind carbon copied as spam. Mail merge puts the recipient's name in the To field, which allows it to pass through many anti-spam filters.

Summary

This hour explained how to use contacts and how to manage them using categories and views. Using categories to manage your contacts has many advantages over using multiple contacts folders. Views make it easier to use one contact folder without being overwhelmed.

You learned how to create distribution lists and how to use categories instead of distribution lists when you need a dynamic address list.

Using contacts in a mail merge to address messages and envelopes or to create letters and labels was also covered in this hour.

Q&A

Q I need to update the area code field on many of my contacts. I tried using the Group By method to change it and changed the entire phone number. Is there a way to change the area code for a large number of contacts without editing each contact?

A No, you aren't doing it wrong; Outlook doesn't support changing the area code this way. As you've discovered, it works when you need to change the entire phone number for a company, but not when only the area code changes.

There are several methods you can use to change the area code. If you only have a few phone numbers to change, use in-cell editing and change the number without opening the contact form. You can also export to Excel and use Replace to change the area codes, or write a VBA procedure to change the area code.

Q When I do a mail merge to email, I get a security dialog and need to allow access for up to 10 minutes, and then I wait and click Yes for each message. What can I do to get rid of the dialogs?

A My crystal ball tells me that you're merging to a plain text–formatted message. If you merge to HTML format, you won't get the dialogs. You can use a script called ClickYes to press the buttons for you, if you really want to use plain text. Look for a link to it at www.slipstick.com.

10

Hour 11

Using Your Calendar

One of the most important modules in a personal information manager (PIM) is a calendar. Like most electronic calendars, Outlook's calendar includes reminders, cross-references to contacts, capability to color-code and categorize appointments or events, and create recurring appointments. Outlook also includes the capability to send meeting requests, view multiple calendars in one window, and use views to control what appointments are visible onscreen.

This hour shows you how to use Outlook 2003's calendar features, including

- Creating appointments
- Organizing your calendar
- Using meeting invitations
- Sharing calendars

New to Outlook 2003's calendar is an alternative calendar feature, which enables you to display information found on calendars used by other cultures, including Hebrew, Arabic, and Asian.

Overview of Calendar Features

Using Outlook, you can set appointments or events or invite other people to meetings. After the events are on your calendar, you can use views to control which events are shown on your calendar and how they're displayed.

The default view on the calendar uses the Day/Week/Month view with the Date Navigator thumbnails on the left, along with a list of available calendars, including all calendars in your message store and shared calendars (see Figure 11.1).

FIGURE **11.1**

The Outlook 2003 cal-endar's default view.

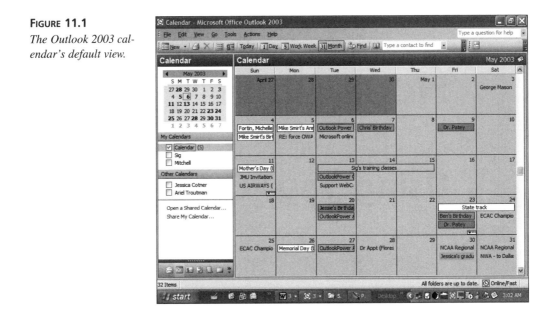

The number of date navigators shown varies with the size of the Outlook window and the width of the Navigation Pane. When you use a very high screen resolution setting and have set the Navigation Pane at its maximum size (one-half the screen width), you might have twenty or more calendar date navigators. When you enable View, Arrange By, Show Views in Navigation Pane, you'll have fewer calendar date navigators in the Navigation Pane.

 Only Exchange Server users can use the Open a Shared Calendar option, but it's listed in the Navigation Pane even if you don't have an Exchange Server account in your profile. The Share My Calendar option is listed only if you have Exchange service in your profile.

The sections in the Navigation Pane aren't adjustable; they adjust automatically as you change the width of the Navigation Pane or add more folders to the My Calendar and Other Calendars sections. If you prefer using the TaskPad with your calendar, enable it using the View, TaskPad menu selection (see Figure 11.2).

FIGURE 11.2

When the TaskPad is enabled, the date navigators on the Navigation Pane disappear.

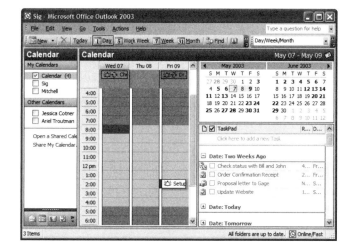

Drag the bar dividing the date navigators and the TaskPad to the top of the screen to hide the date navigators on the right side. Doing so causes the date navigators to reappear in the Navigation Pane.

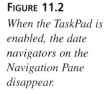

Outlook's calendar is essentially infinite, for all practical purposes, with an ending date of 8/31/4500. When you're scrolling the calendar in Day/Week/Month view, it might appear that the calendar spans two years—one year each before and after "today"—based on the size and position of the scrollbar button. However, unlike other Windows programs, the scrollbar slider is one size and its position at the top or bottom of the window doesn't indicate the beginning or end of the calendar.

To continue scrolling the calendar once you've reached the top or bottom of the scrollbar, you must use the scrollbar arrow buttons or the Page Up and Page Down keys.

Changing Calendar Options

Although Microsoft tries to choose the most common setting for the defaults, you might want to change some of the settings. Begin by opening the Tools, Options dialog.

You can change the default reminder time from the Preferences tab by selecting a time from the Default Reminder drop-down list. If the reminder time you want to use isn't listed, type it in. For example, if you want a reminder 20 minutes before the appointment, type **20m** into the field.

The Preferences tab contains the Calendar Options button, where you'll find all the calendar settings (see Figure 11.3). Some of the settings are also accessible by right-clicking on various calendar elements, including the time scale and the Day/Week/Month calendar grid.

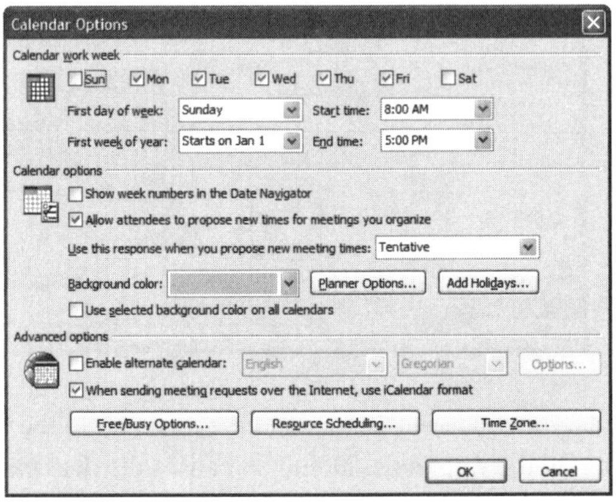

FIGURE 11.3

Use the Calendar Options dialog to control many of the settings used in the calendar display, including the days and times in your workweek, background colors, time zones, and holidays.

The Calendar Options dialog has many settings you might need to customize, including

- Calendar Work Week—Add checks next to the days of the week that you work. The selected days are shown when you choose the Work Week button.

> Outlook doesn't handle nonsequential days well: It shows the selected number of days beginning with the first work day you've checked. For example, if you select Tues and Fri as your work week, selecting the Work Week command button displays Tues and Wed in your calendar. To avoid this problem, select Wed and Thurs as well.

Calendar work week options:

- First Day of Week—Choose the first day of your week. Most calendars begin the week with Sunday or Monday, but you can select any day.
- First Week of Year—Choose from Starts on Jan 1, First 4-Day Week, and First Full Week.
- Start Time—This is the start of your work day. It controls the hours that use the background color in the Day view and in views that show only work times.

- End Time—Like Start Time, this setting affects the hours that use the background color in the Day view and when Only Show Work Hours is selected.

Calendar options:

- Show Week Numbers in the Date Navigator—Shows the week numbers in the small thumbnail calendars in the Navigation Pane and TaskPad.

> Even though Outlook can show week numbers, it doesn't have an option to show day numbers; that is, Jan 1 is day 1, Feb 1 is day 32, and Dec 31 is day 365.

- Allow Attendees to Propose New Times for Meetings You Organize—Determines whether the ability to propose new meeting times is enabled. You can override this setting by choosing Actions, Allow New Time Proposals when creating a new meeting request.
- Use This Response When You Propose New Meeting Times—Choose the default setting from Tentative, Accept, and Decline.
- Background Color—Choose the color that your calendar and your working hours are shown in when you use a Day view. Nonworking hours use a darker shade of this color.
- Use Selected Color Background Color on All Calendars—When selected, all shared calendars and calendars in your message store will use the same color. When this option is left unchecked, each calendar will use a different color.
- Planner Options—Contains options to display appointment details in pop-ups or details in the calendar grid.
- Add Holidays—Import holidays for many countries around the world. Includes holidays for the years 2003 through 2007.

Advanced options:

- Enable alternate calendar—Used to display calendar information used by other cultures—including Hebrew, Far East, or Arabic—in Outlook's calendar.

> Before enabling an alternative calendar, you must enable support for the alternative languages using the Office 2003 Language Settings, found at Start menu, Programs, Microsoft Office, Microsoft Office Tools, Microsoft Office 2003 Language Settings.

- When Sending Meeting Requests over the Internet, Use iCalendar Format—Sends iCalendars by default so that any calendar program can use them.

- Free/Busy Options—Used to configure how much free/busy data is published, how often it's updated, and where it's published (see Figure 11.4).

  Free/Busy information can be published to the Microsoft Office Internet Free/Busy Service, a free service provided by Microsoft. If you prefer to keep your Free/Busy information local, it can published to any server you have read/write access to.

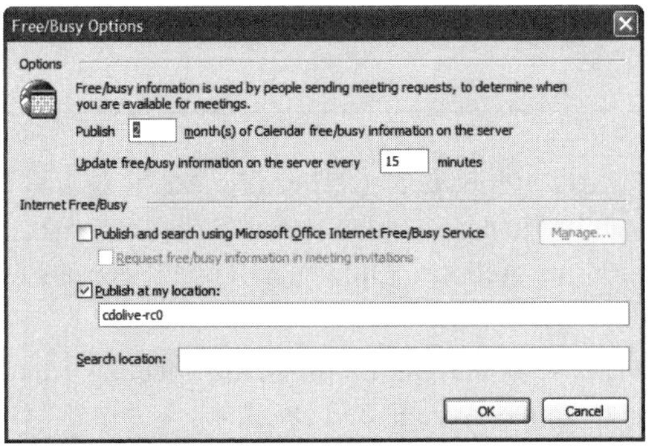

FIGURE 11.4

The Free/Busy Options dialog box enables you to publish your calendar information to the Internet or to a custom server location.

- Resource Scheduling—Use this dialog to enable or disable automatic processing of meeting requests (see Figure 11.5).

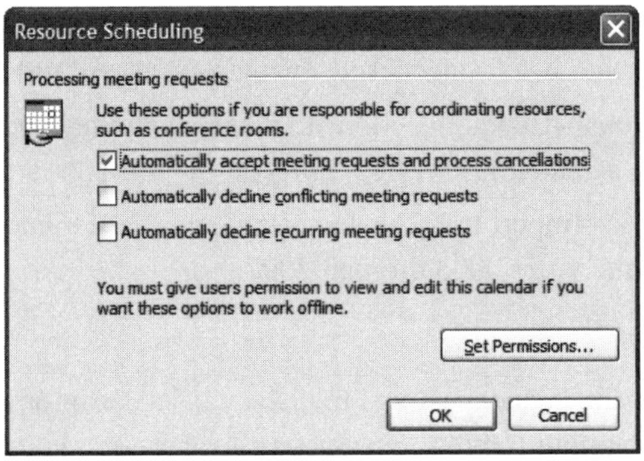

FIGURE 11.5

Automatic accept and decline settings are intended for use with mailboxes assigned to resources. However, you can use those settings to automatically process meeting requests you receive.

- Time Zone—Use this dialog to set up the time zones used by Outlook (see Figure 11.6).

FIGURE 11.6

Outlook supports two times zones. When enabled, the time scale displays both time zones. The current time zone is the default time zone and is used for appointment times.

Understanding Appointments and Time Zones

Outlook's appointment times are based on UTC time, and the appointment times change if you change the time zone settings.

UTC, short for Coordinated Universal Time, is a time scale based on a combination of Greenwich Mean Time and atomic time and refers to the same time zone as GMT.

For example, if you create an appointment in the Eastern time zone for 2 PM and then travel to California and change your computer's time zone to reflect Pacific time, the appointment time changes to 11 PM. All-day events span two days, starting at 9 PM and running for 24 hours. For this reason, it's recommended that you enable the Two Time Zones setting in Outlook and change your computer's time zone settings only when the change will be permanent.

When you're using two time zones and travel, you can use Swap Time Zones to easily switch between your home and local time zones. When you swap time zones in Outlook, the zone settings in Windows change, too.

Changing your computer's clock to reflect the correct time but keeping your home time zone might sound like a good idea, but it causes more problems that it fixes. Email that you send will have the wrong time on it and it might be dropped by spam filters because the times don't match and that often indicates a forged header. Other problems include sorting issues for the

> recipient and the possibility that the message will be grouped with older messages and might not be seen right away. If you're connecting to a corporate network, the server might update your clock to the correct time or refuse to allow you to connect.

When you need to make a permanent change to your computer's clock—for example, if you mistakenly selected the wrong time zone, used the wrong daylight saving time settings, or moved to a new time zone—all appointment times in Outlook change to reflect the new time zone settings.

To prevent problems caused by time changes, first export all appointments and events to either a CSV file or Excel workbook using File, Import and Export, following the steps in the wizard to export the appointments.

Next, change the view on the default calendar folder to a Group By and check the left corner of the status bar to see whether a filter is applied. If so, you must choose another view or remove the filter.

Select one item and then press Ctrl+A to select all the calendar items. Right-click and choose Move to Folder, selecting New on the Move Items dialog. Create a new calendar folder, enter a name, and click OK to create a new folder and move all of your calendar items to the new folder.

Now change the computer's time and make sure that it's correct. Import the CSV or Excel data back into the calendar. All the appointment times should be set at the correct time.

The new calendar folder you created is used only for a back up. When you're sure that the dates are correct in the default folder, you can delete the new calendar folder.

Creating Appointments

There are three methods you can use to create an appointment:

- Open a new calendar form and enter your event details
- Drag a message or other Outlook item to the calendar button or folder
- Select an Outlook item, right-click and choose Copy to Folder, selecting the calendar from the folder selection menu

Creating an appointment using the second and third methods opens the form as an appointment with the next time slot used as the appointment time. For example, if you drag a message to the calendar at 2:50 PM, a calendar form opens with the appointment date and time set for 3 PM today. You can change this, of course.

My all-time favorite time tip is using shortcut keys to enter the time and date. Instead of using the date picker to find 2 weeks from now, type **2w** in the date field. Entering the time as 2:50 PM takes too many keystrokes, whereas 250p doesn't require the use of the Shift key.

Other shortcut letters you can use are d (day), mo (month), and y (year).

The appointment and meeting forms share just one form (shown later in this section), with different controls used depending on the commands you select. When you choose the Recurrence button, the dialog needed to create a recurring appointment opens. When you choose Invite Attendees, you can add email addresses to the form and select other options specific to meeting planning.

Using the New menu to open a form limits you to opening a new appointment form or a new meeting form, but you can use the toolbar button to make a recurring appointment. If you choose the wrong type of calendar form or need an all-day event form, select the toolbar button or option to change the form type.

11

The reminder time for all-day events defaults to 18 hours. If you want a different reminder time, you must select it or type it in when you create the all-day event.

When you right-click on the calendar, you can select the type of calendar item you want to create. They are

- New Appointment—Create a new appointment with start and end times
- New All Day Event—Create an all-day event
- New Meeting Request—Send a meeting request to another person by email
- New Meeting Request With—Available only for Exchange server users and only when a shared calendar is displayed

- New Recurring <u>A</u>ppointment—Create an appointment that recurs

- New Recurring E<u>v</u>ent—Create an all-day event that recurs

- New Re<u>c</u>urring Meeting—Send a recurring meeting request by email

Right-click in any Day/Week/Month calendar and choose from the following context menu items to navigate the calendar:

- Go to This <u>D</u>ay—Used with Seven Day and Day/Week/Month views to open the selected day in a one-day view.

- T<u>o</u>day—Returns you to "today."

- Go <u>t</u>o Date—Opens the Go to Date picker. Select any date and calendar style and that date is displayed in the calendar.

The last items on the context menu are used to customize the calendar views:

- Other <u>S</u>ettings—Opens the Format Day/Week/Month dialog (see Figure 11.7). Use the Format Day/Week/Month View dialog to customize the fonts used on the calendar, to set the time scale, and to control how the time is displayed on appointments. This dialog also includes the option to Compress Weekend Days on the Monthly Calendar. You can also change the time scale by right-clicking on the time scale and selecting a different scale.

FIGURE 11.7

The Format Day/Week/Month View dialog enables you to customize the appearance of your calendar.

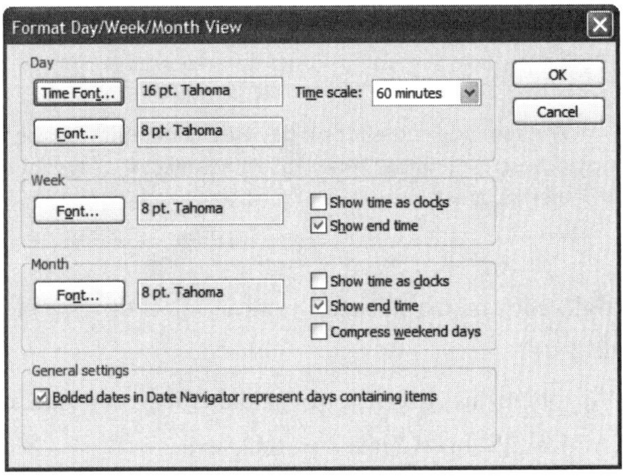

- <u>C</u>ustomize Current View—Opens the Customize view dialog.

- Automatic <u>F</u>ormatting—Sets up rules to apply labels to existing appointments.

The Actions menu in the main calendar window also includes many of the same options listed earlier, plus the following two items:

- Plan a Meeting
- View Group Schedules

Plan a Meeting displays the free/busy information, as shown on the Schedule tab of an appointment form. Enter the attendees' names, check their availability, and choose Make a Meeting to open an appointment form with the time, date, and attendee fields completed (see Figure 11.8).

FIGURE 11.8

Use Plan a Meeting and View Group Schedules to show you the attendees' free/busy information before you begin to plan the meeting.

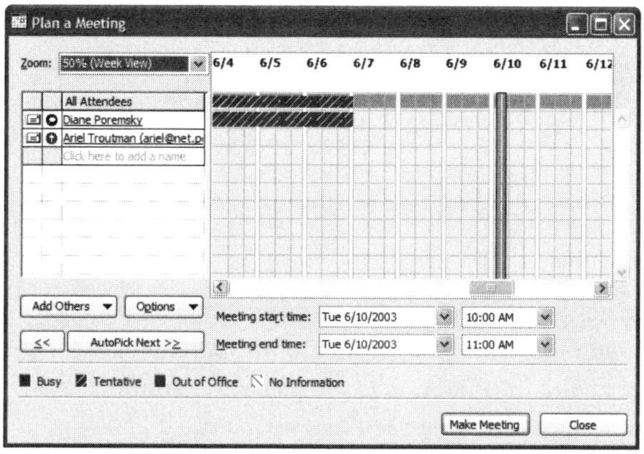

View Group Schedules is available only for Exchange Server accounts. It enables you to create lists of colleagues' calendars. This is similar to a distribution list, but for co-workers whose calendars you open frequently. When you select a group, you'll see the group members' free busy information.

One basic calendar form is used for all appointments, meeting requests, and all day events. Choosing the Invite Attendees button adds a To field for you to enter email addresses. Click the Recurrence button to set up recurring events or add a check to the All Day event box to create an all day event instead of an appointment.

An appointment has a set beginning and ending time. Events last all day and sometimes span several days.

FIGURE 11.9

The appointment form provides you with the fields necessary to input important information about an appointment.

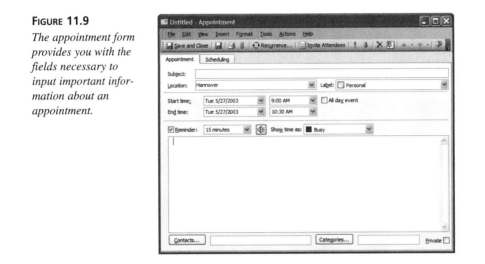

To create an appointment, select <u>N</u>ew or <u>N</u>ew, <u>A</u>ppointment if you aren't looking at the Calendar folder.

1. Fill in the Subject field of the appointment, and press the Tab key to move to the <u>L</u>ocation field. Enter the location of the appointment, if desired. The location list is stored in your profile so that you can select from locations you entered previously, but you can't share you locations with other users.

2. Next, tab to the label field and select a label, if desired. When a label isn't selected, you can use automatic formatting to color appointments by view.

3. Enter a start time. You can type a date in or use date shortcuts, such as 2w for two weeks from now. Enter the time of your appointment, which accepts shortcuts formatted as 245p. Tab to the E<u>n</u>d Time field and enter the time, if the default is not correct.

4. If the item is an all-day event, skip the Start Time field and add a check to the All Da<u>y</u> Event box.

5. Change the default reminder, if necessary, and choose your desired Sho<u>w</u> Time As selection.

<u>S</u>elect Save, close the dialog, and your appointment is added to your calendar.

When you're viewing the calendar, you can double-click on a time in the Day Planner view to create an appointment at that time. Double-clicking in the monthly view creates an all-day event.

Moving Appointments

After you've created your appointments, you might discover the appointment needs to be moved to a new time or date. Other times, you'll need to make a second appointment using the same details. In that case, making a copy of the original appointment is easier than retyping it. There are several ways to perform a move or copy:

- Open the item and change the date. It's boring, but it works.

- Select the item and use the keyboard shortcuts: Press Ctrl+X or Ctrl+C to cut or copy, and then press Ctrl+V to paste it on a new date.

- Select and drag to a new time or date to move, or hold the Ctrl and drag the item to copy it. You can also right-click and drag to choose between copy and move.

- Change the start or end times by dragging the edge of the appointment up or down, when using the Day or Work Week view.

Although dragging and dropping works well when the new times or dates are visible on the screen, it's more difficult to do if you need to scroll very far through the calendar. In most cases, it's easier to open the item and type in a new time when you're moving the item or using cut (or copy) and paste.

11

> It's tricky to use the Day/Week/Month view to move appointments from one time or date to another, or even to another calendar. It's also sometimes difficult to select the appointment without also entering edit mode. If you happen to enter Edit mode, press the Esc key to return to Select mode.
>
> You can also right-click on an item, and after the context menu appears, choose Outlook's Edit menu to return to Select mode.

Although the preceding methods work well when you use the Day/Week/Month view, you can also let Outlook change times or dates for you using a Table view.

1. Select a Table view, such as By Category.

2. Right-click on the row for field names, selecting Group By Box.

3. Drag the Start field to the Group By area. This groups your appointments by the date.

4. Select appointments or all-day events and drag them between groups. The time and/or date changes to what is used by the new group.

You must sort by the start time and drag the item to another group. Although this method doesn't seem very practical because you don't normally want more than one appointment at a specific time and date, it works well to change all-day events on group calendars.

Recurring Appointments

You can create recurring appointments using the same methods you use to create appointments or all-day events: by selecting the Recurrence command button to open the Appointment Recurrence dialog (see Figure 11.10).

Choose the appointment times and the recurrence pattern. The recurring appointment must fit a pattern, such as every *nn* days or every other Monday. Recurring appointments that fall on Monday one week and Wednesday the next week require two appointments, one for each pattern.

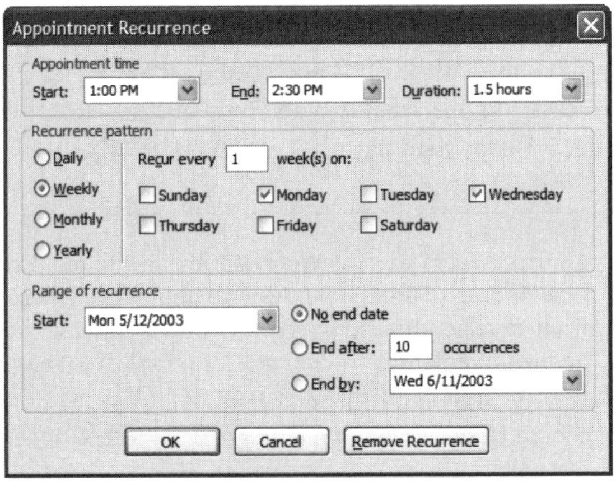

FIGURE 11.10

Use the Appointment Recurrence dialog to set up your recurring pattern. Different options are available when you select Daily, Weekly, Monthly, or Yearly pattern.

If you decide you don't want to create a recurring appointment, choose Remove Recurrence and you're returned to the appointment form.

When you're using a Day/Week/Month view and open, move, or delete an appointment that is part of a recurring series, Outlook warns you that the item is part of a series. In the case of opening or deleting an appointment, you're asked whether you want to open or delete the item or the series.

You receive a similar warning when you move recurring appointments and are offered the opportunity to change only the current item. If you want to change all the items, you'll have to open the series and edit the date.

Meeting Requests

Meeting Requests are appointment forms that you send to someone else. The recipient can accept, reject, or suggest another time. When done properly, the meeting is automatically added to all participants' calendars. Although it's almost always "done correctly" when everyone is using the same Exchange server, meeting requests can also work for non-Exchange users, if certain steps are followed:

1. All attendees must use Outlook

2. All requests must use RTF (rich text formatting) format

It's easy to know whether everyone is using Outlook, but controlling RTF format on messages sent to the Internet is more difficult. If you're sending meeting requests and a recipient is getting them as email messages, open a message from that recipient and double-click the email address to open the E-mail Properties dialog box, as shown in Figure 11.11. (If a contact record opens, double-click the email address on the form.) Choose Send Using Outlook Rich Text Format from the Internet Format drop-down list and click OK.

FIGURE 11.11

Open the E-mail Properties dialog by double-clicking on the name or -mail address in the To field.

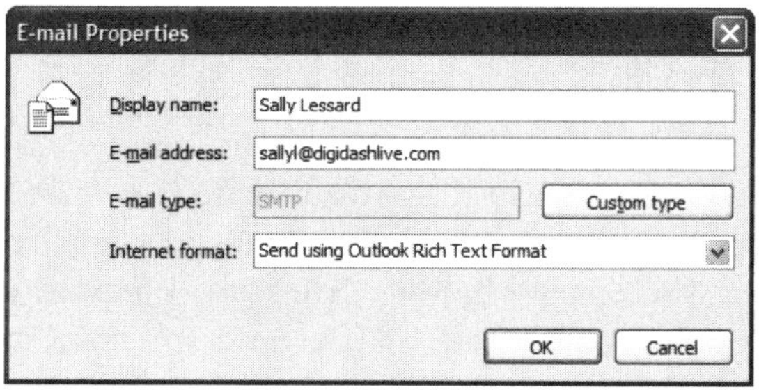

These steps will always send the meeting request properly. In most cases, when the recipient accepts the meeting, you'll receive an RTF-formatted acceptance and your calendar item will be updated properly. Occasionally, the acceptance will arrive in plain text format and you'll have to update the tracking tab yourself, as shown later, in Figure 11.15.

Sending a Meeting Request

Open a new meeting request form using New, Meeting Request or by opening an appointment and choosing the Invite Attendees button. This adds the To field, Meeting Workspace button, and the This Is an Online Meeting Using: check box and drop-down controls to the form (see Figure 11.12).

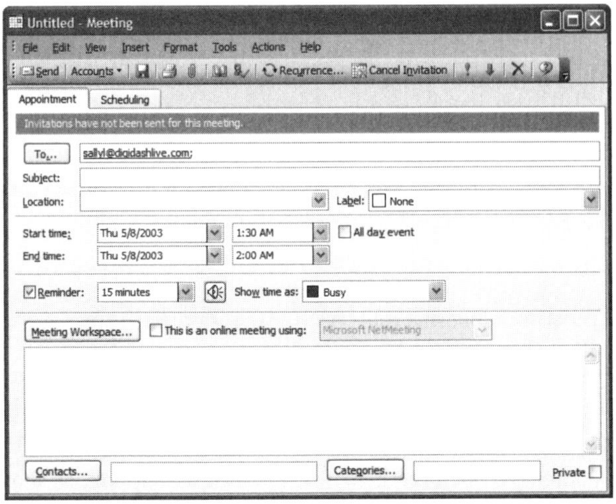

FIGURE 11.12

A meeting request form includes a To field so that you can invite other people to meetings using email.

Meeting Workspace is used with SharePoint Portal Servers (SPS) or Windows SharePoint Services (WSS). This is useful only if both you and the attendees have access to either SPS or WSS. Choosing Meeting Workspace opens the Workspace task pane. If you previously created a workspace, you can select it or create a new workspace from the Workspace task pane.

 If you decide you need the appointment but don't want to invite anyone, click the Cancel Invitation button and the form is changed back to a normal appointment form.

Online meetings can use NetMeeting, Windows Media Services, or Exchange Conferencing Server. After choosing the service you're using, the meeting form expands to show the server fields necessary to connect to your desired service.

The Actions menu enables you to choose to Request Responses and Allow New Time Proposals. The Request Responses menu is useful when you just need to add an appointment to someone's calendar and either it's only for informational purposes or the recipient plans to attend. Select Allow New Time Proposals when you want to allow attendees to suggest a new time if the time you selected isn't convenient for them.

When setting up a meeting, you have the options of making it required or optional for the attendee and of adding the meeting to a resource calendar. Although using resources is generally useful only for Exchange Server users, you can do so as long as the resource (usually a meeting room) has its own mailbox and someone uses Outlook to check the resource's mailbox.

Select the Scheduling tab to check the Free/busy information for your attendees (see Figure 11.13). Add additional attendees by typing their names or email addresses in the attendee column. If you have access to the attendees' free/busy information, existing appointments are blocked out. Hash marks across the calendar indicate that you don't have access to the person's free/busy information.

FIGURE 11.13

Use the Scheduling tab to add attendees or change the options for the attendees.

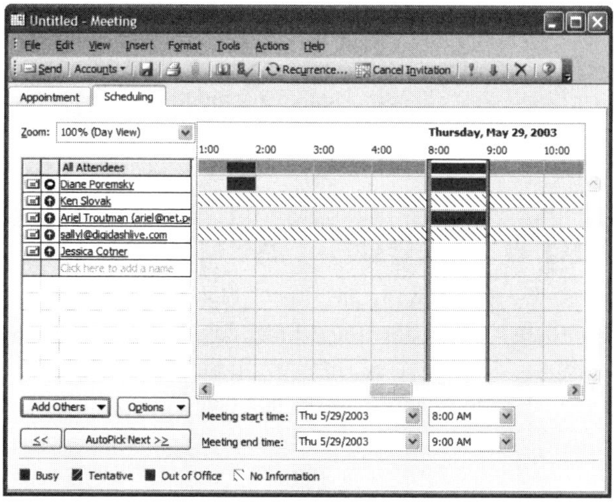

Select an icon in the column to the left of an attendee's name to change that person's status from required to optional. Select the mail icon to send the meeting request. Use the Zoom drop-down list to select different views of the free/busy calendar.

> The To: button on the Appointment tab opens the Select Attendees and Resources dialog. Use it to pick from your address book. Clicking the Add Others button, and choosing the Add from Address Book menu on the Scheduling tab opens this dialog as well.

The Options button on the Schedule tab has four options:

- Show Only Working Hours—Working hours are set in Tools, Options, Preferences, Calendar Options.

- Show Calendar Details—Shows the appointment subject on the free/busy calendar, instead of the colored block. You can always see appointment details if you hover the mouse over the block, unless the private flag is set.

11

- <u>A</u>utopick—Picks a time and date for the meeting, based on the free/busy time.
- <u>R</u>efresh Free/Busy—Updates the attendee's free/busy information.

After you're finished creating the meeting request, choose Send. If all goes well, the recipient will receive a meeting request; when he accepts it, you'll get the acceptance back.

> Using free/busy information isn't limited to Exchange Server users. You can publish your free/busy information to any location to which you have read and write access, including a computer on your network or on the Internet. Microsoft offers a free free/busy server.

Accepting a Meeting Request

When you receive a meeting request, you'll have the option to accept, tentatively accept, decline, or propose a new time for the meeting. If you have the Reading Pane enabled, you can accept or decline the meeting using the buttons on the message header. You can also open the message to accept or decline (see Figure 11.14).

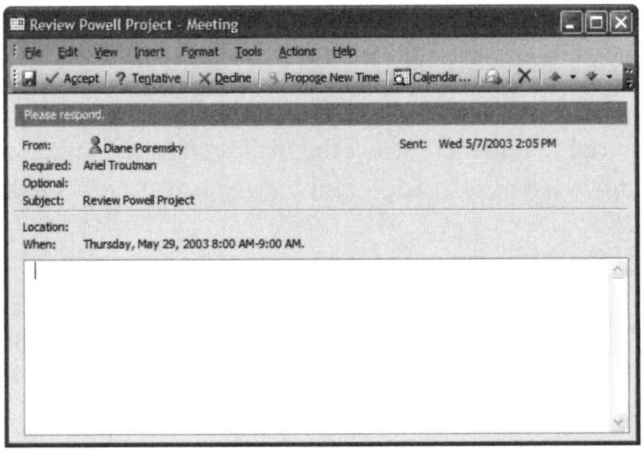

FIGURE 11.14

Respond to meeting requests using the toolbars on the form.

After choosing one of the options, a dialog opens offering three choices:

- <u>E</u>dit the Response Before Sending
- <u>S</u>end the Response Now
- <u>D</u>on't Send a Response

When you edit the response, a standard email reply form opens for you to include comments.

After the meeting's organizer receives the response, the Tracking tab on the calendar item is updated (see Figure 11.15).

Meeting responses in RTF format will have a small calendar icon instead of the envelope found on normal email messages. When you choose Tools, Options, Calendar Options, Resource Scheduling and enable Automatically Accept Meeting Requests and Process Cancellations, as shown in Figure 11.5, the message should disappear from your Inbox within a few minutes. If it doesn't, open the message. If it still won't process, enter the tracking information yourself.

When you have autoprocessing enabled, the meeting request automatically accepts or declines requests, adds accepted requests to your calendar, returns a response (if the organizer wants a response), and deletes the meeting request. Unless you look at your calendar often, you might be unaware that you have the meeting. For this reason, it's best to use autoprocessing only for resource scheduling.

Automatically processing meeting requests for resources, such as meeting rooms, ensures that the resource isn't requested by two groups at the same time.

Using Labels and Categories

Outlook enables you to color-code appointments when you use the calendar grid. This makes it easier to see what types of appointments you have scheduled.

The Label field is on the Appointment tab and includes ten colors plus "none." The colors aren't customizable, but you can change the names used on the labels. You can choose a label when you create the appointment or change the label at any time:

1. Select an appointment, and then use the Edit, Label menu selection to add a label to an appointment or right-click on the appointment and choose Label.

2. Open the item and select a label from the Label drop-down list.

3. Open the Automatic Formatting dialog and use rules to apply labels to many appointments at once. Right-click on the calendar and choose Automatic Formatting to open the dialog.

 You must use a Day/Week/Month view to view the label colors. When you use a Table view, you can add the Label field and see the label name. Use the view's automatic formatting to colorize the items by label name. Right-click on the field names and choose Customize Current View or Custom from the menu to open the Automatic Formatting dialog.

You can change the names used for the labels by using the Edit, Labels, Edit Labels menu selection to open the Edit Calendar Labels dialog.

Using Views

Outlook's default view on the calendar is a Day/Week/Month grid. Most people only ever use this view because it's a familiar format to everyone. When you want to view a shared calendar side-by-side with your calendar, you must use a Day/Week/Month view.

Outlook also has predefined views for Table views. The Table views are handy when you want to see a list of appointments. One advantage of a Table view is that the view is printable, with the fields shown on the screen included in the printout. You can also select and copy a Table view, and then paste it in any other document (see Figure 11.16).

FIGURE 11.16

When using a Table view, you can select rows and then copy and paste them into other documents. The Group By Box is visible at the top of the Calendar pane.

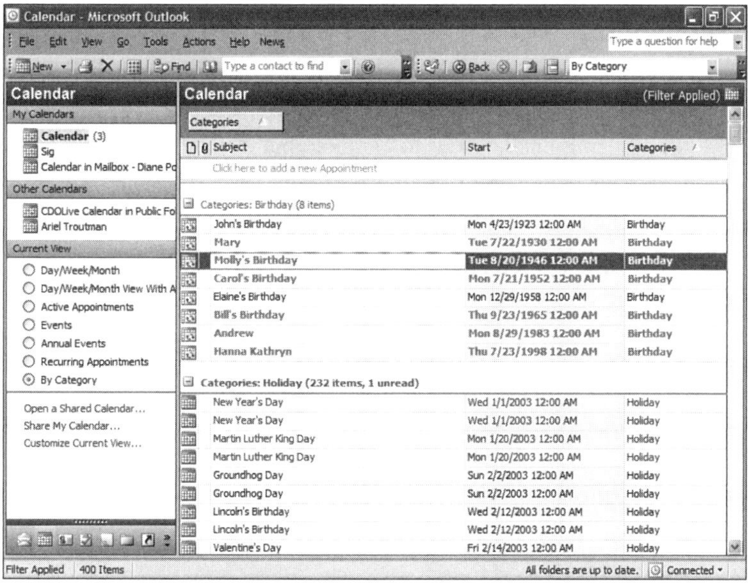

This view uses two automatic formatting rules; both use advanced filter options. One rule colors all appointments with a start date between 1/1/2003 and 2/1/2003 blue. The other rule colors all items in the Birthday category and with a recurrence pattern that contains "June, July, August, September" in red.

Table fields don't support the colored labels, but you can use automatic formatting with views to colorize items in a Table view.

Look for more information on using views in Hour 3, "Navigating the Outlook Interface."

Did you know you that you can copy the data shown on the screen when you use a Table view? Select the rows you want to copy, press Ctrl+C to copy them, and then paste the information in any other program from Notepad to Word or Excel. All visible fields are copied using a tab-delimited format.

11

Sharing Your Calendar with Others

Calendar sharing won't work for about half of all Outlook users because it works only with Exchange Server accounts. SharePoint services enable you to add a read-only copy of a SharePoint calendar to Outlook, but if you don't have Exchange or SharePoint services (including WSS), you can't easily share calendars with other people.

If you use Exchange Server, click on Open a Shared Calendar in the Navigation Pane. You'll add a SharePoint calendar from the portal Web page, not from Outlook.

Exchange Server users can view other people's calendars only when they have permission to both the mailbox and the calendar folder. To change the permissions on a mailbox, right-click the top level of the mailbox (where Outlook Today is), choose Properties, and then select the Permissions tab. Repeat for the Calendar folder.

After you add a shared calendar to your Calendar view, you can view any or all calendars. Add a check to the box beside the calendar in the Navigation Pane to show the calendar; uncheck the box to remove it from the view. To remove the calendar from the Navigation Pane, right-click on the calendar and choose Remove from Shared Calendars.

Only the Day/Week/Month views will show multiple calendars side-by-side. Any other view style displays only one calendar at a time.

If you don't use Exchange Server or SharePoint and need to share your calendar, there isn't any easy way to do it. If you need to share only a few items, sending them as iCalendar or vCalendar works well. Choose Actions, Forward as iCalendar or Actions, Forward after selecting or opening a calendar item. If the recipient receives the calendar item as a message, you'll need to use RTF formatting as discussed earlier in this hour.

When you know you want to share an item with someone as you're creating it, create a meeting request and uncheck Actions, Request Responses.

Forward several calendar items in one message by selecting them, and then choosing the Actions, Forward or Forward as iCalendar menu option. The recipient can drag the items from the message to the calendar.

You can find other techniques for sharing calendars without an Exchange Server at `http://www.slipstick.com/outlook/share.htm`.

Summary

This hour explained how to use Outlook's calendar to help you manage your time. You should now understand the different options available in Outlook and how to use them to your advantage. You learned how to create appointments and meeting requests. You also learned about the limitations to sharing your calendar with others and ways to work around it.

Q&A

Q My co-workers and I share our calendars but we can't see the details of some of the appointments. Why not?

A It sounds as if the Private box is checked on the General tab of the appointment form. When it's checked, you can see only that the appointment exists. If the owners of the appointments want to change the Private setting, they can use a Table view to group by Private field and drag appointments between the Yes and No groups.

To create a new view, select Define View from the Current Views command on the Advanced toolbar. Choose New and select Table View. Choose Group By and then uncheck Automatically Group By Arrangement. Choose All Mail Fields from Select Available Fields From at the bottom of the dialog, and then select Private from the Group Items By menu. Drag items between the Yes and No groups to change the Private setting.

Q We're using Exchange Server and we can't open each other's calendars using File, Open, Other User's Folder. Why not?

A Before you can see a shared calendar, you have to give the other people permission to see the calendar. The easiest way is through Tools, Options, Delegates and adding your co-workers as delegates.

11

Hour 12

Working with Tasks and Notes

Two of Outlook's special items are tasks and notes. Both offer ways to help you organize and prioritize your work. Although tasks have a lot in common with appointments, they're distinctly different from appointments.

Outlook's notes are often underused and misunderstood. This hour teaches you more than you ever wanted to know about using Outlook's notes.

This hour covers

- Using tasks
- Using notes

By the end of the hour, you'll know how to create and use tasks and notes to their fullest.

Overview of Task Features

Use tasks to track events you need to do but not during a specific time period, such as 2 p.m. Tasks can be open-ended with no start or end date, or you can assign start and due dates.

Tasks are also useful for setting reminders for things that aren't necessarily tasks, but that you want to be reminded about. For example, I drag order confirmation or package tracking email messages to the Tasks folder and set a reminder time so that I know when packages are expected to arrive.

Configuring Task Options

There aren't many options you need to configure to use tasks, and the default settings are acceptable to most users.

If you'd like to look at the Task Options dialog, as shown in Figure 12.1, open it by selecting the Tools, Options, Preferences, Task Options menu option.

If Set Reminders on Tasks with Due Dates is enabled on the Task Options dialog, choose a Reminder Time setting on the Tools, Options, Preferences dialog.

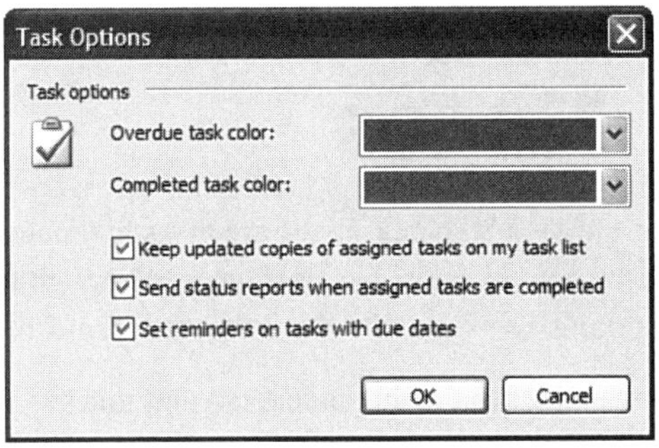

FIGURE 12.1
Use the Task Options dialog to choose an automatic formatting color of overdue and completed tasks, whether to use reminders on tasks with due dates, and how you want to handle assigned tasks.

In addition to setting a default reminder time in Tools, Options, you can choose a specific date and time for your reminder on the task form. These fields accept natural language entries.

Creating Tasks

Although some things can be entered as either calendar or task items, for the most part you'll want to create tasks for items that don't have a set time to be completed. You can set a due date or leave the task open-ended.

To open a task form, select New, Task or press the keyboard shortcut of Ctrl+Shift+K (see Figure 12.2).

You have to complete only the Subject field for your task and save it. But in most cases you'll also want to include a Due Date, and might want to include a Start Date and Reminder Time, or associate Contacts with the task, and assign Categories. As you work on the task, you can update the Status: and % Complete fields.

FIGURE 12.2

The task form needs only a few fields completed: Subject, Start and Due Dates, Status, % Complete and Reminder times. As you complete the task, you can change the % Complete and Status fields.

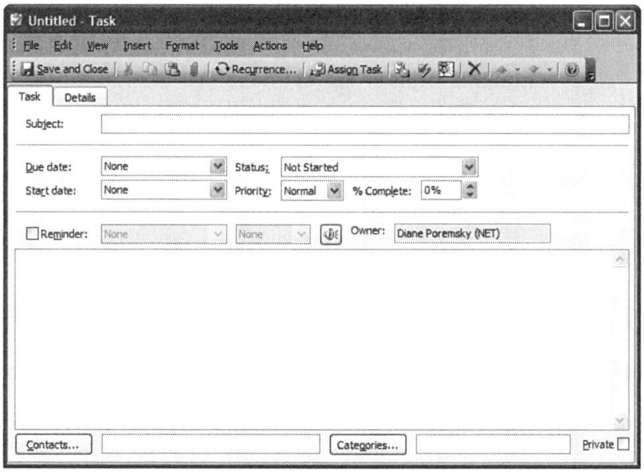

When you enter a contact in the Contacts field, the task is included on the Activities tab of the contact.

You can create new tasks from email messages by dragging messages to the task button at the bottom of the Navigation Pane or to the Tasks folder. When a task is created from an email message, the Subject field is completed automatically (using the email's subject) and the message body is added to the Notes field.

If you'd rather have the message on the task as an attachment, right-click and drag the message to the Task button and then drop it. A menu opens with options for creating a new task using Copy Here As Task with Text, Copy Here As Task with Attachment, or Move Here As Task with Attachment.

In most cases, you'll want to create tasks from email with the message as text, not attachment, because it often results in a smaller file size and you can read the note in the preview pane.

However, if you're creating a task to remind you to reply to a message, adding the message as an attachment means that you can open the message right from the task—you don't have to go looking for it. Adding the message as an attachment also preserves the message source, including HTML formatting, the full Internet header, and any attachments sent with the message.

12

You can also right-click on a message, choose Move to Folder, and selecting the Tasks folder from the folder list. This moves the message and creates a task with the message attached.

You can also create a new task by selecting and dragging text from any application to the Task icon to create a new task with the text entered into the Notes field automatically.

Use the Recurrence button to create recurring tasks (refer to Figure 12.2). Choose the recurrence pattern, the range of recurrence, and whether there is an end date (see Figure 12.3). Click the Remove Recurrence button if you want to remove the recurrence.

When a task is recurring, the next occurrence doesn't start until the current one is marked complete.

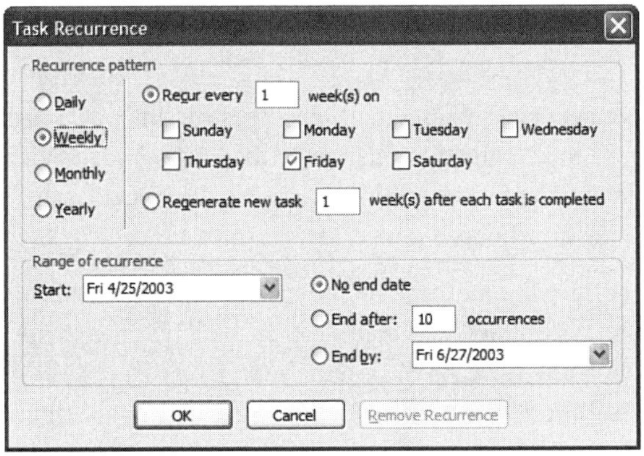

FIGURE 12.3

Use the Task Recurrence dialog to create recurring tasks. Recurring tasks must fit a pattern; you are unable to use this dialog to create tasks that don't fit a pattern.

Click the speaker button following the reminder time fields to choose a specific reminder sound for the task. You can have a different reminder sound for each task if you desire. Select a sound from C:\WINDOWS\Media\ or use sounds you get from other sources or programs.

It's much easier to type the dates in the date and time fields than to use the date and time pickers when you know the shortcuts to use. Among the available shortcuts are 1d (for 1 day), 2w (for 2 weeks), 10a for 10 AM, and 235p for 2:35 PM. The date fields also accept natural language words, which enables you to type such phrases as next christmas, tomorrow, and week from friday and have Outlook enter the correct date in the field. These fields are not case sensitive and you can use lowercase letters for holiday and day names, as I used in my examples.

Outlook can also complete the due date based on the start date, although it's clumsy because the Due Date field is first in the tab order. For example, to create a task that starts next Friday and is due 2 days later, enter **next friday** in the Start field, and then press Shift+Tab to return to the Due Date field and enter **2d**.

When you work on the task, you can change the % Complete field to reflect how much work you've done toward completing the task. Although it's not necessary when working tasks, if you're working on a shared task or were assigned a task by someone else, updating the % Complete field helps others gauge how much is left to do. The drop-down list includes 25, 50, 75, and 100, or you can type any whole number into the field.

You can also set a status for the task, choosing from

- Not Started
- In Progress
- Completed
- Waiting on Someone Else
- Deferred

When the % Complete field is changed and the Status: field is on the default of Not Started, the Status: updates to In Progress or Completed. Status selections are unchanged when another status is selected and the % Complete field is updated to anything except 100 % Complete, at which time the status changes to Completed.

Viewing Tasks

There are three ways you can view your tasks:

- In the Tasks folder (see Figure 12.4)
- Using the TaskPad in the Calendar folder
- On the Outlook Today page

As with all Outlook folders, you can create custom views for both the Tasks folder and the TaskPad.

12

The Tasks folder views can include any view type, including Timeline, Icon, or Day/Week/Month. Although you can't merge calendar and task items, you can create a Calendar view of your task items.

Enable the Current View section of the Navigation Pane using View, Arrange By, Show Views in Navigation Pane.

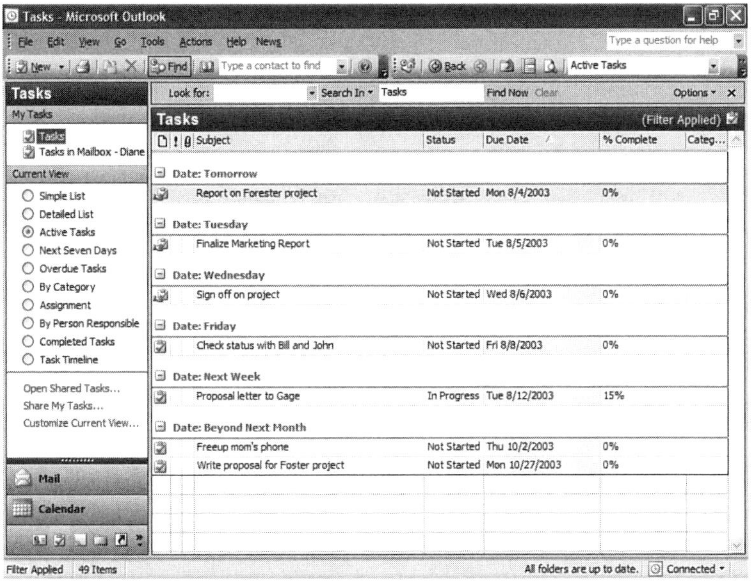

FIGURE 12.4
Use the Tasks folder to view your tasks. The Navigation Pane includes your task folders and you can show the View list in the pane. Icons identify recurring and assigned tasks.

Using the TaskPad with Calendar

Previous versions of Outlook included a TaskPad on the Calendar folder. Although it's no longer the default view, you can restore the view by pulling the right edge of the calendar toward the middle of the screen, moving it at least the width of a calendar thumbnail (see Figure 12.5). When the calendar thumbnails are visible above the TaskPad, the thumbnails on the Navigation Pane disappear. Slide the top border of the TaskPad up to hide the calendars on the right and restore them to the Navigation Pane.

Change the view used in the TaskPad by right-clicking on the row of field names. This brings up the standard view menu that's used in all folders, as shown in Figure 12.6. Use Customize Current View to create a filter for your tasks.

FIGURE 12.5

The calendar thumb-nails are shown on the right side of the win-dow instead of in the Navigation Pane when the TaskPad is enabled.

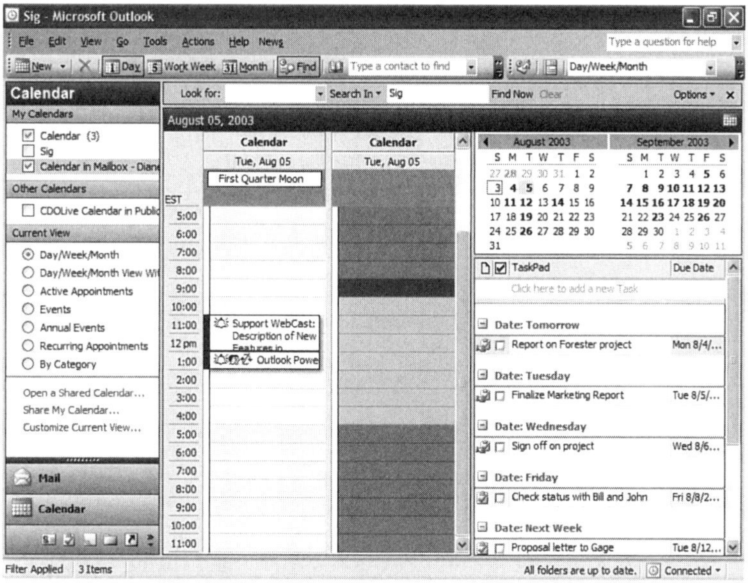

FIGURE 12.6

Right-click anywhere on the row of field names to change the view on your TaskPad.

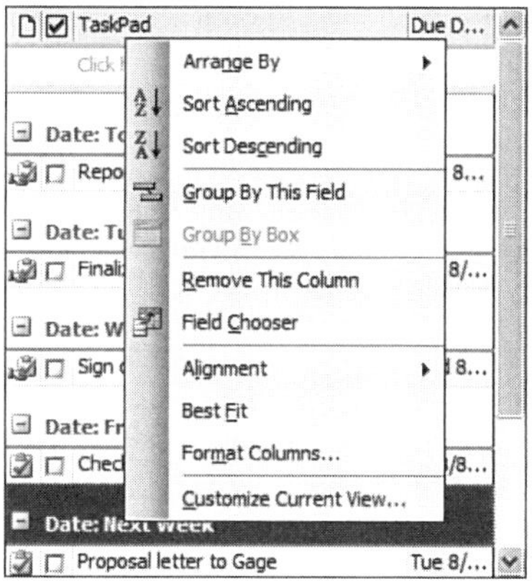

When you right-click in the new item row, you have additional view options. The TaskPad View menu contains a list of six predefined views, including All Tasks, Today's Tasks, Active Tasks for Selected Days, and Overdue Tasks. You can also show or hide tasks that don't have due dates from this menu (see Figure 12.7) .

In addition to creating New Tasks and New Task Requests, you can enable the three-line AutoPreview on the TaskPad and change the current views on the TaskPad.

□ ☑ TaskPad	Due D...
Click here to add a new Task	
New Task	
Date: New Task Request	
Re AutoPreview	Mon 8...
Date: TaskPad View ▸	
Fin TaskPad Settings ▸	Tue 8/...
Date: Wednesday	
Sign off on project	Wed 8...
Date: Friday	
Check status with Bill and John	Fri 8/8...
Date: Next Week	
Proposal letter to Gage	Tue 8/...

Assigning Tasks to Others

One nice feature of Outlook is the capability to assign tasks to others, sending them by email. Although it works best when everyone is using the same Exchange Server, anyone can use the feature. The person you assign the task to must also use Outlook (any version). You must send the task using RTF and when the recipient accepts it, it's added to that person's Tasks folder.

Double-click on the recipient's name and select Send Using Outlook Rich Text Format in the Internet Format field to ensure that the task request is sent using RTF.

You can send a task request by opening the New menu and choosing Task Request or Ctrl+Shift+U (see Figure 12.8). If you have a task form open and decide to assign it to someone, click the Assign Task button on the form and the additional fields used in a task request are added to the form. If you change your mind, click the Cancel Assignment button and the fields are removed.

As the recipient updates the status of the task, updates are supposed to be sent back to you and the copy of the task in your Tasks folder will be updated if you enabled the options when you sent the task. Although that's how it's supposed to work, if both you and the recipient aren't using Exchange Server, many times the task updates are sent as plain-text messages, not RTF, and your copy of the task isn't updated automatically. Instead, you'll receive a message containing the task fields and you have to update the task status yourself.

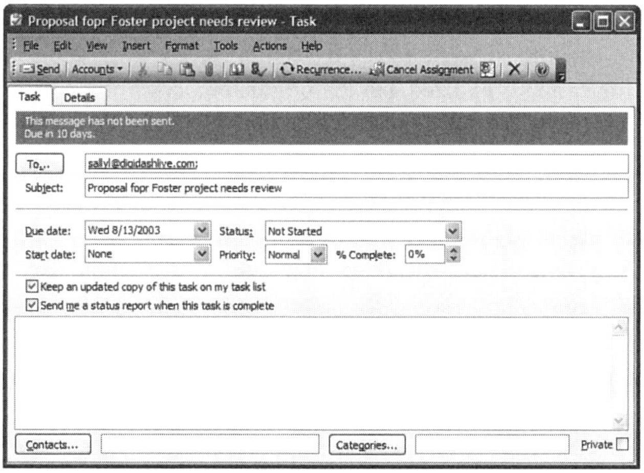

FIGURE 12.8

The task request form is nearly identical to the task form, with the addition of a To field and two check boxes for Keep an Updated Copy of This Task on My Task List and Send Me a Status Report When This Task Is Complete.

When you send a task to two or more people, your copy of the task won't be updated. Outlook warns you before you send the task that if updates are important, you can choose Cancel and remove all but one name.

When you're assigned a task, you'll receive a message similar to the one shown in Figure 12.9. You can accept or decline the task request from the Reading Pane or an open message. After making your selection, you'll be asked whether you want to send the response immediately or edit it first. When you select the Edit Comment option, the task form opens for you to add comments to the Notes field. The notes are saved in the copy in your Tasks folder and included in the response. After accepting the task, it's added to your Tasks folder.

FIGURE 12.9

Select the Accept or Decline button when you receive a task assignment.

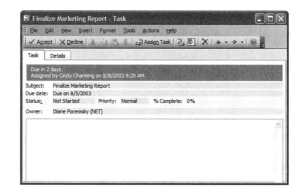

12

Instead of accepting or declining a task, you can reassign it. Open the task assignment message and choose Assign Task instead of Accept or Decline. The task is added to your Tasks folder and is updated, but the originator's copy of the task is not updated.

Making the Most of Notes

Outlook's notes are useful for storing small pieces of text. You can add contacts or categories to your notes and locate the note quickly using Find. Because URLs in notes are clickable, you can paste a URL in a note and include comments about the site. You never have to remember to save notes; Outlook automatically saves them as soon as you move focus away from the note.

Notes resemble sticky notes and can be used to replace the paper version, but they lack a lot of functionality you would expect to find in onscreen sticky notes. That's not to say they aren't useful—they just don't have the features many people expect from electronic sticky notes.

Setting Note Options

The default font, note size, and default note color are set using the Tools, Options, Preferences, Notes Options dialog (see Figure 12.10). The font setting applies to all notes, including existing notes.

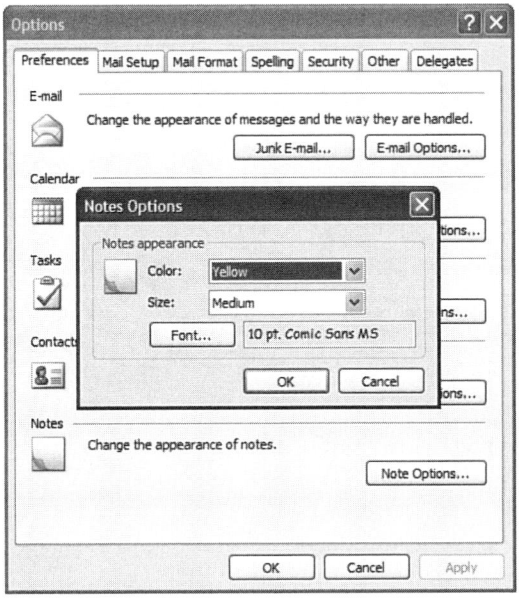

FIGURE 12.10

Use the Notes Options dialog to set the default size and color of your notes and the font. Note color and sizes can be changed when you create a note, but the font is the same for all notes.

Because Notes uses a simple text editor that doesn't support rich text formatting, you can't highlight words or phrases with different colors or fonts or include images in a note.

Notes are yellow by default, with blue, green, pink, and white available as alternative colors. Note size and color changes apply only to new notes. The color and size of existing notes remains unchanged when you make changes to note preferences.

You can change the color of an individual note at any time. If the note is open, click on the note icon in the upper-left corner of a note and then choose Color from the menu. If a note is closed, right-click the note and choose Color.

When you use the Group by Color view, you can drag notes between groups to change their color.

You can display the last modified time and date in the note's status bar. Turn it on with Tools, Options, Other, Advanced Options menu selection, check the box for When Viewing Notes, Show Time and Date. This is a global setting and applies to all notes. It uses the same short date format used by the computer.

The status bar displays the time and date the note was last modified. The Modified Time field is updated to the current time when you edit a note.

12

If it's important for you to know the date a note was created, type the date in the note body—don't rely on the Created and Modified Date fields in Outlook.

Creating Notes

As with all Outlook items, there are several different ways to create new notes.

1. Use the mouse to select File, New, Note from the menu bar or New, Note from the Standard toolbar in Outlook's window. If you have the Notes folder open, the New button opens a new note by default. Or use the keyboard shortcut, Ctrl+Shift+N, to create new notes from anywhere in Outlook. Type or paste text into the note form.

When you use Word as your email editor, you can't use the keyboard short-cut or menus to create notes when composing a message. You must bring Outlook or an Outlook item into focus to use the keyboard shortcut.

2. Double-click between notes in the Notes list to open a new note (see Figure 12.11). If you use an Icon view, simply double-click between the icons or double-click after the last note in List view. The note is now ready for you to enter text.

FIGURE 12.11

Outlook's note has a simple interface and no toolbar. Click on the small icon in the upper-left corner to access the options available for individual notes. This note has the date and time the note was created displayed in the status bar.

8/3/2003 9:06 PM

3. Drag and drop a message to a note folder to save the entire message as a note.

4. Select part of a message and drag the selection to a note folder. You aren't limited to dragging selections from Outlook items; this works for any OLE document, such as Word documents, Excel spreadsheets, and Internet Explorer pages.

Outlook uses the first line of the note for the name of the note. The maximum length for the name is 256 characters, unless you begin a new paragraph. If you want a shorter name, press Enter to begin a new line.

When you drag Outlook items to create notes, drop the text or message on the Note icon at the bottom of the Navigation Pane, on a note folder, or anywhere in the list area.

When you're done creating your note, you can use the Escape key or Alt+F4 to close it.

Assigning Categories to Notes

Although you can't see a Category field on a note form, you can assign categories to notes. When you use categories, you can use the Group By Category view, display the Category field in the Notes List view, or use Advanced Find to find your notes.

There are three ways you can add a category to notes:

- Click on the Note icon in the upper-left corner and select Categories from the menu to display the familiar Outlook Categories dialog.

- Right-click on a note in the folder and choose Categories.

- Turn on in-cell editing and type a category name in List view. In-cell editing is enabled from the View, Arrange By, Custom menu selection, and clicking the Other Settings button.

You can assign a category to several notes at once. After selecting the notes, right-click on the selection and choose Categories. You can also use the Group By Category view and drag notes to category groups.

Assigning Contacts to Notes

You can assign contacts to a note and the note will be listed on the Activities tab of the contact with other Outlook items. I'm not sure how useful it is to associate sticky notes with contacts, but it's an option if you ever need it.

As with categories, the Contact field is not visible on the note form, and the only way to add a contact is by clicking the Note icon and selecting Contacts from the menu.

12

In-cell editing makes it easy to edit items, but many people don't like the feature and worry about accidentally editing a field. This isn't a problem with Notes because Category is the only Notes field that is editable in-cell.

If you want to use in-cell editing but don't want it enabled all the time, create a new view with it enabled. When you want to edit a note, switch to your new view. It's easy to switch views when you show the Advanced toolbar.

Saving Notes

Outlook automatically saves your notes to the default Notes folder when you close the note or focus is no longer on the note.

When you use the File menu or keyboard shortcut to create a note, it's saved in the default Notes folder. If you want to save a note in another note folder, you must open that folder, create the note, or move it from the default Notes folder after it's created.

You can use the mouse to move or copy notes to another note folder. Drag and drop with the left mouse button to move the note, or use a right-click drag and drop to select between <u>M</u>ove or <u>C</u>opy.

When you select two or more notes and right-click, one of the menu options is <u>M</u>ove to Folder. Selecting this option opens the Move Items dialog; select the folder to move the notes to.

You can save contents of a note to the Windows file system as notes, RTF documents, Outlook templates, or text files.

> Instead of copying the content of a large note and pasting it into a document, you can save the note as an RTF file type and open it in a word processor.

Outlook provides two print styles you can use—Table Style and Memo Style—for printing copies of your notes (see Figure 12.12). Use Table style to print a list of your notes or Memo style to print individual notes. For most views, you'll choose your print style; however, Icon view supports Memo Style only.

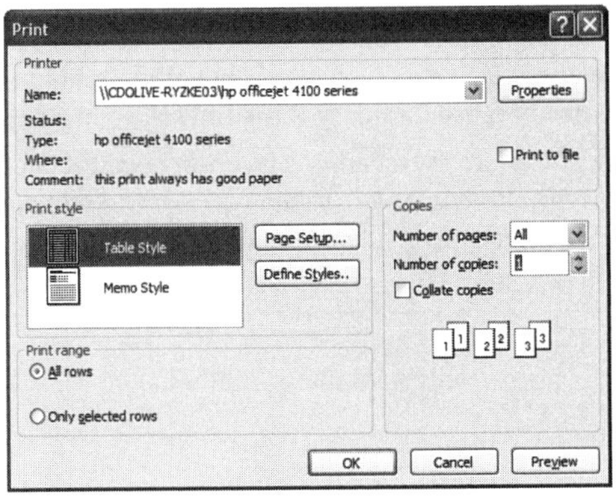

FIGURE 12.12

Notes' Print dialog has two print styles to choose from when you're using a Table view.

Memo style prints just one note per page. When the notes are short, use the Table style to print your notes on one page. This style offers limited configuration settings beyond the type of paper used.

When a Table Style printout is selected, the printout contains all the fields exactly as they're seen on the screen, including AutoPreview, if enabled. Notes that contain fewer than 256 characters of text might print in their entirety when AutoPreview is enabled.

Emailing Notes

It's easy to send your notes to other people: just drag and drop the note on the Inbox or any mail folder. A new message form opens with the text of the note in the body of the message. The first line of the note is used for the subject and the note's last modified date is added to the message.

When you select multiple notes and drop them on the Inbox, one message is created with the contents of the notes in the message body. The subject field is left blank.

You can send notes as attachments, too. If you've already started an email message, choose the Insert File, Item toolbar selection when using Word as your editor or Insert, Item menu with the Outlook editor, browse to the Notes folder, and select the note. When you select the note first, you can use Ctrl+F, or right-click and choose Forward Note.

Organizing Your Notes

After you create many notes, you need to organize them, either using folders or views. In some cases, creating additional note folders makes sense, but you can create custom views to show certain notes. If you get in the habit of using note colors to categorize notes, a simple By Color view might be all you need to be organized.

Outlook includes several predefined views:

- Icon; choose from Small Icons, Large Icons, or List
- Notes list; similar to the view used in the Inbox
- Last Seven Days
- By Category
- By Color

You can customize these views or create new custom views (see Figure 12.13). Right-click on the row of field names to access the Customize Current View dialog or define new views using View, Arrange By, Current View, Define View. When using Icon view, right-click in any open space and select Customize Current View.

FIGURE 12.13

This view uses the Notes List view with the notes grouped by date. Shared Notes is available for Exchange server users only.

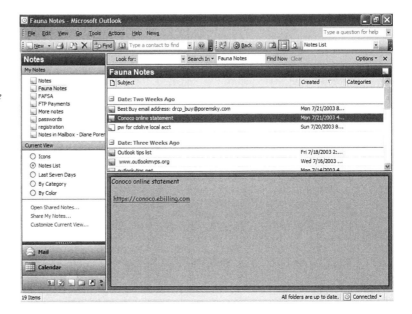

Keyboard Shortcuts

Many users, myself included, use the mouse for everything—sometimes out of habit and others times because it's the only way we know how to access the features. Using the keyboard is faster because you don't need to remove your hands from the keyboard and it's well worth the effort to learn the keyboard shortcuts. Many of these shortcuts work with the other Outlook items, so you need to learn only one set of shortcuts.

Table 12.1 lists the keyboard shortcuts you'll use with Outlook's notes.

TABLE 12.1 Keyboard Shortcuts You'll Find Useful When Working with Notes

Keystroke	Action
Shift+Ctrl+N	New note
Ctrl+N	New note when Outlook is opened to the Notes folder
Escape	Close open note
Ctrl+D	Delete open note
Ctrl+D or Delete key	Delete selected note from list view
Ctrl+E	Center text
Ctrl+R	Block text right
Ctrl+L	Return to left block

Keystroke	Action
Ctrl+I	Insert tab
Ctrl+F	Forward selected note using email
Ctrl+P	Print
Ctrl+S	Save
Shift+Ctrl+V	Move selected note to new folder
Shift+Ctrl+F	Advanced Find

Summary

This hour showed you how to use tasks and notes. You learned how to use tasks, assign tasks to others, and how to view your own tasks. You also learned how to use the features that notes have and how to use notes more effectively.

Q&A

Q The large note is too small. Can I change its size?

A The size of the small, medium, and large default note size is hard-coded and can't be changed. However, you can drag the edges of individual notes to resize them. Because the size and screen position are persistent, the note will open at your custom size or shape and in the same location the next time you open it.

Other options available to you include double-clicking the title of a note to resize it to full-screen size. Double-click the note a second time to return it to its original size. If you save a note as a template, notes created from the template are the size of the note that was used for the template.

Q I dropped an email in Notes and can only see the beginning of the message. I don't have scrollbars. How can I read the entire note?

A As you've discovered, the note form doesn't have scrollbars. There are at least three ways you can read the entire message, though. I prefer to drag the sides of the note and make it large enough so that the entire note is visible. When a note is resized and then closed, the size is remembered and it will always open at the new size.

If you want the note to stay small, you can double-click on the title bar to maximize the note, and then double-click it again to restore the note's size.

If you really want to scroll the note, use the arrow keys or the Page Up and Page Down keys to move around the note. If you want to use your mouse, you must select some text and scroll to select the rest of the message.

12

Q I emailed some tasks home and received them as messages with the task details in it, not a task form.

A When you email tasks—especially when you're sending the task to an Internet email account—you need to ensure that RTF formatting is enabled for the recipient's address. When Outlook sends RTF, it converts the message to HTML format to ensure compatibility with all email programs; however, converting the message to HTML also converts tasks and other Outlook forms to normal messages.

Double-click on the address in the To field and select Send using Rich Text Format in the Internet format field of Internet Properties. If a contact form opens, double-click again in the E-mail Address field to open the Internet Properties dialog.

Hour 13

Keeping a Journal

Anyone who needs to keep a diary of his or her activities will appreciate Outlook's journal. With the journal, you can automatically record specific events such as phone calls, emails sent and received, and documents that were edited (including the length of time they were open), or create journal entries as you work.

In this hour, you'll learn about

- Setting up the journal to record your activities automatically
- Creating journal entries as you work
- Customizing journal entry types
- Using views

By the end of this hour, you'll have a new understanding of the usefulness of the journal and discover new ways to use it.

Overview of Journal Features

The journal can record the phone calls you initiate from Outlook contacts, all your emails, task and meeting requests, and responses for selected contacts. This enables you to easily go back and verify that you sent an email or see when you edited a document or made a phone call.

Included in the activities you can automatically record in the journal are

- Email that you send and receive to selected contacts
- Task requests and responses
- Meeting requests, responses, and cancellations
- Telephone calls you initiate from a contact
- Office documents you work on

By automatically recording the documents you work on, email sent to specific contacts, and phone calls you make, the journal keeps logs of your activity. Journal entries also include the elapsed time along with the event, which is particularly useful to anyone who needs to know how long she worked on a document or spent on a phone call.

When you use the File, New, Journal Entry menu selection to create new journal entries, you're limited in the entry types you can choose. These predefined entry types cover basic business events, such as

- Letters, documents, and faxes you send or receive
- Telephone calls or conversations
- Notes you take
- Remote sessions you participate in

This list is hard-coded and, although you can't type a new entry type in the field, you can edit the Registry to add new entry types. The instructions needed to edit the Registry are later in this hour.

Understanding the Journal Form

The journal form contains only a few basic fields (see Figure 13.1):

- Subject
- Entry Type
- Company
- Start Time—includes time and date fields
- Duration
- Notes
- Contacts
- Categories

After you've entered the information in the fields, click the Save button and your journal item is finished.

FIGURE 13.1

The journal form contains just a few fields that must be filled in. When you use automatic journaling, many of these fields are completed for you.

Using the Journal

You can configure the journal to create journal entries for you when you work on Office documents or Outlook items. When journal items are created automatically, the amount of time the document is left open is also recorded.

Not all activities you might want included in the journal can be automatically created. You'll have to create journal entries for these items if you want to track all of your activities.

Creating a journal entry takes just a small amount of effort and is well worth it. For example, if you need to locate a document, it's often easier to use the journal to go back a few months and find the journal entry for the document you worked on than it is to search your computer's drive. As long as you remember approximately when you created the document, using views or Outlook's Advanced Find to find the journal entry is faster than using the Windows search utility to search your computer's hard drive for a filename you can't remember.

One reason many people give for not using the journal is that journaling causes your mail folder to grow very large. When you configure the journal to automatically create entries for many of your contacts and for all Office documents, you might end up with several hundred entries at the end of each week, many of which offer little or no additional value. Unless you use AutoArchive to clean out the journal regularly, you might have thousands of items in the journal.

13

Configuring the Journal

You can configure the journal to track all emails you send to specific persons, record the Office documents you work on, and track meeting and task requests and responses.

Journaling is disabled by default. The first time you select the Journal folder, a dialog opens asking whether you want to enable journaling. If you need to track only email and other Outlook items associated with specific contacts, the Activities tab on a contact form can be used instead of the journal and you should select No.

If you choose Yes, the Journal Options dialog opens, as shown in Figure 13.2. You can change your configuration for journal options at any time using the dialog in Tools, Options, Preferences tab, Journal Options.

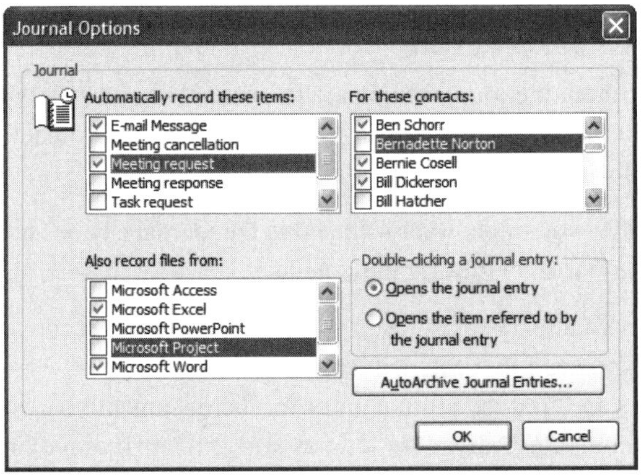

FIGURE 13.2

Use the Journal Options dialog to select the activities you want to automatically record in the journal.

Add a check for the contacts, document types, and meeting and task requests for the journal entries you want to create automatically.

Automatic journal settings apply to the user logon, not to your Outlook profile. When you share your computer logon with another person, changes that person makes to the journal settings affect your profile, too.

The dialog contains three sections you'll use to configure the automatic recording of your activities. The items and contacts you choose in the top sections determine what is journaled automatically.

- Automatically Record These Items—Select the activities that you want to record from this list.

- For These Contacts—Only activities involving the selected contacts are recorded.

- Also Record Files from— Select the programs you want to allow to automatically create journal entries. Only the programs listed support automatic journaling.

For example, journal entries for Automatically Record These Items selections are created only if the contact is selected in the For These Contacts list box, not for every person you exchange email with.

> To be listed in the For These Contacts list, the contacts need to be stored in your default Contacts folder. Contents of other Contacts folders aren't included in this list.
>
> When you add a new name to your Contacts folder, the name is added to the For These Contacts list but isn't checked. You'll have to open the Journal Options dialog and select the new contacts if you want to automatically journal messages to and from your new contacts.

Along with the items checked in the Automatically Record These Items list, journal entries are automatically created for phone calls to the contacts selected in the For These Contacts list when you initiate a call to the contact using the Actions, Call Contact menu on an open contacts form.

The third section, Also Record Files from, contains the list of Office document types that Outlook is capable of tracking and recording. Outlook supports the automatic journaling of documents created with Access, Excel, PowerPoint, and Word. If Project or Visio is installed, documents from those applications can be automatically journaled as well.

> Any VBA-enabled application can be programmed for automatic journaling. See the documentation for the application or search online for the specific VBA code needed because it varies with the source application.

13

The remaining section found on this dialog contains the settings for the default action for opening journal entries when you double-click on an item. The choices are Opens the Journal Entry and Opens the Item Referred to by the Journal Entry.

In most cases, it's more convenient to open the item directly, instead of opening the journal entry. Regardless of your selection, you can right-click on any journal entry and choose whether to Open Journal Entry or Open Item Referred To.

The last setting you need to configure from this dialog is the AutoArchive setting. You should configure AutoArchive Journal Settings if you're journaling activities for a large number of contacts; otherwise, your message store might grow too large.

Task: Enable Journaling for Specific Contacts

Normally, you would use the Tools, Options, Journal Options dialog to enable contacts for automatic journaling. However, it's time-consuming to mark each item. You can also enable contacts for journaling from a contact form's All Fields tab or by using a Table view in the Contacts folder.

Using views to enable or disable your contacts for automatic journaling is the easiest way to set or change the status for a large number of contacts:

1. Open your Contacts folder and choose Phone List view (select View, Arrange By, Current View, Phone List).

2. Scroll to the right; the Journal field is the next-to-last column.

3. Add check marks in the Journal field for each contact you want to be automatically journaled; remove check marks to stop automatic journaling for a contact.

If you have a large number of contacts to change, right-click on the row of field names and choose Group By Box and then drag the Journal field to the Group By box. You can now select and drag multiple contacts between the Journal: No and Journal: Yes groupings, as shown in Figure 13.3.

You can also enable journaling by opening a contact, selecting the All Fields tab, finding the Journal field, and changing the entry to Yes. But that isn't an efficient way to enable journaling for your contacts. However, when you want to enable journaling for all new contacts, you can create a custom form with this field set to Yes:

1. Open the desired contact to the All Fields tab.

2. Choose All Contact Fields in the Select from field.

3. Scroll the list of fields and locate Journal.

4. Enter Yes as the Journal's field value.

▼ 5. Open the Tools, Forms menu selection and then choose Publish Form As.

6. Type a name for the form in the Display Name box.

7. Click Publish and then close the open form, choosing No when asked whether you want to save it.

FIGURE 13.3

Change the journal setting for many contacts at once by grouping contacts by the Journal field. Notice the different icon used on journaled items.

Next you need to make the new form your default contact form:

1. Right-click on the Contacts folder and choose Properties from the shortcut menu.

2. On the General tab, look for the When Posting to this Folder, Use list. Select the form you just published and then click OK.

All new contacts you create will use the form you published with journaling enabled. If you want to stop journaling, repeat the last two steps and select the IPM.Contacts form
▲ instead.

13

Creating Journal Entries

Although many people are drawn to the journal for its capability to record many events automatically, you can create your own entries for anything you want to keep in your journal, including home and car repairs or visits to your doctor. Because Outlook doesn't have entry types for all the types of items you might need, you'll have to make do with one of the existing entry types or create new entry types that meet your unique needs.

See Hour 19, "Managing Your Data," to learn more about using archives.

You might also want to create a second or third Journal folder with different archive settings on each, enabling you to keep business and personal entries separate or to archive your business entries more often than you archive home repairs.

When you use more than one Journal folder, all automatic journal entries are added to the default Journal folder. To use the other Journal folders, you'll have to open the folder before creating the journal entry or move the journal entries to the folder later.

You can't select the folder that Outlook uses as the default Journal folder; Outlook creates it for you.

Task: Create Journal Items Manually

Automatic journaling is the easiest and most reliable way to create journal entries, but not all activities you might want journaled support automatic journaling. For those activities, you'll have to create the journal entries yourself. Because the journal supports automatic creation of entries only from the other Office programs, you might discover that you have to create many entries manually:

1. Select New, Journal entry to open a new journal form (refer to Figure 13.1).
2. Enter a Subject and select an Entry Type for your new journal entry.
3. Enter the Start time and date.
4. Click the Start Timer button if you need to record the duration.
5. Enter notes in the Notes field, insert links to attachments, and associate Contacts or Categories with the journal item.

When you've finished entering notes, click the Save and Close button. The timer stops and the duration field updates to the elapsed time. As you can see, the hardest part is remembering to create the entry when you start the task.

If you journal the same activity often, you can complete the fields that don't change and save the form as a template. When you need to create a journal entry, open the template. To make the template easier to use, you can create a shortcut to it on your toolbar or add it to the Shortcut section of the

Navigation bar. When you publish the form to the Journal folder, it's listed
on the Actions menu when the folder is selected.

Creating Journal Items for Other Applications

When you need a journal entry for an application that isn't listed on the Also Record
Files from list, you can create the journal item manually and then insert a shortcut to the
document.

If you're inserting documents or files, use the Insert button on the toolbar. You can also
use the Insert menu and choose between inserting files, Outlook items, or OLE objects.
When you insert file attachments, you have four insert options:

- Insert—Insert the file as an attachment
- Insert As Text—Available only for text files
- Insert As Attachment
- Insert As Hyperlink

You should avoid Insert As Attachment, especially with larger files; otherwise, your message store might grow very large. Using the Insert As Hyperlink option keeps the size of
your mailbox smaller and is the default when a journal entry is created automatically.

If you use multiple computers or are going to send the journal item to
another Outlook user, you'll want to insert files or Outlook items as attachments because shortcuts might not work correctly.

Inserting objects enables you to display and edit most OLE-aware documents in the
notes field of the journal form. You can insert existing documents or create new documents. However, the journal entries are often larger than they would be if you inserted
the document as an attachment.

You can also insert any item from Outlook's message store as text only, as an attachment, or as a shortcut to the item. In most cases, you'll want to use the As Shortcut to
the Item or As Text Only setting, rather than duplicating an existing item.

Choose As Attachment or As Text to ensure that you always have the original item saved with the journal entry. Hyperlinks fail if you move, rename,
or delete documents or Outlook items that the journal's hyperlinks point to.

13

Not all applications for which you might want to create journal entries are listed in the Journal Options dialog. However, you can add any program to the list of entry types on the journal form by editing the Registry. See the task "Create Your Own Journal Entry Types" later in this hour for instructions. However, although you can add additional applications to the Also Record Files from list, if an application isn't VBA-enabled, the entries aren't automatically recorded without additional programming.

Journaling Appointments and Tasks

Appointments and tasks aren't automatically journaled. However, you can create journal entries for these items with very little typing by dragging the calendar or task item to the Journal folder and dropping it in the journal. This creates a new journal entry with the fields already filled in with information taken from the calendar or task item.

For example, when you drag an appointment from your calendar to the Journal folder, you create a new journal entry with the subject of the appointment used for the journal. The start time, duration, contacts, and categories are also the same as on the appointment. A shortcut to the appointment is added to the notes field of the journal entry. After adding notes about the meeting, you need only save and close the journal entry.

You can also create new journal entries and insert calendar or task items using the Insert, Item menu selection. However, you'll need to complete the journal fields yourself.

Journaling Email

Email is one of the file types available in the Tools, Options, Preferences, Journal Options, Automatically Record These Items list. When you send or receive email to someone who isn't in your Contacts folder or who isn't on your For These Contacts list, you can drag the message to the Journal folder to create an entry for that item.

When you're using the Navigation bar and want to drag a message to another folder to create a journal, task, or contact item from the message, select and drag the message to the folder button at the bottom of the Navigation bar. Let go of the mouse button to drop the message on the folder icon to create an item in the default folder, or hover over the button to open the folders and select a different folder to create the item in.

When you drag an email to the Journal folder, the message subject is used for the journal subject and the date and time the message was received are the start date and time. The Contact field contains the sender's name if a contact exists or the email address if you don't have a contact record for the sender, and a shortcut to the message is added to the journal body (see Figure 13.4).

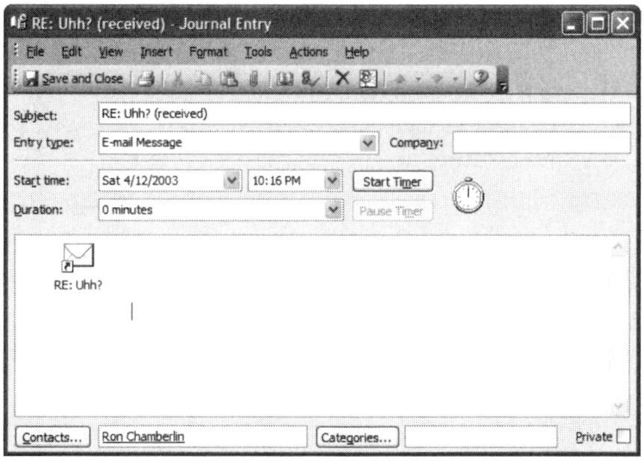

FIGURE 13.4

FIGURE 13.4

A journal item created from a message has all the fields filled in and a shortcut to the message attached. Sent items include (sent) *in the subject line.*

When you hold the right mouse button while dragging the message to the Journal folder, you can choose between creating a journal entry that includes a shortcut to the message, a copy of the message as an attachment, or one that moves the message to the journal entry as an attachment.

> You can move the message to the Journal folder by right-clicking on the message in the inbox, choosing Move to Folder, and then selecting the Journal folder from the folder list. This creates a journal entry with the message attached.

Journaling Your Phone Calls

Although Phone Call isn't listed in the Automatically Record These Items list, when you initiate a call using the Actions, Call Contact menu selection and the contact is in the For These Contacts list, a new journal form loads automatically.

When you have the journal automatically creating journal entries, the journal form's fields pull name and company data from the contact form, the Time and Date fields update to the current time and date, and the timer starts. You don't have to do anything except type notes and save the journal item when the call ends.

The format used in the Subject field is Phone Call—[*contact name*]. If the contact's Company field contains an entry, the Company field on the journal form is completed. The contact also links to the journal item, permitting you to locate the journal entry from the contact's Activities tab.

13

> You can show Phone Call on the Automatically Record These Items list by editing the Registry. Open the Registry Editor, navigate to the `HKEY_CURRENT_USER\Software\Microsoft\Shared Tools\Outlook\Journaling\Phone Call` key, and change the `AutoJournaled` value to `1`.

When you make a phone call to a contact using the Actions, Call Contact menu selection, a journal item isn't created for you unless you add a check to the box Create a New Journal Entry When Starting New Call. If you decide after you begin the call that you need to record the call in your journal, you can open a journal form and fill out all the fields (see Figure 13.5).

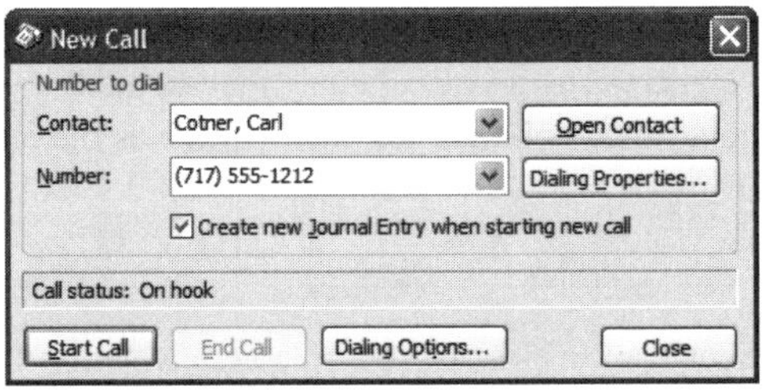

Figure 13.5

Use Outlook's New Call dialog to place calls using phone numbers stored in your contacts.

If you need to call a number that isn't in your contacts, you can type it into the New Call dialog and automatically journal the call when you check Create New Journal Entry.

> You might notice that sometimes the Create New Journal Entry When Starting New Call box is already checked when you start a call and the contact isn't in your For These Contacts list. That happens when you make several calls in a row without closing the New Call dialog. You'll have to uncheck the box to prevent the call from being journaled.

Journaling Incoming and Outgoing Phone Calls

When youdon't use Outlook's dialer to place your calls, you can journal your incoming and outgoing phone calls by creating a journal entry yourself. Open a new journal form using the File, New, Journal Entry menu selection or Ctrl+Shift+J, and complete the form with information about your phone call. If you need to differentiate between incoming and outgoing calls, create custom entry types or use categories. See the next task to learn how to create your own entry types.

Task: Create Your Own Journal Entry Types

▲ TASK

The journal comes with a predefined list of entry types that is limited and might not meet your specific needs. This list isn't editable, restricting you to selecting an entry type from the list. However, the Entry Type list is stored in the Registry and you can change what you see in the Entry Type drop-down list.

> You should always export the section of the Registry you're working on before you begin, just in case you make a mistake.

1. Open the Registry Editor by selecting the Start button. Select <u>R</u>un, type **regedit** in the box, and then click OK.

2. When you have the Registry Editor open, you need navigate to this key: HKEY_CURRENT_USER\Software\Microsoft\Shared Tools\Outlook\Journaling.

   Click on the plus sign (+) beside HKEY_CURRENT_USER to expand it, and then expand Software, Microsoft, Shared Tools, Outlook and finally Journaling by clicking on the plus signs (+) next to the names.

   After you expand the Journaling key, your Registry Editor should look like the screen in Figure 13.6.

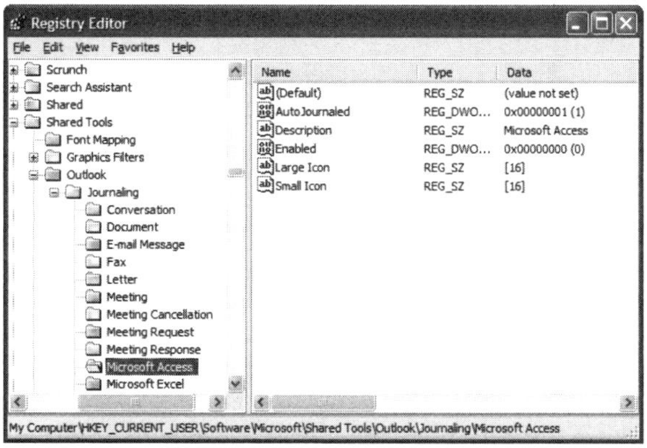

FIGURE 13.6

Create new entry types by adding Registry keys. If you want to remove some entry types, you can delete them from the Registry.

13

Now you're ready to add your new entry type.

3. As a precaution, export the keys by right-clicking on Journaling and selecting Export. If you make a mistake and want to restore the original entry types, find the .reg file you created and double-click it.

▼ 4. Right-click on `Journaling` again and choose New, Key. Type a name for your new key. You'll want to use a short but descriptive name for your key.

5. Now you need to add values to your new key. You'll need a minimum of two values: Description and Large Icon. Right-click in the right side of the Registry Editor and choose New, String Value. Type **Description** to replace New Value #1. Double-click on `Description` and type the text you want to show in the Entry Type field. This text doesn't have to match the name of the key, but it should be similar.

6. Repeat step 3, naming the new string value **Large Icon** and entering a value inside square brackets so that the value data looks like this: [12]. Figure 13.7 shows this example. This value controls the icon that displays in the Journal folder. If you look through the other keys, you'll see what numbers represent other icons.

FIGURE **13.7**

When you've added your key and the values, it should look something like this.

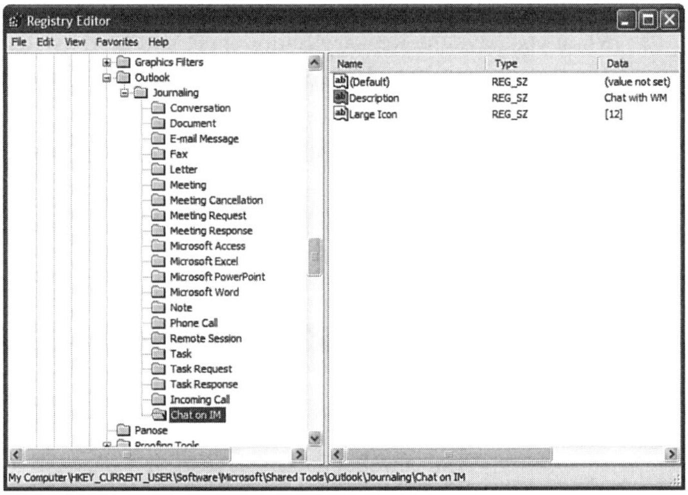

7. Right-click on your new key and export it. You can then use the .reg file to install the key on other computers.

8. Open a new journal form. Your new entry type should be listed in the Entry Type drop-down list.

▲ 9. Close the Registry Editor.

You might have also noticed that there are entries for the other values, such as `AutoJournal` and `Enabled`. `AutoJournal` is a `DWORD` value that controls whether the entry displays in the Automatically Record These Items or Also Records File from lists. If `AutoJournal` is present, a value of **0** means that it's hidden from the lists; a value of 1 means that it's displayed in one of the lists. Enabled with a value 1 means that the box beside the entry is checked and 0 indicates that it's unchecked. Because your custom entry types won't be automatically journaled, you won't need to create these values.

Organizing Your Journal Entries

When you open the Journal folder, you'll see the default By Type view: a timeline grouped by entry type. This view has the date running left to right across the top of the pane, with the journal entries listed under the dates. The timeline view default shows seven days, as shown in Figure 13.8.

FIGURE 13.8

The default view for the Journal folder is a Timeline view.

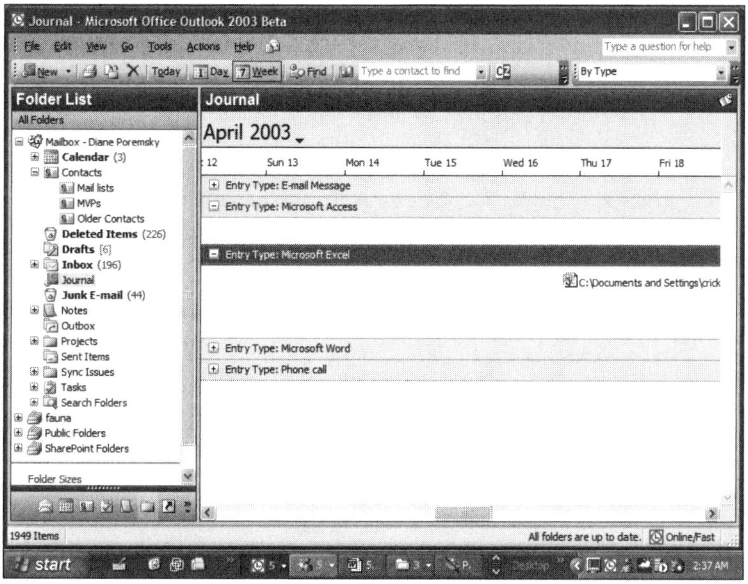

To move around the journal, in addition to scrolling, you can right-click on the row with the month and year to display the date picker or right-click on the date scale and choose Go to Date. Although the Outlook bar has a link for opening shared journals, only Exchange Server users will be able to open or use shared Journal folders.

One of the first changes you might want to make in a Timeline view is to reduce the size of the font used for the month and year. Right-click on the bar where the month and year are displayed, choose Other Settings, and then adjust the size of the Upper Scale Font in the Format Timeline View dialog, as shown in Figure 13.9.

13

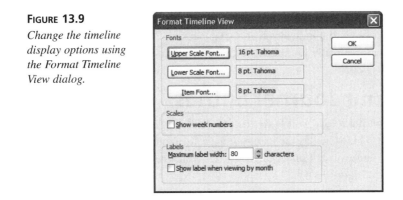

FIGURE 13.9
Change the timeline display options using the Format Timeline View dialog.

Other options you can change from the Format Timeline View dialog include showing week numbers and changing the maximum width of the labels displayed with the icons. You can also control whether the icon label displays when viewing a month in the timeline.

Use the View menu to select different views of your Journal folder, including timelines grouped by contact or by category, Table views showing all items or filtered by the last seven days, or limiting the display to phone calls only.

The Preview Pane is turned off on the Journal folder by default; however, you can turn it on using the View, Preview Pane menu selection. You can use the Preview Pane with any view, including the timeline, and can see all the journal fields in the Preview Pane. For security reasons, you can't open attached Outlook items from the Preview Pane, but you can open attached documents without opening the journal entries. In most views, you'll want the Preview Pane on the bottom of the window to maximize the viewing area for Timeline views, if you use it at all.

Using Views

After you create journal entries, you can use views to organize your journal in these ways:

- By Type—The default view; based on the Timeline view with items grouped by entry type
- By Contact—Based on the Timeline view and grouped by contact
- By Category—Based on the Timeline view and grouped by category
- Entry List—Based on the table list format; initially sorted by creation date
- Last Seven Days—Based on the table list format; filtered to display entries created within the past seven days
- Phone Calls—Based on a table list; filtered to display only phone calls

You might prefer to view your journal in a traditional calendar format. If so, you can create a custom view using a day/week/month format layout.

> The journal can display the week numbers in a Timeline view. Right-click on the bar where the month and year are displayed and choose Other Settings. Then check the Show Week Numbers box in the Scales section.

The journal comes with six predefined views, using Timeline or Table layouts. You can customize these views or create your own custom views. You aren't limited to using Timeline or Table views with the journal: Day/Week/Month views also work well, although Icon and Card views do not.

These Timeline views group the journal entries:

- By Type
- By Contact
- By Category

Each of these views defaults to showing the journaled items for the week. You can change this to one day, segmented by the hour, or one month by clicking the Day or Month toolbar button. You can return to a seven-day view by clicking the Week button.

The remaining preconfigured views use a Table view with filters controlling what you see:

- Entry List—No filter used
- Last Seven Days—Filtered to display entries created within the past seven days
- Phone Calls—Filtered to display only phone calls

You can customize any of these views and create new views using your own criteria.

Customizing the Journal View

Journal comes with several views, all of which are customizable: Right-click on the top row of the journal and choose Customize Current View. The Custom View Organizer opens, enabling you to customize the current view to your liking. If you want to restore the default settings for the view, select the Reset Current View button at the bottom of the dialog.

> When a button or option is dimmed, it isn't available for the type of view you're creating or modifying.

If you don't like the predefined views or need more views, you can create new views:

1. Select View, Arrange By, Current View, Define Views to open the Custom View Organizer.

2. Select New to create a new view.

3. Enter a name for your view and select the type of view you want to create. Day/Week/Month makes a nice Journal view; Icon and Card views aren't very useful Journal views.

4. The Customize View dialog opens and you can set the options you want to see in the view (see Figure 13.10).

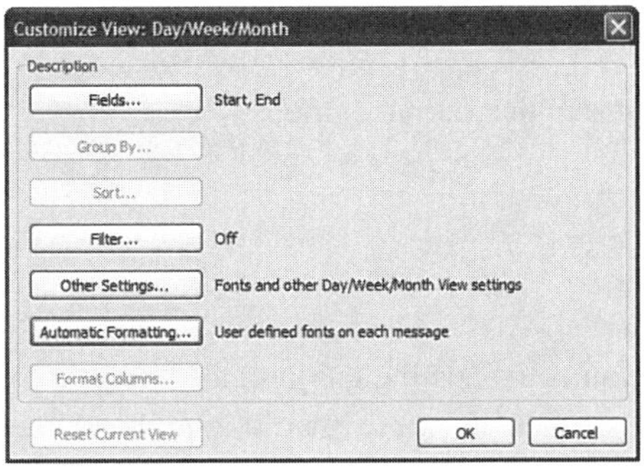

FIGURE 13.10

The Customize View dialog lets you tailor the Journal view to your liking.

Customize View: Day/Week/Month	
Description	
Fields...	Start, End
Group By...	
Sort...	
Filter...	Off
Other Settings...	Fonts and other Day/Week/Month View settings
Automatic Formatting...	User defined fonts on each message
Format Columns...	
Reset Current View	OK Cancel

The options available to customize your view depend on the type of view you're creating. To use the view now, select Apply View when you're finished customizing it. You can apply the view at any time by selecting it by name from the Current View toolbar button or the View, Arrange By, Current View menu selection.

Instead of creating a new view from scratch, you can select an existing view in the Custom View Organizer, click Copy to create a copy of the existing view, and then choose Modify to edit it.

Viewing Journal Items for a Contact

Contacts provide an additional way to view journal entries: from the Activities tab of an opened contact form. In fact, many frequent journal users never use the Journal folder; they use only the Activities tab.

When you want to view the journaled items associated with a contact, open the contact and select the Activities tab. Select Journal from the Show: list to show only journal items.

Summary

In this hour, you learned how to use the journal to record your activities. You discovered how to control what activities are journaled automatically and how to use a Contacts folder view to quickly enable or disable journaling for your contacts. You also found out how to create your own journal entry types.

Q&A

Q My journal entries no longer show up under the Activities tab for my contacts. Can I fix it without opening each journal item and selecting the contact?

A It sounds as if you used import or export to combine PST files or moved the PST to a new location and broke the links between the contacts and the journal. Next time, move the items instead. Moving items doesn't break the links because you aren't creating new items.

You can use a VBA macro called ReconnectLinks to repair the links for most of your contacts. Look for a link to the article "Making Contact" at `http://www.slipstick.com/addins/journal.htm`.

You might need to update some entries by typing in their names, but the majority of the links will be fixed using ReconnectLinks.

13

PART IV

Using Outlook's Advanced Features

Hour

Hour **14**

Organizing Outlook

Outlook contains a lot of data, including all of your email, contacts, appointments, tasks—often at least a couple of years' worth. If you send and receive a lot of email, you could have thousands of messages in your inbox. Keeping up with it is all but impossible. Or is it?

Outlook has a number of features that can help you manage your email and other Outlook items. In this hour, you learn about

- Using Organizer
- Understanding the Rules Wizard
- Using the Junk E-mail filter

This hour includes some information about views because Organizer's Using Colors tab creates views, not rules, to apply color-coding to messages. Organizer also includes a Using Views tab that enables you to apply new views to your folders from the Organize pane. However, please refer to Hour 3, "Navigating the Outlook Interface," for complete information about views.

Using Organizer

Organizer provides a simple interface, with simple options, to move messages, change views, and create automatic formatting rules. It's great for beginners and everyone else to access Outlook's organizational features from one screen or create an automatic formatting view. After a while, the Organize pane lacks the features even beginners need. Using the Rules Wizard or Customize Views dialog provides more options and is accessible from the Organize pane. Choose Tools, Organize to open the Organize pane, as seen in Figure 14.1.

FIGURE **14.1**

Use the Organize pane to move messages to new folders, to use colors to highlight messages, and to use views to control what you see in the message list.

You'll have more options to use with automatic formatting views if you use the Customize Views dialog. Should you have a problem remembering how to get to Customize Views, Automatic Formatting, or the Rules Wizard, you can use the shortcuts on each tab to take you there.

The tab Using Folders enables you to move messages to new folders without creating a rule. Organizer gives you just one choice: moving messages to somewhere. You can select an existing folder to move the messages to or create a new folder. If you want to create a rule to move all future messages to the folder, you'll need to select Rules and Wizards. You can reach the Rules Wizard from the Organize pane by clicking the Rules and Alerts button in the right corner. The Organize pane can be used on any folder and works equally well when you select several messages and then move them as it does with just one message.

An alternative to using the Organize pane to move messages is on the right-click context menu. Select the message or messages you want to move, right-click, and select Move to Folder. You can also create new rules from the right-click menu.

Although it might appear that color-coding is a feature of the Rules Wizard, it's really a view, not a rule. It also involves more than changing the color of the message header shown in the message list: You can change the fonts and formatting as well. You'll need to use the Automatic Formatting dialog to change fonts because Organizer is limited to just applying colors to messages to or from a person.

In Figure 14.2, messages from a mailing list are highlighted in red, whereas messages sent only to me are shown in blue. You can disable highlighting messages sent only to me from Organizer, but you'll need to open the Automatic Formatting dialog to remove other automatic formatting rules.

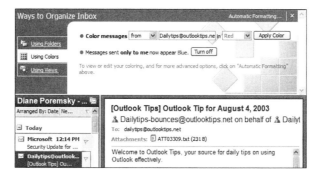

FIGURE 14.2

Use colors to highlight messages for better visibility.

One of the best examples of using color is to create a view in which all messages from someone important, such as your boss, use a large red font. Less important messages can use small gray text.

Refer to Hour 3 to learn more about using views and automatic formatting.

The final tab, Using Views, enables you to select existing views only. If you need to customize a view, use the Customize Views button in the upper right to open the Customize Views dialog.

You'll enjoy more functionality by adding views to the Navigation Pane. Select View, Arrange By, Show Views in Navigation Pane.

Organizer works with each folder type, although the actual options available will vary. Non-mail folders have a Using Categories tab, which you use to assign categories to the selected items or to create new categories.

Because there are several different ways to add categories to items, including right-clicking on any item and choosing Categories, it doesn't make much sense to use Organizer to assign categories, but it's there if you want to use it.

Different views can be applied using the Advanced toolbar's Current View drop-down list or from the Navigation Pane when views are listed in the Navigation Pane, which is enabled using View, Arrange By, Show Views in Navigation Pane. For this reason, using the Organize pane with non-mail folders is less convenient and useful only if you want a very simple screen and limited options.

Using Rules

Rules, or *filters* as they're called in some email programs, are an important method for email management. Uses for rules include moving messages to other folders; adding flags, reminders, or categories to messages; and sending replies to messages that meet specific conditions.

Rules can be used for spam control, although they really aren't the best way to manage unwanted mail, especially considering the large amounts of spam many people get. Instead, you should use the Junk E-mail filter included in Outlook 2003 or one of the numerous third-party anti-spam programs that are available.

 Junk email filters work with POP3 and HTTP (Hotmail) when the full message is downloaded, and Exchange Server when you use a local store (cached mode).

Creating a Rule from a Message

Organizer is simple and builds simple rules, but it's not the only way to quickly make a simple rule. Right-click on any message and choose Create Rule. The dialog shown in Figure 14.3 opens.

Using Create Rules, you can create a rule using the From, To, or Subject field and display the item in the Desktop Alert dialog (shown in Figure 14.10), play a specific sound, or move the message to a folder.

FIGURE 14.3

The Create Rule dialog enables you to customize the conditions of a rule to suit your needs.

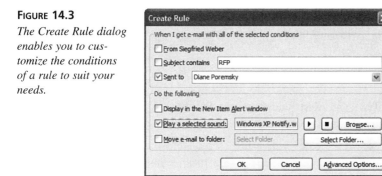

The A_dvanced Options button opens the Rules Wizard at the Select Conditions dialog, as shown later in Figure 14.6. Complete the rule using the wizard.

> You can select a message just by right-clicking on it; it doesn't have to be highlighted in blue. When a message has a dotted outline around it, any option you choose from the context menu applies to the item you right-clicked. This enables you to work with messages without loading them into the Reading Pane.

Using the Rules Wizard

To create more complex rules, you need Outlook's Rules Wizard. You can open the Rules Wizard dialog using the _T_ools, Ru_l_es and Alerts menu selection. Rules and Alerts is shown in Figure 14.4, although your dialog might not have any rules listed yet.

FIGURE 14.4

Use the Rules and Alerts dialog to create rules that help manage your messages.

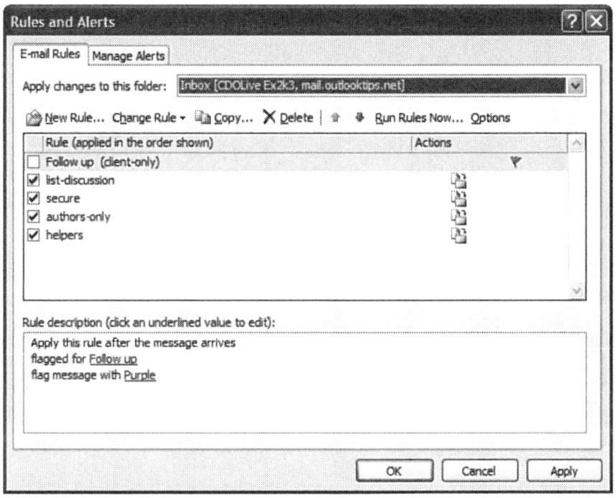

14

Use this dialog to manage your rules. From here, you can create new rules, edit existing rules, and run your existing rules on any mail folder.

Task: Create Rules

TASK ▼

To create a new rule:

1. Select Tools, Rules and Alerts menu (refer to Figure 14.4) and click the New Rule button to open the Rules Wizard.

2. For this exercise, we'll create a rule using a template, which is the default setting. Because I use two computers and send myself files by email, I have the files on both computers. I want to file the messages I send myself in a folder, so I'm choosing the first item, Move Messages from Someone to a Folder (see Figure 14.5).

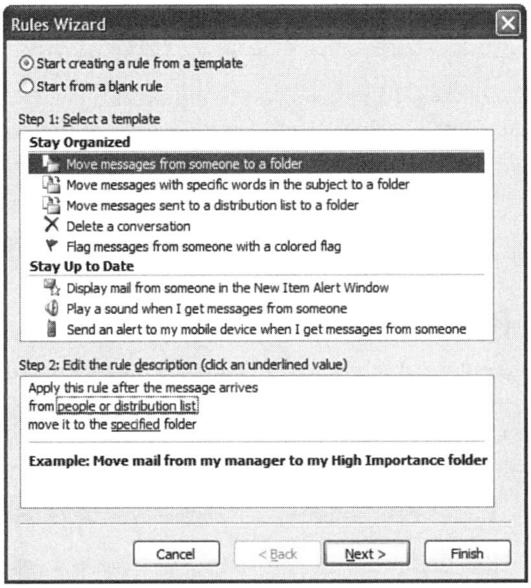

FIGURE 14.5

The rule description shows you what the selected template does.

The template I selected moves mail from people or distribution lists to a specified folder. When you need a rule that doesn't seem to fit any of the items listed, choose Start from a Blank Rule and then choose Check Messages When They Arrive or Check Messages After Sending.

3. If the selected template does exactly what you want, click on the underlined words in the description field. In this example, click on People or Distribution List and Specified folder.

▼

The Rule Address dialog opens so that you can choose people from your address book. You don't need to create contacts to use an address—just type the address in the To field.

Use the condition for specific words in the sender address to apply a rule to a partial address; for example, to flag all messages from Microsoft.com addresses.

4. If these are the only conditions and actions you need for your rule, click Finish. To choose additional conditions or actions, click Next.

5. After you click Next, the Rules Wizard presents you with a list of conditions from which you can choose (see Figure 14.6). When you add a check to a condition, it's entered in the rule description box at the bottom of the screen. Click on the underlined fields in the description box to complete the condition. Click Next when you're ready to select the actions.

FIGURE 14.6

You can choose as many conditions as you need from this list. However, each condition uses the AND operator to connect with the other conditions. The more conditions you have, the fewer messages you'll catch.

6. Now you must choose the action you want Outlook to perform when the conditions you've selected are met. My rule adds a purple flag and moves the messages to a folder (see Figure 14.7). Click Next after selecting the actions and completing the value fields.

14

▼

FIGURE 14.7

Select the actions you want to apply to messages that meet your conditions. Include the Stop Processing More Rules action in all your rules unless you want other rules to apply to the message.

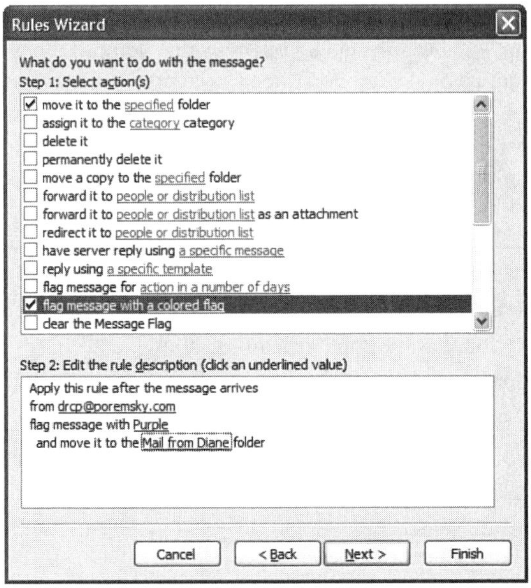

Unless Outlook is told otherwise, it checks every message with every rule, in the order the rules are listed in the Rules and Alerts dialog. When a message meets the conditions in two or more rules, the results might not be what you expected. You can prevent problems by using the Stop Processing More Rules action, found near the bottom of the actions list.

7. On the next screen, you can select exceptions to the rule you've defined. This feature is useful when you want a rule to apply to messages that meet specific conditions, except when a different condition exists. Click Next to continue.

8. You're now on the final page of the Rules Wizard (see Figure 14.8), which enables you to specify a name for the rule and to set a few basic options. In most cases, the default settings are what you want to use, except for the name of your rule. Outlook usually creates a really long name for most rules, and you might want to enter a shorter name. Add a check to Run This Rule on Messages Already in Inbox if you want to run the rule on messages you've already downloaded.

▲

Because you might create rules for future use that you don't currently need, the Turn On This Rule check box enables you to disable the rule temporarily.

FIGURE 14.8

The final step in the Rules Wizard enables you to assign a name to your new rule and run it on existing messages.

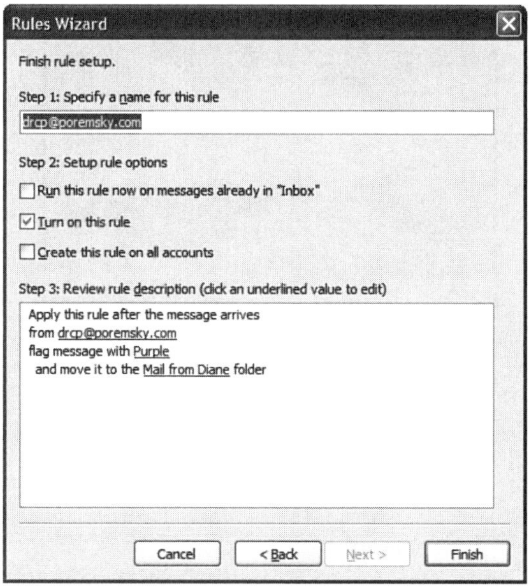

Rules Wizard

Finish rule setup.

Step 1: Specify a name for this rule

drcp@poremsky.com

Step 2: Setup rule options

☐ Run this rule now on messages already in "Inbox"

☑ Turn on this rule

☐ Create this rule on all accounts

Step 3: Review rule description (click an underlined value to edit)

Apply this rule after the message arrives
from drcp@poremsky.com
flag message with Purple
  and move it to the Mail from Diane folder

[Cancel] [< Back] [Next >] [Finish]

The Create This Rule on All Accounts option is available only when you have more than one email account that works with rules in your profile. It creates a copy of the rule for each account.

Keep in mind that rules do not run on HTTP accounts.

Fine-Tuning Your Rules

If you left Run This Rule unchecked and decide later that you want to run the rule on messages already in Outlook, you can choose Run Rules Now from the Rules and Alerts dialog (refer to Figure 14.4). When selected, the Run Rules Now dialog opens, as shown in Figure 14.9.

Run Rules Now enables you to apply rules to any folder at any time. When you create a rule specifically to use it later, deselect Turn On This Rule, shown previously in Figure 14.8. When you want to run the rule, open the Rules and Alerts dialog and choose Run Rules Now.

Run Rules Now is helpful when you want to delete or move sent items. If you create a rule to use when sending, the sent messages are copied, not moved. You can run a rule on the Sent folder later to move the messages.

14

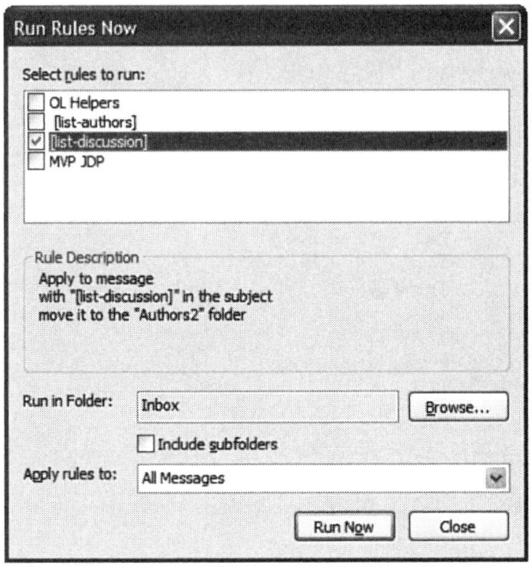

FIGURE 14.9

Use Run Rules Now to apply actions to messages later. You can apply the rule to all messages, only to unread messages, or only to messages marked as read.

Rules are stored in the message store in Outlook 2003. If you open the message store with an older version of Outlook, you risk losing your rules. Use the Options button on the Rules and Alerts dialog, as shown in Figure 14.4, to export your rules for safekeeping or to import to another computer.

Rules are not imported or exported when you use File, Import and Export to copy messages between message stores. You'll have to use the Rules and Alert's Option dialog to import and export rules.

If you're upgrading from an older version of Outlook, you can upgrade your existing rules to Outlook 2003's format from the Options dialog. After the rules are upgraded, they won't work with older versions of Outlook.

In most cases, the first time you run Outlook, it will offer to upgrade your rules. If you choose No and change your mind later, you can use Upgrade Now to convert them.

After you've created some rules, you can use the Rules and Alerts dialog to manage them. Using the buttons above the list of rules, you can open the New Rule dialog, make quick changes to the selected rule, copy or delete the selected rule, change the order in which rules are run, and import or export your rules using the Options dialog.

The Change Rule menu contains a list of the most popular actions and enables you to quickly add an action to an existing rule without opening the rule for editing. It displays only the dialogs you need to complete the rule, such as a dialog to choose the flag color. These menus are toggles, so any action applied using this menu is removed when you select the menu again.

Actions available on the Change Rule menu include

- Edit Rule Settings—Opens the Rules Wizard to the Select Conditions dialog, enabling you to edit the selected rule.
- Rename Rule—Enables you to rename the selected rule.

The following actions apply to the selected rule without opening the actions screen. Hold the Shift or Ctrl key while selecting rules to apply the action to all the selected rules.

- Display in the New Alert Window (see Figure 14.10).

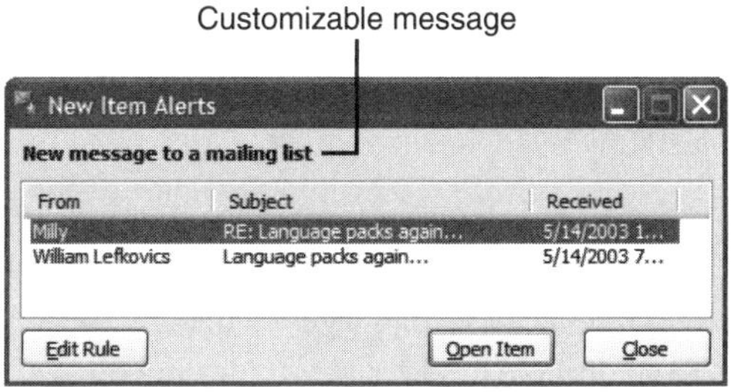

FIGURE 14.10

The New Alert window is a small window that contains a custom message and a list of new mail that meets the conditions of the rule. This isn't the same as the semitransparent desktop alert used for all new mail.

Customizable message

- Play a Sound
- Move to Folder
- Copy to Folder
- Mark As High Priority
- Mark As Low Priority
- Flag Message
- Delete Message

As mentioned previously, selecting an item from this menu toggles the action on or off.

14

Choose Copy when you need to create a rule that's similar to an existing rule because it's often easier to change the fields than it is to create the rule again.

When you no longer want a rule to run, you'll usually uncheck the box beside the rule name. When you're sure that you'll never need a rule again, select it and choose Delete.

Outlook runs rules in the order they're listed in Rules and Alerts. Use the blue arrow buttons to change the order in which the rules are run. The order of rules doesn't usually matter, especially if you use the Stop Processing More Rules action in all of your rules. However, if you're having problems with the wrong rules firing on certain messages, try rearranging the order of the rules. Select the rule, and then click the up or down arrow to move it.

As mentioned previously, look for Import and Export in Options.

Using Rules with Your Email Accounts

You can use the Rules Wizard on POP3 accounts, on Exchange Server accounts, and for the Inbox on IMAP accounts when you download the full message during a send and receive. Rules do not work on HTTP accounts, either as the messages are downloading or by using Run Rules Now.

Using rules with IMAP accounts has two limitations. First, for the rules to run automatically, the messages must be downloaded completely when you check for new mail. Second, you can't use a rule to move messages to another IMAP folder; however, you can move messages from an IMAP folder to a folder in your local message store.

You might notice that your rules have the On This Machine Only condition added. On This Machine Only is an Exchange Server option, and it's automatically added to all rules created for non-Exchange accounts because you can't store rules on the server for the other accounts. Use it when you access your Exchange mailbox from more than one computer and want a server-side rule to work only on one computer or need to force a rule to be client-side.

Outlook 2003 enables you to create rules specific to each account in your profile. These rules will run only on messages received on the specific account. When using this with POP3 accounts, use the Through the Specified Account condition in the Rules Wizard and select the proper account from the list. When the profile has both POP3 or Exchange Server accounts and an IMAP account, you must select the IMAP account in the Apply Changes to This Folder list.

> If you have multiple POP3 and IMAP accounts in your profile, you'll notice that the Apply Changes to This Folder drop-down list displays all of your IMAP accounts separately but all of your POP3 accounts are combined on one entry. This is because all POP3 and Exchange Server accounts use the same message store and the list applies to the Inbox folder used by the accounts.

Exchange Server users have two types of rules available: client-side rules that run only when Outlook is open and sever-side rules that run as new messages arrive.

When used in a rule, the following conditions and actions will create a client-side rule and will run only when Outlook is opened.

Conditions

- With specific words in recipient's address
- With specific words in sender's address
- Flagged for action
- Assigned to category
- With specific words in the subject or message, when multiple phrases are used

Actions

- Display a specific message in the New Alert window
- Display a desktop alert
- Flag message for action in a number of days
- Flag message with a colored flag
- Clear the message flag
- Assign it to a category
- Play a sound
- Start an application
- Run a script
- Print it
- Move it to the specified folder (not found in your mailbox, including public folders or in a PST)
- Move a copy to the specified folder (not found in your mailbox, including public folders or in a PST)

- Reply using a specific template
- Perform a custom action
- On this machine only

Rules used with Exchange server mailboxes are limited to 32KB of data. The exact number of rules available on the server side is dependent on the length of the condition or action used in each rule. You can have a greater number of rules if they're simple with short folder names or addresses, fewer when they're complex or contain long folder names.

Using Alerts

Outlook has three types of alerts: the desktop alert, which is semitransparent and displays when new messages arrive; new alerts, which display a custom message based on rules; and alerts that are sent from SharePoint server sites to alert you when information on the site is updated.

This section is about the alerts sent from SharePoint sites. Alerts that you create using the SharePoint interface aren't listed in Outlook. You must create the alert using the Manage Alerts tab in the Rules and Alerts dialog (see Figure 14.11).

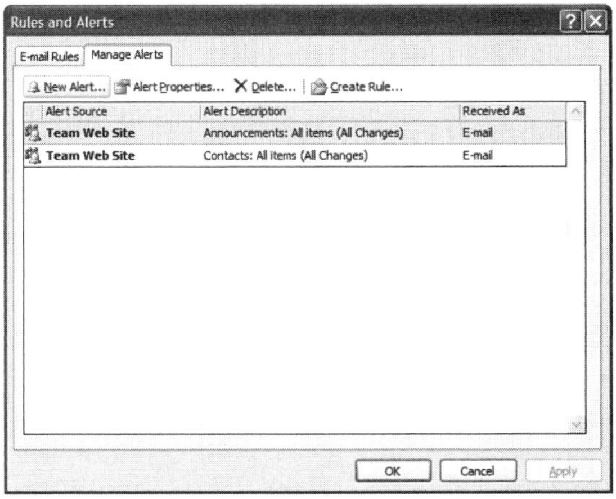

FIGURE 14.11

Use the Manage Alerts tab to view alerts that you created using the New Alert dialog in Outlook.

Select New Alert to create an alert. The New Alert dialog opens with a list of sources currently sending you alerts and a list of sources visited. You can also type the address of your SharePoint site in the Address field. The SharePoint site opens and you can select the alert type you want to create. When you finish, the alert is added to the list in Rules and Alerts.

The Alert Properties button opens the SharePoint site in your browser. View or edit the properties of the alert from there.

Alerts are sent by email and you can use the Create Rule dialog to create a rule to handle the alert messages. Choose between displaying a New Alert window (as shown in Figure 14.3), playing a selected sound, or moving the message to a specific folder. The Advanced button opens the Rules Wizard to the Select Conditions dialog, with the Which Is an Alert E-mail condition preselected. These rules are added to the E-mail Rules list and are identified as alerts.

Managing Your Junk Mail

Junk email and spam are a problem everyone faces. It's not hard to get on a spammer's list, but it's difficult to get off the list. Outlook 2003 includes an improved junk mail filter that includes safe senders, safe recipients, and blocked senders lists.

Microsoft built the junk email filter using information it learned from studying Hotmail's spam. Microsoft plans to provide regular updates to the junk email filters on the Office update site, which is accessible using the Help, Check for Updates menu selection. Let's hope this junk email filter doesn't end up like the ones in previous versions of Outlook, where promised updates never materialized.

Along with safe lists, you can mark messages that are in the Junk E-mail folder as not junk and the message is moved back to your inbox. When you've moved all the messages out of the folder that were caught by the junk filter, right-click on the Junk E-mail folder and choose Empty Junk E-mail Folder to permanently delete the messages in the folder. These messages are not moved to the Deleted Items folder and cannot be recovered, so make sure that you remove all the messages that were moved to the folder by mistake before you empty the folder.

Access the Junk E-mail settings from Tools, Options, Preferences, and clicking the Junk E-mail button or by right-clicking on any message and choosing Junk E-mail, Junk E-mail Options (see Figure 14.12).

14

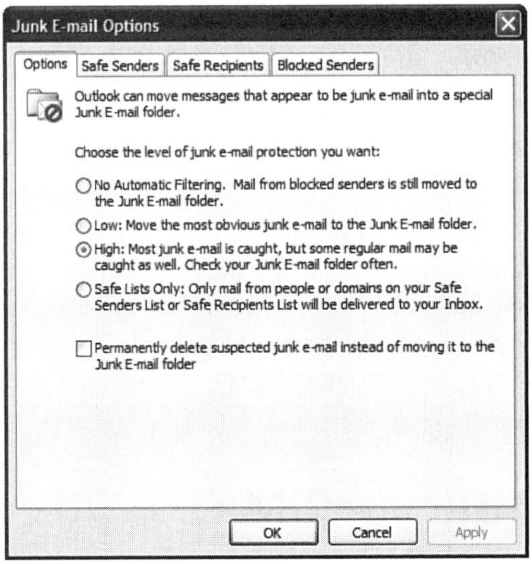

FIGURE 14.12

New to Outlook 2003, the Junk E-mail rules provide much needed spam filtering capabilities. Select the level of filtering you want from this dialog.

Use the Junk E-mail Options dialog to set the level of protection you desire:

- <u>N</u>o Automatic Filtering—Disables the automatic filters but continues to filter messages from addresses on the blocked senders list.

- <u>L</u>ow—Catches some junk mail, but lets a lot through. This setting won't catch many newsletters or advertising you requested.

- <u>H</u>igh—Catches most junk email, including newsletters and advertising you request. The filter misses some spam; specifically, it misses spam that contains only images downloaded from the Internet and little or no text.

- <u>S</u>afe Lists Only—Puts all your email in the Junk E-mail folder, except messages from addresses on your safe lists. This selection will have a high false-positive rate, especially in the beginning as you build your safe filters.

The final option on this tab enables you to permanently delete all messages suspected to be junk. This is usually a bad idea, especially for the <u>S</u>afe Lists Only and <u>H</u>igh filters. Both options have a high false-positive rate and you risk deleting good mail.

When junk filtering is enabled, you can right-click on any message and choose <u>J</u>unk E-mail. The context menu includes menus to

- Add Sender to <u>B</u>locked Senders List

- Add <u>S</u>ender to Safe Senders List

- Add Senders Domain (@example.com) to Safe Senders List

- Add <u>R</u>ecipient to Safe Recipients List
- <u>M</u>ark As Not Junk
- <u>J</u>unk E-mail Options

The first four options add the sender, the recipient, or the sender's domain to the appropriate list on the Junk E-mail Options dialog. Junk E-mail Options opens the dialog of the same name, and Mark As Not Junk opens a dialog from which you can select to always trust email from the sender or to the addresses in the To field (see Figure 14.13). After making your section, the message moves back to the inbox.

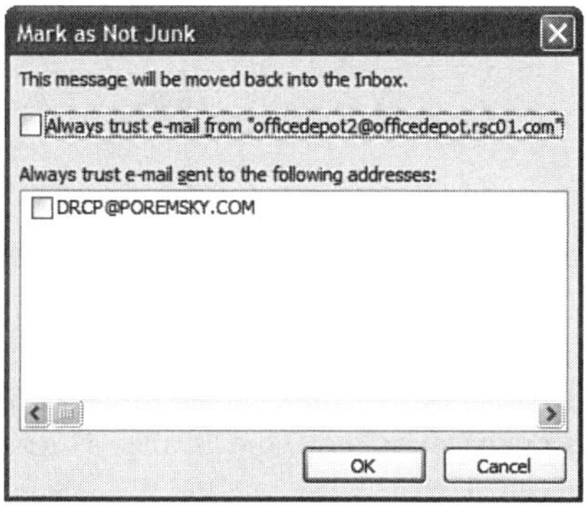

FIGURE 14.13

Use the Mark As Not Junk dialog to add the sender to your safe sender list and move the message back to the Inbox.

Note that when Outlook is first run, the junk filter scans all folders in your message store and messages in other folders might be moved to the Junk E-mail folder. Mark As Not Junk moves the messages back to the inbox only, not to the folder the message was originally stored in.

Understanding Safe Lists

Real spam fighters don't use the term *safe list*; they call the list of addresses and domains that are always allowed to send mail to your address a *whitelist*.

Outlook contains two whitelists: the Safe Senders and Safe Recipients lists. Each list has its own tab on the Junk E-mail Options dialog box, which makes it easier to see who is on which list. The Safe Senders list includes a check box to Also Trust E-mail from My <u>C</u>ontacts (see Figure 14.14). It's enabled by default and should be disabled, especially if you have a contact for yourself. Spammers have already discovered some ways to take advantage of the Safe Senders list and more are expected to follow.

14

FIGURE 14.14

Enter trusted addresses in the lists on the Safe Senders and Safe Recipients tabs. Use Safe Senders for addresses found in the From field; Safe Recipients is used for addresses in the To field, such as mailing list addresses.

Junk E-mail Options

Options | Safe Senders | Safe Recipients | Blocked Senders

E-mail from addresses or domain names on your Safe Senders List will never be treated as junk e-mail.

@b.petfooddirect.com
@email.online.hallmark.com
@ftb.com
@handango.com
buy.com_offers@buy.com
uspr@microsoft.com

Add...
Edit...
Remove

Import from File...
Export to File...

☐ Also trust e-mail from my Contacts

OK   Cancel   Apply

The Safe and Blocked lists accept full email addresses or only the domain part of the address, using (for example) the @microsoft.com format. Wildcards don't work and you'll have multiple entries to allow or block domains such as @microsoft.com, @exchange.microsoft.com, and @newsletters.microsoft.com.

The Safe Senders, Safe Recipients, and Blocked Senders tabs each has Add, Edit, and Remove buttons that you can use to manage your lists. To remove one address from the lists, select it and click Remove; to remove several addresses, select all of them and click Remove.

If you discover that you accidentally added an address to the wrong list, you can copy the address and enter it on the correct list:

1. Select the address, choose Edit, and use Ctrl+C to copy the address to your clipboard. Click Close or OK.

2. Click Remove to delete the address from the list.

3. Select the tab for the list it belongs on.

4. Click the Add button and paste the address in the Add field.

Sometimes it's easier to delete the address and type it in on the correct tab, except when the address is long.

Using Blocked Senders Lists

The opposite of a whitelist, *blacklist* is the term used by spam fighters to refer to blocked senders. The Blocked Senders list works like the safe lists, except that any messages received from an email address or domain on the list are moved to the Junk E-mail folder. Outlook doesn't check the message against the content filter, and the message is not processed by any rules. Because the junk filter processes mail before the Rules Wizard, when you want to delete mail from a person or domain, you should use the Blocked Senders list.

> The dialogs for Safe Senders, Safe Recipients, and Blocked Senders each has an Import from File and Export to File button. For best results, don't import lists created in older versions of Outlook. Let the Junk E-mail filter process the mail and add only the domains or senders it misses. Importing old lists will end up doing two things: duplicate what the filters are already doing and add old domains that no longer send junk email.

Use Export to File to back up your domain list or to share it with other Outlook 2003 users. Naturally, Import from File is used to restore your lists. Each list exports to a separate text file, not one file containing all of your safe and blocked senders.

Working with Categories and Email

Outlook supports categories on all items and, although no one thinks twice about using them on calendars, tasks, and contacts, categories aren't as widely used on messages as they should be.

To add a category to messages using the Rules Wizard, open the Rules Wizard using Tools, Rules and Alerts, New Rule:

1. Create a blank rule to check messages when they arrive and choose your conditions. For this example, we'll choose People or Distribution List.

2. Click on People or Distribution List in the rule description at the bottom of the screen and select the contacts the rule will apply to. Click Next when you're finished adding addresses.

3. Select the action Assign It to the *Category* Category. Edit the rule description and select a category for the message.

4. Click Next and add any exceptions you might need to your rule. Click Finish to create the rule or Next if you need to run the rule on existing messages.

14

Run the rule on any folder in your message store to set categories on messages already in your message store. Turn on the rule and all new messages meeting your conditions will be assigned the category. If you find the default category list lacking, you can add categories to messages by using the Edit, Categories menu selection or by right-clicking on a message and choosing Categories (see Figure 14.15). From there, select categories from the list or type new ones in the Item(s) Belong to These Categories list. Click Add to List to add the category to the Master Category list. You can select more than one message and assign the category to the entire selection.

FIGURE 14.15

Select one or more categories for your messages from the Categories dialog.

Click the Master Category List button to add or remove categories from the master list stored in the Registry. Although you can add categories from the Categories dialog, you can remove them only from the Master Category List dialog.

Add categories to the messages you send by selecting Options, Options as you compose a message using Word or by selecting View, Options when using the Outlook editor. Type your categories in the Categories field or click the Categories button and select from the Categories list.

Categories are not included when you send the message unless you send the message using rich text formatting. In most cases, you need to double-click on the recipient's address and choose Send Using Rich Text Format in the Internet Format dialog. The actual message format doesn't usually matter, as long as the recipient is set to receive RTF-formatted messages.

After your messages are assigned categories, you can use smart grouping, search folders, and Advanced Find to find and view your messages.

Outlook includes a predefined list of categories, but you can add your own categories. Categories you've added to messages can be used on any other Outlook item, as long as the category is added to the Master Category list.

Summary

This hour showed you many things you can do to help manage your email, from using the simple rules created with Organizer, to the more complex and more powerful rules created using the Rules Wizard in the Rules and Alerts dialog.

You learned about the Junk E-mail filter in Outlook and how to use the Safe Sender, Safe Recipients, and Blocked Senders lists to help you handle spam and other unwanted email better.

Q&A

Q I don't like the new mail alert popping up when the new message is spam or is a message that will be moved out of my inbox. I know I can turn it off in Options, but I'd like to see the alert for messages that aren't processed by rules. How can I do that?

A Go ahead and disable the alert in Tools, Options, Preferences tab, E-mail Options, Advanced E-mail Options, and then set up a new rule to display the alert:

1. Open Rules and Alerts and choose New Rule.
2. Select the Start from a Blank Rule option and click Next.
3. Click Next to apply the rule to all messages not handled by other rules.
4. Select Display a Desktop Alert as your action and Finish the rule.
5. Move your new rule to the bottom of the rules list, using the blue arrow on the toolbar.
6. Add the Stop Processing More Rules action to your other rules.

You new rule runs only on messages that remain in the inbox and that don't meet the conditions used in other rules.

Q I used Organize, Using Colors to highlight some messages, but when I moved them to a new folder, the color was gone. How can I get the color back?

A Colors applied using automatic formatting are views. As long as the view is used on the folder, your messages will be colored in any folder.

14

HOUR 15

Searching Outlook

Every folder in Outlook can hold approximately 65,000 items when you use the Outlook 97/2002–compatible PST format. The PST has a limit of 2GB maximum file size—more users hit this limit than hit the 65,000-item limit. If you don't require backward compatibility with older versions of Outlook, you can use the new Unicode PST format in which the sky's the limit both in terms of numbers of items per folder and PST size. Microsoft only tested up to 20GB PSTs for stability and usability, but in theory the only real limit for Unicode PSTs is the amount of free space on your hard drive because the Unicode format supports up to 3 terabytes.

Huge PSTs contain a large quantity of email, and this often means it's easier to find a needle in a haystack than it is to find an email you received last week. You learn to rely on Find and Advanced Find to find messages and other Outlook items. In this hour, you learn how to use Outlook's search tools more efficiently, including

- When to use Find
- The power of Advanced Find
- Using views to filter a folder
- The Search Folder's new view to your email

By the end of this hour, you'll know when to use each method and how to make Outlook's search tools work for you.

The personal store, or PST for short, stores all of your Outlook items in a single file. It's used to store messages for all account types except Exchange Server accounts. Archive uses it to store your archived messages. Outlook 2003 also stores rules, views, and forms in the PST.

Using Find

Outlook's Find is a simple yet powerful tool. For simple searches on any Outlook folder, it does a pretty good job of finding your messages and other Outlook items.

Because Find searches all the basic fields in an item and you can't control the fields it searches, it's often slow going on large folders with thousands of items or when you're searching many folders.

When Find returns results, you must leave the results in the window until you are finished with them or you'll have to run the search again. Fortunately, many times the search remains cached in memory and it takes only seconds to update it.

Outlook's Find is a simple search tool with limited capabilities. Click the Find button on the toolbar or choose Tools, Find, Find to open the Find pane. Enter a name, word, or phrase and click Find Now to begin your search (see Figure 15.1).

The default settings search only the To, From, and Subject fields. You can enable a more thorough search by enabling Search All Text in Each Message.

The Find pane   The Find toolbar

FIGURE 15.1

Use Find for simple searches.

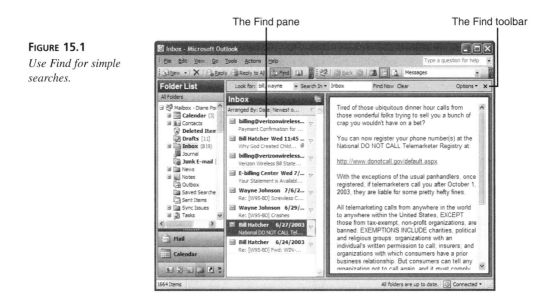

Find searches using multiple keywords when you separate the keywords by commas or semicolons. So, if you're looking for all messages from Bill or Wayne, you can type **Bill, Wayne** and the search finds all messages sent from Bill or Wayne. Find locates all instances of your search words, so messages from the **bill**ing department will also be included in the search results.

If you need a more complete search using all text fields, select Search All Text in Each Message from the Options menu at the end of the Find pane (see Figure 15.2). This is a slower, more thorough search of messages and includes message bodies and the note field in other Outlook items.

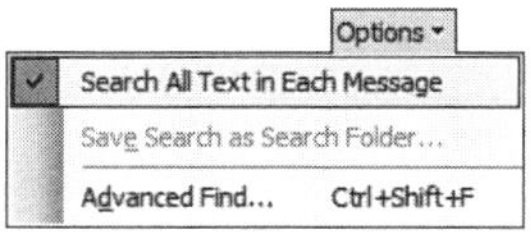

FIGURE 15.2

Use the Options menu to select Search All Text in Each Message, Save Search As Search Folder, or Advanced Find.

The Search In menu has four predefined search locations: the current folder, All Mail Folders, Mail I Received, or Mail I Sent. It also lists recent folders searched and enables you to select the folders you want to search, as shown in Figure 15.3.

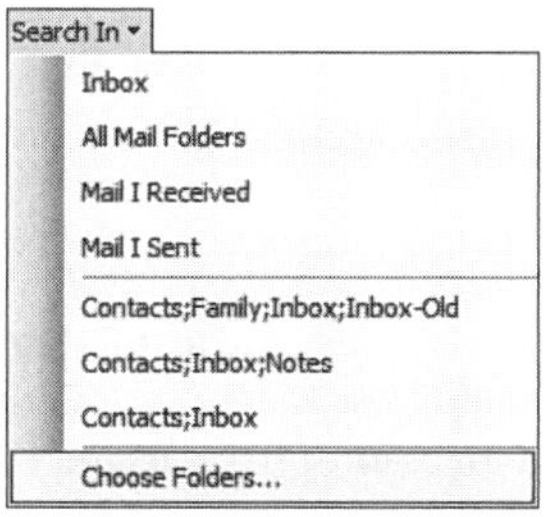

FIGURE 15.3

The Search In menu includes a list of recently searched folders along with the currently selected folder and your mail folders. You can search for any Outlook item type from any folder.

Find can search any Outlook folder type for your keywords and finds all items matching the keywords. Add a check beside each folder you want to search. When Search Subfolders is selected, you only need to select the top-level folders and the subfolders will be searched (see Figure 15.4).

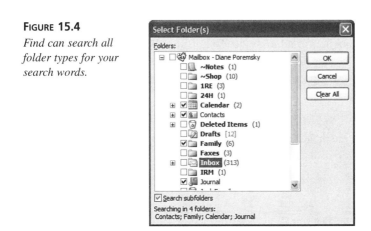

FIGURE **15.4**

Find can search all folder types for your search words.

The Options menu has a new item, Save Search As Search Folder, which is available only for email folders (refer to Figure 15.2). Select this option and enter a name for the Search Folder if you'd like to reuse the search later. If you included other Outlook folders in your search, only mail folders will be saved in the Search Folder. To use the search later, open the Search Folder.

When you're done with the search results, click the Clear button so that you can see contents of your folder. You'll also clear the search results when you switch folders.

After using Find, you can move the found items to a new folder, but you can't use drag and drop. Because of limitations of the viewer controls, you must use <u>M</u>ove to Folder. Select the item or items, right-click, and then choose <u>M</u>ove to Folder.

 Use Find to search your Contacts folder, using a Category as a keyword. Then Select All and choose Send New Message to Contact from the <u>A</u>ctions menu. A new message form loads with the selected contacts populating the To field.

For example, if you wanted to send your old clients a message, you would use Find to show all contacts who you assigned to the Inactive Client category and then use Send New Message to send them a message to remind them of your services.

 ## Task: Use Find

For this task, we're going to find all Outlook items that contain the name *Becky*. If the Find pane is not already showing, click the Find button on the Standard toolbar to enable it.

▼   1. Enter **Becky** in the Search For field.

      2. Select Choose Folders from Search In menu (refer to Figure 15.3).

      3. Check all the folders; also check the box to Search Subfolders (refer to Figure 15.4).

▲   4. Select Search All Text in Each Message from the Options menu (refer to Figure 15.2).

Choose Find Now to find every item that contains the word *Becky*. If your message store is large, it might take a minute for the search to complete. Because this search used the option to search all text, it finds every item where Becky is used in any text field.

> Use the Find a Contact command, located on the Standard toolbar, to find a contact when you're in any folder. The search uses the Name, E-mail Address, and Company fields. Type a full or partial name, email address, or company name and press the Enter key. The Choose Contact dialog opens with a list of matching contacts.

Using Advanced Find

Because I have several contacts whose names are Becky and correspond with other Beckys, I have quite a few search results to sort through when I use Find. I could search for Becky using her last name also, but it would miss the items in which only her first name was used. In this case, it would be better to use Advanced Find because I would be able to use additional criteria in my search and could narrow the results.

Advanced Find has the capability to use multiple conditions so that you can fine-tune your search and eliminate some of the results that aren't what you expected. Advanced Find gives you the opportunity to create searches using any field and use the AND or OR operator in your search strings.

> Outlook includes a predefined Advanced Find, which finds all messages in a thread or all messages from a sender. To use the predefined Advanced Find, right-click on any message, choose Find All, and then select from Related Messages or Messages from Sender. These options open the Advanced Find dialog with search fields filled in to find all the messages in the thread or all the messages from the sender. By default, it searches only in the Inbox, Drafts, and Sent Items folders. If you need to search other folders, use Browse to select additional folders and choose Find Now to rerun the search. You can also add additional criteria to reduce the number of items found.

Task: Create an Advanced Find

In this task, we'll create a simple find using Advanced Find's predefined fields:

1. Open Advanced Find using Tools, Find, Advanced Find or by pressing Ctrl+Shift+F.

2. Select the type of Outlook item you're searching for from the Look for list. Selecting the Look for type clears the search criteria, so you'll want to set the Look for type first.

3. Click the Browse button and select the folders you want to search in.

4. Enter the criteria for your search.

   The first tab uses the name of the Outlook type you're searching and includes a keyword search of subject field, subject, and body fields, or frequently used text fields and by time fields.

   Other options on the first tab are appropriate for the item type, such as Status for task items or Journal entry type for journal items (see Figure 15.5).

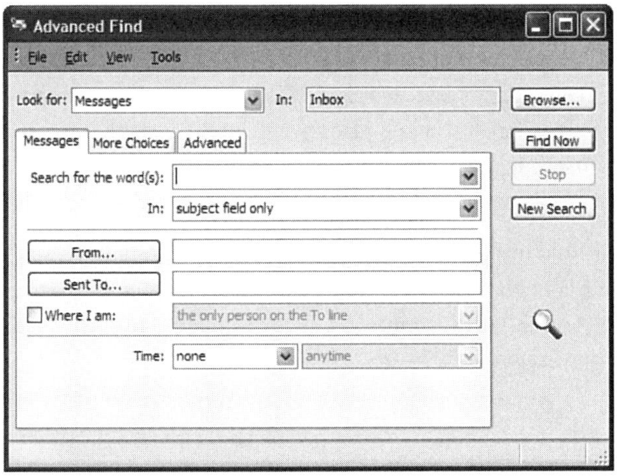

FIGURE 15.5

Select the folder and item type to search for from the first tab.

The More Choices tab (see Figure 15.6) has selections to search by any or all of the following:

- By category.
- Read or unread items.
- Presence of attachments.

▼

- Importance setting.
- Flag style, including colored flags.
- Message size.
- Match the case of the search words entered on the Messages tab. Check this box to force case-sensitive searching.

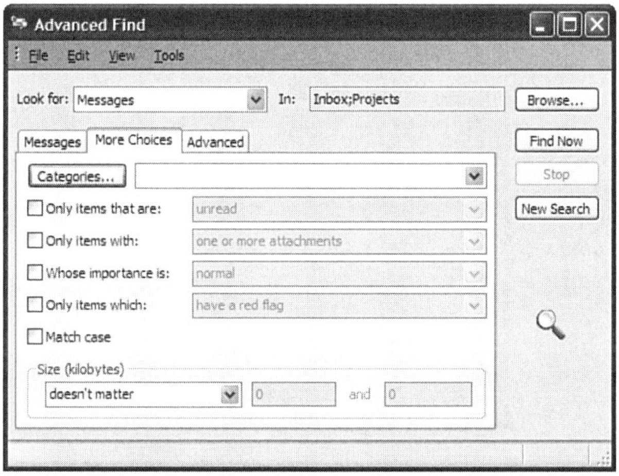

FIGURE 15.6

Select additional criteria from the More Choices tab.

The Advanced tab gives you control over the search criteria, enabling you to select from any Outlook field, choose a condition, and enter values for your search (see Figure 15.7):

- Define your criteria by entering the name of the field you want to search. If you know the name of the field, you can type it in or select it from the Field drop-down list.
- Select the condition from the Condition list. The list includes only conditions that apply to the selected field.
- Enter your search string in the Value field. You can use AND or OR to connect the keywords in your string.
- Choose Add to List to include it in your search. Repeat step 1 to add additional criteria. When you add additional fields to the search, it uses AND, not OR, to connect them.

▼

- Choose Remove to remove criteria from the list for editing.

▼

The Advanced tab includes a More Advanced button that isn't available to use. This button is dimmed in every Outlook version. No one knows why it's there or what fields it might work with.

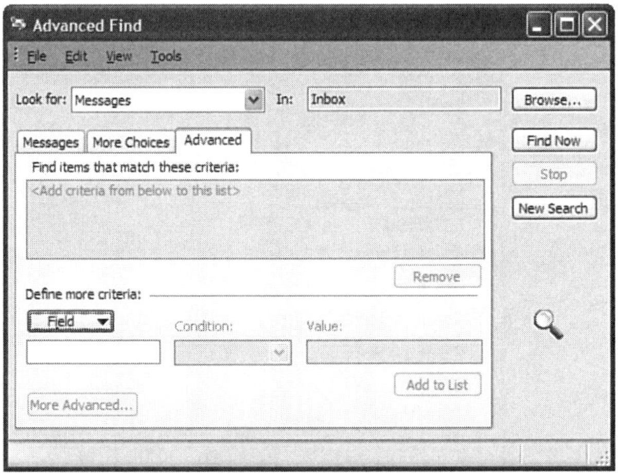

FIGURE 15.7

The Advanced Find dialog includes predefined filters on the Messages and More Choices tabs. You can use the Advanced tab to create your own filter criteria. You can enter search conditions on any or all the tabs.

5. After entering your criteria, choose the Find <u>N</u>ow button.

▲ 6. The search results display in the Advanced Find dialog, as shown in Figure 15.8.

Drag the results window edges or the separator between the conditions and the results if you need a larger pane for your results.

The fields shown in the results pane are customizable using the same options used in folders. Right-click on the field names and select <u>C</u>ustomize Current View from the context menu to change the views. If any of the found items are flagged with Quick Flags, you'll see red flags in the results pane.

A limitation of Find, Advanced Find, and Search Folders is that Outlook can search in only one message store or Exchange public folder at a time. You must rerun the search on each store or public folder separately.

When you use Advanced Find, you can open several Advanced Find windows, run a different search in each window, and then position the windows so that you can view the results side by side.

FIGURE 15.8

*The results of your Advanced Find search are displayed below the search criteria. In addition to the conditions selected on the More Choices tab, I typed **wayne** in the From field on the Messages tab.*

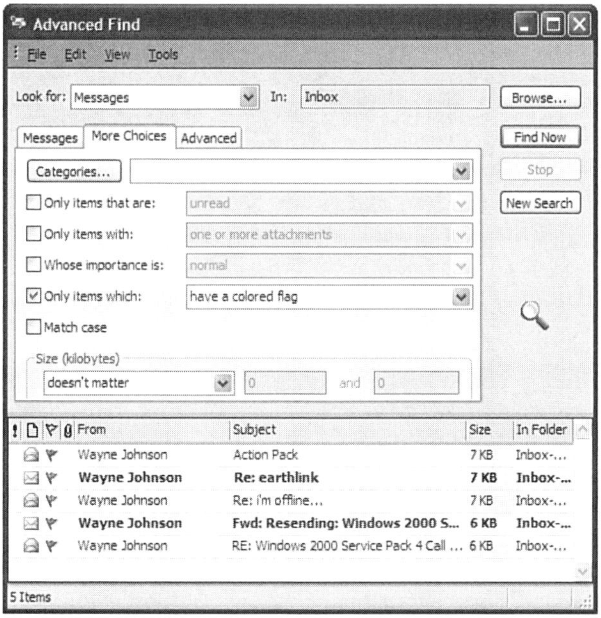

Saving Your Advanced Find Searches

Use File, Save Search or Save Search As Search Folder to save your Advanced Find to use another time.

Save Search saves the search to your drive with the extension .oss (Office saved search). Saving your search as an .oss is appropriate if you won't use the search often need to change the criteria of the search when you use it or search in nonmessage folders. When it's a search you'll use frequently, save it as a search folder. Customized views for the results pane are saved with the .oss.

Save Search As Search Folder creates a Search Folder using your criteria. Save your Advanced Find as a Search Folder if you use the same search criteria often and are using it only for messages.

There are easier ways to use saved searches than opening Advanced Find and using File, Open Search, or locating the search on your drive and clicking to run it.

Create a new Mail and Post folder in your message store and name it Saved Searches. When you save an Advanced Find search, drag it from your drive to your Saved Searches folder (see Figure 15.9).

If you don't want to store the searches in your message store, you can drag the search to the Navigation Pane's Shortcut pane.

Other Ways to Find Outlook Items

Advanced Find uses the same interface as Search Folders and Customize View's filters and automatic formatting, so the criteria you use for Advanced Find can be used with views or in Search Folders.

Although Advanced Find, Custom View's filters, and Search Folders use the same filtering interface and criteria, each one serves a different need:

- Use Advanced Find to search all folders in your message stores and display the results in a separate window. You can save Advanced Find searches and rerun them later.

- Use filters in a customized view to filter items in a folder.

- Search Folders combine the best of custom views and Advanced Find, filtering messages from all of your mail folders and showing the results in one folder.

Using Views

Custom views are commonly used to show a subset of items in a folder, such as all unread messages or all new messages. Custom views can replace Find or Advanced Find to display items matching your criteria. Custom views are often the best way to filter when

15

you know which folder the item is stored in. Unlike Search Folders, custom views work with all Outlook item types.

Right-click the field names in your message list and select Custom. Select Filters and enter your criteria. Click OK twice to apply the filters to your folder.

> For more information about creating custom views, see Hour 3, "Navigating the Outlook Interface."

Using Search Folders

Search Folders were designed for permanent searches. Using Search Folders instead of Advanced Find is a perfect choice when you frequently need to use the same search criteria for messages, such as showing all messages to and from your boss or a client. Unlike Advanced Find, the results display in the message list, not a second window. Because Search Folders work only with message folders, they don't replace Advanced Find for all of your searches. You'll find many uses for them, even with this limitation.

> See "Using Search Folders" in Hour 9, "Keeping Email Organized," for more information about Search Folders.

Summary

By now, you should be able to find anything in your message store. Although Find has only basic features, many users rarely use anything but Find. Advanced Find offers a lot of options and filtering capabilities. As you improve your query building skills creating advanced finds, you can use the knowledge to develop custom view filters and Search Folders criteria.

Q&A

Q I'd like to use Advanced Find to find everyone in my contacts who has a birthday coming up within the next three months. When I create the rule I think should work, it finds all birthdays, not just the upcoming ones.

A Recurring appointments are difficult to filter because Outlook sees them as active all the time, not just once a year. If you use recurrence patterns and categories, you can perform this search using two rules, which you'll need to update as the months change:

Categories contains Birthday

Reoccurrence pattern contains June or July or August

You can use these criteria in a custom view filter; in fact, it might be better used as a custom view instead of Advanced Find.

Q I like the new Outlook 2003 interface, but I am still trying to figure out how to create a search for *all* overdue task items.

A My favorite Outlook feature will handle this for you. Because it's a task item, a custom view might work best:

1. Select the Tasks folder and open the Define Views dialog using View, Arrange By, Current View, Define Views. Select New, Table view and choose All Task Folders. Select OK and the Customize View dialog opens.

2. Select Filter to open the Filter dialog.

3. On the Advanced tab, select Field, Frequently-Used Fields, Due By. The Use Condition equals on or before and Value equals today.

4. To restrict it to tasks not finished, select Complete from the All Task fields menu; the Condition is equals and the Value is No. Choose Add to List.

Your view is fished. Use the Views toolbar to switch between this and other views on your folder.

Hour **16**

Working with Command Bars

Toolbars and menus provide easy access to the commands you'll use with Outlook. These include the menu bar and the Standard and Advanced toolbars, along with context menus that become available when you right-click on folders and items. Although each Outlook folder and item uses similar commands, some commands are available only for certain items or folders.

You'll often discover that you use some menus and commands all the time and rarely use others. When this happens, you can create custom toolbars for your most used commands and hide the default menus or toolbars. You can even create custom toolbar buttons—usually to run macros you've created or to open files or folders you use the most.

In this hour, you'll learn about:

- Using menus and commands
- Customizing command bars
- Creating custom command buttons
- Creating custom toolbars

By the end of this hour, you'll be creating custom toolbars and toolbar buttons containing the commands you use the most.

The Default Display for Command Bars

In the Microsoft Office applications, toolbars and menus are known as *command bars*. The differences between menus and toolbars are blurred, and you can have menus on your toolbars and buttons on the menu bar.

Habits are hard to break, so most people still refer to commands and command bars as *buttons*, *toolbars*, and *menus* based on what they do. A button is pressed, a toolbar has buttons on it, menus fly out when pressed, and menu bars have only menus on them.

> Using the mouse to select commands, including navigating submenus, is slower for many typists because of the need to move your hand from the keyboard and pick up the mouse. Using shortcut keys is easier for many touch-typists and navigating the menus using the arrow keys is faster than using the mouse.

Outlook's command bars are highly configurable and creating custom toolbars with your frequently used commands will help you work faster. As you'll see later in this hour, creating your own toolbars is fun and easy, and it's something that anyone can do.

When Outlook is first started, you'll see the menu bar at the top of the window and the Standard toolbar immediately under it. At the far right of the menu bar is the Ask a Question box. Along with the Standard toolbar, all Outlook items have an Advanced toolbar, as shown in Figure 16.1. The Advanced toolbar is not shown by default, but I recommend showing it because it contains several useful tools (right-click the toolbar area and click Advanced). If you want to save screen space, the Standard and Advanced toolbars can share a row.

> If you upgraded a previous version of Outlook, your previous toolbar settings should be retained.

The buttons and menus shown by default vary depending on the folder type, with the basic commands used by the item type available on the default toolbars. All Outlook folders and forms include a Standard toolbar, and Advanced and Web toolbars, which are not shown by default.

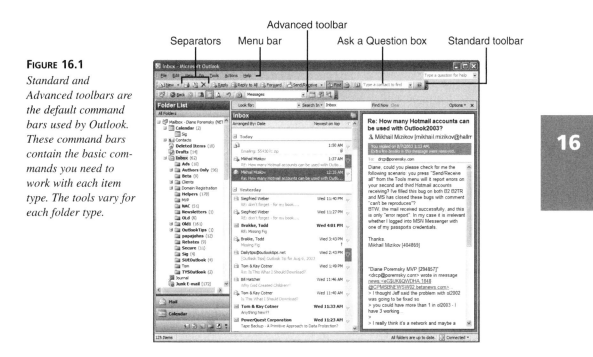

FIGURE 16.1

Standard and Advanced toolbars are the default command bars used by Outlook. These command bars contain the basic commands you need to work with each item type. The tools vary for each folder type.

16

Each Outlook item type uses a different set of toolbars containing the tools Microsoft thinks you'll use the most for that item type. Notes are the exception—there are no toolbars or menus on the note form. The menus and toolbars you'll see when you compose a message depend on whether you're using Word or Outlook's native editor for email.

See the hours about email (Hour 4), calendar (Hour 11), contacts (Hour 10), tasks (Hour 12), and the journal (Hour 13) to learn more about the commands specific to each Outlook item type.

Although Outlook has only one menu bar, you can create as many toolbars as you'd like and put the menus on it. You can also put toolbar buttons on the menu bar. The menu bar can't be disabled, but you can remove menus from it and replace them with other tool buttons, if desired.

The menu bar and toolbars are positioned at the top of the screen by default, but you can dock them on any edge of the Outlook window, including on the left or right side in a vertical position, or have the toolbars float on the screen.

Saving and Restoring Toolbar Settings

When you right-click on a toolbar and choose Customize, you can show and hide toolbars, add and remove commands, and reset the toolbars to their default display. You can also reach the Customize dialog using <u>T</u>ools, <u>C</u>ustomize.

By default, all command bar settings are stored in `C:\Documents and Settings\username\Application Data\Microsoft\Outlook\outcmd.dat`. You might want to make a copy of this file if you make many changes to your command bars. If you need to reinstall Outlook, you can easily restore your customized command bars by replacing the modified file with your copy.

One `outcmd.dat` file is used for each Windows user account. If you use several Outlook profiles with your Windows account, the custom commands will be available in each Outlook profile.

If you make changes to the command bars and want to restore the default settings quickly, you can delete or rename `outcmd.dat`. The next time you open Outlook, it creates a new `outcmd.dat` file and all the toolbars are reset to their default settings.

`outcmd.dat` is often the cause when Outlook crashes or hangs, so your first troubleshooting step should be to rename it and restart Outlook. Unfortunately, you'll lose all customizations and will have to re-create all of your custom toolbars.

Customizing Your Menus and Toolbars

Outlook now has two methods you can use to customize toolbars to show the buttons and menus you use the most and to remove the ones you don't use. If you've customized toolbars in older versions of Office, you're familiar with the first method in which you drag menus and buttons around with the mouse. Choose <u>T</u>ools, <u>C</u>ustomize to open the Customize dialog to create customized toolbars (see Figure 16.2). Select the Toolbars tab to make a new toolbar, <u>C</u>ommands to add new buttons and menus to your toolbars, or <u>O</u>ptions to configure display options such as personalized menus and icon sizes.

While the Customize dialog is open, you're in Edit mode and the normal actions of the buttons and menus are disabled.

FIGURE 16.2

Use the Customize dialog to create customized toolbars.

The second method of customizing toolbars is the <u>R</u>earrange Commands button found by choosing the Customize, <u>C</u>ommands menu selection. The <u>R</u>earrange Commands option is new to Office 2003 and gives users the opportunity to use an interface to add, delete, or move commands. <u>R</u>earrange Commands keeps the menu in view until you're finished editing it, which is especially helpful when you're editing submenus.

Get in the habit of creating new toolbars for your customizations rather than adding custom buttons or menus to the default toolbars. It's too easy to reset the default toolbars before realizing you have custom tools on them.

Using Rearrange Commands Option

Rearrange Commands is a new way to customize tools in Office 2003. Open the Customize dialog using <u>T</u>ools, <u>C</u>ustomize and look for the <u>R</u>earrange Commands button on the <u>C</u>ommands tab. You'll see a dialog like the one shown in Figure 16.3.

FIGURE **16.3**

Rearrange Commands provides a simple interface for customizing command bars.

Using the Rearrange Commands menu, do the following:

1. Choose the menu or toolbar you want to rearrange by selecting the Menu Bar or Toolbar radio button.

2. Choose the menu or toolbar from the drop-down list. The entries are listed in the order they appear on the menu bar and toolbars, from left to right, and include submenus.

3. Add a new command by selecting a command and choosing Add to create the new command above the selection.

4. Select a command and choose Delete to remove it from the menu.

5. Use Move Up or Move Down to change positions on the command bars.

6. Choose the Modify Selection menu, and then select Begin a Group to add separators between the tools to group commands. The separator is added above the selected command, and you can use the Move Up and Move Down buttons to move separators into new positions.

Table 16.1 lists all the options available when you use Rearrange Commands.

TABLE 16.1   Rearrange Commands Options

Button	Action
Add	Opens the Add Command dialog; use it to add additional tools
Delete	Deletes the selected command

Button	Action
Move Up	Moves the selected command up one position
Move Down	Moves the selected command down one position
Modify Selection	Opens a dialog so that you can change how the button or menu looks
Reset	Removes all customizations made to the selected menu or toolbar

The Reset button in the Rearrange Commands dialog restores the command bar shown in the window to its default settings, removing all of your customizations, including any changes made to submenus.

Changing the Toolbar Appearance

When you select a menu and see just a few commands on the menu along with a round button at the bottom, as shown in Figure 16.4, personalized menus are enabled. If the menu doesn't expand after a few seconds, click on the button to expand the menu. If you don't like personalized menus, you can disable the option on the Options tab of the Customize dialog.

FIGURE 16.4

Personalized menus show the most frequently used commands when you first open the menu. When the menu remains selected for more than a few seconds, the menu expands and you can see all the commands on it.

It's often easier to learn where to look for commands if you disable personalized menus until you're familiar with the menus.

Personalized menu usage data is stored in C:\Documents and Settings\username\ Application Data\Microsoft\Office\MSOUTLO.PIP. Each Office program has a *.pip file in this directory that contains the usage data for its toolbars. You can reset the data for the Outlook toolbar by choosing the Reset Menu and Toolbar Usage Data button on the Options tab.

If this is your first time using Outlook, other settings on the Options tab that you might find helpful are Show ScreenTips on Toolbars and Show Shortcuts in ScreenTips. Both of these options help you learn the keyboard shortcuts Outlook uses by displaying them in a small balloon when you hover over a button.

> Changes made in the Options tab of the Customize dialog affect all Office programs, not just Outlook.

Outlook's toolbars dock at the top of the window by default, but they can be placed anywhere on the screen (see Figure 16.5). You can dock them on the sides of Outlook's window or float them on the screen. When a toolbar is floating, you can drag any edge in or out to adjust the height and width of the toolbar, from horizontal to vertical.

FIGURE 16.5

Dock toolbars on any edge of the Outlook windows or float toolbars inside or outside the window.

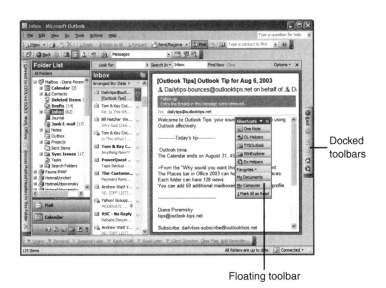

Docked toolbars

Floating toolbar

Move a toolbar by hovering the mouse over the resize handles on the left, holding down the left mouse button, and dragging the toolbar. When you drag a toolbar close to the window edge, it changes shape and docks on the window edge. When toolbars are docked on the left or right window edges, the icons rotate so that they're always in the correct position; text labels on the buttons remain vertical.

Vertically docked toolbars are helpful to anyone who uses a high-resolution monitor setting and has a lot of white space on the right side of the window. Moving the toolbars to the side frees up enough space at the top of the screen to show more lines of text on the screen.

Two or more toolbars can share a row to save screen space. When you place multiple toolbars on one row, you'll have some tools that won't fit on the screen. Look under the Toolbar Options button at the end of the toolbar for the buttons that are hidden. When you choose a hidden button, the button shows and a less-used tool moves to the overflow area. This is part of the personalized menu feature which hides less used menu items but remains enabled if the personalization settings in Tools, Customize, Options are disabled.

Although you can't close the menu bar, you can dock it on any window edge or float it on the screen. When the menu bar is placed at the top or bottom of the window, it cannot share the row with toolbars. But when the menu bar is docked vertically, it can share a row with toolbars.

Using the Modify Selection Menu

Use the Modify Selection menu to customize individual buttons or menus. After opening the Customize dialog from the Tools menu, right-click on any button on the toolbar or menu to show the Modify Selection menu for that command. If you use the Rearrange Commands dialog to edit your menus, select the command and click Modify Selection to show the Modify Selection menu for that command. Finally, selecting any button enables the Modify Selection button in the Customize dialog, which you can use to modify the command. Table 16.2 is a list of the Modify Selection options.

TABLE 16.2   Modify Selection Options

Command	Action
Reset	Resets the button to its default appearance.
Delete	Deletes the selected command.
Name	Names the button. Insert an ampersand (&) in front of the letter you want to use for keyboard shortcut, and then press Alt+ the shortcut key to activate the command.

continues

TABLE 16.2   continued

Command	Action
Copy Button Image	Copies the selected button image.
Paste Button Image	Pastes an image to the selected button.
Reset Button Image	Restores a button image to the default image.
Edit Button Image	Opens the button editor so that you can create your own image.
Change Button Image	Enables you to select from a limited selection of included images.
Default Style	Uses the default style for the button: text only, image only, or text and image. The commands are shown in their default styles on the Commands tab.
Text Only (Always)	Always uses text only.
Text Only (in Menus)	Uses text only when the button is in a menu. For example, the Tools menu has some commands that include images and others that are text only.
Image and Text	Uses both images and text for the button. The Reply and Forward buttons use both image and text on both menus and toolbars.
Begin a Group	Adds a separator above the command if on a menu, or to the left if on a toolbar.
Assign Hyperlink	Adds a hyperlink to change the action of the command.

Among the commands listed here, Assign Hyperlink is a powerful, yet underused feature in Outlook. You can use it to create buttons to open and run almost any program or file, from Windows utilities such as Notepad or Calculator to Word documents or Access databases, open Web sites, and create preaddressed email messages.

For example, you can enter `calc` in the Hyperlink field so that when you click the assigned button, Windows Calculator runs. (Some programs might need the full pathname, but many Windows utilities need only the filename.) You can use a Web address, mailto URL, or network path as a hyperlink.

When you want to create a custom toolbar button, pick any toolbar button from the Commands dialog because Outlook doesn't include blank toolbar buttons. Add a hyperlink to it and then edit its name and image. The hyperlink you use displays as the ScreenTip.

Don't choose a menu button, which has a small triangle at the right side. Use toolbar buttons only.

Task: Create a Custom Command Button

Customizing toolbar buttons enables you to open almost any file or folder and requires no VBA code. One example of the usefulness of this is for users who upgrade from older versions and use the Outlook Bar for shortcuts to frequently used files and folders.

This example shows you how to make a shortcut to an Outlook folder, but keep in mind that you can create a shortcut to any folder or file in the Windows file system:

1. Select the folder you want to use a button to open.

2. Show the Web toolbar (right-click the toolbar area and select Web) and copy the folder path from the Address bar, which will look like this: `outlook:Inbox\OutlookTips\Sent Tips` (see Figure 16.6).

FIGURE 16.6

Copy the folder path from the Web tool's Address bar.

3. Open the Customize dialog (click Tools, Customize).

4. From the Toolbar tab, click the New button to create a new toolbar.

5. Choose any button from the Commands tab and drag it to the toolbar.

6. Right-click on the button you just added and choose Assign Hyperlink. The Assign Hyperlink dialog opens (see Figure 16.7), and you can select from files or enter your own URL.

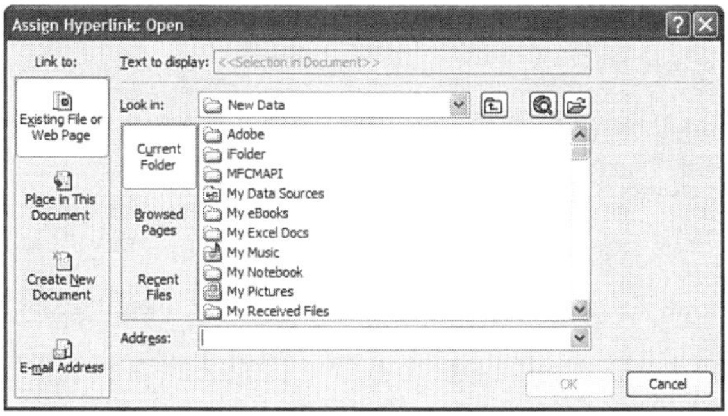

FIGURE 16.7

Use the Assign Hyperlink button to create toolbar buttons for your files.

7. Paste the folder path in the URL field or browse for the folder and close all open dialogs.

8. When you click the button, a new Outlook window opens with the folder in view.

To use a Windows folder or file instead of an Outlook folder, enter the file path to the folder and filename in step 7. You can browse the Assign Hyperlink dialog for the file or folder or copy the folder path from the Address bar in Windows Explorer. If the Address bar isn't showing, right-click on the Windows Explorer toolbar and select Address Bar.

> When you assign shortcuts to buttons and menus, you should try to use a key that isn't already in use or that isn't visible on the screen. When a shortcut is assigned to two different buttons or menus, the first Alt+ keystroke selects the first button that matches the keystroke. When you use the keystrokes a second time, it cycles to the next instance. After it has cycled to the command you want to use, you need to press Enter to activate the button.

Adding and Deleting Tools

To customize your command bars, open the Customize dialog by choosing the Tools, Customize menu selection. When you select a button or menu item, an outline appears around the edge of the button. Clicking the right mouse button grabs the command so that you can move it. You can then drag it to the position where you'd like it to appear and release the mouse button.

If the commands you use the most are missing from the toolbars, you can add them to the existing toolbars or create new toolbars for them. If the toolbars have commands you don't use, you can remove them. To add additional commands to a toolbar:

1. Open the Customize dialog and select the Commands tab.
2. Locate the command you need by first browsing the Categories list and then the Commands list.
3. Drag the command to the toolbar or menu where you want it positioned and drop it.

To delete commands from a toolbar:

1. Open the Customize dialog and select the Commands tab .
2. Select the command you want to remove and drag it away from the toolbar.
3. Release the mouse button when the cursor displays a small x, which indicates you want to delete the command from the command bar.

You can move and remove buttons from command bars without opening the Customize dialog by holding Alt and left-clicking a button. The cursor image changes, and you can drag the button to a new position or drag it off the command bar to delete it .

Adding and Removing Separators

16

Many menus and toolbars have small bars called *separators* between the buttons (refer to Figure 16.1), giving you the ability to organize the buttons into groups. You can create separators using the Begin a Group command found on the Modify Selection menu of a button or just by dragging a command button.

Create separators between two buttons by dragging the rightmost of the two buttons slightly farther from the button to its left. You can remove separators by dragging the rightmost button closer to the button on the left. Create menu separators by sliding a menu item down and remove separators by sliding a menu item up.

Changing How Tools Display

As mentioned earlier, each command has a default display setting. The Commands tab of the Customize dialog displays commands using the default settings. You can change any button or menu to use any of these settings:

- Text only
- Text only when used on a menu
- Text and image
- Image only

After opening the Customize dialog, right-click on the button you want to change and choose the command from the Modify Selection menu (see Figure 16.8). The change is applied immediately so that you can see how it looks.

If you're having trouble remembering what some toolbar buttons do, change the buttons from image only to text and image until you're familiar with them. You can also enable ScreenTips in <u>T</u>ools, <u>C</u>ustomize, <u>O</u>ptions to help you learn the button images.

FIGURE **16.8**

Change the display of the button using the Modify Selection dialog.

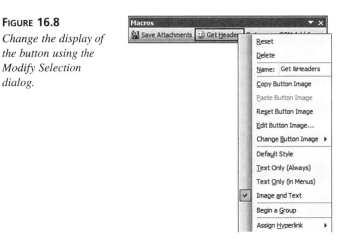

Along with changing how the button name and image are displayed, you can also change the name and the keyboard shortcut used to activate the button. However, it's not a good idea to change the name or shortcut for the default commands. Doing so leads to confusion if someone else uses your computer or if you tell someone to look for a command by name and you forget that you changed the name.

To change a name or keyboard shortcut, open the Customize dialog and right-click on the button. Enter a new name in the Name field and place an ampersand (&) in front of the character you want to use as the shortcut. For example, the hot key for Forward is *w*, which is entered in the Name field as **For&ward**.

To activate the command, press Alt+ the character that follows the ampersand. If the shortcut already exists, pressing Alt+ the character will move you from the first instance to each additional instance, starting at the top of the window. When you use the same shortcut more than once, you must press Enter to activate the highlighted command.

If you don't like an image, you can either edit it or paste an image from another tool or program. All the Office programs have the same Customize dialog and editing options. You can copy a button image from Word or Excel and paste it on a button in Outlook. You can also copy any 32×32 pixel bitmap and paste it as a button image.

To copy a button image from Word to use in Outlook:

1. Open Word's Tools, Customize dialog.
2. Right-click on the button whose image you want to use in Outlook.
3. Select Copy Button Image from the Modify Selection menu.
4. Close the Customize dialog in Word.

5. Open Outlook's <u>T</u>ools, <u>C</u>ustomize dialog.

6. Select the command you want to paste the image on.

7. Right-click on the button and choose <u>P</u>aste Button Image from the Modify Selection menu.

Outlook's button now uses the button image copied from Word.

When copying an image, open the image in your favorite image editor. Select a 32×32 area of the image to copy. Then paste it into Outlook beginning with step 5 in the preceding list.

Use <u>E</u>dit Button Image to edit the button images. Select a color and click in the squares in the Picture field. Double-click to create transparency by erasing color from the squares (see Figure 16.9).

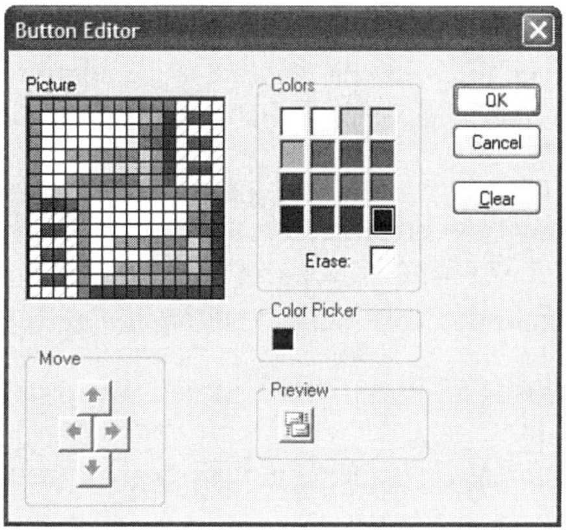

16

FIGURE 16.9

The image editor included with Outlook offers only basic editing features. Select Erase to create transparent areas. Select Color Picker to choose from additional colors.

You can paste a bitmap of almost any size in the paste dialog, but because the button image can only be 32×32, larger bitmaps won't be recognizable. It's better to resize the image to 32×32 using an image editor such as Paint Shop Pro than to paste it as a button image. You'll also want to crop larger images as much as possible before resizing to 32×32.

Moving Tools on Toolbars

You can position commands anywhere you'd like—in a different order on the existing toolbar, on a different toolbar or menu, and even on a new toolbar.

When you're just moving the command, hold the Alt key + left mouse button and drag the button to a new position or toolbar. If you're planning more customizations, use Tools, Customize and open the Customize dialog. Drag the buttons around to reposition them.

> When you use the personalized menu feature, Outlook remembers the most frequently used commands and displays them, hiding the less used commands. You might need to disable this feature if you have problems finding commands or if your custom buttons don't seem to stay where you position them.

Modifying the Display of Drop-Down Lists

Along with normal command bar buttons, Outlook includes command buttons that contain drop-down lists. You're already familiar with the New button on the Standard toolbar, as well as the menus on the menu bar and the menu commands on some of the menus with triangles pointing to the right to indicate that they contain more menus.

When you create hyperlinks using a standard button, you can edit any command button without affecting the behavior of other buttons that were created using the same button. For example, if you need three buttons, you can drag three copies of the same button to a toolbar and assign different hyperlinks to each button.

However, you can't edit the predefined drop-down buttons—if you drag a drop-down button to a toolbar and edit it, the changes are mirrored in the original button. In the case of the New menu, the changes are reflected in both the New button on the Standard toolbar and the New menu on the File menu.

When you want to create custom drop-down buttons, you need to use the blank New Menu button found in Tools, Customize, Commands. Scroll to the bottom of the Categories list to locate the New Menu category and then drag a New Menu button from the Commands list to a menu or toolbar.

When you place a New Menu button on a toolbar, the button has the small triangle pointing down. When you place it on the submenu, the triangle points right, as shown in Figure 16.10. When it's put on the menu bar, it looks like the other menus and doesn't have the triangle.

All New Menu drop-downs have most of the Modify Selections menu options dimmed, and you're limited to deleting the button, resetting it, editing the name, or beginning a new group. You're also limited to using text for the buttons, not images.

FIGURE 16.10

FIGURE 16.10

When you use menu commands on a tool-bar, the commands include triangles to indicate they include submenus. You can position menus and tool buttons on a tool-bar, menu, or submenu.

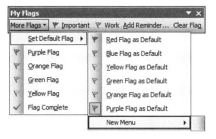

16

After you've added and named the New Menu command, you can drag buttons to sub-menus. When you hover the mouse over a menu, it opens and you can then move the mouse over the opened menu and drop the tool on it. You might find it easier to use the Rearrange Commands option on the Commands tab to arrange the submenus.

Resetting Toolbars

After you make changes to your command bars, you might decide that you want to restore the default settings. You can easily reset the command bars:

1. Open the Customize dialog (choose Tools, Customize).
2. Select the Toolbars tab.
3. Select the menu or toolbar by name.
4. Click the Reset button.

If you have many changes to reset, close Outlook, delete `outcmd.dat`, and restart Outlook. This restores the toolbars and menus to the default settings and removes every custom toolbar you created.

Creating Your Own Command Bars

One of the most powerful features in Office is the capability to customize your work-space so that you can have the tools you need the most at your fingertips and remove the tools you don't use.

Creating a Custom Toolbar

Creating a custom toolbar is as easy as opening the Customize dialog, selecting the Toolbar tab, and choosing New. Enter a name for your toolbar in the New Toolbar dialog box that appears, click OK, and you've created a new toolbar (see Figure 16.11). For the toolbar to be useful, you must add tools to it, either by dragging tools from other toolbars or by adding new tools to it.

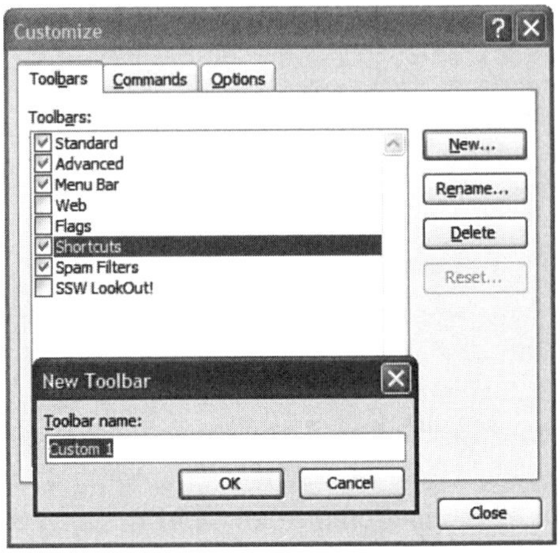

FIGURE **16.11**

Use the Toolbars tab to create or delete custom toolbars and to reset the default toolbars to their original settings.

By default, a new toolbar floats on the screen; you'll have to move it to one of the edges of the window if you want it docked. Custom toolbars are listed with the other toolbars when you choose <u>V</u>iew, <u>T</u>oolbars or use a right-click to show the toolbar list. You can use this menu to show or hide your toolbars.

Custom toolbars aren't just for the main Outlook window. You can create them for any Outlook folder or form except note forms. When you create folder-specific toolbars, only the tools that can be used in that folder will display on your toolbar. For example, when you're in the Notes folder, a custom Quick Flag toolbar will display without buttons because Notes doesn't support Quick Flags.

Adding Tools to Custom Toolbars

After you've created a custom toolbar, it's time to add tools to it. Switch to the Commands tab and browse the categories and commands to find the tools you want on your new toolbar. For example, if you'd like to make a toolbar that contains just the tools you use from the Standard and Advanced toolbars, you can drag tools from those two toolbars to create a single custom toolbar.

When you're creating hyperlink buttons, drag any button from the Commands list or choose one with an icon that will match your hyperlink, such as a document icon if you're going to hyperlink to a document or a folder icon for a hyperlink to a network folder.

Renaming and Deleting Custom Toolbars

If you discover the name you gave your custom toolbar isn't descriptive or is misspelled, select the toolbar by name from the Tools, Customize, Toolbars tab list and choose the Rename button, as shown in Figure 16.11.

If you decide you really don't need your custom toolbar any longer, select it and click the Delete button, and the toolbar is gone. After you delete a custom toolbar, you can't restore it—you'll have to create a new one.

Task: Create a Custom Toolbar

When there are commands you use often, you might want to create custom toolbars so that your frequently used commands are together on one toolbar.

One custom toolbar you'll probably find very useful is a toolbar containing buttons for the different colored Quick Flags. You can label each flag color with a name, such as Important, ASAP, Read Later, or another descriptive label:

1. Open the Customize dialog using the Tools, Customize menu selection.
2. Select the Toolbars tab, if it's not already selected, and choose the New button.
3. Enter a name for your toolbar. Because I'm making a custom toolbar for Quick Flags, I'm calling my toolbar Flags. Click OK after entering a name. A new toolbar is created next to the Customize dialog.
4. Choose the Commands tab.
5. In the Categories list, choose Actions.
6. Scroll down the Commands list and look for the flag commands.
7. Drag each of the flag color commands to the Flags toolbar.
8. Drag the Clear Flag and Add Reminder commands to the toolbar (see Figure 16.12). You don't need to add a Flag Complete button because one click on a flag completes it.
9. Right-click on each flag button on the toolbar and change the Name field to the description you want to use for the flag color. For example, I'm using Important for the red flag. Add an ampersand (&) before the character you want to use as the Alt+ shortcut, for example, Impor&tant.
10. Select Image and Text so that you can see the name and flag color on the button.
11. Close the Customize dialog when you're finished editing the toolbar.

Drag the toolbar to any edge of the window to dock it or let it float on the screen.

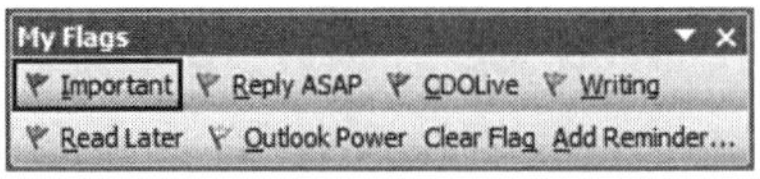

FIGURE **16.12**

Create a custom toolbar for Quick Flags.

Summary

In this hour, you learned how to use and customize the command bars included with Outlook. You also learned how create your own custom tools and custom toolbars.

Q&A

Q When I create custom toolbars, the changes I made are gone almost every time I close Outlook and reopen it. Am I doing something wrong?

A Outlook stores the toolbar information in a file called `outcmd.dat` in the `C:\Documents and Settings\username\Application Data\Microsoft\Outlook` folder. Outlook occasionally replaces the file with a new copy and you lose your custom toolbars.

If you can't find the folder where `outcmd.dat` is stored, you'll need to enable Show Hidden Files and Folders in Windows Explorer's Tools, Options, View menu selection.

Q I'm having a hard time finding some of the menu commands. When I look on the menu where I think I'll find a command, it's not there. In fact, many times there are just a few commands listed.

A That's how personalized menus are supposed to work. They're designed to help you work faster and smarter because they show you only the commands you use the most. You can disable this feature by setting the toolbars to expand automatically or reset the usage data using the Tools, Customize, Options tab.

Q I want my toolbars to look like they did when I first installed Outlook. What do I need to do?

A If you want only some toolbars reset to the default look without affecting other toolbars, you can right-click on a toolbar and select Customize. From the Toolbars tab, select the toolbar or menu and click the Reset button. If you want to reset all the menus and toolbars throughout Outlook, including customized toolbars on forms, close Outlook and delete the `outcmd.dat` file. The next time you open Outlook, it will create a new `outcmd.dat` file and all menus and toolbars will be restored to their default settings.

HOUR 17

Printing from Outlook

Although Outlook is a good electronic personal information manager, there will be times when you'll want a printed copy of your messages and notes or day planner–style printout copies of your appointments or tasks.

This hour covers

- Printing styles
- Printing options
- Printing single items or lists

Outlook supports printing your calendar and contacts in formats used by popular planners, including Day-Timer, Day Runner, and Franklin Planner, using a wide range of paper sizes and layouts.

What Are Styles?

A *print style* is a combination of paper and page settings that controls the way items print. Outlook comes with some built-in print styles, which you can customize to create additional styles.

You can print individual items or a list of all items in the folder. For example, you can print the details of an individual appointment or you can print a list of appointments in the Calendar folder.

Each item or list uses a print style that controls the layout, font style and size, and other formatting options. You can control how an item or view is printed by modifying a print style to create your own custom print styles.

All Outlook items use two basic print styles and all custom styles you create use one of these styles as the underlying format. The two styles are

- Table Style—Prints Outlook items in a table format similar to the table style view you're familiar with in Outlook folders.
- Memo Style—Used when you need to print out an Outlook item on a single sheet of paper—one Outlook item per sheet.

Calendar and contacts have additional print styles, which are similar to layouts used in day planners. In addition to Memo and Table Style, the following print styles are available for calendar items when you use a Day/Week/Month view:

- Daily Style—Prints your appointments in a daily appointment-style list, similar to the 1 day view available in Outlook and used in day planners.
- Weekly Style—Prints your calendar using a weekly format, similar to the weekly format Outlook uses onscreen.
- Monthly Style—Creates a printout of your calendar in a monthly style, similar to the monthly style used onscreen.
- Tri-fold Style—Prints a trifold calendar. By default it contains appointments for a specific date, along with your tasks or a blank area for handwritten notes and a weekly calendar. The content of each section is configurable.
- Calendar Details Style—Prints your appointments grouped by date. The printout includes appointment details.

When you use an Address Card view, the following additional styles are available for printing Contact items:

- Card Style—Prints your contacts using the same fields that are visible in the Address Card view.
- Booklet Style—Available in small or medium booklets. Use this style to print your contacts in a convenient address book you can carry with you. Use this style to print on both sides of a sheet of paper that folds into a booklet.
- Phone Directory Style—Prints your contacts in an alphabetical list, such as you'll find in commercial phone books.

The availability of print styles is dependent on the view used on each folder. When you use a table view, Memo and Table Style printing are available. When you use an icon or timeline view, only Memo Style printing is an option. The additional print styles for calendar and contacts are present only when you use Day/Week/Month view or Address Card view.

If you don't have these additional print styles listed when you choose File, Page Setup, change the view on the folder.

Information about the styles used in Outlook is stored in a file called OutPrnt, located in C:\Documents and Settings\username\Application Data\Microsoft\Outlook. All of your Outlook profiles will use the same OutPrnt file and, as a result, use the same print styles, including custom styles.

Printing errors in Outlook are corrected by deleting or renaming the OutPrnt file. Outlook creates a new OutPrnt the next time it runs, but you lose any custom settings or styles.

Printing Outlook Items

When printing most Outlook items from table views, including email messages, tasks, notes and lists of calendar or contacts, the default print settings are often acceptable. You can print one or more items in memo form, with the body and important fields printed, as a list of the selected items, or with all items in the folder. When you choose to print a list, the fields visible in the folder are included in the printout.

Table views print the fields shown when you turn off or slide the Reading Pane to the right, reducing the list pane to a one-line view. You don't need to turn off the reading pane to print, unless you want to confirm the fields that will be included in the printout.

All formatting shown in the view is printed when you use Table Style. This includes icons, dates, and bold fonts for unread items. The Quick Flag field is included in Table Style printouts, as are colored flags when Quick Flags are disabled.

Group headings are included in the printouts. When using Group By views, the group titles are included in the printout. The group headings print exactly as shown on the screen, including shading, if enabled.

> If you have specific fields that should be included in Table Style printouts, create a custom view and select it before printing.

Use Memo Style to print messages or items in full, one item per page. When you open an item and choose File, Print, the only style available is Memo Style.

When using Memo Style, you don't have control over the fields that are included. The header fields will print, including all the recipients listed in the To and CC fields. Attachments included on the message can be printed along with the message.

> When you want to print a message but don't want to include the list of recipients, click the Forward button, remove the names and addresses from the message body, and print the message.

Selecting File, Print opens the Print dialog, as shown in Figure 17.1 (in the next section). The basic elements of the Print dialog include

- Page Setup—Opens the page setup dialog. Use this to change fonts, footers, and paper sizes.
- Define Styles—Opens the Define Styles dialog so that you can create a new style or edit the existing style.
- Print Options—The options listed are determined by the selected Print Style.
- Preview—Previews the pages before printing.

The Page Setup and Define Styles buttons are disabled if you select more than one item to print and use Memo style. The Print option to Start Each Item on a New Page is available for contacts only.

> Messages received with Information Rights Management (IRM) enabled have the print menus disabled and are not printable.

Task: Print a List of the Items in Your Contacts Folder

A table list of your contacts makes a handy phone or address list to carry with you.

1. Begin by creating a custom view that includes only the fields you need. When the folder contains only the fields you want to include in the printout, you're ready to print it out.

 See Hour 3, "Navigating the Outlook Interface," for more information on creating custom views.

2. Select the items you want to print unless you want to print all the items in the folder.

3. Choose File, Print to open the Print dialog.

4. Select Table Style from the Print Style list (see Figure 17.1).

17

FIGURE 17.1

Printing a Table Style list of Outlook items using the default settings.

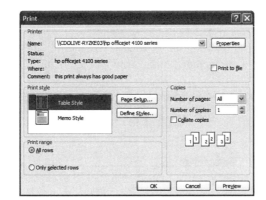

5. Select All Rows from Print Range options if you want to print a list of all the items.

6. Choose Preview if you'd like to see what the printout is going to look like (see Figure 17.2).

▲ 7. Choose OK when you're ready to send it to your printer.

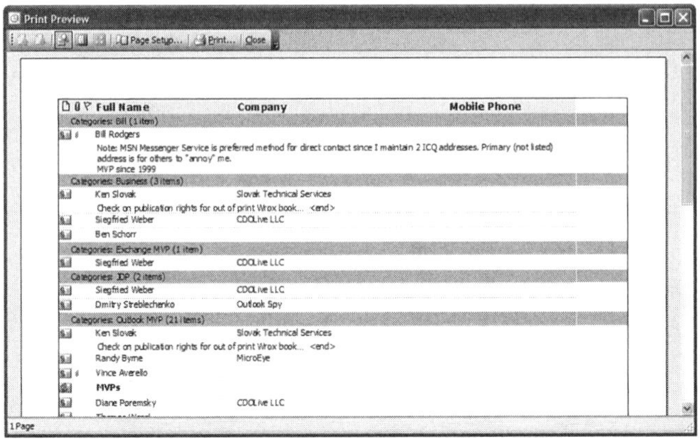

FIGURE 17.2

I printed a mobile phone list, using Group By Category view with AutoPreview and the default print settings.

The finished printout includes the fields you included in your view. If you left the icon or attachment field in the view, the icons are in your printout.

When you want to include the Notes field, you can choose View, AutoPreview to enable the three-line AutoPreview. This includes the first 256 characters of a message or the Notes field of the other Outlook items (refer to Figure 17.2).

Use the Memo style printout to print messages. When printing other Outlook items, fields that contain data are included in the printout (see Figure 17.3).

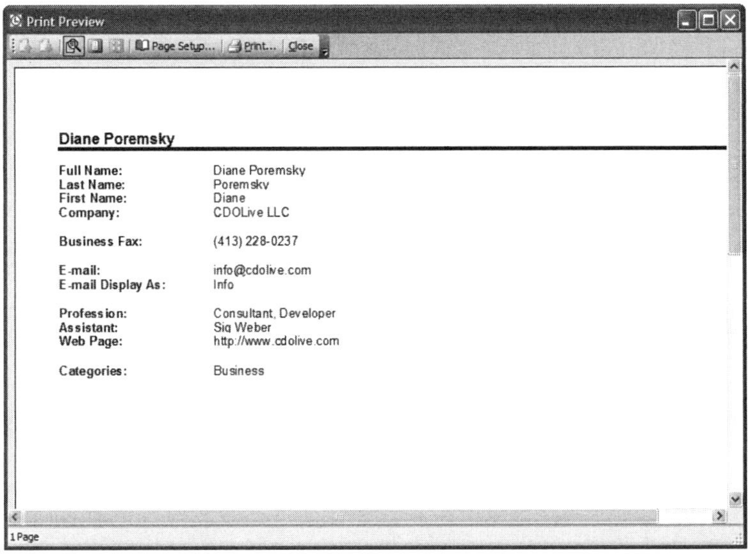

FIGURE 17.3

If you chose the Memo Style print style, your printouts include the fields that contain data.

You can print each contact on a separate sheet of paper or print several on one sheet to conserve paper. Other Outlook items always print on separate sheets of paper.

Configuring Printing Options

Outlook comes preconfigured with print styles and many people never change the defaults. However, you can change them if you want to or you can create your own print styles.

> If you want to use the print style another time, choose Define Styles and Copy. Give your style a name and close the Define Styles dialog.

17

Open the Page Setup dialog using File, Page Setup and select the print style you want to use. In most cases, you'll have a choice of Table Style or Memo Style in addition to Define Print Styles. If you created your own styles or are using a view based on Day/Week/Month or Address Card layouts, you'll have additional styles to choose from.

When you choose a print style by name or choose Define Print Styles, and Edit or Copy, a print dialog resembling the one shown in Figure 17.4 opens.

FIGURE 17.4

This dialog is identical for all print styles and enables you to customize the style's properties.

Page Setup: Table Style

Style name: Table Style

Format | Paper | Header/Footer

Paper
Type:
Letter (8.5 x 11 in.)
Legal (8.5 x 14 in.)
A4 (210 x 297 mm)
A5 (148 x 210 mm)
B5 (182 x 257 mm)
Index Card (4 x 6 in.)

Dimensions:
Width: 8.50"   Height: 11.00"

Paper source:
Auto

Margins
Top: 0.50"   Left: 0.50"
Bottom: 0.50"   Right: 0.50"

Page
Size:
Day-Timer Junior Pocket
Day Runner Entrepreneur
Day Runner Classic
Day Runner Running Mate
Franklin Day Planner Monarch
Franklin Day Planner Classic

Dimensions:
Width: 5.50"   Height: 8.50"

Orientation
A   A   ◉ Portrait
            ○ Landscape

OK | Cancel | Print Preview | Print...

The Format tab of the Page Setup dialog includes the Fonts settings and column shading settings.

Use the Paper tab, as shown in Figure 17.4, to choose the paper type, the size of the printed page, and the page orientation. Many paper types are included in the list, but you also can create a custom type. The page size reflects the size of the finished page, with many sizes defined, including pages for popular planners. As you select different page sizes, a preview of the page is shown in the orientation preview section.

The Header/Footer tab has your options for headers and footer (see Figure 17.5). Click your mouse in any of the sections and click the icons at the bottom of the footer area to insert the page number, date and time, and username. Text entered into the left block is blocked left, text in the center section is aligned center, and text on the right is blocked right.

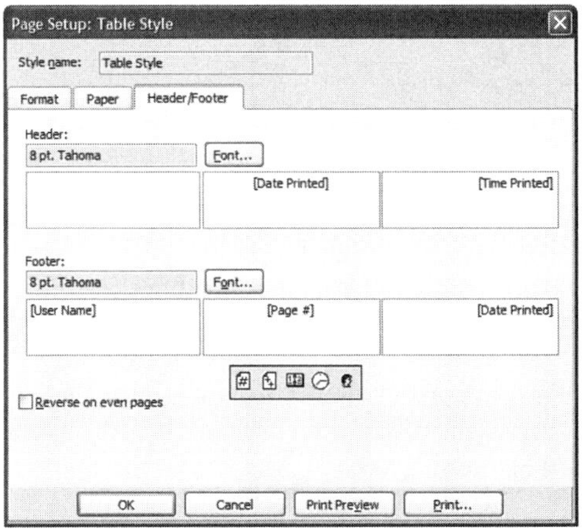

FIGURE 17.5

Add page numbers, number of pages, printed date, printed time, and username to the headers and footers.

Page Setup: Table Style			☒
Style name:	Table Style		

Format | Paper | Header/Footer

Header:
8 pt. Tahoma   Font...

	[Date Printed]	[Time Printed]

Footer:
8 pt. Tahoma   Font...

[User Name]	[Page #]	[Date Printed]

☐ Reverse on even pages

[OK]   [Cancel]   [Print Preview]   [Print...]

You can also type anything in the header and footer blocks, such as your name, company name and other information. Font changes apply to the entire header or footer.

You can edit the style from the Print dialog using the Define Styles button, but if you want to create a new print style, choose Define Print Styles. This opens the Define Print Styles dialog, which enables you to select the default style that you want to work in creating your new style (see Figure 17.6). Select the style that's closest to your needs and click Copy.

When you choose Edit or Copy, the Page Setup dialog opens, as shown in Figures 17.4 and 17.5. Use it to create the style you need. For example, if you often print out copies to carry in your planner, you'll want to create a style with the paper options set for your planner.

FIGURE 17.6

Use the Define Print Styles dialog to Edit, Copy, Delete, or Reset a style. The Delete button is hidden until you've created a new style.

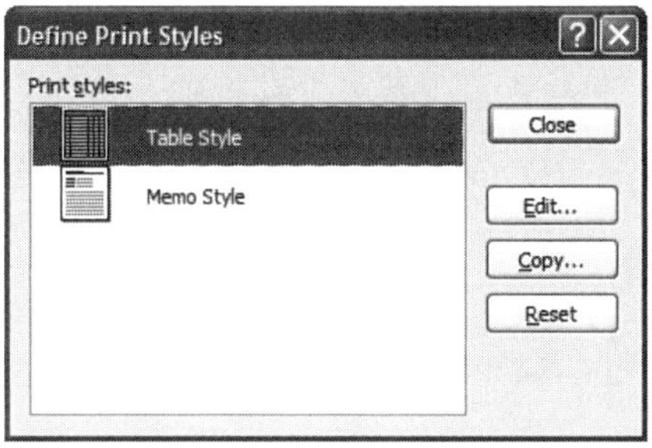

When you choose Copy, you can enter a name for the print style, while Edit changes the configuration of the currently selected style. For this reason, you should use Copy for your custom styles.

17

Printing Calendars

The layout options you'll have to choose from when you print your calendar vary with the print style you choose. Among the options you can select is the number of pages to use per selected time period, which is usually one or two pages per day, week, or month. You'll also use this dialog to include a task list or a blank area for handwritten notes.

When you have the option to include a notes area, it's for handwritten notes, not Outlook notes.

Calendars have additional print styles available when you use the Day/Week/Month view on the folder. When you use a Table view, you'll have memo and table styles only.

Although the options you'll have available depend on the print style you choose, some of the options include

- The time range to include for daily calendars; the default is 7 a.m. to 7 p.m.
- Exclude weekends on monthly calendars.
- Force a full month per page when you select a date range that spans months.
- Arrangement used for days in a weekly calendar (left to right or top to bottom).

Using the trifold style, you can select the calendar element that prints in each section:

- Daily calendar
- Weekly calendar
- Monthly calendar
- TaskPad
- Notes area, blank or lined

The paper type and size selections and header/footer options are the same used for Table and Memo styles.

You can print your calendar using a wide range of styles, options, and paper sizes.

1. Open your Calendar folder and apply a Day/Week/Month view if you're currently using a Table view. As with table styles, the configuration of your calendar might affect the printout. For example, if you use compressed weekend days, a printout of your calendar will include compressed weekend days. Open the File menu and select Print (see Figure 17.7).

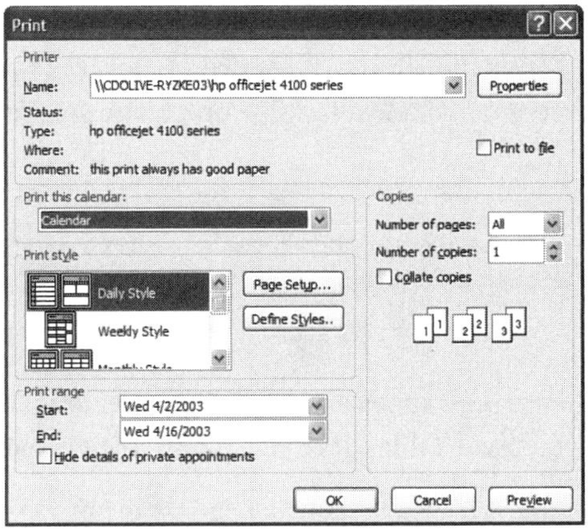

FIGURE 17.7

The Print dialog used for the calendar has some options not found in the Print dialog for Table and Memo views. In addition to several styles to choose from, you can also choose which calendar to print when you display multiple calendars.

2. Select the calendar you'd like to print from the Print This Calendar drop-down list. The list will contain multiple calendars when you have more than one displayed side-by-side in Outlook.

3. Select the date range to print.

4. Add a check to Hide Details of Private Appointments if you want to hide the details of appointments marked private.

5. Select the print style you want to use. You can choose from
   - Daily Style
   - Weekly Style
   - Monthly Style
   - Tri-fold Style
   - Calendar Details Style

6. After selecting a style, choose Page Setup to set additional options (see Figure 17.8).

7. After selecting all of your options, choose Print from the Page Setup dialog or click OK in the Print dialog.

That's all there is to printing out your calendar. When you make your own styles, you can print out your calendars in just three steps: Choose the File, Print command; select your style from the Print Styles list; click OK to print it.

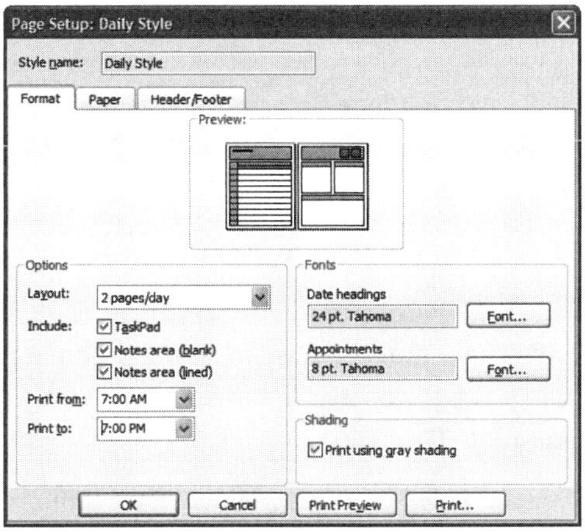

17

FIGURE **17.8**
Use the Page Setup dialog to control the layout of your printed calendar. You can double-click on the style when you select it to open the Page Setup dialog.

Printing Your Contacts

As with the calendar, there are print styles specifically for contacts. You must view your Contacts folder using an Address Card view to access the special print styles. The special print styles available for contacts are

- Card Style
- Small Booklet Style
- Medium Booklet Style
- Memo Style
- Phone Directory Style

The Card and Booklet Styles are similar and have the same Page Setup options (see Figure 17.9). Phone Directory Style prints a phone book–style list of your contacts.

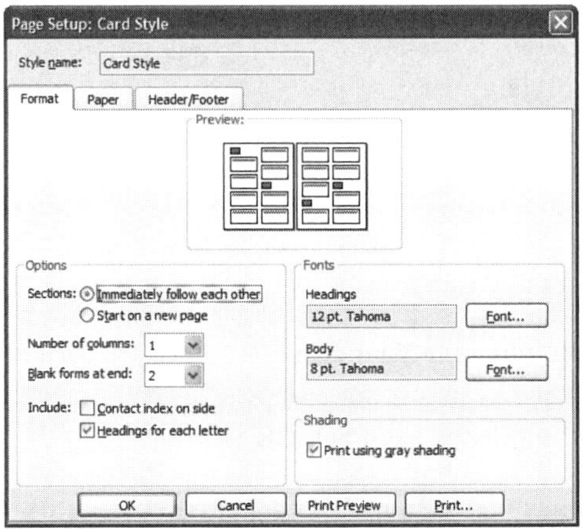

FIGURE **17.9**

Use the Page Setup options to control the look of your printout. In many cases, the fields in your view are used in the printout.

A section is created using the first letter or number of the File As name. If you want the sections on separate pages, choose Start on a New Page; otherwise, leave it set to Immediately Follow Each Other.

Choose the number of columns you want to use. Unless you're using landscape format, you'll want to limit this to three or fewer.

Blank Forms at the End prints forms you use to add new contacts to your booklet. Naturally, you'll have to write the contact information into the fields by hand. Later, you can enter the information into Outlook.

You can include the contact index on your printout. This is the index shown at the right of the window when using Address Card view. It's probably better to use the default setting of Headings for Each Letter, which adds a letter between each contact section.

Use the Paper tab to select the paper types, sizes, and layouts for your printout. Customize the header and footer using the Header/Footer tab.

If you think you'd like to use the style you created again, choose Define Styles, select the style you customized, and choose Copy to save your custom print style. Finally, choose OK to send it to your printer.

The Phone Directory Style prints a list of your contacts in a format similar to traditional phone book listings. The page setup options available for Phone Directory Style are limited to the number of columns and whether to use headings for each letter or the contact index.

> Default print styles are associated with views, not folder types. For example, if you want to print your Journal folder using the weekly format available for calendar items, create a custom view for the Journal folder using the Day/Week/Month layout.

Summary

This hour showed you how to use print styles to print out Outlook items, including using Table and Memo views. You also learned about the different print styles available for the calendar, including how to print the daily, weekly, and monthly calendars. Using the Address Card view in the Contacts folder enables you to print booklets and phone book–style lists. More importantly, you learned how to customize the print styles and save them for use another time.

Q&A

Q I want to print appointment details in a monthly calendar. Is there a way to do it?

A The Monthly calendar style is somewhat limited in functionality and as you've discovered, it doesn't include calendar details. However, Microsoft has a Word template that includes the appointment subject and location you can use. Because it's a Word document, you can adjust the size of the cells before printing it.

An added benefit to using this template is that it creates calendar thumbnails for last month and next month, whereas Outlook uses this month and next month for its calendar thumbnails.

Because you can insert background images before printing or fill cells with a background color, this template makes an excellent choice when you need to print a calendar for clubs or organizations.

Download the template from `http://office.microsoft.com/downloads/9798/olcalndr.aspx`.

17

Q I'd like to remove the name that prints at the top of my email. Where does it get the name from?

A Sorry, no. You can't remove it for the normal printout. Use Word as your email editor, choose the Forward command to open a new message, and then print it—the header isn't added to the message. This also enables you to remove long lists of To and CC addresses. When you use the Outlook editor, the header is added when you print from a compose message form.

The name printed in the header is your display name on the account. Look in Tools, E-mail Accounts to change it. However, Outlook won't allow the display name to be blank.

Hour **18**

Understanding File Management

Outlook uses a lot of information, from connection settings, navigation, and toolbar customizations to custom forms and, of course, email, calendar, contacts, and other Outlook data.

This hour will help you understand

- Which files Outlook uses
- Where Outlook stores them
- Which files are most important to back up

On occasion, some of these files cause problems for Outlook, I'll tell you some of the more common problems and how to fix them.

Files That Outlook Uses

Outlook uses files to store information it needs. Some of the files are stored on your drive, other data is stored as hidden messages in your mail folders, and some configuration data is stored in the Registry. This hour discusses the files Outlook creates on your hard drive.

Outlook creates the following files and stores them in one of two folders in your Windows user profile. Some of the files are specific to your Outlook profile. So, if you have two profiles, you have two files, each named for a profile. Others files are shared by all of the Outlook profiles used with your Windows logon, including your custom toolbars, Outcmd.dat and VbaProject.OTM.

The following files contain your Outlook data and customization configurations:

- Personal store (*.PST)—Required to use Outlook, unless you use Exchange Server
- Offline store (*.OST)—Used only with Exchange Server mailboxes
- Offline Address Book (*.OAB)—Present only if using an Exchange server mailbox in offline or cache mode
- Personal Address Book (*.PAB)—Old address book file; not recommended for use with Outlook 2003
- Send and receive settings (*.SRS)—Controls how often Outlook checks for new messages
- Nickname file (*.NK2)—Stores addresses used for AutoComplete
- Navigation Pane settings (*.XML)—Stores customizations to the Navigation Pane
- Outcmd.dat—Toolbar customization information
- OutlPrnt—Printer settings
- VbaProject.OTM—VBA project file
- Extend.dat—Information about your installed add-ins

Your email, calendar, and contacts are stored together in one PST if you use POP3 email accounts. If you use HTTP or IMAP email accounts, you have one personal store for each account.

The personal stores used by HTTP and IMAP accounts are for email only. You'll have a second personal store file in your profile to store your contacts, calendar, journal, tasks and notes.

IMAP servers aren't able to support the special forms and folders needed for the special Outlook items—or they couldn't until recently. InsightConnector (www.bynari.net) is an Outlook add-in that copies your Contacts, Calendar, Journal, Tasks, and Notes folders to your IMAP server and synchronizes the folders for you. It works with any IMAP server. You'll still need two personal stores in your profile, but all of your Outlook items will be stored on the IMAP server.

Working with Outlook's Message Store

By default, Outlook stores your PST files at `C:\Documents and Settings\username\Local Settings\Application Data\Microsoft\Outlook`. You can and should move your message store to a better location—one that gets backed up regularly and is easier to find.

To move the PST files used with your POP3 accounts, close Outlook, find and move the PST to a new folder, and reopen Outlook. When Outlook complains that it can't find your personal store, browse to the new location and open the PST.

HTTP (Hotmail) and IMAP folders can be moved using this method; however, they sometimes revert to the default location for reasons only Outlook knows. When this happens, Outlook creates a new PST for the account in the default location. Because messages for HTTP and IMAP are offline copies of the contents of your online mailbox, backing up the PST used for these account types is not as important as it is for your default message store.

Outlook uses two hidden folders in your user profile to store data and configuration files. You'll need to select Windows Explorer's Tools, Folder Options, View and select the option to show hidden files and folders. When you use Window's Search, you should choose the advanced option to search all hidden files and folders.

Personal folders and address books are stored in `C:\Documents and Settings\username\Local Settings\`, whereas configuration files are in `C:\Documents and Settings\username\Application Data\`.

18

Outlook uses a new file format, often referred to as *Unicode*, for the message stores so that it can support character sets that aren't supported in the local code page, such as Chinese, Japanese, and Arabic fonts. If you've ever received a message full of question marks, it's because the sender used a character set your installation doesn't support. Using Unicode prevents these types of problems.

Outlook uses Outlook97–2002 PST format for HTTP and IMAP local stores. You are unable to convert it to a Unicode PST.

Unicode format also supports larger file sizes. If you have a large message store, you'll want to use a Unicode format PST. If you also use your personal store with older versions of Outlook, you'll need to use the ANSI format (which Outlook refers to as the Outlook 97–2002 PST format) because Unicode format won't work with older versions of Outlook.

> Although the theoretical limit to a Unicode message store is 33TB, Microsoft has tested it for stability and reliability only up to 20GB. As a result, Microsoft limits the size to 20GB by using a Registry key.

A Unicode PST exports only to another Unicode PST. When you need to use a Unicode PST and want to use your PST with an older version of Outlook, move or copy messages or folders to a new PST that you create using the Outlook 97–2002 PST format. You might lose some data as all instances of Unicode characters are converted to question marks, as shown in the note in Figure 18.1.

FIGURE **18.1**

This note was created using the extended characters from a Unicode character set, and at some point the Unicode information was lost from the note.

```
?? ??????? ?????? ??????????? ??
??????? www.msddb.ru
??? ??????? ? ???????, ???????????
??????? ?????????? ??????????????
???????, ??? ??????? ????????????
????????? ????????? ???????????:
    User Name: drcp
    Password : ehvagg



1/23/2002 10:14 PM
```

It's important to understand that even though it's now stored in a Unicode message store, the character data was lost and the text can't be converted back to the original letters. It will always be question marks.

> Many of the fonts included with Windows, Office, and other Microsoft programs support Unicode. If you'd like to see what characters are included in a Unicode font, open the Start menu, select the Run command, and type **charmap** in the Open field to open Window's character map. It should open with the Arial font in view. If not, select Arial from the Font list and scroll through the list of characters available in a Unicode font.

Outlook won't export or archive from Unicode format to ANSI format for two reasons:

Lack of Unicode support in older personal stores. You might have messages using the extended characters found in Unicode and aren't aware of it. The unsupported characters are converted to question marks and the message is unreadable.

File size limitations. Your Unicode PST could easily exceed the 2GB file size limitation found in the ANSI PST format.

In both cases, undesirable data loss occurs.

Outlook won't convert your existing personal store to Unicode format. If you need the large file sizes available with Unicode personal stores, you must create a new personal store using Unicode format and move your existing messages and other items to the new personal store. The next two tasks will lead you through the creation of a new set of personal folders, setting it as the default personal store, and moving your existing items to it.

Task: Add a New Personal Store to Your Profile

You can have as many personal stores (PST) in your profile as you need. Many people have just one, but I often have several personal stores in my profile. I use one for each of my projects and when the project is complete, I close the personal store to remove it from my profile.

These steps will guide you through adding additional PSTs to your profile:

1. Select File, New, Outlook Data File to open the personal store format dialog and select the personal store format that you want to use (see Figure 18.3). Choose the PST format listed first, Outlook Personal Folders File, unless you need backward compatibility with Outlook 97–2002.

2. After selecting the personal store format you want to use, the Save As explorer opens. Select a different folder if you want to store your personal store in another location and enter a filename for your personal store.

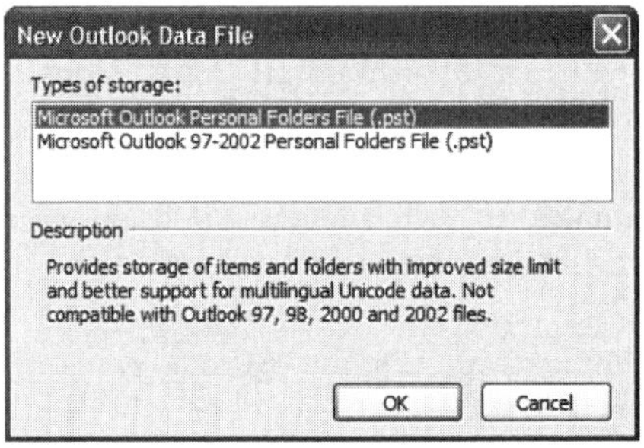

▼ **FIGURE 18.2**

Outlook 2003 supports two PST formats: Unicode, which supports PSTs up to 33 terabytes in size and works with Outlook 2003 only, and ANSI format, which is backward compatible with all versions of Outlook.

I highly recommend storing your personal stores in a subfolder of My Documents so that they are backed up when you back up your other documents. On occasion, Outlook has been known to overwrite personal stores during a reinstall, and when they aren't stored in Outlook's default location, Outlook can't overwrite them.

Using a unique filename for the personal store also prevents Outlook from accidentally overwriting it and you'll also know at a glance which personal store is yours.

3. Next, you'll have the opportunity to enter a display name (see Figure 18.4). Having two folders named Personal Folders is confusing when you open another personal store in your profile, and a unique display name makes it easier to tell which personal store is your current mail folder and which is your old one.

   Also, leave Compressible Encryption selected and add a password, if desired. If you choose to enter a password, use one you won't forget.

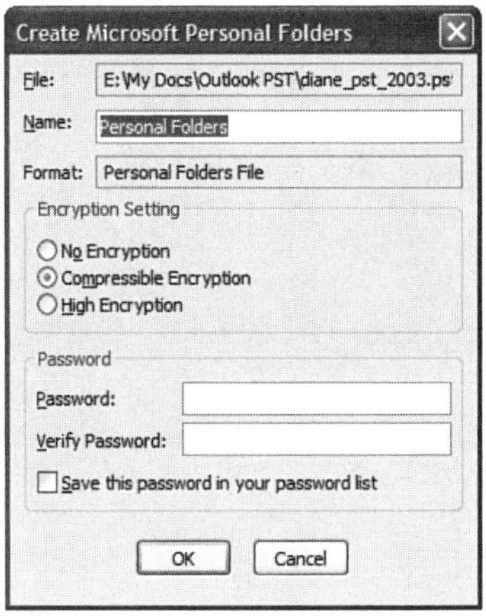

FIGURE 18.3

When you use a personal store for archiving your older mail, change the name to something more informative than Personal Folders.

▼

▲   4. Once you click OK, Outlook creates your personal store and adds it to your profile.

What Do the Encryption Settings Mean?

Encryption encodes the file to make it unreadable by other programs and after you create the PST, you can't change the encryption setting. Outlook offers three options for encoding the information in your personal store file:

No Encryption—Does not encode the personal store. It might be possible to read the personal store file using a text editor or a hex editor. This is the least secure option.

Compressible Encryption—The personal store can't be read using a text editor or a hex editor. It also encodes the personal store in a format that allows compression if you have a compression program set up on your computer. This is the recommended encryption option.

Best Encryption—The PST can't be read by a text editor or a hex editor, and it encodes the PST in a format that offers the greatest degree of protection. The file can be compressed if you use a compression program, but to a lesser extent than with compressible encryption.

In most situations, the default setting of Compressible Encryption provides sufficient security. Use Best Encryption and a password for your PST if security is very important to you.

18

That's all there is to it: You've just created a new PST in your profile. You can move or copy messages to it. When you no longer need it, right-click on the top level of the personal store and choose _C_lose _folder name_.

If you want you new mail delivered to the folder, you have to set it as your new default delivery location.

1. Open _T_ools, E-mail _A_ccounts. Select _V_iew or Change Existing Accounts and then click _N_ext.

2. Select the personal folders you just added from the Deliver _N_ew E-mail to the Following Folder drop-down list and select Finish.

Outlook warns you the changes you made won't take effect until you close and reopen Outlook. The next time you use Outlook, it'll add the special folders to the new PST and all new messages will be delivered to the new Inbox.

Changing the default delivery location won't affect Hotmail and IMAP accounts. When these accounts are present, the default folders are used for nonmail items. Changing the delivery location applies only to the location used when creating new appointments and other Outlook items.

If you use an Exchange Server account, you should not change their default delivery location unless instructed to do so by your administrator.

If you have an old or archive personal folder that you need to open, use File, Open, Outlook Data Files to open an Explorer window. Browse to the folder where you store your Outlook files and select the personal store you want to open. It's added to the folder tree and remains there until you close it.

When you have more than one personal store in your profile, Outlook automatically shows the folders from all the personal stores in the appropriate folder group on your navigation bar.

Task: Move Contents to a New Unicode PST

After creating a Unicode PST and setting it as your default delivery location, you'll want to move the contents from older PSTs to the new one. It's especially important to move tasks and appointments because reminders work only in the default folders.

In most cases, it's better to move the folders and Outlook items instead of importing or copying the items.

1. If the old message store is in your profile, close Outlook, locate the PST, and copy it to a new location. This ensures that you have a copy if you ever need to access it using an older version of Outlook. Open Outlook after the old PST file is copied.

2. The default folders (Inbox, Calendar, Tasks, Notes, and Journal) cannot be moved. You'll have to move the folder contents. Select an item in your Inbox folder and use Ctrl+A to select all the messages. Then right-click and choose Move to Folder. Select the Inbox in the new PST and your messages are moved.

3. Repeat step 2 for each default folder type, choosing By Categories View and selecting the correct folder in the new PST.

4. Folders you've created can be moved as a folder and contents in one step. Select the folder, right-click, and choose Move "[*Folder Name*]". Select the location in

▼   the new PST and the folder and contents, including subfolders, are moved to the
        new PST. When you move folders, custom views and forms in the folder move
        with the folder. Repeat for each folder.

        The reason why you should use Move, not Copy or Import, is because any links to
        other Outlook items are broken when you copy or import and are retained when
        you move. This is especially important if you use the journal or link contacts to
        other items.

5.   When you finish moving the items and folders, right-click on the old personal fold-
▲   ers and choose Close "[*personal folder name*]".

Compacting Your Message Store

After using your message store for several weeks or months, it might contain white space,
or wasted space, that opens up when you delete messages. The structure of the message
store is a database. Emptying the Deleted Items Folder deletes the items from the index,
but doesn't remove the actual content. When the message store has at least 20% white
space and Outlook is idle, it compacts the message store automatically. If you delete a
large number of items or several large attachments, you can compact the store yourself.

18

> Even though emptying the Deleted Items folder removes the items from the
> index table but leaves the item, the items can't be recovered after they're
> deleted from the index. Items that are deleted using the Shift and Delete
> keys bypass the Deleted Items folder and are also not recoverable.
>
> Exchange Servers could have deleted item recovery enabled. If it's enabled,
> items deleted from the mailbox might be recoverable using the Tools,
> Recover Deleted Items menu selection.

Task: Compact Your Message Store

Both OST and PST stores benefit from compacting. When the message store is large,
your PST might have several hundred megabytes of white space before you reach the
20% threshold at which automatic compaction kicks in. After Outlook begins to compact
your message store, it can take several minutes for compacting to complete.

To compact your personal store manually:

1.   Open the Personal Folders dialog, using Tools, Options, Mail Setup, Data Files.

▼ 2.   Select the message store you need to compact and then choose the Settings button.

▼ FIGURE **18.4**

Compact your PST using the Personal Folders dialog.

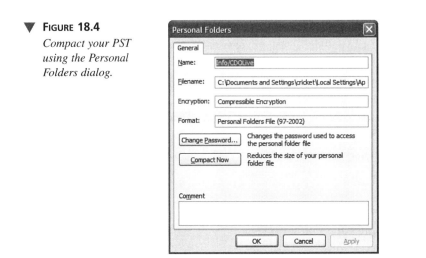

3. Choose Compact Now. You can set a password on your PST from this dialog or change the display name, but you cannot change the filename from this dialog.

Depending on the size of your PST and the amount of white space in it, it could take several minutes for the compacting process to complete.

Offline folders (OST), for cached Exchange or traditional Offline mode, are compacted from the Advanced tab of the Exchange Account Settings dialog.

1. Right-click on the top level of your Mailbox folder and choose Properties for Outlook Today.

2. Click the Advanced button and then the Advanced tab.

3. Click Offline Folder File Settings and then Compact Now (see Figure 18.5).

If your OST is large, this could take several minutes.

FIGURE **18.5**

Compact your OST using the Offline Folders File Settings dialog.

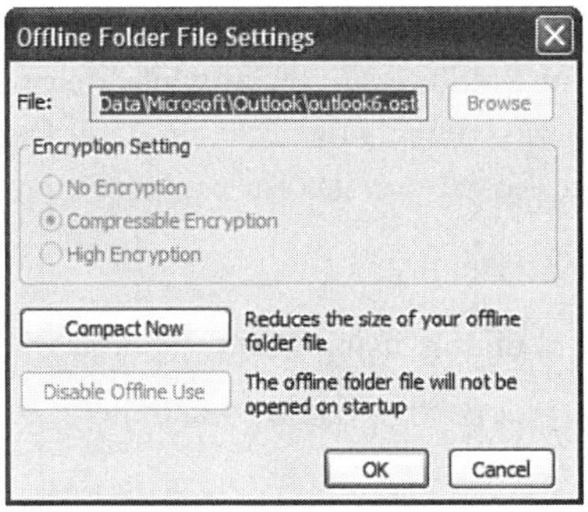

▲

Using Exchange Offline

Exchange Server accounts use an offline message store (OST) when they're using Cached Exchange or offline mode. Offline mode typically is used to store a filtered copy of your mailbox, usually on your laptop. You need to choose which mailbox folders you'd like to store in your local copy, and then set filters to limit the size or age of messages that are stored locally when working offline. Your entire mailbox is available to you when you work online, but you have access to only selected folders when you work offline. Offline mode is most often used by employees who travel so that the most important Outlook folders and content is available locally.

> Offline availability and filtering options are configured using the Send/Receive dialogs and the folder properties dialog for each folder.

New to Outlook 2003, Cached Exchange mode stores a copy of your mailbox on your computer. Unlike offline mode, which is more appropriate for remote users, Cached Exchange mode was developed to benefit desktop users. When you use Cached Exchange mode and your server goes down, you still have access to your email, calendar, and contacts because all the content in your Exchange mailbox is stored in the offline folders.

18

Cached Exchange mode was developed to provide a better user experience by eliminating problems caused by network outages and delays. When Outlook is using the classic online mode, accessing your mailbox is slow when the network is slow. If the network goes offline, you lose access to your mailbox. Using Cached Exchange mode, a copy of your mailbox is cached on your workstation and you continue to have access to your mailbox if the network is down. Cached Exchange mode keeps a local copy of your mailbox, so it reduces the network load because only new items are downloaded when you open outlook.

Cached Exchange mode is enabled by default when you set up your Exchange account in your profile. To verify that you are using Cached Exchange mode or to disable it, choose Tools, E-mail Accounts, View or Change Existing E-mail Accounts. Then select your Exchange Server account and choose Change. As shown in Figure 18.6, make sure that the Use Local Copy of Mailbox option is enabled (which it is by default).

Cached Exchange mode downloads a complete copy of your mailbox, and it might take some time for the process to complete when you first connect to your mailbox.

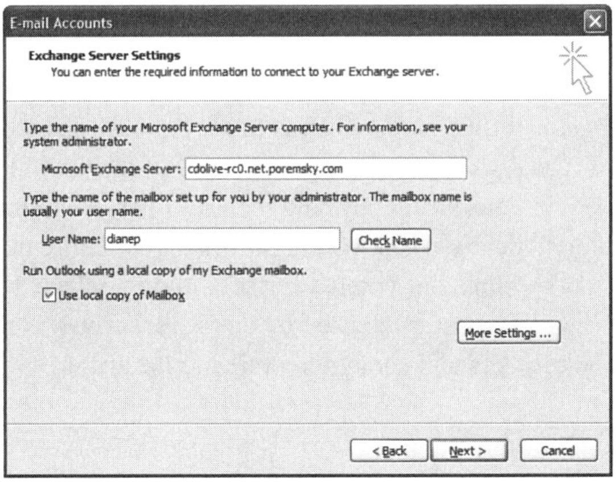

FIGURE 18.6

When you set up an Exchange profile, Use Local Copy of Mailbox is enabled by default. Administrators can choose to disable this with group policy settings.

When you use Cached Exchange Mode, you can choose to include public folder favorites in your local cache. When the folders contain large numbers of items, synchronizing with your server can take a long time. However, when you're working remotely, these folders are included when Outlook checks for new messages and they are available to you when Exchange Server is not available.

When public folder favorites aren't cached, you won't have access to the contents when you don't have access to Exchange Server.

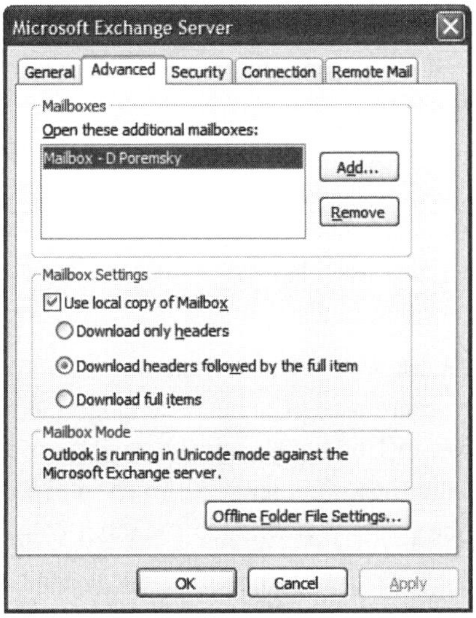

FIGURE 18.7

Change your mailbox settings using the Exchange Server Properties dialog. Open the dialog by choosing the More Settings button shown in Figure 18.6.

When Outlook downloads your messages, it does so using one of three modes:

- Download Only Headers—Downloads only the headers until you retrieve the message body by opening the message or marking it for download on the next message check.

- Download Headers Followed by Full Item— Also known as *drizzle mode,* Download Headers Followed By Full Item downloads all the headers and then message bodies are downloaded. This enables you to see all of your message headers while the message bodies download. This option is available only with Exchange 2003 and works well when your connection to Exchange Server is slow.

- Download Full Items—Downloads the complete messages at one time. Unlike the Download Headers Followed by Full Item option, you don't see the message headers until the full message is downloaded. This option works best when you have a fast and reliable connection to Exchange Server.

You can access and choose between these modes by clicking the Connected icon in Outlook's status bar or using File, Cached Exchange Mode.

> Cached Exchange mode can use the same filtering options as traditional offline use. However, filtering is not recommended for normal usage because you'll have access to all of the items in your mailbox only if you log on to your mailbox using classic Exchange.

18

Along with the offline store containing your locally cached Exchange items, the global address book is stored locally in several offline address book files (`*.oab`) at `C:\Documents and Settings\username\Local Settings\Application Data\ Microsoft\Outlook`.

The offline address book (OAB) stores a copy of Exchange's Global Address Book on the local machine when Outlook is set up for offline usage. This is used for both cached and offline usage. Your send and receive settings control the OAB download. In most cases, you'll want to leave them on the default.

The Personal Address Book (PAB) has been around for years. Now that Contacts folders can store distribution lists, there's little need for PABs. If you have one, you should import it into your Contacts folder.

Outlook doesn't use the Windows Address Book (*.WAB)—the address book used by Outlook Express. All Outlook addresses are stored in the PST, OST, or PAB (if you still use one).

Outlook's Customization and Configuration Files

Outlook stores some customization and configuration information in files; other information is stored in the Registry. Outlook stores the configuration files at C:\Documents and Settings\username\Application Data\Microsoft\Outlook (see Figure 18.8).

FIGURE 18.8

Outlook uses your profile name as the filename for its configuration files. If you move, rename, or delete the files in this folder, Outlook automatically creates new ones the next time you open Outlook using that profile.

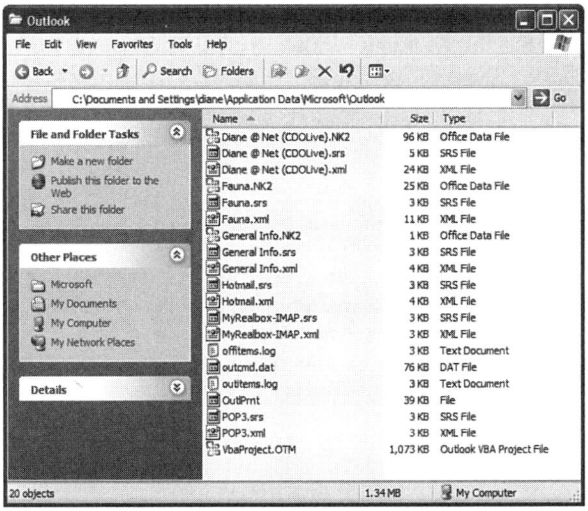

Send and Receive Settings (*.SRS)

Send and receive group setting files use the file extension *.SRS. When you customize your send/receive settings in Tools, Options, Mail Setup tab, Send/Receive button, (or using Ctrl+Alt+S) the changes are saved to the SRS file for your profile. If you have problems viewing the send/receive groups or using the Tools, Send/Receive menus, delete or rename this file.

When Outlook leaves messages on an email server, Outlook stores information about the last downloaded message in a hidden message form in your mailbox. Views, rules, and published forms are also stored as hidden messages in your mailbox or personal folders.

If you need to delete any of these items, you should use the Outlook interface. However, you can also use Outlook Spy (www.dimastr.com) to view or delete any of the hidden files. Always back up your personal folders before using tools such as Outlook Spy because items deleted in this manner cannot be recovered.

Hours 3, 14, and 20 provide more information about managing your views, rules, and forms.

Nickname Cache (*.NK2)

The first time you send either a new message or reply email to an address, that address is added to the Nickname cache (*.NK2) file. This file stores the addresses used by AutoComplete to populate the address fields when you begin typing an address. If you have an error in an address in your AutoComplete field, delete it from the cache by using the arrow buttons to select it and then pressing your Delete key. If Outlook crashes when you address new mail, delete or rename the NK2 file for your profile and Outlook will create a new one.

Navigation Pane Settings (*.XML)

The navigation pane on the left of Outlook's window displays your Outlook folders and shortcuts or favorites you've added to it. The configuration for the navigation pane, including Favorite Folders or shortcuts you've added, is stored in an XML file.

You can open the file using Notepad if you want to look at it, but don't edit it unless you know exactly what you're doing. If you have a large number of shortcuts to delete, you can delete this file. You should back up this file on a regular basis.

You can also start Outlook using the /resetnavpane switch to clear the *.XML file, reset the navigation bar buttons, and remove shared folders from the folder groups.

To use the switch to clear your navigation bar, open the Run dialog from the Start menu and type "C:\Program Files\Microsoft Office\OFFICE11\OUTLOOK.EXE" /resetnavpane in the Open: field .

Custom Toolbar Settings (outcmd.dat)

Data for customized toolbars is stored in outcmd.dat file. It contains all command bar customization information for changes to the default command bars and custom command bars you've created. This file should be backed up each time you create new command bars or make extensive edits to existing ones.

18

outcmd.dat occasionally becomes corrupted, which causes Outlook to hang at startup. If this happens, you need to delete outcmd.dat. If you have a back up, you won't lose your custom toolbars.

Printer Settings (OutlPrnt)

Print settings are stored in OutlPrnt. If you receive errors when you attempt to print from Outlook, close Outlook and delete this file. Outlook will rebuild the file the next time you print an Outlook item.

VBA Projects

Macros and VBA projects are stored in VbaProject.OTM. Beginning with Outlook 2003, VBA code contained in your project file is trusted by Outlook's object model and won't trigger security warnings or prompts. When you create your own macros, you should either back up this file or export your code.

Add-in Configuration File (extend.dat)

Information about add-ins installed on your computer is contained in extend.dat. This file shouldn't be backed up. If you uninstall an add-in and restore an old extend.dat, you'll get errors when Outlook starts that it can't find a missing add-in.

If you see an error message that says Outlook can't find an add-in, delete extend.dat or reinstall the add-in.

Occasionally you'll install an add-in that's supposed to add toolbar buttons or menus to Outlook, but they aren't added to the toolbars. Verify that the add-in is installed by looking for the add-in on the add-in list in Tools, Options, Other, Advanced Options, COM Add-In and Add-In Manager buttons. If the add-in is listed and checked, delete extend.dat and restart Outlook.

When you use multiple Outlook profiles, they all use the same OutlPrnt, VbaProject.OTM, and extend.dat, files.

Working with Folders

Outlook stores all of your items in a single message store unless you added additional personal folder stores. To make it easier to manage your messages, you can create additional folders to supplement the default ones created by Outlook. Using the Outlook 97–2002 PST format, there is a limit of approximately 65,000 items and folders per folder, whereas a Unicode format PST can contain an unlimited number of items and folders.

Using some folders to file your messages helps improve message management, but when you have too many folders and subfolders, it's often harder to find your messages. How many is too many? If you have so many that you can't remember some of their names or where you created them, you probably need to consolidate your folders. You can move some of the folders to a new personal store and reduce the number of subfolders in subfolders.

> I like to limit my mailbox to about 20–30 mail folders—one for each project I'm involved in and several for general organizational use. I also try to avoid making subfolders more than two folders deep. It's too much work to expand a lot of subtrees when I'm looking for a folder.
>
> Soon after a project ends, I move the folders and messages into a personal store for archiving. I name the personal store after the project and store copies of Word documents or other files in the personal store along with all messages, copies of contacts, calendar events, and journal entries.

Task: Create New Folders

Outlook includes one folder of each Outlook item type when you create a mailbox PST. Although you can use just one folder for your mail, most people like to add additional folders and create a filing system for their messages and other Outlook items. When you add a second PST, Outlook includes just the Deleted Items folder and you need to add folders to it. Don't move items to the top level of a new PST—add folders and create a file system.

1. Right-click on any folder and choose <u>N</u>ew Folder to add an additional folder (see Figure 18.9). By default, new folders are added to the folder you right-clicked on to select New Folder, but you can select a location from the Create New Folder dialog or you can move the folder at any time.

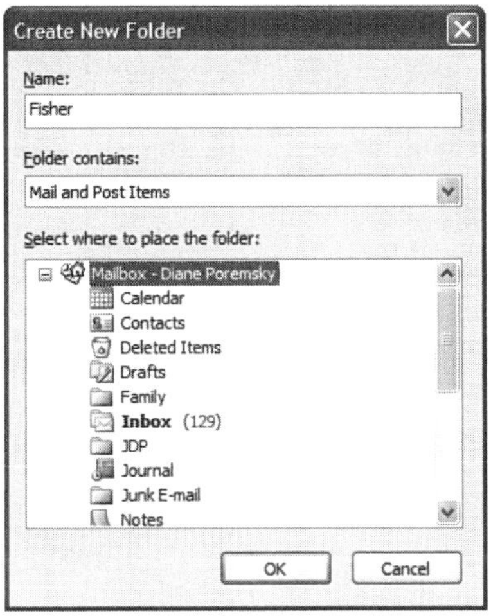

FIGURE 18.9
Use the Create New Folder dialog to add new folders to your message store.

▼   2. Choose a folder type for your folder from the Folder Contains menu. You can
        choose from any of the Outlook folder types: Calendar, Contacts, Mail and Post,
        Journal, Tasks, or Notes.

     3. Choose a location for your folder. If you don't select a folder, your new folder is
        added as a subfolder in the folder you last selected. Any folder type can be a sub-
        folder of any other folder type. For example, I often add a tasks folder as a sub-
        folder of a project folder.

▲   4. Click OK to add your new folder your message store, and right-click and choose
        Add to Favorite Folders if you'd like.

You can add as many folders as you want to your message stores, although too many
folders—especially when you use a lot of subfolders—often makes it harder to find your
messages.

Task: Moving Messages and Folders

When you need to move or copy the contents of a folder between message stores, move
or copy the entire folder:

1. Select the folder you want to move.

2. Right-click and choose Move *folder name*, where *folder name* is the name of the
   selected folder.

3. Select the new folder or personal store from the Move Folder list (see Figure 18.10).
   If you need to create a new folder, click the New button.

FIGURE 18.10

*The Move Folder and
Copy Folder list enable
you pick a folder or
message store to move
or copy folders to. You
can also drag and drop
folders to move them
or press Ctrl and drag
to copy. When you
right-click and drag,
you have the option to
Move or Copy your*
▼ *folders.*

Summary

This hour introduced you to the new Unicode message store format, which provides support for many of the character sets used worldwide. A side benefit of Unicode is the ability to store more items in your personal folders than the ANSI format used by older versions of Outlook. Because the Unicode format doesn't have a file size limitation, you won't have to worry about losing data if you let your personal folders get too large. You also learned how to set up a personal folder and move your folders between personal folders.

In addition, this hour explained what the different files Outlook stores on your hard drive are used for and which ones should be backed up. It also included some troubleshooting tips to try when Outlook misbehaves.

Q&A

Q Should I use a Unicode message store?

A If you're new to Outlook, you should use Unicode format. It's the future. When you upgrade from earlier versions of Outlook, the answer depends on your email habits.

Do you correspond with people from other countries? Do their messages often have question marks where text should be?

If you answer either question with yes, you'll benefit from using Unicode format.

Is your personal store more than 1GB or close to 2GB? Do you archive or delete attachments from messages to keep your mailbox from reaching 2GB?

If you answer yes to either of these questions, you should use Unicode format.

Do you use your personal store with older versions of Outlook?

If you answer no, you should use Unicode format. Backward compatibility is the only reason not to use Unicode. By the same token, if you answered yes only to this question, stick with the Outlook97–2002 format. You can use file management techniques such as archiving to keep your personal store small.

If you answered yes to all three sets of questions, you should use Unicode and copy items to an Outlook97–2002 format personal store or upgrade to Outlook 2003 on all of your systems. The benefits of using Unicode for foreign character support and large message store outweigh compatibility issues. You can always copy most items to an older format personal store if you need to. However, items that use Unicode characters won't be readable when copied to an Outlook97–2002 PST.

18

HOUR 19

Managing Your Data

You can create and store a lot of information in Outlook—more than 20GB when you use the new Unicode PST format. Even the older PST format, with a limit of just 2GB, could hold a large number of Outlook items. As a result, it can be difficult to find the information you need when it's mixed in with so much information you no longer need.

Backing up your Outlook data is important; otherwise, you risk losing everything if your computer dies or is stolen. Although you could easily re-create the accounts, the messages might be gone forever.

This hour shows you how to manage your messages and other Outlook items using

- Archiving
- Importing and exporting
- Backing up your Outlook data
- Saving your Outlook settings

You'll learn how to use archive to remove your old items from Outlook and how to use Import and Export to merge PSTs. You'll also learn where Outlook stores all of your data and how to make copies of it.

Archiving

After several months of using Outlook, you'll have a lot of older information that you no longer need in your day-to-day work, but that you don't want to delete either—you never know when you'll need to reference it later.

It's Archive to the rescue by providing an easy, automated way to move your older items to another PST.

By default, after you use Outlook for a couple of weeks, it will ask whether you want to use AutoArchive. Select the AutoArchive button to view your AutoArchive settings, choose Yes to archive or No to cancel (see Figure 19.1).

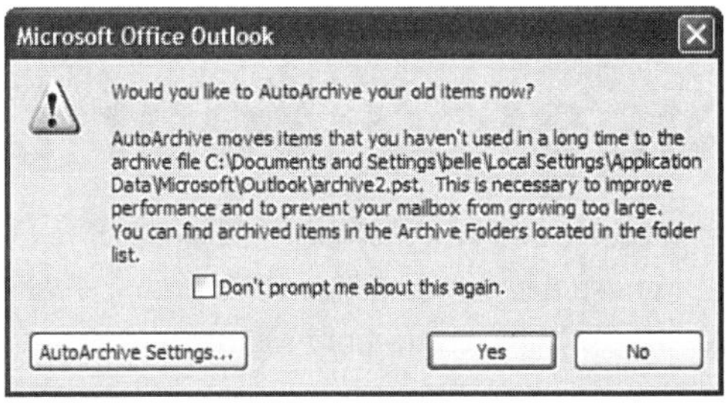

FIGURE 19.1

AutoArchive offers to archive your old messages about two weeks after creating your account.

Whether you choose Yes or No, you can choose Tools, Options, Other, AutoArchive at any time and enable, disable, or change your settings (see Figure 19.2).

FIGURE 19.2

Use the AutoArchive dialog to configure your global archive settings. Many of the settings can be set per folder by opening each folder's property sheet.

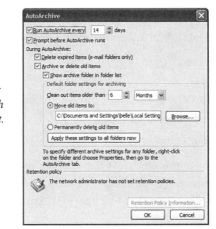

Among the settings you can configure are the following:

- Run AutoArchive Every 14 Days—Determines how often you want to archive. In most cases, one or twice a month is often enough.

- Delete Expired Items (E-Mail Folders Only)—Deletes messages that expired.

- Archive or Delete Old Items—Archives or deletes old items based on the default folder settings for archiving.

- Show Archive Folder in Folder List—When enabled, the archive folder is listed in the folder list and you can browse old items.

- Clean Out Items Older Than 6 Months—Select how many days, weeks, or months you want to keep items in your message store.

- Move Old Items To:—By default, the archive folder is `C:\Documents and Settings\username\Local Settings\Application Data\Microsoft\Outlook\archive.pst`. You can browse to create the archive PST in a new folder and change the name of the PST, if desired.

- Permanently Delete Old Items—Choose this option to delete items instead of moving them to the archive folder. Items deleted using this setting are not recoverable.

Choose Apply These Settings to All Folders Now to set the global settings. You can change the settings for individual folders as needed. For example, you might want to keep older journal items or not archive some folders at all.

> Configure AutoArchive on the Deleted Items and Junk E-mail folders to delete older items and you won't have to empty those folders.

19

Retention policy settings are used for Exchange Server accounts only. Configured by the Exchange administrator, the retention policy controls how long messages remain in users' mailboxes. It's usually done to control mailbox sizes.

After it's enabled, AutoArchive runs immediately and, in the future, on the schedule you selected.

Should you want to archive one folder or archive your items between the selected archive times, you can force an AutoArchive on all folders or a selected folder at any time by choosing File, Archive (see Figure 19.3).

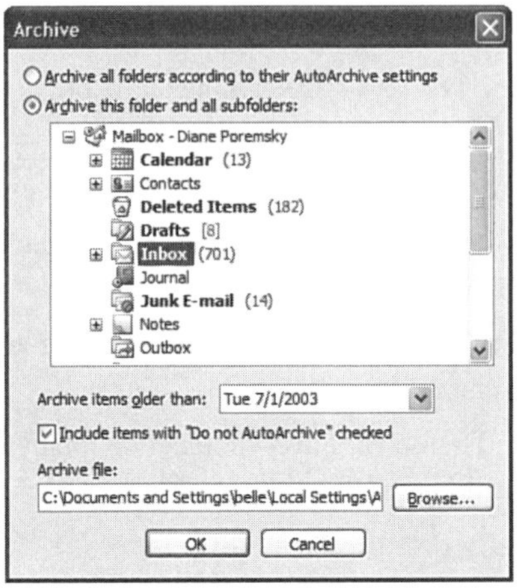

FIGURE 19.3

Use Archive to archive any folder or your entire message store at any time. When you select a single folder, you can choose any date for the archive.

Archive

○ A̲rchive all folders according to their AutoArchive settings
◉ Archi̲ve this folder and all subfolders:

   ⊟ 📧 Mailbox - Diane Poremsky
     ⊞ 📅 **Calendar** (13)
     ⊞ 📇 Contacts
       📄 **Deleted Items** (182)
       📝 **Drafts** [8]
     ⊞ 📥 **Inbox** (701)
       📓 Journal
       📧 **Junk E-mail** (14)
     ⊞ 📒 Notes
       📤 Outbox

Archive items o̲lder than: Tue 7/1/2003

☑ Include items with "Do not AutoArchive" checked

Archive f̲ile:

C:\Documents and Settings\belle\Local Settings\A | B̲rowse...

     OK   Cancel

Use Advanced Find to find items to delete because you cannot use File, Archive to delete items from an individual folder. Select the items in the Advanced Find window and delete them. Use Modified as the field name on Advanced Find's Advanced tab. Choose `on` or `before` as the C̲ondition and enter a date in the Val̲ue field.

Archive looks at the last modified date on an item and uses that to determine what to back up, based on the premise that if you haven't touched the item in months, it can safely be archived. This often causes unexpected results when you expect items to be archived and they aren't. In addition to opening or editing an item, Import and Export changes the modified date and will cause Archive to fail.

Working with Archived Folders

When you need to read the items in your archive folder, use F̲ile, O̲pen, Outlook Data F̲ile to open the file in your folder tree. Don't use Import—you'll just need to archive them again, which is difficult because the modified date is the date of the import.

If the archive was moved to a CD-ROM for storage, you'll have to copy it to your hard drive and remove the read-only flag by right-clicking on the archive file in Windows Explorer, choosing Properties, and then removing the check from the R̲ead-Only box.

To remove an archive PST from your folder list, right-click it in the Navigation Pane and choose C̲lose from the context menu.

Alternatives to AutoArchive

Although AutoArchive makes it easy to keep your message store compact, it might archive items you don't want archived. Plus, by default, it archives items to just one file: `archive.pst`.

> AutoArchive doesn't work with IMAP or HTTP accounts.

You can control the items you want to archive and choose to move them to different PSTs by moving the items yourself.

Task: Create Your Own Archive PST

▼ TASK

When you want to group items by project, date, or other criteria, or need to archive your HTTP or IMAP messages, you'll have to move the messages yourself.

This enables you choose the messages you want to move out of the message store and put them in any PST you choose. You can use this method to store all files associated with a project, including documents from your file system, in one PST.

1. Add a new PST to your profile by choosing File, New, Outlook Data File and select the file format for your personal folders. Choose Unicode unless you need to retain backward compatibility with older versions of Outlook.

> If you plan to store documents in the PST, remember that the Outlook 97–2002 PST format has a maximum size of 2GB.

19

2. Browse to the location you want to store the folder in, usually your My Documents folder, and enter a filename such as **Johnson_2003** or **2003_2Q**. This helps you find the right archive set if you need it months later.

3. Enter a short but descriptive name for the folder set, such as **Johnson Project** or **2003 April-June** (see Figure 19.4). Click OK and Outlook creates the personal folder and adds it to your folder list.

4. Create new folders in the PST, if necessary. You can move folders (and their contents) from your message store to the PST.

▼

▼

FIGURE 19.4

Create a new personal folder to use for your archive. Use a name that describes the contents and add a password if desired. Remember: If you forget the password, you won't be able to recover your data.

Create Microsoft Personal Folders

File: D:\2003_2Q.pst

Name: 2003 (April-June)

Format: Personal Folders File

Encryption Setting

○ No Encryption
● Compressible Encryption
○ High Encryption

Password

Password:

Verify Password:

☐ Save this password in your password list

OK   Cancel

5. Select the item(s) or folder, choose Edit, Move to Folder, and then select the folder in your archive PST. Use move, not copy, to preserve the message ID, which is what Outlook uses to track messages and replies.

▲

Use Advanced Find or Find All (on the context menu of a selected message) to help you locate all the messages you want to move to your archive folder.

You can store files as well as Outlook items in the PST, including documents, spreadsheets, or graphics. This enables you to create archives by project and store all the related material together. If the PST exceeds 2GB, use the Unicode format to ensure you can store all of your files together.

After you've moved all the items to the folder that you want to move, right-click on it and choose Close to remove it from your folder list. When you need to review the items or files, use File, Open, Outlook Data File to reconnect it to your profile.

There are a number of third-party utilities to archive your messages and Outlook items. Look for the list of currently available programs at `http://www.slipstick.com/addins/housekeeping.htm`.

Using Mailbox Cleanup

Outlook 2003 includes a new feature that helps you keep your mailbox size under control: Mailbox Cleanup. Select Tools, Mailbox Cleanup to open the dialog shown in Figure 19.5.

Using Mailbox Cleanup, you can

- View your message store size (see Figure 19.5).
- Use a predefined Advanced Find search to locate items based on their age or size.
- Initiate AutoArchive.
- Empty your Deleted Items folder and check its folder size.
- View the conflicting items resulting from synchronizing your mailbox and server if you're an Exchange Server user.

FIGURE 19.5

Mailbox Cleanup groups some of Outlook's file management features on a dialog.

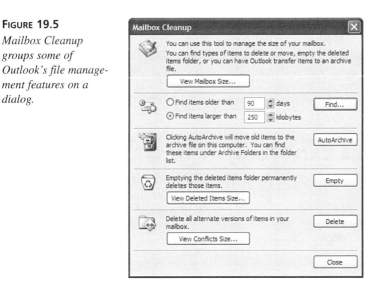

The View Mailbox Size and View Deleted Items Size choices display a list of your mailbox folders and their sizes (see Figure 19.6). Although the figures are fairly accurate, deleting everything in your message store might not reduce the mailbox size very much. This is because Outlook stores a lot of data in the mailbox, including views, custom forms, and rules.

FIGURE **19.6**
Use View Mailbox Size to see how big your mailbox is.

Only your default mailbox is listed in the View <u>M</u>ailbox Size dialog. You can still check the folders' sizes for additional personal folders: Right-click on the personal folder file, choose Properties, and then choose <u>F</u>older Size. You'll see a list of all subfolders and their file sizes.

Importing and Exporting Your Data

Although Impor<u>t</u> and Export isn't the best method to use when backing up your messages, calendar, and contacts, or when you move to a new computer and need to set Outlook up with your old messages, it's the method most people discover and use.

Suggested uses for Import and Export include

- Use it when you want to share your calendar or contacts with someone else. Export to a PST and others can either import the items or use File, Open, Outlook data file to view the items.

- Use it when your appointment times are messed up because of time zone or daylight saving time settings. Set the computer's time so that the appointment times are correct, and then export to Excel or Comma Separated Value (Windows). Delete the calendar items or move them to a new folder before correcting the computer's time and importing the items back into the calendar. After you're satisfied that the appointments were imported correctly, delete the old appointments.

- Export your contacts to Excel or a CSV file to use in a mail merge that doesn't support Outlook address books.

> Don't use Import and Export to back up your data. See the next section for the proper way to back up or move to a new computer.

Task: Use the Import and Export Wizard

▼ TASK

The Import and Export Wizard supports many file types and, in most cases, handles importing or exporting data very well. There are some limitations when you export to other file types; for example, the receive date is not exported.

1. Start the Import and Export Wizard by choosing File, Import and Export. If you have Outlook's Business Contact Manager installed, select Outlook to open the wizard.

2. Choose the action to perform (see Figure 19.7). Although you'll choose Export to a File for this exercise, you can import from a number of sources using this wizard.

FIGURE **19.7**

Use the Import and Export Wizard to import vCards, vCalendar, and iCalendar files, import from another program or file, and import account settings and addresses from Outlook Express.

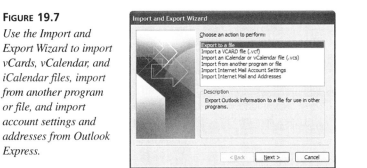

19

3. After selecting Export to a File, you'll be able to choose the file type to export to, including

- Comma Separated Values (*.CSV)
- Microsoft Access Database
- Microsoft Excel Spreadsheet
- Personal Folder File (*.PST)
- Tab Separated Values

▼ For this task, choose Personal Folder File.

▼   4. After selecting the file format, the folder browser dialog opens for you to select the folder or folders from which you want to export. To export the entire message store, select the top-level folder of your mailbox, shown here as Hotmail (see Figure 19.8).

FIGURE **19.8**

Select the folders to export. When you select the entire mail-box and include sub-folders, Deleted Items and Junk E-mail will export if the folders contain deleted items or junk email.

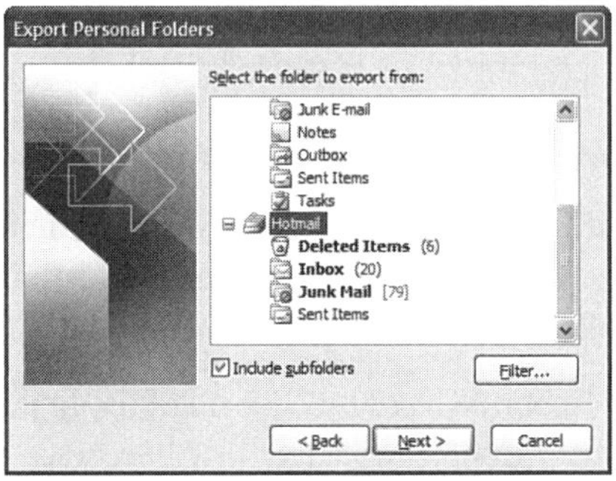

You can create filters to restrict the items exported. The Import and Export Wizard uses the filter dialog used by Advanced Find and Search folders.

5. Select the file that you want to Save Exported File As. It can be an existing file or you can create a new one. Choose how you want to handle duplicates.

▲   6. Click Finish and Outlook exports the items.

> The Excel Spreadsheet format is a good choice for backing up appointments or contacts. It's the recommended format to use when you need to export your appointments before correcting time zone problems.

When you need to import the items, repeat the steps and choose Import from Another Program or File. Choose Personal Folder File (PST) and browse to locate the file (see Figure 19.9).

Like Export, you can create filters to control what is imported. Import enables you to select where the items are imported. Choose Finish when you're ready to complete the import.

FIGURE 19.9

Select the folder or folders to import. When you have more than one folder in your profile, you can choose which folder to import the items into.

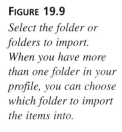

Backing Up Your Data

Many people don't think about backing up their data until something happens and they need to restore it. Don't be one of them: Back up your PST regularly, as often as once a day or once a week.

People who back up Outlook typically use Import and Export to back up their Outlook data or move it to a new computer. That's the wrong way to do it. Import and Export imports and exports only Outlook items; it doesn't touch custom forms, views, or other hidden items in the folders.

When you want to back up your data or move it to a new computer, find the PST and copy it. Unless you moved your PST to a new location, Outlook stores the PST at `C:\Documents and Settings\`*username*`\Local Settings\Application Data\ Microsoft\Outlook`. Close Outlook, find the file, and make a copy.

> To make it easier to back up your PST, move it to your My Documents folder. Close Outlook, find the PST, and move it. Reopen Outlook and when it complains about the missing PST, browse for the PST in the new location.
>
> There's little reason to back up your HTTP and IMAP PSTs because they contain copies of the messages still on your server. You need to edit the Registry to move them, but because Outlook often re-creates new PSTs in the default location, it's not recommended.

The Outlook folder under Local Settings contains Offline address book files (if you use an Exchange Server account) and `extend.dat`. Neither of these files needs to be backed up. Because `extend.dat` contains information about installed add-ins, using it on other machines could cause errors if the add-in isn't installed.

If the Outlook folder isn't visible, enable Show Hidden Files and Folders using Windows Explorer's Tools, Folder Options, View. When using Windows Search, always use the Advanced option to Search All Hidden Files and Folders.

The other Application Data folder in your Windows user profile, `C:\Documents and Settings\`*username*`\Application Data\Microsoft\Outlook`, contains the remainder of the Outlook data you might want to back up.

In most cases, the customization files in this folder path use the name of your profile. Each profile has its own set of files. The exception is the toolbar customization file: `outcmd.dat`. The same custom toolbars apply to all profiles used with your Windows user account. Copies of `outcmd.dat` should be made after creating toolbar customizations. Because it's not profile-specific, you can use this file on any machine with any profile.

- XML—Stores your navigation pane settings. This file can be backed up or deleted when you want to remove customizations and Outlook will create a new default XML.
- NK2—Stores the AutoComplete addresses seen when you type addresses into the To field. This file does not need to be backed up. Delete it to start with a new AutoComplete list.
- SRS—Send and receive settings. This file can be backed up, although it's most useful only when the same accounts are restored.

Any of these files can be renamed to match the name of any profile and, in most cases, they work just fine in any profile.

Rules are stored in your message store—they aren't included when you use Import and Export. For that reason, Import and Export is not recommended. You can export your rules for safekeeping: Select Tools, Rules and Alerts and choose Options, and then Export Rules or Import Rules. Rules are tied to the name and location of your PST, and you might need to repair the rules by selecting a new folder for each rule that moves or copies messages when you import it into another computer or profile.

Views and custom forms are also stored in the mailbox or personal folders file and are not imported and exported. Many times, views are folder specific and forms are published to a specific folder. In such cases, moving or copying the entire folder also copies the view and forms associated with the folder.

Saving Your Settings

Profiles are stored in the Registry, at `HKEY_CURRENT_USER\Software\Microsoft\Windows NT\CurrentVersion\Windows Messaging Subsystem\Profiles`. Because of all the information stored in the profile, exporting the Registry to save your profile doesn't always work well. You can back up your profile using the Office Save My Settings Wizard, found on the Start menu at All Programs, Microsoft Office, Microsoft Office Tools, Microsoft Office 2003 Save My Settings Wizard.

Follow the prompts to back up all of your Office settings or to restore saved settings.

If you have Windows XP, you can use the File and Settings Transfer Wizard to copy your profile. It doesn't copy your personal folders, just the profile settings. You can't select just Outlook, so you need to use to save the settings of many applications.

Summary

The hour introduced you to archiving and backup. You learned how to configure your AutoArchive settings and use AutoArchive to move older items out of your mailbox. You also learned about backing up your Outlook data, including what files to back up and where to find them.

Q&A

Q What's the best way to back up my Outlook data?

A Many people use the Backup program included with Windows or Shadow Volume copy. You can use Windows scripts or batch files to copy the PST before opening or after closing Outlook. Microsoft has a backup utility, and although it works OK, it's often easier to use Windows Backup or a script.

19

PART V

Getting More Out of Outlook

Hour

Hour 20

Custom Forms and Templates

One of the strengths of Outlook is the capability to create custom forms. No other popular consumer email client enables users to easily create custom forms and templates. Although it helps if you understand some basic programming concepts, you don't need to be a programmer to create simple custom forms. More complex forms often require scripting or VBA code, but anyone who is interested in learning scripting can find many code samples on various Internet sites, including Slipstick.com and Outlookcode.com.

This hour introduces you to the basics of designing and using custom forms and templates, as well as how to publish and manage your forms.

- Customizing forms
- Using templates
- Publishing forms
- Managing published forms

Custom forms and templates aren't just for developers and programmers. They're simple to create and can save you time. You don't need to be an expert to create templates and custom forms, but if you don't feel skilled enough using Outlook now to try your hand at designing a custom form, come back to this hour in a few weeks.

Creating Custom Forms

Although the standard Outlook forms are often good enough, there are times when you'll wish the form had different fields. You might want to remove some of the default fields, add some of your own, or just rearrange what's there.

You might want to create a boilerplate message to use in response to inquiries, or pre-address a message form to a group of people with whom you often correspond. You can do all of this and more using custom forms.

You can create templates and forms containing boilerplate text by editing the fields in the form. But when you want to add or remove fields or use scripting with the form, you need to use Design mode to open Outlook forms so that they can be edited.

You don't need a special program to use Design mode; it's part of every form included with Outlook and is enabled when you tell Outlook you want to design a form.

You can open a form in Design mode two ways: by using Tools, Forms, Design a Form and selecting a form from the dialog; or when a form is already open, by using its Tools, Forms, Design this Form menu option. In any case, when it's a message form, it will look similar to Figure 20.1.

You need to use Outlook as your email editor to design email forms or templates. When Word is your editor, you can't go into Design mode for email forms.

When forms are in Design mode, the Form Design toolbar is visible (see Figure 20.2). This toolbar has many of the design tools you'll use the most. The Form and Layout menus also contain design tools.

Customize the Forms toolbar to add the Run This Form button to it. Doing so makes it easier to test your forms as you design them.

Along with the Form Design toolbar, you'll also use the Field Chooser and Control Toolbox to create your custom forms. Right-click on any control to access the Properties and Advanced Properties dialogs. The Properties dialog contains display, value, and validation information for the control, whereas Advanced Properties has more advanced display properties.

FIGURE 20.1

A message form in Design mode. Hidden pages have parentheses around their names. Drag fields from the Field Chooser to add them to a form or create your own fields.

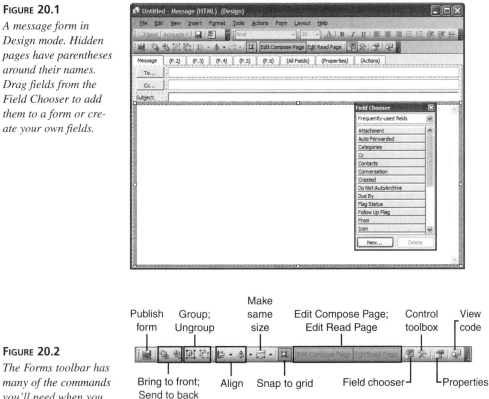

FIGURE 20.2

The Forms toolbar has many of the commands you'll need when you customize your forms.

To design forms, drag controls from the Control Toolbox or fields from the Field Chooser and configure the properties. Select the control and drag it to the form, dropping the control when the mouse cursor is over the area where you want the control placed. When you drag fields to the form, the fields are automatically arranged on the left edge of the form.

A feature many people request is to list a person's age on the contact form, so I'll show you how to create a custom form with the contact's age on it.

Task: Design a Form

Designing a custom form is actually pretty easy, at least for simple forms. You can customize any Outlook form, except for message forms, when you use Word as the editor.

20

▼   1. Open the Design Form dialog using the Tools, Forms, Design a Form Menu (see
         Figure 20.3). The Standard form library contains the form types that can be
         customized.

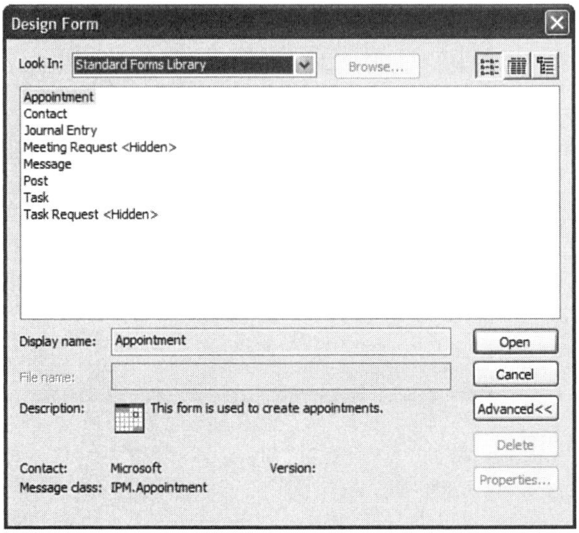

FIGURE 20.3

*The Design Form dia-
log lists all forms cur-
rently installed on your
computer or in your
Outlook message store.*

Outlook's notes, known in form language as `IPM.StickyNote`, are not customizable and can't be used for custom forms. You can save notes to use as
templates.

2. Select a form to edit or customize. For this example, I'm going to choose a contact
   form to open (see Figure 20.4).

The first page of each of the appointment, journal, and task forms is not
customizable. The All Fields, Properties, and Actions tabs are not customizable on any form.

Editable pages have a grid to help you align the controls and page names in parentheses indicate that the page is hidden on published forms.

The Field Chooser lists all available fields that can be used on the forms and displays when a form opens in Design mode. You can create new fields if you need

▼   them (click the New button).

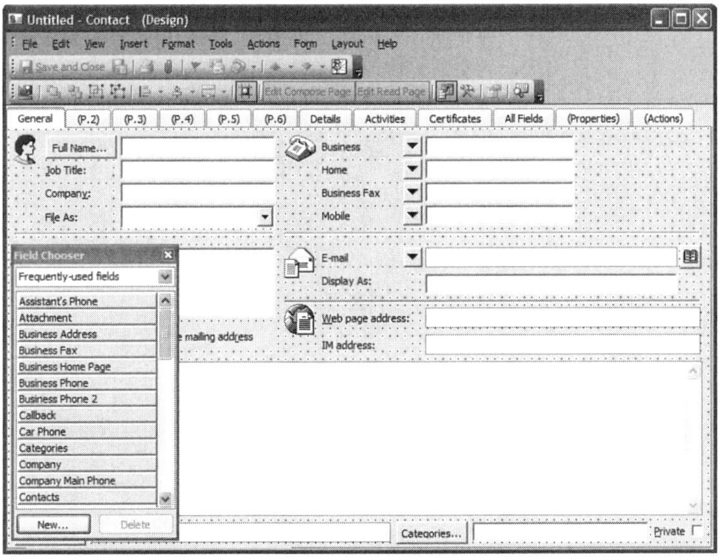

FIGURE 20.4

A contact form in Design mode.

You won't see the picture control when you're designing a custom form but it remains on the forms unless you change the first page of a custom contact form. Making any changes to the first page removes the picture control and the form reverts to the style used by Outlook 2002 and older versions. If you need to add fields and want to keep the new look of the form, add the fields to another page.

3. Our age form uses a TextBox to display a formula that calculates a person's age, so we need to choose the Control Toolbox button to display the controls.

   Because I like the contact form with the picture control, I'm going to add the Age field to (P.2). When the first control is dropped on the page, the parentheses disappear.

4. Drag a Label and a TextBox control to the form. These are the second and third icons in the Control Toolbox, identified by the uppercase A icon and the lowercase ab icon.

5. Right-click on the control identified as Label1 and choose Properties (see Figure 20.5).

   You can change other properties, such as the font and colors. Because this field is used as the name for the TextBox, we don't need to change anything on the other tabs.

20

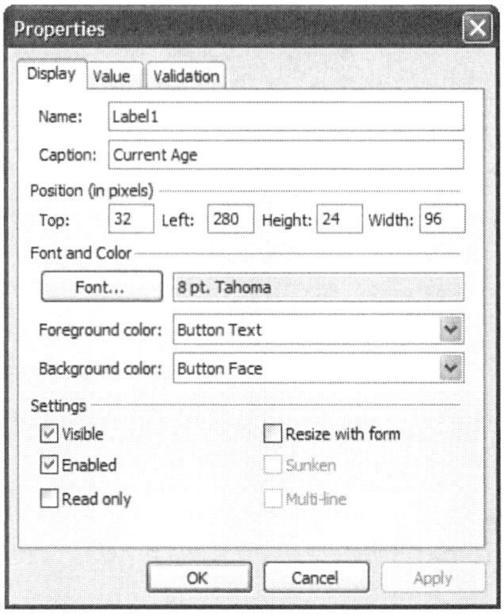

▼

FIGURE 20.5

Change the properties of a control using the Properties sheet. In this case, we're leaving the label named Label1 and changing the caption to Current Age.

6. Right-click on the TextBox and choose Properties. Change the Name to txtAge and select the Value tab. Click New to create a new field for Age, using Number for the Type: and changing Format: to All Digits (see Figure 20.6).

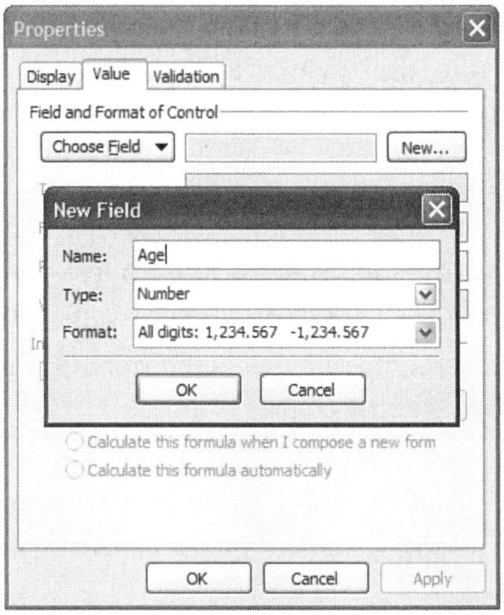

FIGURE 20.6

Create a new field for displaying the age.

7. Add a check to the Set the Initial Value of This Field To: box and choose Edit. Enter the formula to calculate the age (see Figure 20.7):

```
IIf([Birthday]<>"None",DateDiff("yyyy",[Birthday],Date())
-IIf(DateDiff("d",CDate(Month([Birthday]) & "/" & Day([Birthday]) & "/" &
Year(Date())),Date())<0,1,0),"")
```

▼

FIGURE 20.7

Use the Edit dialog to enter the formula for the field.

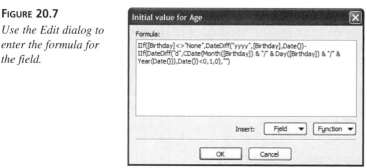

> **Initial value for Age** ☒
>
> Formula:
>
> IIf([Birthday]<>"None",DateDiff("yyyy",[Birthday],Date())-
> IIf(DateDiff("d",CDate(Month([Birthday]) & "/" & Day([Birthday]) & "/" &
> Year(Date())),Date())<0,1,0),"")
>
> Insert: [Field ▼] [Function ▼]
>
> [OK] [Cancel]

8. Choose Calculate This Formula Automatically and click the Value tab. Select the Validation tab and add a check to Include This Field for Printing and Save As. Click OK.

> ⓘ A less accurate, but easier to type formula is (Now() - [Birthday]) /365.
> This formula rounds to the contact's nearest birthday, with the age off by as much as six months.

Now it's time to test your form. Choose Form, Run This Form to open a new form using your new form. Enter 1 **test** in the File As Field, select the Details tab, and type your birth date in the Birthday field. Save the form using File, Save (Ctrl+S) and check the Age field.

> ⓘ You could add this to an appointment form that you use for birthdays and anniversaries.

Does it show your age as of your last birthday? If the age is correct, congratulations: You created your first custom form. If the age is not correct, check the formula for typographical errors. If you want to copy the formula and paste it into the field, the formula and sample forms are at http://www.outlook-tips.net/samples.htm.

Before publishing or saving the form, you'll want to change the tab name from P.2 to something more informative. Choose Form, Rename Page and enter a new name for your page.

The new page uses an ugly gray color. You can change this by right-clicking on the Current Age label and choosing Advanced Properties. Select the BackColor field, type

20

00f7f7f7 in the text box at the top of the form, and then click Apply, as shown in Figure 20.6. This changes the label field to the silver color used on the other pages. You can double-click on the BackColor property to open the color picker, if you want to use a different color.

Click again anywhere on the page to switch to the Properties dialog for the page (see Figure 20.8). Change the BackColor property to 00f7f7f7, apply it, and close the Properties dialog.

Use the Advanced Properties dialog to change the display properties for the control.

Properties

Apply	00f7f7f7 - Unknown	▼	...

BackColor	00f7f7f7 - Unknown
BorderColor	80000012 - Button Text
BorderStyle	0 - None
Caption	
Cycle	0 - AllForms
DrawBuffer	32000
Enabled	-1 - True
Font	8pt MS Sans Serif
ForeColor	80000012 - Button Text
KeepScrollBarsVisi	0 - None
MouseIcon	(None)
MousePointer	0 - Default
Picture	(None)
PictureAlignment	2 - Center

The final step before saving the form is entering a version number. This helps to prevent corruption in the forms cache when you increment the version number after editing the form and republishing it using the same name.

When you don't use a version number and republish the form, you might cause the form to become one-offed. *One-offed* means that the form uses a form definition stored with the form, not the global definition. This results in larger item sizes and the possibility of mismatched fields.

Select the (Properties) tab and enter a number in the Version field. In most cases, you'll use 1, but any number will do. Enter a number in the Form Number field.

Although it's not necessary, you can also select custom icons to use for the large and small icons. Choose a 32×32 icon for each size, with the large icon filling the 32×32 square and the small icon using a 16×16 image in the upper-left corner.

Custom icons usually won't be visible on forms in your Outlook folders until you restart Outlook. Occasionally, you'll also need to delete `C:\Documents and Settings\username\Local Settings\Application Data\Microsoft\ FORMS\FRMCACHE.DAT` before the icons will be visible.

If you can't find the folder, you have hidden files and folders enabled. Use Search and enable Search Hidden Files and Folders under More Advanced Options.

The other options you can configure on the dialog include password protecting the form so that others can't customize it and sending the form definition with the item.

Check Send Form Definition when you are creating a form you're going to share with other people, or when you use Exchange Server and didn't publish the form to the Organizational Forms library. When it's enabled, the complete form is sent, resulting in a larger item but enabling the recipient to see and use your customizations. If you don't send the form definition, Outlook uses the default form to display the item.

Although you can create many nice custom forms using only controls and fields, at some point you might need code to do what you want the form to do. You'll need to know how to write VBScript, or at least know where to find code samples on the Internet.

Task: Add a VB Script to a Form

I'm going to customize another contact form, this time with a command button that enables you to add the time and date to the Notes field.

1. Open a new contact form in Design mode and click on the Control Toolbox toolbar button to display the toolbox.

2. Drag the CommandButton control to an empty area on the form. I'm putting it under the Address fields on my form (see Figure 20.9).

3. Right-click on the button and choose Properties. Enter a descriptive caption in the Caption field and click OK.

4. Choose Form, View Code to open the Script Editor. Enter the following script in the editor then click on the X to close the window:

```
Sub StampDate()
Item.Body = Now() & vbCrLf & vbCrLf & Item.Body
End Sub
Sub CommandButton1_Click()
Call StampDate()
End Sub
```

20

FIGURE 20.9
Add the CommandButton to your form,

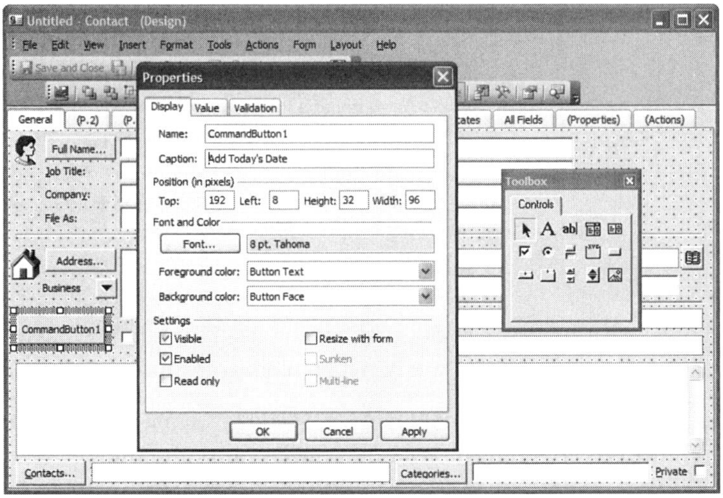

5. Choose **F**orm, Run This Fo**r**m to test your code. Pressing the command button should enter the current time and date.

> You'll find it's easier to use a third-party script editor or the Visual Basic IDE when you're working with complex scripts. You'll have better tools to verify your code and can copy and paste the finished script into the Script Editor window.

Because the form contains code, it must be published. Outlook's security prevents the code from running.

Publishing Custom Forms

After the form is completed, you obviously need to save it somewhere. In most cases, the preferred method is publishing it to an Outlook folder or library. It's also good practice to save the form as a template to your file system so that you have a backup copy. Use **F**ile, Save **A**s, and select Outlook Template (*.oft) as the file type.

Use the **T**ools, **F**orms, Publish **F**orm menu selection to bring up the Publish Form As dialog (see Figure 20.10). Select the folder the form will be published in from the Look In list. Use the Browse button to select folders that aren't listed.

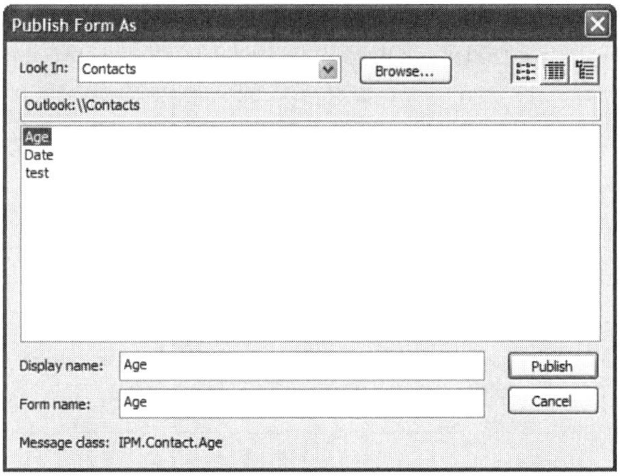

FIGURE **20.10**

Use the Publish Form dialog to publish forms to your Outlook folders. Type a display name and Outlook enters it into the Form Name field for you.

Publish Form As

Look In: Contacts

Outlook:\\Contacts

Age
Date
test

Display name: Age

Form name: Age

Publish

Cancel

Message class: IPM.Contact.Age

Publish forms to the folder you're planning to use them in, such as the Age form to the Contacts folder, and you can select the form from the bottom of the Actions menu after opening the folder.

When you're using Exchange Server, you can publish to the Organizational Forms library if your administrator allows it. When forms are in the Organizational Forms library, anyone in the organization can use them. Do this when you want to share the form with your co-workers.

Using Templates

A *template* is a custom form you save in your Windows file system, instead of publishing it to an Outlook folder. A template can be used for everything that a form is used for. Create a custom form, and then choose File, Save As, Outlook Template instead of publishing it to a folder.

You can also create a template without entering Design mode by choosing File, Save As, Outlook Template (*.oft) from any form. Use this method when you're creating a template with fields filled in or a message that contains boilerplate text.

20

A good use of a custom template is explained at
`http://www.slipstick.com/dev/olforms/skedrpt.htm`. Follow the instructions to send a message to the same group of people on a schedule.

Many users find templates easier to work with than forms for several reasons. You can copy templates to a folder in Outlook and double-click to use them. When you no longer need a template, it's easy to delete it. You can create toolbar buttons hyperlinked to templates or add templates to the Navigation bar's Shortcut bar.

When you use scripting in your form, you'll have to publish the form to avoid Outlook's security features or use ClickYes (`http://www.express-soft.com/mailmate/clickyes.html`) to avoid the security prompts.

> You must use Outlook as your email editor to design email forms or templates.

Managing Published Forms

After you've published a form, you might want to always use it when you create an item in your folders, convert all existing items to use the new form, or delete old forms that you no longer use.

As I mentioned previously, when the form is published to a folder, it's listed in the Actions folder when you open the folder. This works well for a form that you don't want to use for every item, but it won't work when you automatically create items without opening the folder, such as dropping messages in a folder to create contact, task, or calendar entries.

When you want the new form set as your default, select a folder, right-click on it, and choose Properties (see Figure 20.11). Select the new form from the When Posting to This Folder, Use drop-down list. To test it, drag a message to the folder. It should use your new form.

If your form wasn't published in this folder, you'll have to copy it to the folder.

1. Switch to the Forms tab and select Manage (see Figure 20.12).
2. Choose Set and browse to the folder you need to copy a form to or from.
3. Select the form you want to copy and choose Copy.
4. Delete forms you no longer use by selecting the form and choosing Delete.

Use the Properties button to look at and edit the properties of the selected form. If you didn't enter categories, contact, or description information before you published the form, you can add the information using the Form Manager. The description displays on the Forms Manager dialog and in the description field on the Forms tab. Choose Clear Cache to delete the forms cache file and create a fresh one.

FIGURE 20.11

Use the Properties dialog to manage your custom forms. Set the default form for the folder from the General tab and manage your forms from the Forms tab.

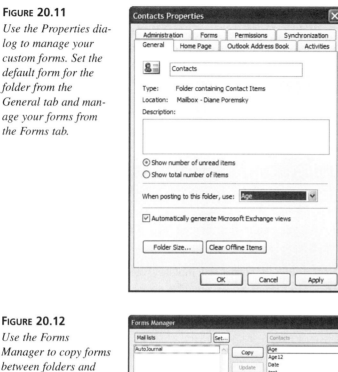

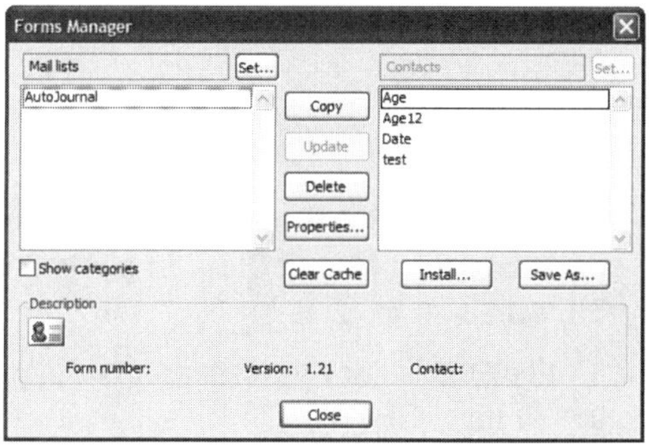

FIGURE 20.12

Use the Forms Manager to copy forms between folders and delete forms you no longer want.

Changing existing items to use the new form requires VBA code or a utility to change the old MessageClass to the new MessageClass. I use Change Forms, a utility included in the Office 2000 Resource Kit. It was written for Outlook 2000 and works well with Outlook 2003, although you'll have to unzip ChangeForms.exe and run Changeforms.msi to install it.

After installed, select an item you want to change to use the new MessageClass, and run Change Forms from the Tools, Forms, Change Forms menu. Type the name of the new MessageClass in the field and run the utility. Only the items using the old MessageClass are changed to the new MessageClass.

20

Another utility is Omsgclas, which is available from Microsoft's Knowledge Base Article 201089. It changes all items in the folder to the new message class. As a result, when you run Omsgclas on a Contacts folder, it destroys all distribution lists in the folder. You can use Omsgclas to identify the different message classes you have in a folder, and then use Change Forms to change specific message classes.

For more information and utilities you can use to change the MessageClass, see http://www.slipstick.com/dev/newdefaultform.htm.

Summary

The hour introduced you to designing and using custom forms. You learned how to open and use the Forms Designer, how to create custom fields, and add a VB script to a form.

Publishing your new forms or saving the forms as templates was also explained. You can use the new form as the default form for a folder and change the existing items to use the new forms. Managing the forms you created with Forms Manager allows you to copy forms between folders and delete old forms.

Q&A

Q I created a custom form, changed the icon, and restarted Outlook. I then used Change Forms to change the MessageClass on all the items in the folder, but only a few items use the new icon.

A There's a bug in Outlook that causes some items to display the default icon. There doesn't seem to be any rhyme or reason to it—some old contacts are affected as are some newer ones. When you check the MessageClass or open the item in Design mode, the icon it's supposed to use is the correct one.

HOUR 21

Creating Macros

Creating macros in Word or Excel is as simple as turning on the Macro Recorder and recording your keystrokes and mouse movements. Although it creates messy code with many unnecessary commands, it works quite well and serves its purpose.

Outlook doesn't have a Macro Recorder, so you need to learn how to program and write your own code. Fortunately, there are plenty of Web sites and forums that provide tutorials and code snippets to get you started.

In this hour, I'll introduce you to the basics of creating macros and create a couple of simple macros in Outlook.

- Using the VB Editor
- Introducing the Outlook Object Model
- Creating macros with Visual Basic for Applications (VBA)

Even if you don't consider yourself a programmer, you should try the sample macros included in this hour. In the end, you'll have two useful, time-saving macros. And even if you never write a line of code on your own, the macros you create here will be useful in your day-to-day work.

Understanding Outlook's VBA

Programming and VBA scares a lot of people off. It's really not hard and many code samples are available on the Internet for you to use, so you don't even have to know how to program. But if you're unsure of whether you're ready for this, put it down, get yourself an introductory Visual Basic programming book, and come back to this hour when you feel you're ready.

Typing code samples from books isn't a favorite hobby of mine, even for short code snippets. It's too easy to make a typing error and hard to notice the mistake when the code errors, resulting in frustration and a feeling that you can't do it.

For this reason, I have a text file with the code used in this book available at www.poremsky.com/samples/ for you to download. Copy and paste the code into the VB Editor as you read this hour and you'll discover you can do it. You might even discover you like doing it.

There are many differences between how you create macros in Outlook compared to Word and Excel. First, you have to write the code yourself; you can't record it using a Macro recorder. Secondly, Word and Excel enable you to create a lot of modules that you can easily distribute to others. Outlook uses one module, `C:\Documents and Settings\ username\Application Data\Microsoft\Outlook\VBAProject.OTM`, which contains all the macros the user created. All forms and modules are stored within this one file. If you give this file to someone and he uses it to replace his copy, he loses all previous macros he had.

Projects and Modules

All OutlookVBA code is contained in a single project, coincidently named VBAProject.OTM. This project is associated with a Windows user account, so all users of a computer have their own VBAProject. You can have just one VBAProject and all code used with Outlook is contained in this file.

A project contains code modules and UserForm modules. Don't confuse Outlook forms with UserForms. UserForms are used to create the dialog boxes you respond to, not only in Outlook, but in all Windows programs.

Code modules contain your VBA code, which is also referred to as a *routine*, *procedure*, *macro*, *function*, or *subroutine*. To the untrained eye, these all mean the same thing—a bunch of code "that's all Geek to me." Seasoned developers use the terms to describe different types of code. In Outlook, the main code module is called ThisOutlookSession.

For a list of Outlook programming resources and code samples, see
http://www.slipstick.com/dev/index.htm.

There's so much to learn about writing your own Outlook code that it's better suited for a book specifically about Outlook programming. For that reason, I won't go over the object model or programming in depth; rather, I'll begin with entering your first macro. If you want to learn more, there are many resources and code samples available on the Internet.

Because Outlook can do so much with code, Microsoft added security features to the object model to block unauthorized access to a number of Outlook features by other programs and VBA. Outlook 2003 eliminates the security prompts in properly constructed Outlook COM add-ins and published Outlook forms. Code in Outlook VBA also does not trigger security prompts because it's implemented as a COM add-in. However, using the code to access other COM add-ins or libraries will trigger the security warning.

Using the Visual Basic Editor

Before you can write VBA macros, you need an editor. Outlook, like the other Office applications, includes the Visual Basic Editor. Open the editor interface by choosing Tools, Macro, Visual Basic Editor or by pressing Alt+F11 on your keyboard.

The Visual Basic Editor should be installed by default with a typical or complete installation. If it's not available, you'll have to use the Add/Remove Programs applet in Windows Control Panel and change your installed features.

The Visual Basic Editor has all the tools you'll need. Use the Project Explorer to see all the modules you've associated with Outlook and the Properties window to add or change properties, including the project name and other properties.

Type your code in the large window. Selecting Application in the Object drop-down list, shown as (General) in Figure 21.1, lists the available procedures in the right field and automatically enters the selection in the code window.

The Visual Basic Editor interface includes the Project and Properties browsers, the main code window, and the Standard toolbar. Right-click on the toolbars and show the Edit and Debug toolbars. Figures 21.2 through 21.4 detail the buttons found on these toolbars.

21

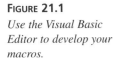

FIGURE **21.1**

Use the Visual Basic Editor to develop your macros.

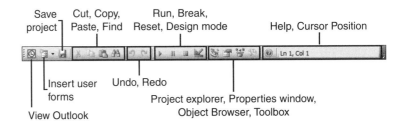

FIGURE **21.2**

The Standard toolbar has the standard Windows commands along with commands you can use to switch back to Outlook, select a module, form, or class, run your code, and show the object browser and control toolbox.

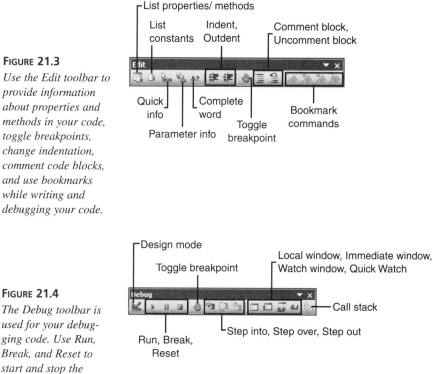

FIGURE 21.3

Use the Edit toolbar to provide information about properties and methods in your code, toggle breakpoints, change indentation, comment code blocks, and use bookmarks while writing and debugging your code.

FIGURE 21.4

The Debug toolbar is used for your debugging code. Use Run, Break, and Reset to start and stop the macro, and use Step In, Out, and Over to run the code line by line or skip lines. Use the windows and watches and see the results your code returns.

One of the most important features of the VB Editor is the Object Browser. Using the Object Browser, you can see all the properties, methods, and objects referenced in your project and available for you to use (see Figure 21.5).

Add or remove libraries from your project using Tools, References. Only references that have checkmarks are available for use in your project.

21

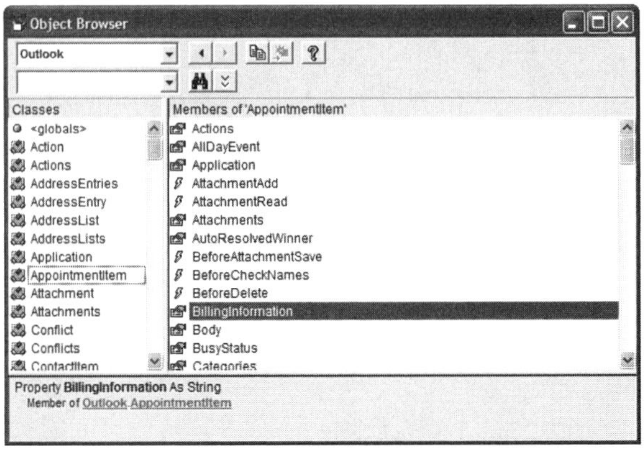

FIGURE 21.5

Use the Object Browser to view the object model and libraries referenced in your project. Select the library from the Project/Library list or enter search words in the Search field.

Now that you know where to find the main parts of the editor, it's time to write your code. The general steps are

1. Make a copy of or back up your mailbox before testing your code. Although it's safer to test against a test account, the results might be different when you test against real data and it's very risky if your code doesn't work correctly. Backups are especially important when you're writing code that changes items.

2. Name the Sub procedure. This is the project name you'll look for when you run the macro from Tools, Macros, Macros. Don't use spaces and keep the name short.

3. Declare your objects, strings, and so on. You need to define the name and data type of a variable used in your code.

4. Type your code in the module.

5. Test your code to see if it works without error.

> Use the Save button often and either exit Outlook and confirm the prompt to save the VBAProject.OTM, or copy the code to Notepad or an Outlook post form and then save. If Outlook hangs on your code, you could lose your work.

Task: Create Your First Macro

When there is a feature Microsoft forgot that you'd like to have in Outlook, many times you can create a macro yourself. Some macros are complex, but others just look complex. The macro we're going to create falls into the second group; it looks complex, but it's really simple.

▼ This macro provides a time-saving feature that Outlook should have, but doesn't: the ability to easily save attachments to a specific folder on your hard drive and then delete the attachment from the message. In addition, we add a clickable link pointing to the attachment on the bottom of the message.

> Attachments that are blocked by Outlook's Attachment Security features will not be saved or removed from the message.

Before you can enter VBA code, you have to open the VB Editor, using the Tools, Macros, Visual Basic Editor menu selection. If you prefer keyboard shortcuts, use Alt+F11.

1. Click on ThisOutlookSession to open it in the code window, if it's not already open.

2. Choose Insert, Procedure to open the Add Procedure dialog (see Figure 21.6). Enter a name for the procedure. I'm calling mine SaveAttachments. Leave the options on their defaults and choose OK. Use an underscore to replace spaces in names.

FIGURE 21.6

Use the Add, Procedure dialog to enter the name of the procedure automatically or type it in the code window yourself.

> You can download a text file containing the code sample from http://www.poremsky.com/samples/. Copy and paste the text into ThisOutlookSession, and then follow along with the text.

21

3. Declare your variables. This macro removes attachments from selected messages, so we know we'll need to define what Application, MailItem, Attachments, and Selection are. Any variables we discover we need later will be added here.

▼

Type the following code into your subprocedure in `ThisOutlookSession`, as shown in Figure 21.7.

```
Public Sub SaveAttachments()
    Dim objOL As Outlook.Application
    Dim objMsg As Outlook.MailItem 'Object
    Dim objAttachments As Outlook.Attachments
    Dim objSelection As Outlook.Selection
    Dim i As Long
    Dim lngCount As Long
    Dim strFile As String
    Dim strFolderpath As String
    Dim strDeletedFiles As String
```

FIGURE 21.7

Define the objects you'll use in your macro.

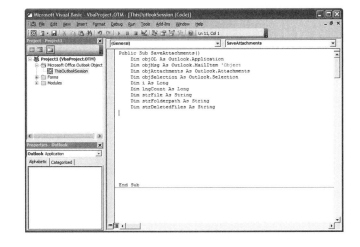

4. We need a location to save the attachments. In my case, I wanted them saved to a subfolder in My Documents. I could easily hardcode the path, but if I give it to someone else, her path would be different. Add a line for error handling and comment out or remove the `MsgBox` line when you are satisfied that it's getting the correct path.

A hardcoded path would look something like this, where My Outlook Attachments is the full path to the folder location:

```
strFolderpath = "D:\My Data\My Outlook Attachments\"
```

Because I want to share this code with others, I'm using the user's My Documents folder, which is a special Windows folder whose full path is stored in the registry.

```
strFolderpath = CreateObject("WScript.Shell").SpecialFolders(16)
MsgBox strFolderpath
    On Error Resume Next
```

▼

> Add an apostrophe to the front of a line you want to comment out. VB
> ignores all comment lines, which are used as notes to the person reading
> the program code. You can also select a block of code and use the Edit tool-
> bar's Comment Block and Uncomment Block buttons to quickly add and
> remove comments from your code.
>
> Use comments liberally throughout the code so that you can remember why
> you did it like that months later.

5. Instantiate an Outlook `Application` object and get the collection of selected objects. This tells the code what folders and items we want to use. In this sample, we want whatever Outlook item is selected. Later, we'll verify it's a mail item.

```
Set objOL = CreateObject("Outlook.Application")
Set objSelection = objOL.ActiveExplorer.Selection
```

6. Set the path to the attachment location. I created a subfolder to save the attachments in. Again, remove or comment out the `MsgBox` line when you're satisfied that it returns the correct path.

```
    strFolderpath = strFolderpath & "\OLAttachments\"
MsgBox strFolderpath
```

Message boxes, or `MsgBox` in VBA, are useful to show you if a piece of code is returning the results you expect. When a `MsgBox` is used, the code stops until you press OK (see Figure 21.8). Other methods, such as using the Immediate window to display the results and continue running, are often better for debugging, but for small projects, MsgBox is quick.

FIGURE 21.8

Use `MsgBox` to display the results of strings while you test your code to learn whether a string contains the data you expect it to.

Microsoft Office Outlook ☒

D:\New Data\OLAttachments\

OK

7. This code checks the selected message for attachments. If attachments are found, it counts how many there are. Comment out the `MsgBox` line after you verify that it works.

```
For Each objMsg In objSelection
    If objMsg.Class = olMail Then
        Set objAttachments = objMsg.Attachments
        lngCount = objAttachments.Count
```

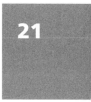

▼

```
MsgBox objAttachments.Count
```

8. Use this next section of code to loop through the selected messages, saving and removing the attachments. We count down (`Step -1`), not up, because the index changes each time an attachment is deleted and only every other item would be removed otherwise.

```
If lngCount > 0 Then
    For i = lngCount To 1 Step -1
```

9. We need the filename next. First, we get the filename of the attachment and store it in the `strFile` string. Then we append it to the string that contains the folder path. When we're done, we save the attachment and delete it from the message.

```
strFile = objAttachments.Item(i).FileName
strFile = strFolderpath & strFile
objAttachments.Item(i).SaveAsFile strFile
objAttachments.Item(i).Delete
```

10. This next piece of code is used to save the file path on the message. First check to see whether the message is HTML formatted. If it's plain text, we'll use a simple `file://` hyperlink, but we need to use HTML tags if the message is HTML formatted. The path is added to a string and a message box shows us the full string while we're debugging the code (see Figure 21.9).

```
If objMsg.BodyFormat <> olFormatHTML Then
    strDeletedFiles = strDeletedFiles & vbCrLf & "<file://" & _
    strFile & ">"
Else
    strDeletedFiles = strDeletedFiles & "<br>" & "<a href='file://" & _
    strFile & "'>" & strFile & "</a>"
End If

MsgBox strDeletedFiles
```

FIGURE 21.9

The message containing the attachments used HTML formatting, so the `StrDeletedFiles` *string contains the filenames and HTML formatting and is used to create links to the files.*

Microsoft Office Outlook

<a href='file://D:\New Data\OLAttachments\CDOLive Training Objectives.doc'>D:\New Data\OLAttachments\CDOLive Training Objectives.doc</a>
<a href='file://D:\New Data\OLAttachments\Denise Checchia.msg'>D:\New Data\OLAttachments\Denise Checchia.msg</a>
<a href='file://D:\New Data\OLAttachments\Hilton Philadelphia City Avenue.msg'>D:\New Data\OLAttachments\Hilton Philadelphia City Avenue.msg</a>
<a href='file://D:\New Data\OLAttachments\Holiday Inn - City Line.msg'>D:\New Data\OLAttachments\Holiday Inn - City Line.msg</a>
<a href='file://D:\New Data\OLAttachments\QC Revision Report.oft'>D:\New Data\OLAttachments\QC Revision Report.oft</a>

OK

11. Loop back to remove the next attachment. After all the attachments are removed, the loop ends and the macro continues to the next step.

```
    Next i
End If
```

▼ 12. Check the body for HTML formatting. If the message is HTML, write the file path
string to the message body using HTML formatting tags. Then save the message.

```
If objMsg.BodyFormat <> olFormatHTML Then
    objMsg.Body = objMsg.Body & vbCrLf & _
    "The file(s) were saved to " & strDeletedFiles
Else
    objMsg.HTMLBody = objMsg.HTMLBody & "<p>" & _
    "The file(s) were saved to " & strDeletedFiles
End If
```

```
objMsg.Save
```

13. If more than one message was selected, the macro loops back and processes the
next message. The filename string, `strDeletedFiles`, must first be reset to nothing; otherwise, each additional message will have links to all previous attachments
or you'll be limited to selecting one message at a time.

```
    End If
strDeletedFiles = ""
Next
```

14. This code exits the macro early if there is an error and clears the objects from
memory when it exits due to an error or after it's finished removing the attachments.

```
ExitSub:
    Set objAttachments = Nothing
    Set objMsg = Nothing
    Set objSelection = Nothing
    Set objOL = Nothing
End Sub
```

Press F8 or use <u>D</u>ebug, Step <u>I</u>nto to walk through the macro and watch it work on copies
▲ of your messages or using a test message store.

> You should always set the objects you use to nothing before exiting a pro-
> cedure so that the memory they hold is released. If you don't release the
> objects each time you run the macro, more memory is held and you'll have
> to reboot your computer.

You could refine this macro to ask for the file location, either prompting you with a simple input screen or with a folder browser dialog. Although adding a folder browser dialog
appears to defeat the purpose of using a macro because it mimics Outlook's File, Save
Attachments command, Outlook doesn't allow you to select multiple messages, add the
file path, and delete the attachment in one step.

21

You could also check for existing files using the same name, create new subfolders based on the date, or save the attachments in different folders based on file type.

After you save the procedure, customize your Outlook toolbar and add a button to run the macro. Choose Macros from the Customize dialog and drag your macro to the toolbar. Edit the display name and it's ready to use.

> Always make backups before testing code on your items. If there is an error, you might lose the data.
>
> Use the Search Folder to locate items in your mailbox that contain attachments. Then create a test folder and use Edit, Select All, Edit, Copy to Folder and make copies of the messages. If you don't have many messages containing attachments, make several copies. Use the copies when you test your code.

Task: Get the Internet Message Header

Anyone who trying to report spam or is curious about suspicious messages wants to look at a message's Internet header. It contains information about the sender, who he says he is, the route the message took to get to you, and the location it was sent from. You can learn a lot from viewing a message header, but Outlook makes using the Internet header difficult.

As you know, viewing the Internet message header on a message is not as easy as it could be. You need to right-click on the message in the message list, choose Options, and then try to read the header in a tiny text box. You might need to paste it in the message to forward to your email administrator, or need to Select All, Copy and then paste the header into a new message. The process is an annoyance and requires too many steps for many people.

You can use a few lines of VBA to make the process much simpler. If you often need to paste a header in a message, two additional lines of code will copy the header to the Windows Clipboard. You can view the header in a message box or create a form and display it in a text box.

1. Open the VBE (Alt+F11) and choose `ThisOutlookSession`, if it's not in focus already.

2. Click in the code window and choose <u>I</u>nsert, <u>P</u>rocedure. Enter the name of your procedure. I'm going to use `GetInternetHeaders`. Click OK and the sub is created for you.

▼

▼ 3. You first need to set the references to the libraries you're going to access. Using Tools, References, scroll down and select Microsoft CDO 1.21 Library (see Figure 21.10). When you receive an error that says `Compile error: User-defined type not defined`, you're missing references.

Collaboration Data Objects (CDO) is used for some Outlook programming tasks, such as displaying some message and address book properties.

FIGURE 21.10

Your list might have more or fewer libraries checked. Occasionally, you'll have to browse the file system to locate the file you need.

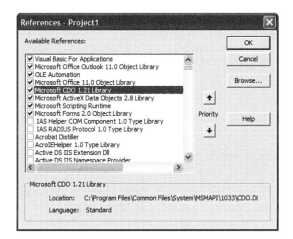

If you don't see Microsoft CDO 1.21, it's probably not installed. Use Add/Remove Programs applet in the Windows Control Panel to run Office setup and install it.

4. Enter your code, beginning with error handling. Because this is a simple procedure, I'm going to use only basic error handling, `On Error Resume Next`.

```
Public Sub GetInternetHeaders()
On Error Resume Next
```

You can download a text file containing the code sample from http://www.poremsky.com/samples/. Use File, Import File to import the frmHeader form.

▼

▼ 5. Because we use CDO to get the message header, we need to declare it as a constant.

```
Const CdoPR_TRANSPORT_MESSAGE_HEADERS = &H7D001E
```

6. Next, we must declare the objects that we need to use. When you write a procedure from scratch, you might not know what you need to declare and will add more objects or variables to the list as you code. You should always have these grouped at the top and in the order you use them. It makes the code easier to read and understand later.

```
Dim objSession As New MAPI.Session
Dim objExplorer As Outlook.Explorer
Dim objSelection As Outlook.Selection
Dim objItem As Outlook.MailItem   'Object
Dim objMessage As MAPI.Message
Dim objFields As MAPI.Fields
Dim strheader As String
Dim InetHeader As New MSForms.DataObject
```

7. Now it's time for the nitty-gritty. The code needs to log on to Outlook.

```
objSession.Logon , , False, False, 0 ' Use the existing Outlook session
```

8. Once we're logged on, we need to instantiate an Outlook Application object and get the selected objects.

```
Set objExplorer = ThisOutlookSession.ActiveExplorer
Set objSelection = objExplorer.Selection
```

9. Each item in Outlook's message store has a unique EntryID. We need to pass the selected message's EntryID to CDO so that the code knows exactly which message to get.

```
Set objItem = objSelection.Item(1)
Set objMessage = objSession.GetMessage(objItem.EntryID,
objItem.Parent.StoreID)
```

10. When we know which message we need, we ask for the field in a text string called strheader. We use error handling here, just in case we try to get a message header from another item, such as a contact. When an error is found, the code skips to step 15, otherwise, it continues on.

```
' Get message fields
Set objFields = objMessage.Fields

' Get SMTP header
Err.Clear
strheader = objFields.Item(CdoPR_TRANSPORT_MESSAGE_HEADERS).Value
```
▼
```
If Err.Number = 0 Then
```

▼   11. If there is a message header, we can display it immediately in a message box (see
         Figure 21.11). Message boxes display just 256 characters, so you'll see only part of
         the header. This line can be commented out later.

```
'Verify code gets header
MsgBox strheader
```

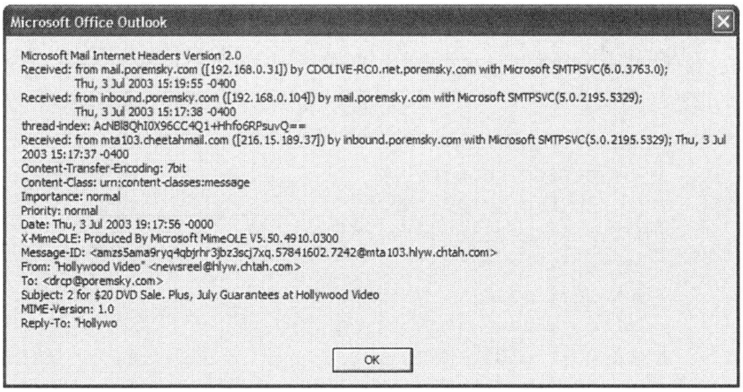

FIGURE 21.11

The message box displays the contents of strheader. *Because the message box displays only the first 256 characters, the complete header isn't visible.*

12. If you want both the message header and the body, this code snippet gets the body
    and adds it to the header string. If you only need the message header, comment this
    section out.

```
If objItem.HTMLBody = "" Then
    strheader = strheader & objItem.Body
Else
    strheader = strheader & objItem.HTMLBody
End If
```

13. This copies the header string to the Windows Clipboard. If you don't need the
    string on the Clipboard, comment out this section.

```
InetHeader.SetText (strheader)
InetHeader.PutInClipboard
```

14. This sends the header string to a text box in a form that we'll create later. If you
    use the message box and/or copy the header string to the Clipboard, you could
    comment out this section and paste the header into a new message or Notepad. You
    must have a form in the project for this line to work.

```
frmHeader.txtHeader.Text = strheader
▼    frmHeader.Show
```

21

▼ 15. If an error is found in step 9, the code skips ahead to this line and displays a message box on the screen.

```
Else
    MsgBox "No SMTP message header information on this message",
vbInformation
End If
```

16. Now that the code is done, the code needs to log off the Outlook session and release the objects it stored in memory. If you don't set the objects to Nothing, your computer will eventually require a reboot to free up resources.

```
'Logoff and clean up
objSession.Logoff
Set objExplorer = Nothing
Set objSelection = Nothing
Set objItem = Nothing
Set objSession = Nothing
Set objMessage = Nothing
Set objFields = Nothing
Set objField = Nothing

End Sub
```

Your procedure is now complete. You can test it now, if you comment out the lines in step 13. Otherwise, before the code will work correctly, we have to create a UserForm,
▲ which we'll do next.

Task: Create a UserForm

You're already familiar with UserForms, even if you don't think so—every application in Windows uses at least one as a Help, About dialog.

In this task, we're going to create a UserForm of our own to display an Internet header in a larger box than Outlook uses.

1. Select Insert, UserForm or use the Insert button on the Standard toolbar and choose UserForm. Drag the lower-right corner to make the form a little bigger.

2. Enter a name for the form in the (Name) field of the Properties window. Because the code refers to frmHeader, we need to name the form frmHeader or change the code. The Caption field holds the text that is displayed in Windows title bars. I'm
▼ using Internet Headers for my caption (see Figure 21.12).

FIGURE 21.12

Create your own dialog boxes using UserForms. Use the Properties window to change the form name, title, and other attributes.

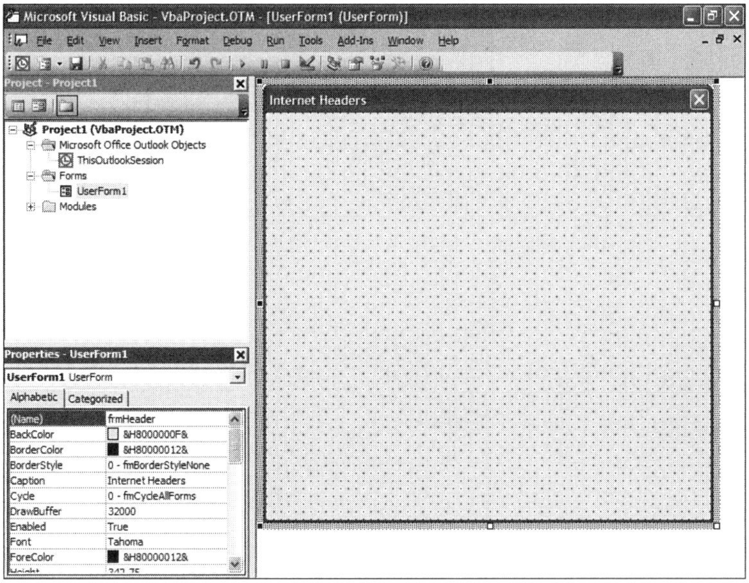

3. Show the Toolbox by clicking the Toolbox toolbar button or selecting <u>V</u>iew, Toolbo<u>x</u>. Add a command button to the bottom of the form. Change the (Name) to cmdClose and the caption to Close.

4. Drag the TextBox control (lowercase ab icon) to the form. Drag the corners so that the control fills most of the form (see Figure 21.13). Change the (Name) to txtHeader.

5. Right-click on any part of the form and choose View Code. Enter the following code to exit the form when you're done looking at the message header:

```
Private Sub cmdClose_Click()
    Unload Me
End Sub
```

You're done. Now it's time to see whether it works. Run or step through the code. You might want to show the Immediate and Local windows so that you can see what the code is doing.

If you receive errors, first check for typographical errors—it's a problem even seasoned developers have. Next, check your Dim statements. Did you include statements for each object you used? Did you set the references you need?

21

FIGURE 21.13

FIGURE **21.13**

Add a text box and command button, and your form is almost complete.

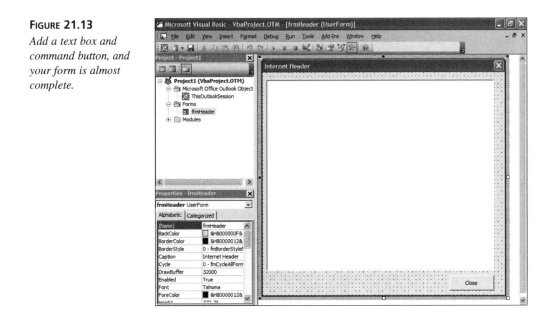

Because the code uses the CDO library, you'll get the security prompt when you run the procedure and you'll need to allow access. The 1 Minute setting is more than enough time for the macro to run.

After you save the procedure, customize your Outlook toolbar and add a button to run the macro. Choose Macros from the Customize dialog and drag your GetInternetHeader macro to the toolbar. Edit the display name and it's ready to use (see Figure 21.14).

If you regularly report spam, you could refine the procedure to paste the message header and body in a new mail message.

For links to many ready-to-use code samples, see `http://www.slipstick.com/dev/code/index.htm` and `http://www.outlookcode.com/`.

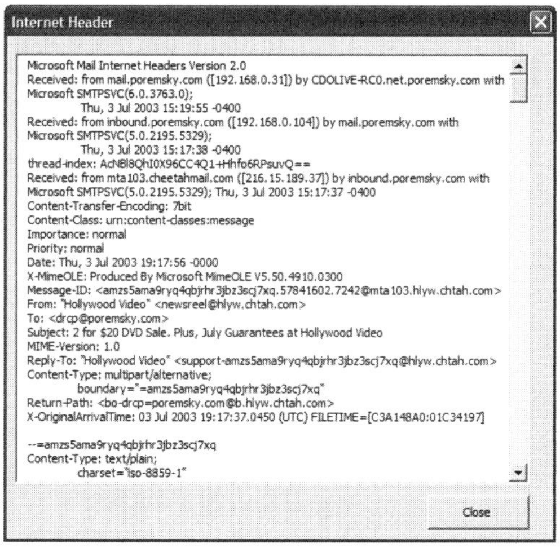

FIGURE 21.14

*The macro's final
result. Use it to view
headers on spam or
view the message body
of suspect messages.*

Summary

This hour covered a lot and probably took you into a second hour. Although we didn't get into in-depth programming techniques, the text introduced you to the very basic levels of programming. If it helped you catch the programming bug, congratulations and good luck. Outlook is a powerful program and you're on your way to taking full advantage of its capabilities.

If this hour convinced you that programming is not your cup of tea, use the SaveAttachment and GetInternetHeader macros you created. They'll save you a lot of time.

Q&A

Q I need to use CDO, but it brings up the dialog that something is trying to access my address book. Is there anyway to disable the message?

A No, you can't disable it. Any time an outside application is trying to access certain properties, you'll receive the warning. Outlook 2003 trusts properly constructed add-ins and VBA, but even though CDO is called by the trusted code, it's not trusted. You'll have to use a program called Redemption (http://www.dimastr.com/redemption/) to avoid the prompts completely.

For the most up-to-date information on the security features in Outlook, see http://www.slipstick.com/outlook/esecup.htm.

21

HOUR **22**

Sharing Outlook Information

One thing many people want out of Outlook is the ability to share their appointments and contacts with other people. Although Outlook does this very well when used with an Exchange client, many people believe it performs poorly when sharing over the Internet. In this hour, you'll discover some of the ways you can share your Outlook data with other users, including

- Using vCal and iCal to share appointments
- Using online services
- Using vCards to share contacts
- Using SharePoint Portal Server and Windows SharePoint Services to share your Outlook calendar and contacts
- Other services you can use with Outlook

By the end of this hour, you'll have a better understanding of just what Outlook can and cannot do when it comes to sharing data.

Sharing Your Calendar

For Exchange Server users, sharing your calendar is as simple as giving another person delegate permission to access it. Exchange Server users can use public folders to create group calendars and contact folders to share with their co-workers.

Non–Exchange Server users wish they had it as easy. A standalone Outlook user is unable to easily share her entire calendar in real-time with another Outlook user, other than forwarding individual items or exporting the calendar to a file.

Outlook can display a calendar hosted on a SharePoint Portal or Windows SharePoint Services Web site, but it's a one-way share: from a SharePoint calendar to Outlook. In addition to SharePoint, other Web-based calendar services are capable of sharing Outlook's calendar data. Some use synchronization software to automate the data transfer, whereas others rely on exporting a comma-separated values (CSV) file from Outlook and importing the CSV into the Web-based calendar.

If none of these methods is satisfactory, there are some third-party applications available that might help. Look for these at `http://www.slipstick.com/outlook/share.htm`.

Outlook can save your calendar items in two formats that are supported by a number of calendaring programs: iCalendar (iCal) and vCalendar (vCal).

If you've used older versions of Outlook, you might be familiar with NetFolders and MS Mail workgroup post office. Although both applications were useful for sharing Outlook items, they aren't available in Outlook 2003.

NetFolders caused a number of problems, from duplicated messages to deleting items it was supposed to share. Because of this instability, Microsoft removed it from Outlook 2002.

MS Mail is no longer supported by Microsoft, nor is it Y2K compliant, although that doesn't seem to affect it.

Task: Use iCals to Send Appointments by Email

The best way to share appointments with other Outlook users is by using iCal. This is an Internet standard format for calendar files and is used by other calendaring programs in addition to Outlook. It's easy to use: Save your appointment as an iCal and forward it others. You can use the Actions menu to create and forward the iCal.

1. Select one or more calendar items.

> Hold the Control key as you select items in the Day/Week/Month view to select multiple items. It's often easier to switch from the Day/Week/Month view to By Category view and select the items.

2. Choose <u>A</u>ctions, Forward as iCa<u>l</u>endar.

A new message form opens with the selected calendar items as *.ics files—ready to enter the recipient's name and your message (see Figure 22.1).

FIGURE 22.1

Send your appointment items to others using the iCalendar format.

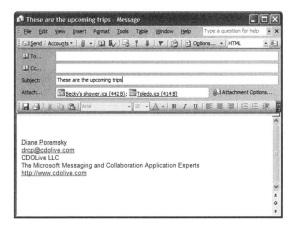

> vCals and iCals are text files that use a specific format for the text and have a *.vcs or *.ics extension. After saving a vCal (.vcs) or iCal (.ics) file to your hard drive, you can open it using Notepad to see how the text is formatted.

Using Meeting Requests to Share a Calendar

Another way to share an appointment with others is by sending it to them as a meeting request. Although it's easiest to do this when you create the appointment, you can also open any calendar item and choose I<u>n</u>vite Attendees.

After selecting I<u>n</u>vite Attendees, the To field is included on the appointment form. Enter the email addresses you want to send the meeting request to, complete the appointment details, and select <u>A</u>ctions, Reque<u>s</u>t Responses to remove the check from the menu selection. You won't get a reply when the recipient accepts the meeting, but it will be added to the recipient's calendar and any changes you make to your calendar will be sent to the recipient so that you won't have to send another meeting request.

Using MSN, Yahoo!, and Other Web Services

MSN and many other Web sites provide online calendaring options. Many also offer ways to synchronize with Outlook. Some of the methods used to share data between a Web calendar and Outlook are nothing more than using import/export functions and are not true synchronization. Sharing the data involves exporting the Web calendar as a CSV file and importing it into Outlook, or exporting Outlook's calendar to a CSV file and then importing it into the Web calendar.

> Learn more about importing and exporting in Hour 10, "Managing Your Data."

MSN and Yahoo! use custom versions of Intellisync to synchronize Outlook with the Web-based calendar. Using Intellisync enables you to automate the synchronization of your calendars with a Web-based interface that you can access from anywhere.

> At the time this book is being published, there is a fee to use MSN Calendar whereas Yahoo! Calendar is free.

Yahoo!'s calendar supports synchronizing multiple Outlook calendar, tasks, notes, and contacts folders. You can share your Yahoo! calendar with family and friends who use Yahoo!; the only requirement at this time is that you maintain a free Yahoo! account.

Using Web Publishing

One of the easiest ways to allow others to see your calendar is to publish it as a Web page and view it in Internet Explorer. You can save the files to any folder and view the calendar on your computer or local network; a Web server is not required. If you copy the HTML pages to a Web server, other people can view it as well.

If you want to share you calendar with friends and family, you'll need a Web host. Many ISPs provide some free Web space to their subscribers. Or you can use a free service, such as Yahoo! GeoCities.

The HTML calendar is a monthly calendar with list of daily appointments and details included.

1. Choose the File, Save As Web Page.

2. In the Save As Web Page dialog, select the start and end dates for the date range of the appointments you want to include in the calendar (see Figure 22.2). This determines the dates of published appointments. The finished calendar displays a calendar grid containing the entire month.

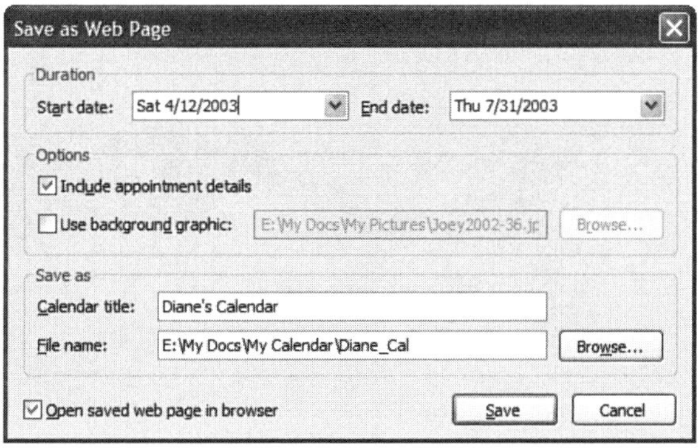

FIGURE 22.1

Use File, Save As Web Page to save your calendar as a Web page. Save it to your computer and upload it to a Web server, if desired.

3. Select the other options as desired. If you choose to use a background image, it will work better if you use one that is light-colored and small enough to tile.

4. In the Filename field, enter the path and a filename as shown in Figure 22.2. The Save As Web Page Wizard adds the file extension for you. When you click the Save button, the wizard creates 18 files, so you might want to include a subfolder in the calendar path.

The calendar uses a somewhat ugly aqua color scheme. You can change the color scheme only by editing the cal.css file in Notepad.

The colors are listed in cal.css in hexadecimal format, with entries similar to this: color:#669999. You can replace the hex codes with color names; such as color:LightYellow. Many natural-language color names will work, from the basic colors like Red, Blue, and Yellow to DeepSkyBlue, HotPink, and ForestGreen.

If you want to use hex codes, search the Internet for *hex color picker* to find lists of hex codes.

When you're finished, make a copy of the `cal.css` file (because Outlook replaces it each time you use Save As Web Page), and then restore the copy after you save the calendar.

The Save As Web Page Wizard creates an okay calendar, but it has lots of limitations and is really lacking in many areas, including how it handles multiple appointments on the same day. It's difficult to customize, even using FrontPage or another HTML editor. It's also unsuitable for creating printed calendars (see Figure 22.3).

FIGURE 22.3
Outlook's calendar published as a Web page.

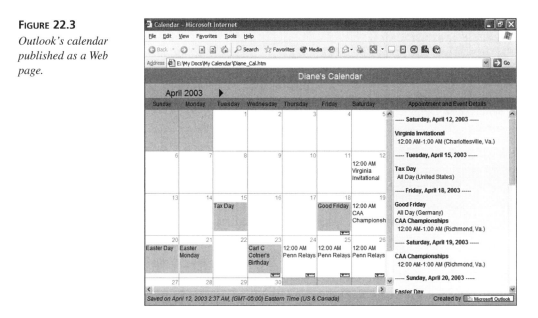

If you want better control over your calendar, including the option to print it out and save it on your Web site, try the Calendar template that Microsoft released for Outlook 97/98 and Word 97. It works great with Outlook and Word 2003. Look for the template installation file, called `olcalndr.exe`, on the Office downloads site at Microsoft.com:
`http://office.microsoft.com/downloads/9798/olcalndr.aspx`.

The template uses tables to lay out the calendar grid and you can insert pictures or shade individual cells. Because it's in Word, you can resize and rename the fields and customize the calendar before printing or saving as HTML.

Because the template uses macros to import your Outlook calendar data, you'll have to change your macro security in Word to Medium (using Tools, Macro, Security) to use the template.

After you open the template in Word, you're presented with a dialog to set up the calendar (see Figure 22.4). You can choose from your default calendar, the currently selected calendar folder or, if you're using Exchange Server, another person's calendar.

FIGURE 22.4

Use the Calendar Setup dialog to select the calendar to print, the calendar format, and the week or month you want to include in your calendar.

Choose a weekly or monthly format and the date the calendar covers. Click OK to start the macro and create your calendar. After it ends, you can customize the calendar with borders and shading or pictures. When you're finished, use File, Save As Web Page to convert it to HTML.

> When you use the calendar template, change the file properties with File, Properties. The Title field is the name for the calendar when it's published as HTML. If you do a Web search for *Outlook Calendar Template for Word*, you'll discover all the organizations that are using the template.

Sharing Your Contacts

Outlook is great for storing your contact records and if you use Exchange Server, it's great for sharing your contacts with co-workers. You can even share your contacts with people who don't use Outlook by saving your contacts as vCards.

Like vCals, vCards are an Internet standard for sharing contact records and a number of programs in addition to Outlook use vCards. A vCard is a plain-text file with the `*.vcf` extension. When you open a vCard in Notepad, it is formatted as shown in the following example:

```
BEGIN:VCARD

VERSION:2.1

N:White;Collette

FN:Collette White

TITLE:Sales Manager

TEL;WORK;VOICE:(423) 555-1212

ADR;WORK:;;;123 E Main;St;;United States of America

LABEL;WORK;ENCODING=QUOTED-PRINTABLE:123 E Main, St=0D=0AUnited States of
America

EMAIL;PREF;INTERNET:collette@digidashlive.com

REV:20030626T025116Z

END:VCARD
```

You could create a vCard using Notepad and save it with the `.vcf` extension and it would work in all programs that support vCards. However, it's easier to let Outlook do the conversion for you.

After selecting a contact from your Outlook contact list, use File, Save As to open the Save As dialog box. Then select vCard (*.vcf) from the Save As Type drop-down list and click Save. Alternatively, select one or more contacts and use Actions, Forward As vCard to send your contacts by email to another person.

Along with sharing your contacts digitally, you can print phone directories or address lists to give to others. One of the easiest ways to print a list is directly from Outlook. Create a custom view with the fields showing that you want to share. Use Outlook's built-in printing capabilities to print a directory, or Select All, Copy and Paste into Notepad, Word, or Excel and print.

Using SharePoint with Outlook

You've probably heard a lot about SharePoint Portal Server or Windows SharePoint Services and are wondering whether it might just be what you need to solve your problems. Although

SharePoint Portal Server is overkill for small companies or workgroups, Windows SharePoint Services provides nice collaboration features and is included with Windows Server 2003.

SharePoint sharing capabilities are only one-way—from SharePoint to Outlook—and not as dynamic as some would like. Using SharePoint, you can view calendar data side-by-side in Outlook and view contacts synchronized from a SharePoint server (see Figure 22.5).

FIGURE 22.5

When a SharePoint or Windows SharePoint Services calendar or Contacts folder is linked with Outlook, you can view the events or contacts along side your calendars.

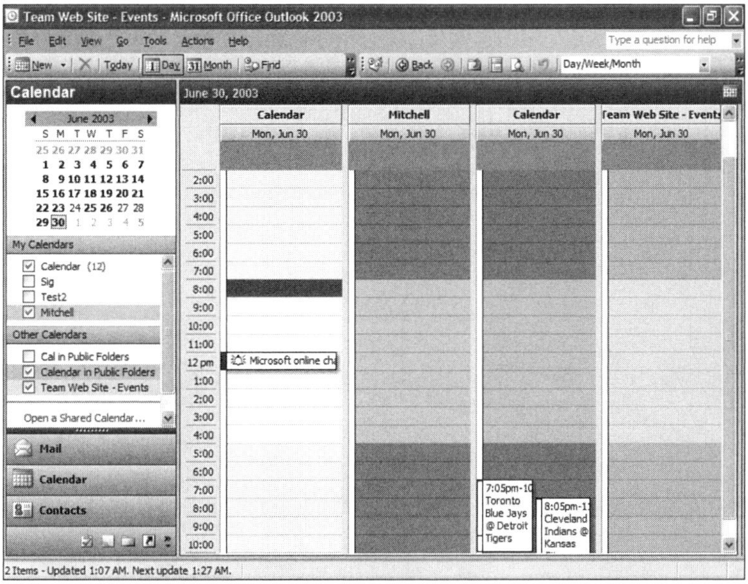

Add a SharePoint calendar or contacts to your Outlook view by opening the SharePoint Services site in your browser and browsing to the list you want to show in Outlook. Choose Link to Outlook from the toolbar (see Figure 22.6).

After you choose Link to Outlook and confirm your desire to create a link, as shown in Figure 22.7, the folders are added to Outlook in the Other Calendars and Other Contacts section.

After creating the link to SharePoint, a local copy of the calendar or contacts is created and added to your profile. SharePoint links are read-only; changes made to the items locally are not reflected in the originals on the SharePoint Web site.

Each time you open Outlook or open the folders contained in the SharePoint PST, the folder contents are synchronized.

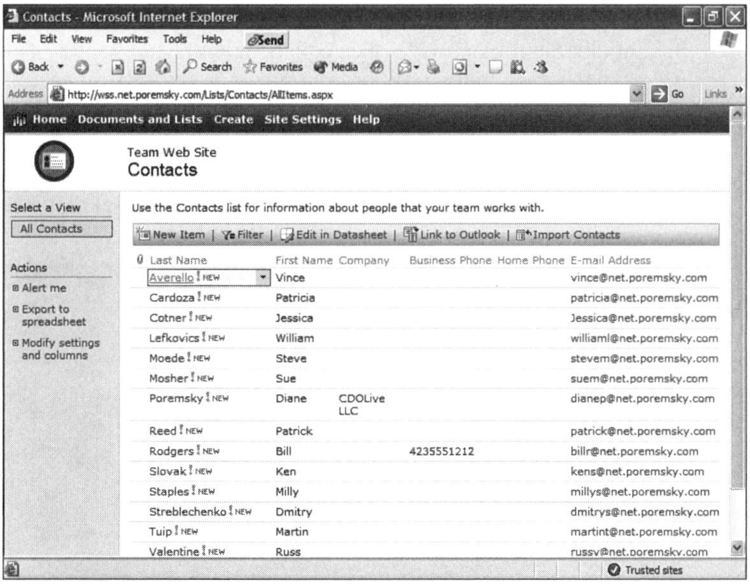

FIGURE 22.6

Use the Link to Outlook button to link SharePoint calendar or contact lists to Outlook. Outlook contacts can be imported into SharePoint, but you're limited to linking calendar events from SharePoint.

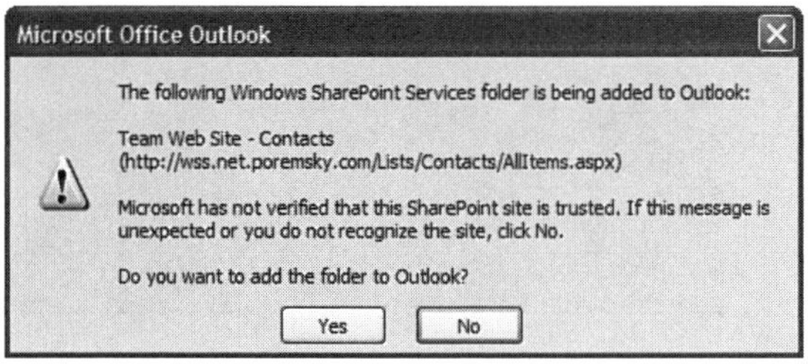

FIGURE 22.7

Okay the dialog to link a calendar or Contacts folder to Outlook. If you're a member of more than one SharePoint site, you can add calendars and Contacts folders for each site.

Third-Party Solutions

Small organizations or small office/home office (SOHO) networks that need to share contacts should consider using a Lightweight Directory Access Protocol (LDAP) server. The software can be installed on a spare computer or on your desktop computer. It should be installed on a computer that is left running all the time. An LDAP server provides a central location to store contact information and when installed in conjunction with an email server, it gives your organization intranet email as well.

If you'd like to explore the options available to you to share calendars and contacts without using Exchange Server, see the latest information and applications listed at http://www.slipstick.com/outlook/share.htm.

22

Summary

Although sharing Outlook information isn't always easy when you don't use Exchange Server, this hour showed you some of the ways you can share your Outlook data with other people. In many cases, they don't need to even use Outlook.

Using iCals, vCals, and vCards to share your calendar and contacts in an Internet standard format allows the items to work for many calendars and address book systems, not just Outlook.

Q&A

Q I sent contacts to friends who use Outlook and they didn't receive the contents of the contact in the message body. Why?

A For Outlook's special items to arrive using Outlook's forms, you must send the message using RTF formatting. Although Outlook is usually smart enough to send messages using RTF, when they're sent to the Internet, messages are normally converted to HTML. If this causes problems, you'll have to force the message as RTF by clicking on the email address and setting the Internet Format option to Send Using Rich Text Format in the E-mail Properties dialog.

Q We got some new computers in our office and they have Outlook 2003 installed. We use NetFolders to share our calendar but I can't find that option in Outlook 2003. Where is it?

A NetFolders is not included in Outlook 2003. They are unstable and unreliable. If Exchange Server is not an option, use an IMAP server and InsightConnector to share your calendar and contacts. You'll be happier with it and have fewer problems.

Hour **23**

Office 2003 Integration

We often need much of the information stored in Outlook in other programs. We can use the information to make a phone directory, send personalized letters, or use the data in Excel or other programs.

You can create tasks or calendar entries associated with files created in other programs or email files you're working on. This hour covers

- Using mail merge
- Sending email from Office applications
- Working with embedded documents

Outlook is fairly well integrated with other Office programs, and all of the preceding activities are possible and easy to accomplish. This hour shows you how to do all of this and more.

Using Contacts for Mail Merge

Mail merge is possibly the most popular reason for accessing Outlook data from Word. Mail merge makes it easy to create address labels, personalized letters, and address books. You can start mail merges from either Outlook or Word, and a number of options are available to you for configuring the mail merge.

By opening Word and using the Tools, Letters and Mailings, Mail Merge menu selection to begin the merge, you limit the number of contact fields available for use as merge fields to common mail fields. When you start the merge from Outlook, it makes all contact fields available to use in the merge, although you have the option to include only the fields used in the current view.

Beginning the merge from Outlook also enables you to select a group of contacts to use in the merge, instead of filtering your contacts using the basic filtering options available from the Mail Merge dialog in Word.

Regardless of how you begin the mail merge, you can change the merge type or fields used at any time. To avoid the security prompt in Outlook, you'll want to merge to HTML-formatted messages.

Task: Start a Mail Merge from Outlook

When you begin your mail merge from Outlook, you can use its filtering capabilities to select the contacts you want to include in your merge. Use custom views or Find to filter your contacts, and then select the contacts you want to include in the merge.

After the contacts are filtered or selected, you're ready to create your mail merge:

1. Select the contacts you're going to merge and choose Tools, Mail Merge. This opens the Mail Merge Contacts dialog, as shown in Figure 23.1.

FIGURE 23.1

Selecting the contacts to use in Outlook often results in faster merging in Word because the mail merge data file contains only the contacts you're using in your merge.

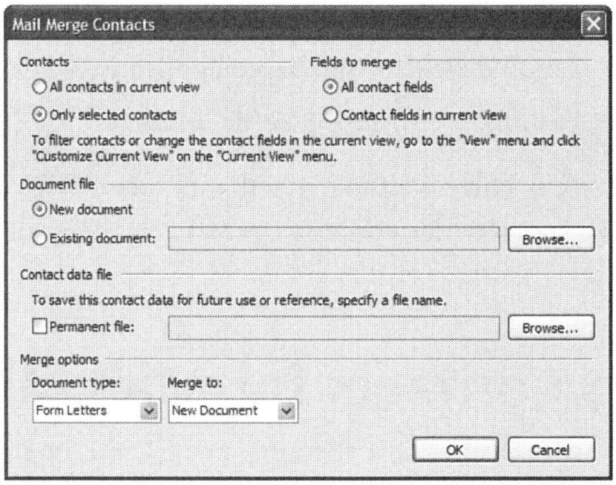

2. If you selected a group of contacts before choosing mail merge, Only Selected Contacts is enabled. Choose All Contacts in Current View if you created a filtered view containing the contacts you want to include in the mail merge.

▼

Use Advanced Find to find your contacts meeting specific criteria, choose Select All, and use the Edit, Categories menu selection to add a unique category to the contacts. Next, use the Group by Category view to group by categories and select the category for your mail merge.

23

3. By default, all contact fields are included in the merge. However, if you're merging a large number of records, it's faster if you include only the fields you're going to use. Create a view containing the fields you plan to use before beginning the merge.

4. Select the document you want to merge to. In many cases, you'll want to keep the default new document. However, you can merge to a predefined document, such as a fax cover sheet or form letter.

5. If you plan to use the contact data another time or need to keep it for reference, add a check to the Permanent File field and enter a filename. When the merge is completed, Outlook will save the file.

6. Select the document type to which you're going to merge. Your choices are form letters, mailing labels, envelopes, and catalog. Select the merge format you want to

▲   use, choosing from new document, printer, and email.

If you change your mind about the document type or merge options you want to use, you can change the merge options after the contact data is loaded into Word.

After you choose OK to begin the merge, Outlook processes the contacts and writes them to a file named `OMM*.doc`, saving it at `C:\Documents and Settings\username\ Local Settings\Temp`.

If you want to save the data file, use Windows Explorer to find it. Copy it to your My Documents folder and rename it.

Word opens with the OMM document attached as a data source and is on step 3 of the Mail Merge Wizard. You can use the Mail Merge toolbar to add merge fields or display the wizard by choosing Tools, Letters and Mailings, Mail Merge.

Add merge fields to your document and then complete the merge, selecting the Merge To document type from the wizard or toolbar.

> If you're new to mail merge, using the wizard to lead you through the process the first few times is very helpful.

Should you realize that you selected contacts you don't want to include in the merge, you don't need to redo it. Uncheck the contacts you don't want included or filter the contacts by selecting the arrows beside the field names, as described in the next section.

> Mail merging to email triggers security alerts that must to be allowed for each address on your mail merge list if you merge to plain text message format. When you merge using HTML-formatted messages, you won't have to respond to the security prompts.

Starting Your Merge from Word

You can begin a mail merge from Word by choosing Tools, Letters and Mailings, Mail Merge. Step through the Mail Merge Wizard, choosing Outlook as your data source in step 3. Choose Select from Outlook's Contacts, and then click Choose Contacts Folder to open the Select Contacts List Folder dialog. Select the Contacts folder and choose OK.

The Mail Merge Recipients dialog is populated with all the contacts in the Contacts folder, which might take a couple of minutes if you have a large number of contacts. Click on the field names to change their sort order, or set up filters by clicking the black arrows (as shown in Figure 23.2) and choosing from (All), (Blanks), (NonBlanks), or (Advanced).

Choosing Advanced Filtering Options opens the Filter and Sort dialog, as shown in Figure 23.3. You can use this dialog to create filters, but it's generally easier to filter in Outlook and begin the merge from Outlook rather than use the Filter and Sort dialog.

Complete the steps in the wizard and finish the mail merge.

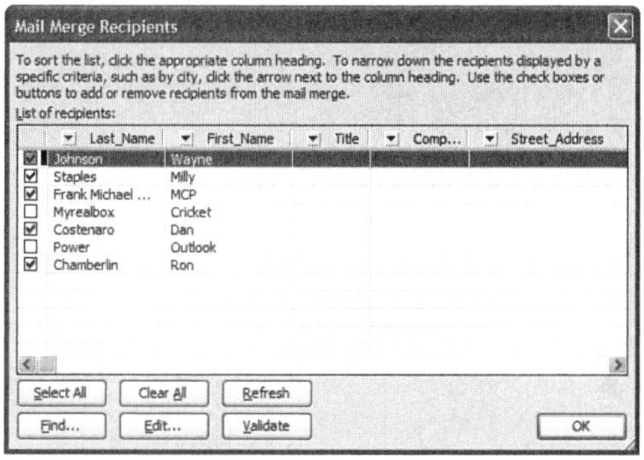

FIGURE 23.2

Remove the check from the records you don't want to include in your merge or use the arrow buttons to filter the records. Black arrows indicate no filter; blue arrows are used for fields where filters are set.

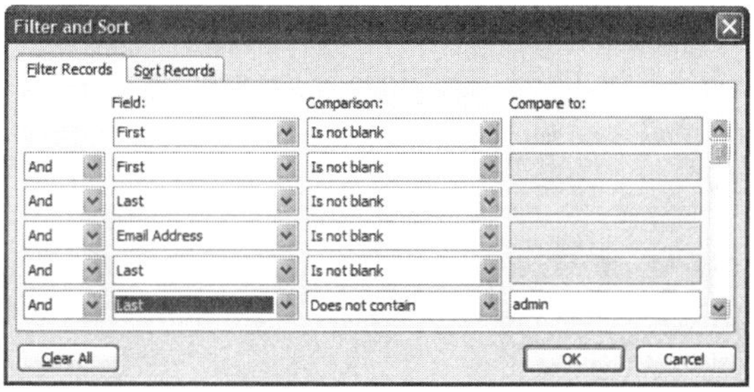

23

FIGURE 23.3

Use the Filter and Sort dialog to filter your mail merge records.

Using the Office Envelope

Many Windows applications are email-enabled and include a File, Send E-mail menu that enables you to send the current document by email. Some applications, such as Word, have several send options and you can send a file as an attachment or embedded in the email message, whereas others can send a file only as an attachment.

When you click on the E-mail icon in the toolbar or choose File, Send To, Mail Recipient and a message header is added to the file, you're using the Office Envelope to send the file. If you want to send it as an attachment, choose File, Send To, Mail Recipient (As Attachment) instead (see Figure 23.4).

Using the File, Send menu from any application will always use the Outlook editor, even if you have Word selected as your email editor.

FIGURE **23.4**

Word's File, Send To menu includes options to send Word documents for review, as attachments, save in an Exchange folder, or send using Internet Fax—all these options send the document using Outlook.

Word, Excel, Publisher, OneNote, and Access have the capability to send open files using the Office Envelope. This enables you to send the file in the message body, instead of as an attachment. When the Office Envelope is available, you'll see File, Send To, Mail Recipient or an email icon on the toolbar (see Figure 23.5).

> The Mail icon on the toolbars in Office applications is either an open envelope or includes a paper clip, which usually means the file will be added as an attachment.

Each Office program handles Office Envelopes differently:

- Publisher converts the publication to a JPG and embeds it in HTML, resulting in a larger message.
- Word converts the document to HTML.
- OneNote converts the note to HTML and has the option to send the note file as an attachment. When used with a Tablet PC or graphics tablet, Ink is converted to images.
- Access uses the Office Envelope on a limited number of objects, such as forms. An ActiveX control is embedded in the message, which is blocked in the restricted zone Outlook uses for email.
- Excel sends the current sheet or a selection as the message body. Some elements, such as text boxes and buttons, are converted to JPG. Sending the current sheet or large selection can result in a very large message and takes several minutes for Excel to render and send it.
- FrontPage sends the current page as HTML.
- Picture Manager has an option to send the selected images embedded in an HTML message and include the image as an attachment.

Office envelope

Email button   Email toolbar

FIGURE 23.5
The Office Envelope sends the current file as the message body. Use the E-mail button to toggle the message header and E-mail toolbar on and off.

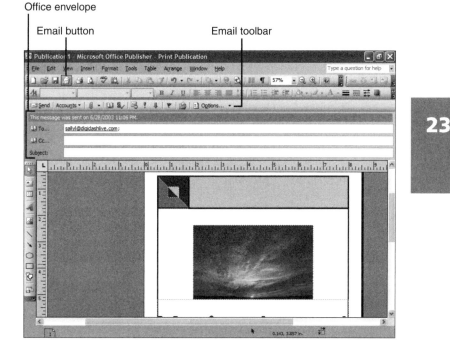

23

Although Office Envelopes are an easy way to send information, the resulting message can be much larger than sending the document as an attachment.

When you send messages using the Office Envelope, they often can be opened for editing in the application that created them. Look for Open in [*program*] on the Edit menu or on the context menu when you right-click in the message body.

In addition to sending documents using the Office Envelope, you can use the Insert File dialog to insert a file either as an attachment or—for Word documents, HTML, and other text-based documents—insert the file as inline text by selecting Insert As Text (see Figure 23.6).

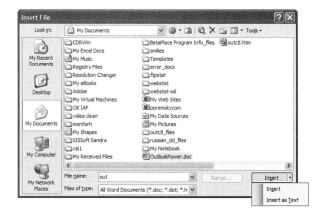

FIGURE 23.6

Use the Insert File dialog to insert attachments or inline text to your messages. Insert As Text works well when you send HTML newsletters created in an HTML editor.

Using For Review or As Attachment

In addition to using Office Envelopes to send files, you can send files as attachments. The File, Send To menu uses two types of attachments: attachments sent for review and standard attachments. Standard attachments are just that—it's the same as sending a file using the Insert File option in Outlook.

Sending an attachment for review includes document information that enables you to merge the changes when the reviewer sends the file back to you. In addition, the Reviewing toolbar is visible and Track Changes is turned on.

Recipients are able to reply with changes if the Add Properties to Attachments to Eenable Reply with Changes is enabled in Outlook's Tools, Options, Preferences, E-mail Options, Advanced E-mail Options. With this feature turned on, Outlook includes information about the original file so that when it's sent back to you the documents can be merged.

Sending from Other Applications

Many other applications are MAPI-aware and can be used to send open files by email. Users occasionally have a problem using the File, Send To menu (some applications call it File, E-mail) and sending attachments using Outlook. After opening a new mail form using the File, Send To menu, you can't do anything in Outlook until you save and close or send the message. Additionally, when you save the email message, it's saved in the inbox, not in Drafts. This is a limitation of MAPI and is just how Outlook works.

Common problems users face when sending Web pages or links to Web pages from Internet Explorer using Outlook include

- Pages are sent as attachments, not in the message body. This is because you're using plain text as your default message format. When you use HTML as your default format, Web pages are embedded in the message body.

> When you use Internet Explorer and send links by email, you can install a small script called Mailto_URL that adds a Send Link by Email item to the context menu when you right-click on a page. The script is available at slipstick.com.
>
> This script works with any email program and does not keep focus in Outlook like using the File, Send To menu does.

- Early versions of Windows XP do not send text URLs, only attachments, which Outlook's security model blocks. Windows XP SP2 corrects this behavior by adding a text URL to the message body. Until SP2 is available, use Mailto_URL to send text URLs.

Using OneNote with Outlook

OneNote is a nifty new program in the Office family used for taking notes. It's useful for notes that document a meeting, whereas Outlook's notes are generally better for smaller notes. OneNote doesn't have anything to do with Outlook's notes and there is very limited integration between Outlook and OneNote. OneNote 2003 can send mail using the Office Envelope and create a task out of selected text, but that's it.

Send a OneNote page by email using the same steps you use to send other Office documents: Choose the File, E-mail menu to open an Office Envelope. Selecting more than one note page enables you to send all the pages in your email. OneNote sends them as one long message, with each page converted to HTML and in sequence in the message body.

> Email options for OneNote, including the signature line added at the end of OneNote's email and whether the original note (*.one) file is attached to the message, are configured in OneNote's Tools, Options, E-mail menu.

OneNote also supports creating task entries from your OneNote notes. Select the note text and choose the Task button on OneNote's Standard toolbar to create a task containing your selection. The first line of the selection becomes the task's subject, leaving you to fill in the dates and set a reminder.

Summary

This hour showed you some of the ways you can use the Office applications and Outlook data. You learned how to use mail merge to prepare letters, email, and other documents using Outlook's contact data.

This hour also included information on how to use the Office Envelope to send email from any Office program that supports the Office Envelope feature. Only Microsoft Office programs support the Office envelope, but many other applications can open files as attachments.

Q&A

Q **My Send button no longer works when I try to send using the File, Send menu in other applications. Why?**

A Did you install a pop-up stopper program? This is the most common cause of the Send button not working.

Q **When I mail merge to email, a dialog tells me that something is trying to access my addresses and I need to allow it for up to ten minutes. Then I have to click Yes for each address. Can I turn this annoying dialog off?**

A You can't turn the security dialog off, but if you merge to HTML-formatted messages, you'll avoid the prompt. If you really need to use plain text formatting, look for a utility called ClickYes from `http://www.express-soft.com/mailmate/clickyes.html`. It will respond to the security prompts for you.

Hour **24**

Migrating from Outlook Express

There comes a point in time for many users when Outlook Express no longer offers enough of the features they need. Others decide to give Outlook a try when they purchase Office and discover Outlook that is installed by default.

This hour guides you through the steps needed to convert your accounts, rules, and messages from Outlook Express to Outlook and helps you understand the differences between Outlook and Outlook Express. You'll learn

- Migrating accounts and settings
- Exporting messages to Outlook
- Outlook Express features missing from Outlook

Moving from Outlook Express to Outlook is not an upgrade because Outlook Express is not a light version of Outlook. Many users aren't aware that Outlook Express is not a stripped-down Outlook and complain when their favorite features from "the free version" are not available in Outlook, even though it's expensive software.

The programs come from different product groups within Microsoft and share only the name Outlook and the capability to send and receive email.

Migrating Accounts and Settings

After the Office or Outlook installation is complete and you open Outlook for the first time, it'll ask whether you want to import the email accounts it found. If you choose Yes, your account settings are imported to Outlook. If you choose No, you can import the account settings at a later date, using File, Import and Export.

> When you have multiple email accounts in Outlook Express, the dialog enables you to choose between importing all of your email accounts or selecting one of the accounts to import.

When you choose to import your Outlook Express accounts, Outlook imports your account settings, email, and rules into Outlook.

> Saved passwords aren't imported, so the first time you check for email using Outlook, you'll have to re-enter your password for each account.

After the import is completed, a dialog asks whether you want to make Outlook your default email client. Although Outlook works just fine for most things when Outlook Express is the default email client, if you want Outlook to handle mailto URLs or use Word's mail merge, you must set it as the default.

> The default mail program setting applies to all user accounts on the computer.

If you chose No or imported only one account when you first opened Outlook and now want to import the other account settings, use Outlook's File, Import and Export menu selection to open the Import and Export Wizard.

> To use Import or Export, you must have both Outlook and Outlook Express accounts configured on your computer.

Choose Import Internet Mail and Addresses on the Import and Export Wizard to open the Outlook Import tool (see Figure 24.1). From this screen, you can choose whether to import your email, address book, or rules from Outlook Express to Outlook.

FIGURE 24.1

You can use the Import and Export Wizard to import your Outlook Express account settings or to import just your email, address book, and rules.

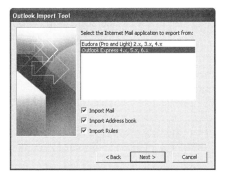

To confirm that the account settings that Outlook imports are correct:

1. Open the accounts dialog using Tools, E-mail Accounts.

2. On the E-mail Accounts screen that appears, select View or Change Existing Accounts and click Next.

3. Select the imported account and choose Change.

4. When the Internet and E-mail Settings dialog opens, you can use the available fields to re-enter your password.

5. Choose More Settings and select the Advanced tab to confirm your other account settings. If you're using IMAP accounts, verify that the port settings on the Advanced tab are correct.

When importing contacts, you can let Outlook check for duplicates as it imports or import all contacts, which might result in duplicate contacts.

In some cases, you might choose to import duplicates and compare and delete the duplicates yourself. The easiest way to know which items are new and potentially duplicated is to add the Modified Date field to your view. All imported items have a current modified date, so you can use a custom view to group or sort duplicates together and then use the Modified Date field to identify the new contacts.

To add the Modified Date field to your Outlook view:

1. Close the Reading Pane or slide it to the right so that the message list uses single lines.

2. Right-click on the row of field names, choose <u>C</u>ustomize Current View, and then choose <u>F</u>ields.

3. From the Selec<u>t</u> Available Fields from list, choose Date/Time fields, and then <u>A</u>dd the modified field to your view.

4. Click OK twice to return to the folder and sort by the Modified Date field .

> You'll need to continue to use Outlook Express for reading newsgroups. You can open it using any shortcut in Windows or edit the shortcut to make it work only as a newsreader. You have the choice of two switches to convert Outlook Express to news-only mode: /outnews and /newsonly. The only difference is what the title bar and startup page call the newsreader. Add either switch to the command line so that it looks like this:
>
> `C:\Program Files\Outlook Express\msimn.exe /newsonly`

Moving Email to Outlook

Exporting messages from Outlook Express to Outlook gives you the option to choose the folders that you want to copy to Outlook. Access the Export dialog from Outlook Express's <u>F</u>ile, <u>E</u>xport, <u>M</u>essages menu choice.

Choose <u>A</u>ll Folders or <u>S</u>elected Folders. If you choose Selected Folders, hold down the Ctrl key to select multiple folders (see Figure 24.2).

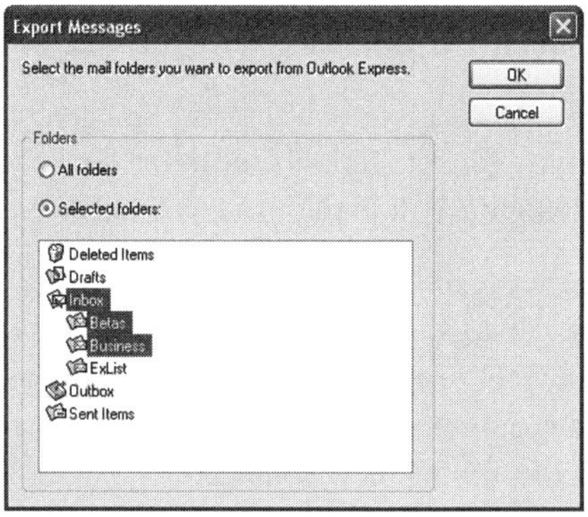

FIGURE 24.2

Use the Export Messages dialog to export messages from Outlook Express to Outlook. When the export is initiated from Outlook Express, you can select the folders you want to include in the export.

With previous versions of Outlook, importing into Outlook using Outlook's File, Import and Export menu selection often resulted in the import date replacing the received date.

Exporting from Outlook Express to Outlook retained the correct dates. Although this bug appears to be fixed in Outlook 2003, if you use Import in Outlook and the import date is displayed instead of the correct received date, export from Outlook Express instead.

> Rather than exporting all of your old email from Outlook Express to Outlook, create archive folders in Outlook Express for your older email and export only the newest messages to Outlook. You can use a utility called DBXtract to scan Outlook Express's DBX files, break them into messages, and then burn the messages onto a CD for safekeeping. You can open the messages in Notepad if you ever need to read them from a system that doesn't have Outlook Express installed.
>
> Look for links to DBXtract at www.tomsterdam.com .

Task: Move Accounts and Messages from Outlook Express to Outlook

You don't need to re-create your accounts in Outlook. You can copy many of the settings to Outlook and save yourself a lot of time and aggravation:

1. Begin by setting up your Outlook profile. When no one has used Outlook yet, you'll be presented with the Account Setup Wizard when you first open Outlook. If another person is already using Outlook and you want to use it also, create another profile using Control Panel, Mail applet. You can find the Mail applet in the User Accounts category if you're using Windows XP.

> If you previously created a profile in Outlook and chose No when Outlook offered to import your accounts and messages, use the File, Import and Export menu selection to import Outlook Express accounts at any time.

2. When you're asked whether you want to import Outlook Express accounts, choose Yes.

Follow the steps in the Import Wizard screens and your account information will be imported into Outlook.

Different or Missing Features

Although Outlook and Outlook Express are both email clients owned by Microsoft, different product groups developed them and, as a result, there are some differences in how some features work in Outlook compared to Outlook Express.

Outlook Express is a nice little email program; it does many things well and it's small and fast. It has some features that many users enjoy, but some of those features work a bit differently or are not available in Outlook. This section attempts to cover most of the differences so that you don't waste time trying to figure out how to turn on the feature in Outlook.

View Images Inline

The Outlook Express feature that most people seem to miss the most is inline preview of images. This feature previews images attached to messages at the end of the message, eliminating the need to open the attachment. Outlook doesn't support inline previews. When selected, an image should open in the Windows Image and Fax Viewer when you use the default Windows settings.

Automatically Add Addresses to the Address Book

Outlook Express has an option in Tools, Options, Send that enables you to automatically add to your address book anyone to whom you've sent a reply. Outlook 2003 doesn't have the capability to do this, and for good reason: Doing so often results in a folder full of addresses that you might never need again.

When you want to add an address to your address book, right-click on an address and then choose Add to Contacts Folder. You aren't limited to adding only addresses in the To and CC fields when you reply—this trick works on the To, From, or CC fields in any message in your inbox.

If you need to automatically save addresses to your address book, add-ins that use rules to automate this for you are available. Look at `www.ornic.com` for Exlife or custom actions for Outlook's Rules Wizard, or at `www.slipstick.com` for a list of current add-ins. Using a rules-based method gives you more control over the addresses that are added, such as only those that use certain keywords in the subject.

View Contacts in the Outlook Express Window

Outlook Express enables you to include a Contacts pane in the Outlook Express window, just below the folder list in the lower left of the screen. Outlook doesn't support this feature.

Signatures

Signatures are not imported when you import an Outlook Express account to Outlook. You'll have to re-create the signatures in Outlook.

Hour 5, "Working with Email," shows you how to create signatures in Outlook.

Understanding AutoComplete and Automatic Resolution

AutoComplete is the feature that remembers an email address that has been typed into the To, CC, or BCC field. In Outlook Express, AutoComplete remembers addresses stored in the Windows Address Book. Outlook's AutoComplete remembers every address you type into the address fields. As you begin typing an address in an address field, a list of previously used addresses is displayed (see Figure 24.3).

24

FIGURE 24.3

Outlook's AutoComplete feature displays previously used addresses as you type.

To...	bob; Carol Mitchell
Cc...	o
Subject:	outlook-users@yahoogroups.com
	outlook@outlooktips.net

Right-click on names underlined with a wavy red line and select the correct person from the menu. The next time you enter the same text, it will resolve to the last used address and will be underlined with a green dotted line.

Outlook also includes automatic name resolution, which attempts to resolve names typed into the address fields with entries found in the Outlook Address Book. When you type in a name, or even just part of a name, Outlook looks for a match in your address book. If it finds a single match, it automatically resolves the address for you. If more than one match is found, Outlook underlines it with a wavy red line, as shown in Figure 24.3.

Addresses that Outlook resolves are added to the AutoComplete cache list. The next time you need to send a message to that address, type just the first few letters of the name and select it from the AutoComplete cache list.

When a misspelled or old address appears in the AutoComplete list, use the arrow keys to select the incorrect entry and press the Delete key. If you have a lot of incorrect entries, find and delete the *.NK2 file for your profile. You'll find it at `C:\Documents and Settings\username\Application Data\Microsoft\Outlook`.

You can also copy the AutoComplete list and use it with other profiles.

Receiving Blocked Attachments

Both Outlook and Outlook Express now block some types of attachments in an attempt to prevent the spread of viruses. In Outlook Express 6, you can disable this feature at Tools, Options, Security, Do Not Allow Attachments to Be Saved or Opened That Could Potentially Be a Virus. You can leave it enabled and choose Forward when you need to access a blocked attachment and then open or save the attachment.

Accessing blocked attachments isn't quite so easy in Outlook. It doesn't have a setting to completely disable attachment blocking, and you have to edit the Registry to unblock attachments. If you're not into Registry editing, get Attachment Options from `www.slovaktech.com`.

See `http://www.slipstick.com/outlook/esecup/getexe.htm` for more ways to work with blocked attachments and `http://www.slipstick.com/outlook/esecup.htm` to learn more about the security features in Outlook.

Using Group Address Lists

The Windows Address Book uses what it calls a *group* when you want to create an address list that contains several individual addresses. Outlook calls this feature a *distribution list*. They are identified as bolded entries in the Outlook Address Book and, with the Reading Pane enabled in the Contacts folder, you can see the distribution list members without opening the distribution list.

Saving Your Account Settings

Outlook Express saves and restores your account settings from the Tools, Accounts menu selection. Outlook does not offer explicit save and restore options for your account settings.

However, you can use the Office Save My Settings Wizard located at Start, Programs, Microsoft Office, Microsoft Office Tools to save and restore your Office settings. This enables you to save all of your Office settings to an .OPS file, including the settings for all installed Office programs. You cannot select only Outlook settings using this wizard.

Summary

This hour showed you how to migrate your email, address book, and rules from Outlook Express to Outlook.

You learned about the differences between the features found in Outlook compared to Outlook Express. When a feature is not available in Outlook, you learned how to work around the differences, if a workaround exists.

Q&A

Q I imported my messages from Outlook Express and the dates on the messages are the date of the import, not the date I received the message.

A This happens occasionally. Delete the messages you imported, open Outlook Express, and then export the messages to Outlook. If you already had messages in Outlook, add the Modified Date field and sort by it. Select and delete the messages with the same modified time and date.

Q I accidentally imported my contacts from Outlook Express twice. What can I do to remove the duplicates?

A Add the Modified Date field to your view, sort by the modified date, and select items that were imported at the same time.

If you have a lot of duplicates that were created at different times, there are utilities you can use to identify and delete them, including Outlook Contacts Scrubber from www.teamscope.com. You can find a complete list of utilities to remove duplicates at http://www.slipstick.com/addins/contacts.htm#dupes.

24

Appendixes

Appendix

APPENDIX A

Installing Outlook

Before using Outlook, you have to install it. If you purchased an Office suite and used the default installation, Outlook is installed along with the rest of the Office applications.

Some users purchased only Outlook or received it in the software package included with a PDA. The installer installs Outlook with the same basic configuration options used to install it as part of Office 2003, except for the use of Word as your email editor. Because Outlook requires the same version of Word for the email editor, these versions won't have Word enabled as the editor.

If you purchased a new computer and Office was bundled with your system, congratulations, Office is preinstalled for you, but you can keep reading. You might want to install some missing options.

The last section of this appendix details how to use the Office Save My Settings Wizard to move some of your settings to your new machine when you're migrating from a previous version of Office to Office 2003. You can also use the Save My Settings Wizard to back up your Outlook profiles.

Installing Outlook 2003

Office 2003 requires Windows 2000 Service Pack 3 or higher or Windows XP or later operating system. Although Outlook will install on an older computer with a CPU of at least a Pentium 133 and as little as 64MB of RAM, it will be very slow.

You'll have a much better experience if you install Outlook on a computer with a Pentium III 400 or greater CPU and at least 256MB of RAM. (Adding more memory is usually cheaper than getting a new computer, although not nearly as fun. Memory is also easy enough to install that you can do it yourself.)

You'll need at least 245MB of free hard disk space on your computer, with at least 115MB free on the same disk that Windows is installed on.

> Before installing Office 2003, create a system restore point in Windows XP.

After accepting the licensing agreement in the Installation Wizard dialog, you have three choices:

- Complete Install—All features are installed for each application. This is the best choice if you are installing Office or Outlook on a laptop and travel a lot. All features are installed and you don't need the CD to install them later. This choice is the most convenient, if you have plenty of free space on your hard drive.

- Minimal Install—Only the basic features are installed. Many features are installed on first run and you might need the CD to install the features you need. Choose this option if you don't have a lot of free hard drive space.

- Custom Install—Choose the features you want to install (see Figure A.1).

> To show you the options you can choose from, we're going to choose Custom Install.

The next screen lists the Office applications and includes a check box for Choose Advanced Customization of Applications (see Figure A.2). Add a check to this option to see the installation options for a minimal installation and to add options. Uncheck any applications you don't want installed and choose Next.

When you aren't sure what a feature does, select it and look in the Description field (shown in Figure A.2), where you'll see a short description of each feature.

FIGURE A.1

Use the Custom Install option so that you can choose the applications and features you want to install. The options installed with a minimal install are selected when you choose Custom.

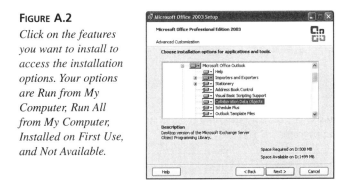

The wizard displays the list of applications from which you can choose.

FIGURE A.2

Click on the features you want to install to access the installation options. Your options are Run from My Computer, Run All from My Computer, Installed on First Use, and Not Available.

The icons indicate what the installation settings are.

- White drive icon—The feature (or features included on submenus) will be installed.
- Gray drive icon—Some features listed on the submenus will be installed, but not all.
- Yellow number 1—The item will be installed the first time you need the feature (Run on First Use).
- Red X—This item or group of items is not going to be installed and will not be available.

Install all options available for Outlook by clicking on the Microsoft Outlook for Windows item and choose Run All from My Computer. The dialog shows you how much space the selected options require; installing all of Outlook's options requires a grand total of 4MB additional disk space. However, the default selections are suitable for most users, with the exception that you may want to install Collaboration Data Objects (CDO) or set it to First Run; by default, it's unavailable.

CDO is used by many third-party applications to access information in your mailbox. When it's set to first run, Outlook warns you when an application needs CDO and you have to provide the installation CD at that time.

Browse the Office Shared Features and Office Tools sections and choose the features you need. Installing all the Office shared features requires nearly 200MB of disk space, and installing all the Office Tools requires about 30MB.

Choose <u>N</u>ext after selecting all the options you want to install. Choose Install from the review dialog when you're ready to begin installing Office or choose Back if you want to make changes to your installation.

Sit back and have a cup of tea while you wait for the installation to complete. It can take 30 minutes or more to complete the installation if you have an older, slow computer.

After Office is installed, the final screen offers to check for updates online and remove cached installation files. If you have Internet connectivity, you should enable the Check the Web for Updates and Additional Downloads check box to check the Office update site for updates.

> Check for updates at any time by choosing <u>H</u>elp, Chec<u>k</u> for updates while using any Office program.

If you have plenty of free space on your hard drive, you should leave the cached installation files installed. These files are used when you need to install a Use on First Run feature or when you need to repair the installation. The cached installation files are stored in the MSOCache folder on your hard drive. If you have more than one drive, these files are placed on the drive with the most free space.

Choose Finish to close the wizard and begin using Outlook.

You don't have to reboot after completing the installation, but it's good practice to reboot at your earliest convenience.

That's all there is to it. Office is installed and Outlook is ready for you to configure your profile. See Hour 2 to learn how to setup an Outlook profile.

The first time any Office program is used, you'll be reminded that you need to activate it. Activation is an anti-piracy measure to prevent users from installing their copy on more computers than the EULA permits. Office 2003 includes a 50-use grace period before activation is required. If you don't activate after that period expires, the programs drop into reduced functionality mode and you can read documents but not edit, save, or send them.

I recommend waiting until you have used Office about 40 times before activating to ensure that it works correctly and doesn't need to be reinstalled.

While you are activating your copy, you'll have a chance to register your copy with Microsoft. It's up to you if you want to register it. If you choose to, you'll need to give them your name and address during registration.

> Microsoft stores the activation information for Office in a hidden file: C:\Documents and Settings\All Users\Application Data\Microsoft\ OFFICE\DATA\opa11.dat. Make a copy of this file and restore it if you need to reinstall Office. This file is tied to the computer hardware and the installation key (CD key) used to install Office. You can't use this file to activate Office on another computer.
>
> If you need to reinstall or have other problems, you'll be able to activate Office after installing it by placing a copy of this file back in the folder without completing the Activation Wizard. If you replace several pieces of your computer hardware or use a different installation key, you'll have to reactivate.

Using the Office Save My Settings Wizard

Office includes a Save My Settings Wizard that saves your Office and Outlook settings and enables you to move them to a new computer or restore the settings if you reformat your computer. The wizard saves the settings for all the Office programs you have installed, and you might see strange behavior or error messages if the same programs, including add-ins, are not present on both machines.

Open the Save My Settings Wizard by choosing the Start menu, Programs, Microsoft Office, Microsoft Office Tools, Microsoft Office 2003 Save My Settings Wizard. After quickly checking your system for installed Office programs, the wizard asks if you want to save the settings used on the computer or restore previously saved settings.

Before restoring settings, you need to save your settings, so we're going to choose Save the Settings from This Machine this time (see Figure A.3). Choose a file location and filename in the next screen and click Finish. You'll have to close all open Office programs before the wizard will run. If you forget, the wizard will tell you which programs are open and remind you to close them.

When you're ready to restore the settings, copy the file to your hard drive, open the wizard, and choose Restore Previously Saved Settings to This Machine. Browse to the file you created earlier and run the wizard.

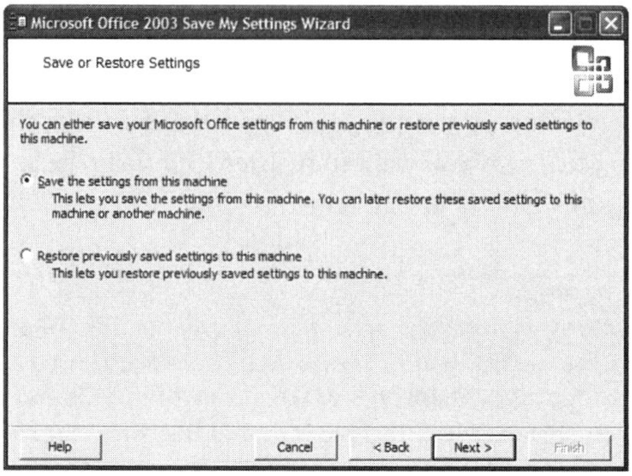

FIGURE A.3

*Use the Save My Settings Wizard to back up and restore your Office settings. After the *.OPS file is saved, save it to a floppy disk and use it on another computer or keep it as a backup.*

Microsoft Office 2003 Save My Settings Wizard

Save or Restore Settings

You can either save your Microsoft Office settings from this machine or restore previously saved settings to this machine.

○ Save the settings from this machine
This lets you save the settings from this machine. You can later restore these saved settings to this machine or another machine.

○ Restore previously saved settings to this machine
This lets you restore previously saved settings to this machine.

Help   Cancel   < Back   Next >   Finish

Windows XP includes a File and Settings Transfer Wizard. If you use this to back up your settings, make sure that you install the same Outlook add-ins that you had on the computer that you saved the settings from. If not, you'll receive errors mentioning missing files when you start Outlook.

The File and Settings Transfer Wizard can move your Outlook files, including the *.PST and other files. The Office Save My Settings Wizard saves only settings—you have to save the files yourself.

APPENDIX B

Outlook's Command-Line Switches

Outlook has a number of command-line switches you can use to control how Outlook starts, to perform maintenance, and to help diagnose problems.

You can use switches to create shortcuts for frequently used tasks or enter them in the Start, Run command dialog. This appendix covers

- Opening Outlook items from a command line
- Controlling how Outlook opens
- Using diagnostic switches

Working with Switches

Switches are used with the file path to the Outlook program file. If you used the default installation path, it's found at `C:\Program Files\Microsoft Office\Office11\Outlook.exe`. Enter this line in the Target field of a shortcut or in the Open field of the Start, Run command and append the switch at the end of the line.

When it's a command you'll want to use often, creating a shortcut is often the best way. Command lines you type into the Start menu, Run dialog are persistent, but you can put shortcuts on the Quick Launch menu and your desktop, or pin them to Windows XP's Start menu.

When making shortcuts for command lines, I prefer to copy the shortcut on my Quick Launch toolbar and add switches to the shortcut properties. To make a copy of a shortcut, right-click on it and choose Create Shortcut. The new shortcut, which you might want to rename, is named Launch Microsoft Office Outlook (2) by default.

If you're not using the Quick Launch toolbar, use the wizard to create a shortcut on your desktop and use copies of it for your commands. Right-click on the desktop and choose New, Shortcut and follow the steps in the wizard.

Now that you have a shortcut ready to work with, right-click on it and choose Properties. The Properties dialog for the shortcut opens, as seen in Figure B.1. Because I used a copy of the shortcut on Quick Launch, it has the /recycle switch already appended; I'll replace it with a new switch.

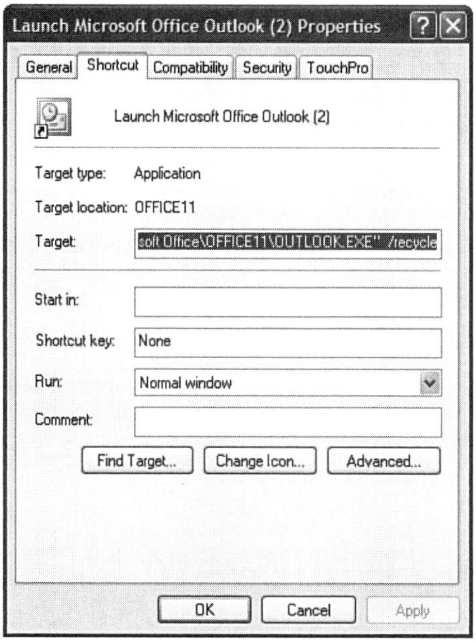

FIGURE B.1

Create new Outlook shortcuts on your Windows desktop. Don't forget to change the shortcut's name on the General tab.

After creating the shortcut, you can drag it to Outlook's Shortcuts bar on the Navigation Pane or to the Start menu's All Programs menu.

Using just `Outlook.exe` as the command line (without the folder path) often works. However, if you receive errors that the file can't be found, use the full path and enclose it in quotes when the path contains spaces. You'll see both formats used in the examples.

> The switches are not case-sensitive; I used capital letters to make the commands easier to read. When you're typing a switch, you can use all lowercase.

Open Outlook Items from the Command Line

The collection of switches covered in this section works with Outlook forms and files. You can open a specific form or file or open a form and include an attachment or an email address.

You can create desktop shortcuts to quickly load a form, putting them on the shortcut Navigation Pane or create toolbar button hyperlinks.

Possible uses of these switches even include Quick Launch shortcuts to frequently used forms or with Windows Task Scheduler to automatically create an item at a specific time.

- /a—Creates a new message with the specified file as an attachment. For example, this command line creates a new message with `report.doc` attached:

```
"C:\Program Files\Microsoft Office\Office11\Outlook.exe "
/a "C:\My Documents\report.doc"
```

> The command-line examples might be printed on two or more lines, but when typing them in, use one line and leave a space before the slash (/), as seen in the shorter examples.

When you don't specify an item type, Outlook uses the `IPM.Note` form, which creates a new email message. Other item types are listed in the next bullet.

- /c *messageclass*—Creates a new item of the specified message class:

```
Outlook.exe /c IPM.Note
```

The default message classes included with Outlook are

/c IPM.Activity—Creates a journal entry

/c IPM.Appointment—Creates an appointment

B

`/c IPM.Contact`—Creates a contact

`/c IPM.Note`—Creates an email message

`/c IPM.Stickynote`—Creates a note

`/c IPM.Task`—Creates a task

Or you can use the `/c` switch with a custom Outlook form that you've created:

`/c IPM.Note.MyForm`

> See Chapter 20, "Creating Custom Forms," to learn how to create and publish custom forms.

> You can combine the `/a` and `/c` switches to open a form and add an attachment:
>
> `"C:\Program Files\Microsoft Office\Office11\Outlook.exe "`
>
> `/c IPM.Note.Report /a "C:\My Documents\report.doc"`

- *`/m emailname`*—Provides a way for the user to add an email address to a message. You can use an email address or any resolvable name or distribution list in your address book. Use it with the `/c` command-line parameter as in this example:

  `Outlook.exe /c IPM.note /m diane@poremsky.com`

  This opens a new message form addressed to `diane@poremsky.com`. If you have a contact for me in your address book, you could use `"Diane Poremsky"`, enclosed with quotes because the name includes a space.

  Unfortunately, you can't string this switch with both the `/a` and `/c` switches. The `/c` switch is required.

Use the following switches to open files stored on your computer's hard drive, not files that are stored in Outlook's folders. In many cases, the following group of commands is more appropriate to use to programmatically use a feature, rather than for regular use.

The format of the command line needed for these switches is similar to this:

`Outlook.exe /f "C:\My Documents\savedsearch.oss"`

Replace the switch and filename with the appropriate switch.

- /Embedding—Embeds the specified message file (.msg) as an OLE (Object Linking and Embedding) object in a new message. Also used without command-line parameters for standard OLE co-create. Use with the /c switch to create Outlook items with embedded messages. This example creates a new contact form with a message embedded as an OLE object:

  ```
  Outlook.exe /c IPM.Contact /Embedding "D:\Data\Account.msg"
  ```

- /f msgfilename—Opens the specified message file (.msg) or Microsoft Office saved search (.oss) which is in the Windows file system. Create saved search files when you save an Advanced Find search and use the shortcut to run the search at a later time.

  ```
  Outlook.exe /f "D:\Data\Mitchell_Project.oss"
  ```

- /hol holfilename—Opens the specified Holiday (.hol) file. Use this to add holidays to the calendar.

  ```
  Outlook.exe /hol "D:\Data\company.hol"
  ```

- /iCal icsfilename—Opens the specified Internet Calendar (.ics) file. Use /vCal to open vCalendar (.vcs) files.

  ```
  Outlook.exe /ical "\\Shared\Documents\Independence Day.ics"
  ```

  ```
  Outlook.exe /vcal "D:\Data\Christmas_Party.vcs"
  ```

- /l olkfilename—Opens the specified Outlook Address Book (.olk) file. Word creates this file when you perform a mail merge using Outlook as your data source.

  ```
  "C:\Program Files\Microsoft Office\Office11\Outlook.exe " /l "D:\promo.olk"
  ```

- /t oftfilename—Opens the specified template (.oft) file.

  ```
  Outlook.exe /t "D:\templates\invoice.oft"
  ```

- /v vcffilename—Opens the specified vCard (.vcf) file.

  ```
  Outlook.exe /v "C:\ \\Shared\Documents\Jenny Smith.vcf"
  ```

- /x xnkfilename—Opens the specified Outlook link (.xnk) file. Links are shortcuts to Outlook folders in your profile, created by right-clicking and dragging a folder to the file system, and choosing Copy Here when you release the mouse button.

  ```
  Outlook.exe /x "\\Shared\Documents\Team Calendar.xnk"
  ```

B

Controlling How Outlook Opens

Use the following switches to control how you start Outlook, including switches that enable you to disable the Navigation Pane or reading pane. You can also use switches to select a specific profile when Outlook loads, disable Outlook's capability to check whether it's the default mail client, and disable an automatic mail check.

Additional startup switches are discussed in the "Diagnostic Switches" section, including /Safe switches and switches used to clean special items, such as reminders or rules.

- /AltVBA *otmfilename*—Opens the VBA program specified by *otmfilename*, instead of your VbaProject.OTM file.

  Outlook.exe /altvba cleanup.OTM

- /Autorun *macroname*—Opens Outlook and immediately runs the macro specified in *macroname*. The macro needs to be in the OTM file Outlook is using. You can use this switch with the /AtlVBA switch to automatically run a specific macro. This command runs the SaveAttachment macro stored in the cleanup.otm file.

  Outlook.exe /altvba cleanup.OTM /autorun SaveAttachments

- /Designer—Starts Outlook without checking to see whether it should be the default email client. Use this switch when Outlook isn't the default mail client and you won't receive the prompt asking whether it should be the default.

- /Explorer—Opens the new window in Explorer mode (Navigation Pane on).

- /FirstRun—Starts Outlook as if it were being run for the first time (which creates a new welcome message).

- /Folder—Opens a new window in folder mode (Navigation Pane off).

- /LaunchTrainingHelp *assetid*—Opens a Help window with the Help topic specified by *assetid*. This could be used by administrators to point users to a specific help file. The *assetid* is identified in the HTML help source by a META ID tag. The following command line should open Help to the mail merge topic.

  Outlook.exe /LaunchTrainingHelp *HP03073411*

- /NoPollMail—Starts Outlook without checking mail at startup.

- /NoPreview—Starts Outlook with the Reading Pane off and removes the option from the View menu.

- /p *msgfilename*—Prints the specified message (.msg). If Outlook is closed, loads in the background and closes after preparing the print job. Does not work with HTML-formatted messages when Outlook is closed.

  Outlook.exe /p "D:\Data\document path.msg"

- /Profile *profilename*—Loads the specified profile. When your profile name contains a space, use quotation marks (") to enclose the profile name:

  `Outlook.exe /profile "Diane Poremsky"`

- /Profiles—Opens the Choose Profile dialog regardless of the setting in Control Panel, Mail, Show Profiles:

  `"C:\Program Files\Microsoft Office\Office11\Outlook.exe " /profiles`

- /Recycle—Starts Outlook using an existing Outlook window, if one exists. Can be used in combination with /Explorer or /Folder. This switch is used on the Outlook shortcut added to the Quick Launch toolbar:

  `Outlook.exe /recycle /explorer`

- /RPCdiag—Opens Outlook and displays the remote procedure call (RPC) connection status dialog. Used with Exchange Server when troubleshooting connection problems.

- /S *filename*—Loads the specified shortcuts file (.fav). Use this to install Outlook Bar favorites on Outlook 2003's Shortcuts pane:

  `Outlook.exe /s "C:\My Documents\new_shortcuts.fav"`

- /Select *foldername*—Opens Outlook to a specific folder. For example, to open Outlook and display the default calendar, use this command line:

  `Outlook.exe /select outlook:calendar`

 If you aren't sure of the folder path, open the folder in Outlook, show the Web toolbar using <u>V</u>iew, <u>T</u>oolbars, and copy the path from the Address bar.

B

- /Sniff—Starts Outlook, forces a detection of new meeting requests in the inbox, and then adds them to the calendar.

Diagnostic Switches

Use the switches listed in this section for diagnostic purposes.

Some, like the /Safe switches, disable features when you start Outlook. Use these switches to troubleshoot problems.

Other switches, such as /CleanFinders, delete or clean up various settings or items and give you a fresh slate. You'll use these switches when a specific feature doesn't work correctly, including when your reminders don't fire, your rules don't work, and so on.

Use the clean switches with caution. In some cases, they delete your customizations, including the clean rules and clean views switches. Others, like
the clean reminder switch, are safe to use because they clean items that
Outlook re-creates.

The final switches in this group are those that reset Outlook to use default settings,
including `ResetNavPane`, which removes all of your shortcuts from the Navigation bar
and resets the buttons to their original positions.

- `/CheckClient`—Prompts for the default manager of email, news, and contacts. Use
  this when another email client is set to default and Outlook doesn't ask whether it
  should be the default.

- `/CleanClientRules`—Starts Outlook and deletes client-based rules. Works with all
  mail account types.

- `/CleanDmRecords`—Deletes the logging records saved when a manager or a delegate declines a meeting (Exchange Server only).

- `/CleanFinders`—Removes Search Folders from the Microsoft Exchange Server
  store.

- `/CleanFreeBusy`—Clears and regenerates free/busy information. This switch can
  be used only when you're able to connect to your Microsoft Exchange server.

- `/CleanProfile`—Removes invalid profile keys and re-creates default Registry keys
  where applicable.

- `/CleanPST`—Launches Outlook with a new Personal Folders file (`.pst`). The existing PST is not affected; it's just replaced in the profile for one use.

- `/CleanReminders`—Clears and regenerates reminders.

- `/CleanRules`—Starts Outlook and deletes client- and server-based rules. Use with
  care—this switch deletes all existing rules.

- `/CleanSchedPlus`—Deletes all Schedule+ data (free/busy, permissions, and `.cal`
  file) from the server and enables the free/busy information from the Outlook calendar to be used and viewed by all Schedule+ 1.0 users.

- `/CleanServerRules`—Starts Outlook and deletes server-based rules (Exchange
  Server only). Use with care—this switch deletes server-based rules.

- `/CleanSniff`—Deletes duplicate reminder messages.

- `/CleanSubscriptions`—Deletes the subscription messages and properties for subscription features.

- `/CleanViews`—Restores default views. Use with caution; this switch deletes all custom views you created. Use with care—this switch deletes all views, including any custom views you've created.
- `/ImportPRF` *prffilename*—Launches Outlook and opens/imports the defined MAPI profile (`*.prf`). If Outlook is already open when you run the command, the new profile is imported on the next clean launch.
- `/NoCustomize`—Starts Outlook without loading `outcmd.dat` (customized toolbars) and `*.fav` files. Use this to troubleshoot problems when Outlook hangs or crashes when you first start it. If Outlook loads using this switch, delete `outcmd.dat`.
- `/NoExtensions`—Starts Outlook with extensions turned off, but listed in the Add-In Manager.
- `/ResetFolderNames`—Resets default folder names (such as Inbox and Sent Items) to the default names in the current Office user interface language. This is used when you connect to an Exchange Server which uses a language different from your Office installation.
- `/ResetFolders`—Restores missing folders for the default delivery location. Use this switch if you use OWA to access your mailbox and accidentally delete a folder.
- `/ResetNavPane`—Clears and regenerates the Navigation Pane for the current profile. All shortcuts on the shortcut bar are deleted.
- `/Safe`—Starts Outlook without extensions, Reading Pane, or toolbar customization.
- `/Safe:1`—Starts Outlook with the Reading Pane off. Use this if you have a message in the inbox selected and it causes Outlook to hang or crash.
- `/Safe:2`—Starts Outlook without checking mail at startup. Use when you don't want Outlook to check for new email, but don't want to disable automatic checking in Tools, Send/Receive.
- `/Safe:3`—Starts Outlook with extensions turned off, but listed in the Add-In Manager.
- `/Safe:4`—Starts Outlook without loading `Outcmd.dat` (customized toolbars) and `*.fav` files.

B

INDEX

Symbols

+ (plus sign), 174

A

Access, Office Envelopes, 424

accessing
  HTTP, 29
  profile dialog boxes, 38

Account Settings dialog, 34

Account Setup Wizard, 433

accounts
  email, 69-71, 79
  HTTP, 28, 79-81
  IMAP, 28
  migrating, 430-433
  POP3, 28-34

Profiles, 34-37
RPC, 80-81
  Exchange Server, RPC
   (Remote Procedure
   Call), 70
  HTTP, 70, 78-79
  IMAP (Internet Mail
   Access Protocol), 69,
   75-77, 138
  naming, 31
  passwords, 30
  POP3 (Post Office
   Protocol version 3),
   69-74
  rules, 280-282
  send/receive groups,
   136-138
  setting up, 27-29
  settings, 431, 436

Accounts button, 97

Actions menu, 187

C

COM (Component Object Model), 142

command bars

default display, 304-305

drop-down lists, displays, 318

menus, customizing, 306

appearance, 309-311

Modify Selection menu, 311-312

Rearrange Commands option, 307-309

separators, adding/deleting, 315

toolbars

commands, moving, 317

custom command buttons, creating, 312-314

custom, 319-321

customizing, 306-312

docking, 310

moving, 310

resetting, 319

saving/restoring, 306

tools, 314-317

command-line switches, 447

diagnostic, 453-455

Outlook, opening, 452-453

Outlook items, opening, 449-451

shortcuts, 448

Command Prompt, SecureTemp folder, 115-116

commands

Actions menu

Call Contact, 251, 257-258

Change Picture, 189

Forward, 226

Forward as iCalendar, 409

Forward as vCard, 414

New Mail Using More Stationery, 93

Recall This Message, 106

Change Rule menu

Edit Rule Settings, 279

Rename Rule, 279

custom toolbars, creating, 320

Edit menu

Categories, 288, 421

Label, 224

Move to Folder, 362

Select All, Edit, 398

File menu

Archive, 359

Copy Folder Design, 179

Export, Messages, 432

Import and Export, 134, 196, 212, 365, 430

New Messages, 91

New, Journal Entry, 248, 258

New, Note, 239

New, Outlook Data File, 341, 361

Open, Outlook Data File, 41

Permission, Restrict Permissions, 160

Print, 326

Save as Web Page, 411

Save Search, 299

Send To, Mail Recipients, 423

Format menu, Plain Text, Rich Text, 94

Forms menu, Run This Form, 382

Insert menu

File, 110

Procedure, 393

Signature, 97

UserForm, 402

New menu

Appointment, 216

Journal, 254

Meeting Request, 219

Task Request, 236

Tasks, 230

toolbars, moving, 317

Tools menu

Advanced Find, 190

AutoCorrect Options, Smart Tags, 127

Customize, 168

E-mail Accounts, 34, 131, 135, 431

E-mail, Options, 103

Find, 292

Find, Advanced Find, 296

Forms, 253

Letters and Mailings, Mail Merge, 420-421

Macros, Macros, 392

Macro, Security, 413

Folder, Copy Folder Design command (File menu), 179

folders, 352

adding, 176-177

All Mail, 12

archived, 360

Calendar, 52

contacts, enabling, 98

creating, 353-354

custom toolbars, creating, 320

default attachment folders, selecting, 113-114

Deleted Items, 177-178

deleting, 177-178

design, copying, 179

email, moving to, 270

Favorites, 173-176

found items, moving to, 294

Journal, 254

moving, 178-179, 354

Navigation Pane, 12-13

Junk E-mail, merges, 283

purging, 77

Search, 170-173, 176, 301

SecureTemp, 114-117

Sent Items, 110

Startup, 41-42

Tasks, 51

Unread, 176

Views, Journal, 262

Virtual, Search Folders, 170

fonts

email, 93

month/year, Journal, 261

Unicode, 340-341

footers, printing, 330

For Follow Up Search folder, 170

Form Design toolbar, 374

Format Columns option (Custom View dialog), 56

Format menu commands, Plain Text, Rich Text, 94

Format Timeline View dialog, 262

formats. *See also* **quoting formats**

address cards (contact views), 50

Day Planner-style, 49

email, 81-84

email voting, 130-131

hexadecimal, colors, 411-412

formatting. *See also* **automatic formatting**

RTF, 94-95

Rules, views, 60-61

Formatting toolbar, 94

forms. *See also* **custom forms**

contacts, 187-188

Journal, 248, 252-255

security, Exchange Server, 144

UserForms, creating, 402-404

Forms command (Tools menu), 253

Forms menu commands, RunThis Form, 382

Forms, Publish Form command (Tools menu), 382

Forward as iCalendar command (Actions menu), 409

Forward as vCard command (Actions menu), 414

Forward command (Actions menu), 226

forwarding email, 102-104, 110

Free/Busy Options (Calendar Options dialog), 210

FrontPage, Office Envelopes, 424

FUS (Fast User Switching), 37

G

General tab, 186

Getting Started task pane, 20

Google, 20-22

graphics. *See* **images**

group address lists, 436

Group By dialog, 53

Group By option (Custom View dialog), 53

grouping

automatic, fields, 53

Smart Grouping, 16

groups

collapsing, 195

send/receive, 136-138

P

PAB (personal address book), 100, 136
adding, 39
connecting to profiles, 135
importing, 134-135
Page Setup dialog, 330
Page Setup option (Print dialog), 326
pages. *See* folder home pages
panes. *See also* task panes
Find, 292
Navigation Pane, 206
All Mail folders, 12
buttons, 10-11
calendar, 13-15
Current View, 12
customizing, 10-11
folders, 12-13
layouts, 9-10
settings (.XML), 351
shortcuts, 15
views, adding, 271
Organize, 52, 269-270
Preview, Journal, 262
Reading Pane, 16-17, 144-145
Research Pane, 22
Passport Wizard, 158
passwords, email accounts, 30
Permission button, 158
Permission, Restrict Permission As command (File menu), 160

personal address book (PAB), 100, 136
adding, 39
connecting to profiles, 135
importing, 134-135
Personal Folders dialog, 345
personal message stores (PSTs), 12, 40-41, 71
encryption, 343-344
profiles, adding, 341-344
storing, 342
Unicode, 339-341, 344-345
phone calls, journaling, 251, 257-258
Phone Directory Style (print style), 324
Phone List view, 194
photos (contacts), adding, 188-189
Picture Manager, Office Envelopes, 424
plain text format, 81, 84-85
Plain, Text, Rich Text command (Format menu), 94
Planner Options (Calendar Options dialog), 209
plus sign (+), 174
Pocket PCs, categories, 191
POP3 (Post Office Protocol version 3), 28, 69-74
creating, 29-32, 34
rules, 280-281
port 80, 79
ports, nonstandard, 35
Post Office Protocol version 3. *See* POP3

PowerPoint, IRM (Information Rights Management), 157
Preferences tab, 207
Prefix Each Line of the Original Message, 103
Preview Pane. *See* Reading Pane
previewing, inline previewing, 434
Print command (File menu), 326
Print dialog, 326
Print Options (Print dialog), 326
print styles, 323-324
Calendar, 331
contacts, 333-335
creating, 329-330
Memo, 326
notes, 242-243
Table, 325
Printer Settings (OutlPrnt) files, 352
printing
Calendar, 331-333
contacts, 327-329, 333-335
headers/footers, 330
options, configuring, 329-330
paper setup, 329
print styles, 323-324
Calendar, 331
contacts, 333-335
creating, 329-330
Memo, 326
Table, 325
troubleshooting, 325

Q–R

Your Guide
to Computer
Technology

www.informit.com

Sams has partnered with **InformIT.com** to bring technical information to your desktop. Drawing on Sams authors and reviewers to provide additional information on topics you're interested in, **InformIT.com** has free, in-depth information you won't find anywhere else.

ARTICLES

Keep your edge with thousands of free articles, in-depth features, interviews, and information technology reference recommendations—all written by experts you know and trust.

POWERED BY

Safari

ONLINE BOOKS

Answers in an instant from **InformIT Online Books'** 600+ fully searchable online books. Sign up now and get your first 14 days **free**.

CATALOG

Review online sample chapters and author biographies to choose exactly the right book from a selection of more than 5,000 titles.

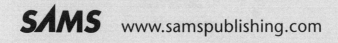

SAMS www.samspublishing.com